ARIEL
DORFMAN

AN AESTHETICS OF HOPE

Sophia A. McClennen

DUKE UNIVERSITY PRESS
DURHAM AND LONDON 2010

© **2010 DUKE UNIVERSITY PRESS** All rights reserved. Printed in the United States of America on acid-free paper ∞. Designed by Amy Ruth Buchanan. Typeset in Minion by Keystone Typesetting, Inc. Library of Congress Cataloging-in-Publication Data appear on the last printed page of this book. Parts of this book previously appeared in the following: "Ariel Dorfman" *The Review of Contemporary Fiction* 21, no. 3 (2000): 81–132; "The Diasporic Subject in Ariel Dorfman's *Heading South, Looking North*" *MELUS* 30, no. 1 (spring 2005): 169–88; "Torture and Truth in Ariel Dorfman's *Death and the Maiden*," forthcoming in *Revista Hispánica Moderna*; "Beyond *Death and the Maiden*: Ariel Dorfman's Media Criticism and Journalism," forthcoming in *Latin American Research Review* 45, no. 1 (2009). Frontis photo: Julio Donoso, 2006.

THIS BOOK IS FOR
ISABEL AND SEBASTIAN,
STORYTELLERS OF DREAMS,
AND FOR **HENRY.**

CONTENTS.

PREFACE.

This book is about breaking rules. Ariel Dorfman has spent his life breaking rules—refusing to be told who he is, what he should feel, how he should write, and what it should mean. Through his work he tells his readers to ask questions, refuse definitions, and think alternatively. But, he cautions, do not do this alone. Reach out, learn about your community, connect with humanity, be full of patience and compassion, and be full of rage and resistance. Be fallible. Be courageous. Take risks. And, most important, a message he repeats again and again is that literature, the arts, and culture play an essential role in the way we understand our world and in our struggles to change it.

One of the cardinal rules that Dorfman breaks is to passionately insist that art and politics are integrally connected. Dorfman's work challenges conservative views of art that suggest that it should be "free" of the taint of politics. Even though this debate has a long history, Dorfman has been forced to confront it repeatedly. For instance, in an exchange about the role of poetry in understanding the Abu Ghraib torture photos, David Ball claimed that poets who "try to express horror at the practice [of torture] run the risk of writing bad poems" (Ball et al., 6). Dorfman responded that poetry enables a vision of torturer and victim that reveals their mutual contaminations (ibid., 7). For Dorfman, the aesthetics of engaged literature offer the reader an opportunity to see the world from a new angle, one that has been lost or forgotten, re-pressed or silenced, censored or ignored by mainstream worldviews.

Dorfman has also broken another rule regarding the artist. He has promis-cuously mixed criticism with creativity, refusing the division between the critic and the creative writer. He has written an almost equal number of nonfiction works as literary texts. Moreover, he has written in every major literary genre (novel, short story, poetry, drama) and has adopted the voice of a variety of literary forms, including (among others) the picaresque, the epic, the noir, and the theater of the absurd. He has also refused common identity categories, understanding himself as a writer, an activist, a Chilean, a North American, and more. His works are read alternately and simultaneously as part of the Latin American literary canon; as examples of human rights literature; within the tradition of bilingual, cross-cultural, ethnic writing; and as part of a trans-national community of exiled and displaced writers.

Dorfman's work constantly tests limits, challenges assumptions, and refuses preconceived categories. He finds hope in the most devastating moments, such as the Chilean coup of 1973 and its aftermath or the terrorist attacks on the World Trade Center in 2001, because such moments of horror allow the victims to learn, to connect, and to grow. Similarly, he feels compelled to be critical of the most seemingly innocuous popular culture, such as the cartoons of Donald Duck or the movie *ET*, revealing the dangers inherent in their embed-ded ideological assumptions. The common thread throughout all of these activities is that hope depends on a permanent state of reflection, critique, and engagement.

Dorfman's work has also been controversial, often sparking radically dif-ferent responses from his audience. For instance, Maya Jaggi writes that Dorf-man has been "dogged by the charge that he has profited from others' experi-ences from the safety of exile" (n.p.). But she further notes that "for the Mexican writer Carlos Fuentes, who deemed *Death and the Maiden* Sopho-clean in its power and simplicity, no other play in Latin America has achieved its universal resonance" (n.p.). Despite the fact that Dorfman engages in a variety of social issues, he is most often associated with human rights, and it is in this arena that his work has received the most contrasting responses.

Once in exile, Dorfman's ability to write in English and his visibility as a writer associated with Salvador Allende positioned him as a voice for Chile to the English-speaking world. Such a position is never easy, and any writer who occupies it is likely to attract intense scrutiny. As Dorfman's career as a writer became increasingly successful, it was inevitable that some would wonder whether that success meant that he had capitalized on the trauma of the

Augusto Pinochet years. Dorfman's tendency to address critical social issues with a combination of bald truth, relentless hope, literary imagination, and complex questioning has also frustrated and alienated some of his readers. In addition, his practice of alternating across many types of writing has often confused his readers, who return to his work expecting a particular Dorfman mode only to find a radically different sort of work. For instance, the baroque, picaresque, Don Juanesque, hybrid literary form of his novel *The Nanny and the Iceberg* (*La nana y el iceberg*) frustrated those readers who favored the passionate, poignant voice Dorfman often adopts when he speaks as a human rights defender. For instance, Shashi Tharoor laments in his review of the novel that it doesn't offer "any greater meaning" (n.p.). One of my central arguments in this book is that Dorfman's decision to constantly experiment with new forms and to challenge his readers has been a purposeful, albeit risky, aesthetic strategy.

Dorfman's multiple projects over a broad range of genres and discourses in addition to his complicated relationship with his reading public may explain why this is the first book on Dorfman's work to appear in English and why it is the first book in any language to treat the full spectrum of his creative and critical texts. To this end, this book has two interrelated goals: to provide readers with a broad overview of Dorfman's life and work and to offer a critical assessment of his writing. My analysis shows that despite Dorfman's vast and varied artistic forms and literary genres, he presents readers with a cohesive and organic aesthetic theory, what I have termed his *aesthetics of hope*. Rather than follow the model that applies theory to texts, this book turns such practice around and uses Dorfman's works as a basis for developing a theory about art and life.

The first chapter, "The Political is Personal," gives an overview of Dorfman's life in relation to historical developments, providing a brief introduction to the arc of his literary career. The chapter suggests that Dorfman's background and his literary works serve as an example of the complexity of a bilingual, cross-cultural, hybrid identity. His life and work also allow readers to understand the Americas hemispherically, where the north and the south engage in continuous cultural, political, and economic entanglements. Documenting how crucial historical moments—such as anti-Semitism in 1940s Argentina, the death of Franklin Delano Roosevelt, the execution of Ethel and Julius Rosenberg, McCarthyism, Berkeley in 1968, and the Chilean coup of 1973—directly affected Dorfman's life, this chapter offers important insight into the ways that historical events have influenced Dorfman's writing.

The second chapter, "On Becoming a Storyteller," traces Dorfman's literary and cultural influences, which range from William Shakespeare to Pablo Picasso to Harold Pinter to Julio Cortázar. Key to this chapter is the idea that the novelty of these influences lies not in their range but rather in the ways that Dorfman incorporates the voices of these texts into his own work. The chapter further suggests that Dorfman envisions the writer as a storyteller, someone who cultivates oral tales and performs a social role, rather than as an author, who writes alone and isolated from society. Dorfman's faith in storytelling reveals how he has been influenced by Jewish and Native American traditions that depend on the power of oral communication to maintain customs and preserve history. But Dorfman's view of the writer also includes incessant questioning of the problems of representational practices. Thus his view of the writer as a storyteller also takes into account postmodern ideas about the difficulties inherent in writing for social change.

The third chapter, "An Aesthetics of Hope," uses Dorfman's writing, both fictional and critical, as a starting point for elaborating an aesthetic theory based on his work. The chapter traces his influences from critical theorists, such as those associated with the Frankfurt School, and Latin American intellectuals in order to detail Dorfman's theory of the social role of art. Even though the chapter suggests that Dorfman's aesthetic theory has much in common with other Latin American writers from his generation, my analysis highlights specific features of Dorfman's writing that reveal how he links literary form to content. With analysis that ranges from sentence structure to textual structure to the use of language, I show that Dorfman's formal experimentation is a crucial part of his aesthetic strategy but that within that experimentation there are consistent textual practices that flow throughout his work. Synthesizing his critical writings with his literary practices, this chapter proposes that Dorfman's aesthetics of hope is dedicated to the conviction that art plays an essential role in how we remember the past and imagine the future. Art with an aesthetics of hope is provocative and disturbing, intimate and collective, historical and utopian. Such art also has high expectations for the reader—expectations that are not so easily fulfilled by a mass media society accustomed to easily digestible culture. These high expectations coupled with Dorfman's self-reflexive, experimental mode of writing, I argue, expose the serious challenges such an aesthetic strategy faces.

The next two chapters chronologically trace Dorfman's literary career. Chapter 4, "Anything Else Would Have Tasted Like Ashes," covers Dorfman's literary works during the years of Salvador Allende's presidency (1970–73) and the years of Dorfman's exile from Augusto Pinochet's dictatorship (1973–90).

The chapter analyzes his novels, poetry, and short stories from this period with emphasis on his investigation of the relationship between the artist and social struggle. Early in his writing career Dorfman wrestled with what he perceived to be a conflict between literature and politics. Even though he was convinced of the social role of literature, when he began to actively work in politics prior to and during Allende's presidency, he felt torn between the immediacy of political activism and the more ethereal nature of literary writing. Doubts about the political efficacy of art haunt him throughout his career, but they are of particular concern during these years. Picking up on how this theme runs throughout his literature during this period, this chapter analyzes how the early works correspond to personal and historical events in Dorfman's life.

The fifth chapter, "I Am a Liar Who Always Tells the Truth," covering the period 1990–2005, begins its analysis with the international hit play *La muerte y la doncella* (*Death and the Maiden*) and examines Dorfman's transition from exile to diaspora by focusing on his interest in the relationship between literary language and aesthetics. This chapter also explores the complex combination of local and global references in his writing. During this period there is an increasing global turn in Dorfman's work, in addition to an attunement to an audience that goes beyond the Latino/Latin American, a shift that may account for the increasing international success of Dorfman's literature. After the end of his official exile, Dorfman narrates transnational contexts in an effort to find a language that can communicate human interactions and issues of social justice to a cross-cultural audience. Simultaneously, though, he produces some of his most distinctly Chilean texts, including the novel *The Nanny and the Iceberg*; his travel memoir to the north of Chile, *Desert Memories*; and his account of the Pinochet case, *Exorcising Terror*. This chapter traces how the transition to diaspora pushes Dorfman's work in two different yet complementary directions—the global and the local. Both of these narrative trends converge, though, in a shared concern for the role that language plays in the construction of identity. Consequently, this chapter follows this theme as it runs through the works of the second part of Dorfman's career.

The sixth chapter, "Creative Criticism/Critical Creativity," centers on Dorfman's essays, journalism, and media projects, exposing the interconnectedness between his critical activities and creative work. The chapter outlines the main components of his major works in media theory. These critical works are also considered in light of Dorfman's own cultural products. Few media critics also produce media. In this sense Dorfman's work is unusual. He constantly balances his criticism with constructive practice. These dual intentions—to consistently criticize the alienating effects of mass media and to create viable cultural alternatives—are at the core of his work. Yet most studies of Dorfman ignore or gloss over his essays and focus solely on his literature. I argue that his literary production must be understood as part of a larger project that includes a critique of the negative effects of media culture. Calling attention to the full range of Dorfman's creative activities, my analysis briefly examines the variety of other types of cultural production in which he has engaged, such as work with fine arts, film, photography, and music, in order to point out its discursive diversity and the relationship of these activities to his overall aesthetic project. The chapter then analyzes Dorfman's cultural journalism and proposes that he has developed a lyrical form of periodical writing.

Chapter 6 further suggests that what may be seen as a strength can also be considered a flaw: the variety of Dorfman's cultural practices can be read negatively as the result of an almost frenzied need to communicate, or they can be read positively as a multifaceted, concerted effort to create culture that can have a social impact. In fact, as the analysis of this book shows, Dorfman's writing combines unflagging faith in progressive culture with a penchant for creating dense, complex texts that runs similar risks of contrasting critical responses. As I argue, Dorfman is well aware of the dangers inherent in such a project, and they form a central part of his aesthetic theory. The question of whether or not such a project succeeds, though, is not at the center of this book. Rather, I hope to have shown that what may appear as disparate and disconnected practices actually coalesces around a coherent and innovative aesthetic project.

The concluding chapter returns to the thesis that Dorfman's cultural production reveals a combination of creative activism and aesthetic experimentation that collectively forms his aesthetics of hope. The chapter ends with a discussion of Dorfman's aesthetics of hope in comparative context. I suggest that Dorfman can be productively compared to other writers affected by diaspora and globalization who use formal experimentation to communicate political commitment and concern. Here I place Dorfman alongside other writers who engage in aesthetic innovation at the service of social commitment. The connections between these writers and Dorfman suggest that a number of writers working in the latter part of the twentieth century and the early twenty-first century have often turned away from literary realism and have considered complex aesthetics to be an essential literary tool for critiquing society. In this way the work of Dorfman is exemplary of a global countercultural trend.

The appendices provide two crucial tools for future research on Dorfman's work. The first is a chronology that documents important dates and events in

Dorfman's life. The second is a full bibliography of Dorfman's work, including his extensive periodical publications in both English and Spanish. Throughout the book I draw attention to the connections and distinctions between originals, translations, and later transformations of his texts. It is my hope that this book will serve as a springboard to more scholarship on Dorfman's work.

ACKNOWLEDGMENTS.

I wish to thank all of those who provided me with support and guidance during the writing of this book. Two colleagues, Steven Totosy and Djelal Kadir, deserve special thanks. Steven has supported my work for over ten years, and I continue to be thankful for his guidance as well as his sense of humor. Djelal has been a wonderful friend, mentor, and interlocutor. My deepest thanks to both of them for their support at crucial moments in my career and for their continued engagement and commitment to my work.

I am especially grateful for Henry Giroux's support and his dynamic intellect. His notions of social agency and educated hope helped me refine my ideas about Dorfman's aesthetics and politics. I found that simply talking to him gave me renewed energy, and I am thankful for his generous spirit.

While teaching at Illinois State University, I had the good fortune to connect with a number of colleagues who continue to give me guidance. I am especially grateful to Robert McLaughlin, who supported the article on Dorfman that appeared in the *Review of Contemporary Fiction* and that ultimately led me to begin writing this book. Diane Urey read chapters and gave her wise advice and warm friendship. Ron Strickland has been guiding this project for years, beginning with our co-edited issue of *Mediations* and culminating recently when he helped me sort out some of my thoughts about the connections between Dorfman and Shakespeare.

At Penn State I have been grateful for the extraordinary support of Carey Eckhardt, who has repeatedly taken time from her busy schedule to read chapters or to chat about this book. Tom Beebee helped me understand how Dorfman used Bob Dylan and Schubert in his work, and Bob Blue gave me insight into the postmodern picaresque. Both Lisa Surwillo and Shu Kuge gave me careful and thoughtful readings of chapters, offering fresh perspectives for my tired eyes. I am also grateful for financial support for this project from Penn State's Institute for the Arts and Humanities.

Sergio Waisman and María Laura Sofo helped me understand special nuances to words and phrases from the Southern Cone. David Schroeder, whom I met while I was Fulbright Research Chair in Globalization and Cultural Studies at Dalhousie University, gave me considerable insight into Dorfman's use of Schubert in *Death and the Maiden*. George Shivers, who translated a number of Dorfman's works, graciously shared his notes and experiences with me.

I thank Henry James Morello for teaching me about theater and trauma. His theory of post-traumatic theater shaped some of the central ideas in chapter 5 and influenced my understanding of the relationship between literary expression and historical crisis. Earl Fitz refined my understanding of inter-American culture, and I am very grateful for his intellectual collaboration and warm camaraderie. Dan Simon at *World Literature Today* and Chad Post at *Context* and Dalkey provided excellent venues for my interviews with Dorfman in conjunction with much energy and enthusiasm for this project. Reynolds Smith at Duke University Press has been a patient and supportive editor in addition to a good friend. I also thank the anonymous reviewers who read for the press. Their insights greatly improved the book. When I was in the midst of working out ideas on politics and aesthetics, I was fortunate to come across an essay by Michael McIrvin that led me to blindly send him an e-mail. That message prompted an ongoing exchange of ideas. Michael has also been a patient and careful reader of many of these chapters.

A number of colleagues and good friends lent an ear and provided important dialogue to some of my ideas. Pius Adesanmi, Biagio D'Angelo, Gene Bell-Villada, Michael Berubé, Debra Castillo, Deb Cohn, Greg Dawes, Jonathan Eburne, Claire Fox, Moira Fradinger, Ricardo Gutiérrez-Mouat, Natalie Hartman, Eric Hayot, Alex Huang, Manuel Jofré, Neil Larsen, Don Lazere, Jonathan Marks, Bill Mullen, Silvia Nagy-Zekmi, Aldon Nielson, John Ochoa, Raquel Olea, Julio Ortega, Danny Postel, Daniel Purdy, Matt Restall, John D. Riofrio, Maria Helena Rueda, Claudia Sadowksi-Smith, Malini Johar Schueller, Susan Searls Giroux, Christina Shouse-Tourino, Joseph Slaughter, Steve Thomas, Santiago Vaquera, and many others have been wonderful sources of engaged critique, intellectual community, and friendship.

In 2004 the University of St. Thomas's English department selected Dorfman's *Heading South, Looking North* as the common text for the entire freshman class, and I was privileged to give that year's Common Text Lecture. Thanks to Kanishka Chowdhury and Carmela Garritano and to the students of the University of St. Thomas for making that a wonderful and enriching experience.

This book would not be what it is without the tremendous efforts of a number of research assistants who painstakingly helped to construct the bibliography, track down obscure texts, and aid in various other ways. Special thanks to Marta Vidal, Ericka Parra, Irene Robles-Huerta, Sara Armengot, and Justin Halverson. Thanks also to the wonderful students who tested my theories, adding their own brilliant insights into Dorfman's work, especially Tasha Walston, Nicole Sparling, Bridget Fahrner, and Tim Meneely. I have included a text by Dorfman in almost every class I have taught over the past few years, and the students from those classes have given me a chance to refine my critique and learn from their observations. Thanks to all of them.

Special mention must go to Jennifer Prather, Dorfman's assistant at Duke University, who answered numerous e-mails and helped me track down a number of crucial texts. Patient and always helpful, she was an extraordinary resource during this process. I am also most grateful for the friendship, support, and insider information provided by Rodrigo and Joaquín Dorfman. Their constant collaboration with their father has made it difficult to see where his work ends and theirs begins. And that is just the way they like it.

It goes without saying that this book wouldn't exist without the work of Ariel Dorfman. But this project owes thanks to him that go beyond the obvious. He began as my teacher and mentor and has become a close friend and colleague. Contrary to what some might imagine, he has consistently pushed me to be more critical of his work. He has also been incredibly generous with his time, providing me with countless details and documents, including a number of unpublished manuscripts. He spent his precious moments on trips to Chile, for instance, looking for old articles from the 1960s or tracking down his thesis at my request. There is no question that it has been hard for me to write this book, both because at every moment that I thought I had found a good place to stop, he seemed to finish another work that needed to be included, and because it can be difficult to write about someone's work when one deeply cares about the human being behind the public writer. It seems to me, though, that it is just that type of passionate engagement with our objects of study that is lacking from so many other academic pursuits, and I am happy to have faced the challenge. I also believe that I learned much from Ariel about what it means to be an inspired, engaged, and committed intellectual. From the time I was his student to today he continues to teach me how to combine intellectual commitment with warmth, humanity, and compassion.

I could never have found the time or the mental clarity to write this book without knowing that my children were being well cared for. I have been extremely fortunate to have had a number of warm and wonderful women who have given Isabel and Sebastian love and care. Sofía Champac, Jazmín Villamil, Agustina Peralta, Amanda Pheeney, María Laura Sofo (and her daughters Agustina and Lucía), Agustina Roca, and Adriana Vázquez all made it possible for me to write. Their loving care helped curtail my feelings of guilt at precious moments lost, and I am sure that Isabel and Sebastian are better people for knowing them.

The last and most important thanks go to my friends and family, who always help put things into perspective. Special thanks to my mom, who always inspires me with her wit, intelligence, and dynamism. I have enjoyed answering my grandmother Mim's probing questions about this book, and I am also grateful to my aunt Stephania, whose passion for learning has given me a chance to talk about my work. I thank Isabel and Sebastian for giving me daily reminders of joy and innocence and for teaching me about patience and spontaneity. This book could never have been written without Henry's support. He always rescues me with optimism and strength when I need it most. He is the love of my life.

NOTE ON CITATIONS AND TRANSLATIONS.

At the first mention of each literary work in a chapter, I give the original title in italics, followed by the title in English when the original is in Spanish. When translations are available, I give their titles in italics. Subsequent references to the text use only the English title of the work when an English translation is available. Otherwise, subsequent references are to the original Spanish followed by translation into English in roman type within parentheses. For example:

1. Original in English: *Heading South, Looking North*
2. Original in Spanish, no translation published in English: *El absurdo entre cuatro paredes: El teatro de Harold Pinter* (The Absurd within Four Walls: The Theater of Harold Pinter)
3. Original in Spanish with a translation published in English: *Para leer al pato Donald: Comunicación de masas y colonialismo* (*How to Read Donald Duck: Imperialist Ideology in the Disney Comic*).

Citations, except where otherwise noted, always include the original version. When that version is in Spanish, it is followed by a translation into English. Page references are given in the text for all citations. When a page number follows the English translation, it refers to the published translation, which, accordingly, is set inside quotation marks. When the translation into English does not have a page reference, the translation is mine and is therefore not set inside quotation marks.

1. THE POLITICAL IS PERSONAL

Ariel Dorfman's personal biography is inseparable from inter-American history, and his life has been connected in uncanny repetition to many of the region's most significant historical events. Beyond being tangentially influenced by events taking place in his environs, however, Dorfman's life continually confronts and is confronted by history. His life is the story of multiple exiles, historical ruptures, and profound despair. It is equally the story of passionate social commitment and relentless hope. The story of Dorfman's life is remarkable not only for its profound connection with the hemispheric history of the Americas, but also because it is the story of a man who not only witnessed history but also felt compelled to write about it.

Vladimiro Ariel Dorfman was born on May 6, 1942, in Argentina. Throughout his life, the man known today as Ariel Dorfman has used three distinct first names: Vladimiro (Vlady), Edward (Eddie), and Ariel. Dorfman's name changes run (almost) parallel to the three nations (Argentina, the United States, and Chile) in which he lived as a young man, and they indicate some of the reasons why Dorfman's literature often deals with problems of identity. These name changes further evoke the linguistic shifts of his multiple exiles and their cultural contexts. He moved from Spanish to English as a young boy exiled from Argentina to New York (1945–54), from English to Spanish when his family was expelled from the United States to Chile due to McCarthyism (1954–73), and then finally to bilingualism as an exile from Pinochet's dictatorship (1973–90); a condition he only came to fully embrace after 1990, when Pinochet no longer ruled Chile. The name changes also reveal that Dorfman was extremely invested from a young age in his ability to shape identity through naming. Well before he had read theories about language and power and well before he became intellectually versed in the connections between naming and social control, Dorfman was acutely sensitive to the ways that names project meaning.

His initial, given name, Vladimiro, was assigned to him by his parents, who named him after Vladimir Lenin. This unwieldy name signals his parents' commitment to politics and their close ties to Eastern Europe, especially to the Russian Revolution. (His father remained faithful to the Bolshevik Revolution after he left Russia in 1920.) Later, as we learn from Dorfman's 1998 memoir, *Heading South, Looking North*, when the family lived in the United States, the "flaming moniker" Vladimiro became a tremendous liability (23). It was a name easily butchered during children's renaming games, and Dorfman was verbally attacked with perversions of his name such as Bloody, Flatty, and even Laddie and Lady (79). Vladimiro was also a name that prevented his complete immersion into U.S. culture. So in 1951, while on a cruise to Europe at the age of nine, Dorfman launched a plan that he had been concocting for some time. He introduced himself to everyone he met as "Edward" or "Eddie," and before his parents knew what was happening, Dorfman had been "baptized" with an Anglo name that eschewed his Jewish, Latino, and leftist heritage. "Edward" came to Dorfman by way of a comic book edition of Mark Twain's *The Prince and the Pauper*, a fitting sign of his "conversion" to U.S. culture (79). The comic book may also have been Dorfman's first introduction to the literary theme of the doppelganger, which would later influence much of his work (79). Remade as "Edward the Prince," Dorfman announced to his startled parents that he "would not answer if called Vlady ever again" (80).

The eventful cruise in which "Vlady" was abandoned and "Eddie" emerged was a watershed moment in Dorfman's quest for acceptance in U.S. culture. Prior to this trip Dorfman had grown up in a leftist household in Manhattan, where his father worked with the United Nations and the family had strong connections to many political activists and intellectuals who often visited the Dorfman home. In contrast to his parents' world of foreign languages, young Vlady favored English and U.S. cultural assimilation, immersing himself in the life of an *all-American* kid: "I wanted to melt and dissolve . . . into the gigantic melting pot of America" (*Heading*, 78). How did a nine-year-old Argentine boy come to desire such radical self-transformation?

Dorfman's parents, Fanny Zelicovich Vaisman and Adolfo Dorfman, were both the children of Jewish émigrés who came to Argentina to avoid European anti-Semitism and to seek financial success. His mother's grandfather was murdered in the pogrom of 1903 in Kishinev (now Moldavia). Subsequently her family decided to leave the country, choosing Argentina as a consequence of Baron Maurice de Hirsch's Jewish Colonization Association, which helped many East European Jews emigrate to Argentina and Brazil. Dorfman's maternal great-grandmother, Clara, and his great-aunt, who had stayed behind because the latter was sick with meningitis, were killed by the Nazis (*Heading*, 15). On his father's side of the family, emigration was largely due to financial pressures. In 1914 Adolfo went back to Russia with his mother and witnessed the beginnings of the First World War and the Russian Revolution, returning to Argentina in 1920. In relation to Dorfman's personal history it is crucial to understand that his parents' families had endured massive dislocation as a consequence of historical conflicts. Dorfman was born into a legacy that was already deeply marked by exile, loss, and intolerance. His Jewish heritage, which is more cultural than spiritual, signals patterns and tropes that continue to influence his life: exile, wandering, loss, struggle, and the search for a community. Referring to his time in Chile, where he felt at home, he writes, "There is a place, one place, where you truly belong" (*Heading*, 275). Yet he also suggests that to "start anything worthwhile, one must leave the place of one's birth" (276). Connecting his exile to the Jewish tradition, he writes that "salvation can only be attained by wandering" (276). These themes that link geography and identity, wandering and exile, struggle and joy, persecution and oral history, indicate the ways that his life and work highlight common Jewish motifs.

After a pro-Axis coup led to a change in government in Argentina in 1943 and stripped marxist Adolfo Dorfman of his position as a professor of industrial engineering at the Universidad de la Plata, Dorfman's family moved to the United States, where his father was a Guggenheim fellow. The ironies of life were emphasized for the young Dorfman by the fact that the anti-imperialist Adolfo came to the United States, "the most powerful capitalist country in the world, protected by a foundation built with money that had come out of one of the world's largest consortiums" (*Heading*, 24). When Fanny, Vlady, and his older sister, Eleonora, joined Adolfo over a year later, Adolfo was distant and preoccupied.[1] He had been called to military service and was expected to report for duty four days after his family arrived in Manhattan. In a key example of the ways that historical events would shape their lives, Adolfo was reclassified because Nelson Rockefeller, founder of the State Department's Office of Inter-American Affairs, determined that Adolfo Dorfman's work for their office was "essential."[2] This reclassification gave the family a reprieve from another dislocation and separation.

Shortly after his family had moved into their first Manhattan apartment, Vlady Dorfman, then a young exile nearing three years of age, caught a terrible case of pneumonia and was hospitalized and quarantined. He was isolated from his family for three weeks, and when he returned home from the hospital, he spoke only English, refusing to communicate in Spanish altogether. Dorfman describes this complete immersion into English as a desire for coherence and unity, as part of a will to wholeness: "I instinctively chose to refuse the multiple, complex, in-between person I would someday become" (*Heading*, 42). In contrast to other immigrants and exiles who tend to live bilingually, young Vlady sought monolingualism as a way to exercise control over his identity. Or at least that is the way the adult Ariel describes his immersion into English, since much of our knowledge of his early life comes from the reconstitution of that experience in *Heading South, Looking North*.[3]

This event, the pneumonia and hospital quarantine that led to his adoption of English, becomes a defining moment in Dorfman's life. It not only signals a linguistic tension between Spanish and English, but also reveals another pressing tension that haunts his identity: that between understanding the self as a subject of free will or as a socially and historically determined entity. When one's life and the lives of one's family have been scattered by the winds of history and the upheavals of politics, it is tempting, if not necessary, to seek some measure of agency in understanding identity. While Dorfman describes his isolation in the hospital and its inevitable connection to English, he wavers between emphasizing his control—that is, the degree to which adopting English was his choice—and admitting his submission to external forces requiring, or at least encouraging, him to use that language only. This struggle to make sense of the forces that shape personal lives, to understand history as either malleable by the human will or beyond our control, persists throughout Dorfman's writing.

After Dorfman's initial isolation in the hospital, he was to endure another separation that caused him further anguish and confusion. Shortly after the death of Franklin Delano Roosevelt on April 12, 1945, Dorfman's mother, Fanny, suffered a bout of severe depression. The stresses of being separated from her exiled husband for over a year, of being thrust into the unwelcoming environment of New York City, and of losing the one political figure who she felt could steer the world to a better place overwhelmed her, and she had a breakdown. Once again, the twists of history had intense consequences for Dorfman and his family: "My mother felt as if Roosevelt's death were wresting a father from her, as if what was about to end was not the war but the world, as if nothing would ever be sane again. . . . She could not deal with what the orphaned world was sending her way" (*Heading*, 47). She was institutionalized, and Vlady and Eleonora spent six months in a foster home, where English was, again, essential for survival. By the time his parents came to pick him up on November 1, 1945, to move the family into a new apartment on Morningside Drive, they discovered that they had lost their son "to the charisma of America" (47).

In these early years of his life, Dorfman eagerly consumed U.S. media culture: "Listen to me in the car as we drive home . . . : I was coming around the mountain when she comes. . . . I was rowing the boat ashore, I was working on the railroad all the live long day, even if I sometimes felt like a motherless child, still, Zip-A-Dee-Doo-Dah I had the whole world in my hands . . . and it was marching on to the green grass of home. Home. That's where I was, where I had chosen to be. . . . I was home, home on the range . . . this land was my land and it was made for you and me, but especially, I felt, it had been made for me" (*Heading*, 48).[4] It is no surprise that this young boy felt culturally lost, completely unmoored from any sense of a stable cultural background, and reluctant to use his parents as models for his own future identity. In addition to feeling abandoned by his father when Adolfo first was forced to flee Argentina, Dorfman also had to endure the trauma of being isolated in the hospital, only to quickly lose his mother to depression.

Exiled families often experience similar challenges, and the rate of divorce and separation among them is extremely high (see Grinberg and Grinberg). Added to the ordeal of exile, young Vlady became sick with an illness that made breathing difficult and painful, an event that gave him an extreme sense of his mortal vulnerability. As he desperately craved stability and security, he was separated from both his father and his mother and momentarily lost their support, comfort, and the cultural grounding of their language. In addition, Dorfman's family was fractured at a moment in history when the United States had launched a massive global campaign for international prominence and had refashioned itself, after the Second World War, into a model society that contrasted starkly with the so-called evil of the Soviet bloc, an identity that would not only persist throughout the Cold War but would also spread with incredible speed and intensity during the 1940s and '50s. "The United States had turned me into one of its children by offering me comfort and safety and power during its most expansive and optimistic post-war phase" (*Heading*, 162). In this way, the cultural instability caused by Dorfman's exile and illness was exacerbated by his personal, historical, and geographical context. The desire to belong to a community is a logical consequence to Dorfman's early social dislocation and cultural loss. And even though the desire to belong to a community and to understand the self as whole and complete is a theme that runs throughout Dorfman's work, the reality of his hybrid, cross-cultural life thwarted even his earliest plans to shape his destiny.

In 1949, two years before he executed his plan to change his name to Eddie and become an all-American kid, Dorfman began attending PS 117, a New York City public school located in Queens.[5] He was no longer sheltered in the multicultural world of the UN Children's School, which he had attended after his father became deputy head with the Council for Economic Development at the newly formed United Nations in 1946. At the same time, the mass hysteria and fear of the Cold War was erupting in the "red scare." Until then Dorfman had been able to lead a double life: at home, leftist activism and communist politics; away from home, capitalist consumption and U.S. nationalism. Attending public school during a period of extreme political paranoia caused him substantial distress because he was no longer able to keep these worlds apart. His teacher told his class about people who were a danger to the "American" way of life, people who were like "rotten apples" (*Heading*, 68). After a fight with his father, where he threatened to tell his teacher that his father was a communist, he finally realized the gravity of his dilemma. He could no longer love his father and his adopted country equally because with each passing day the United States was increasingly targeting men like Adolfo Dorfman as enemies of the state.

Returning to the importance of Dorfman's cruise aboard the *De Grasse* where the author changed his name and sought a unity of self, if even for a brief moment, a third key element of his personal history and writing surfaces: the role of literature and language in shaping his identity and his relationship to the world. He tells his readers that on this trip "literature was revealed to me as the best way to surmount the question of how to hold on to the language that defined my identity if I did not inhabit that country where it was spoken" (*Heading*, 81). On the ship, Dorfman met Thomas Mann, and the meeting sparked Dorfman's interest in the power of literature ("I wanted the power to reach all of humanity"), the role of language in literature ("In what language does he write?"), and the ways that exiles use literature to recreate their ties to their home (86). After embarking on the ship, his parents gave him a journal as a gift. Writing in it was the first time that he recalls using words to freeze time. What would have been ephemeral now had permanence, and the notion that the written word has a way of recording time and of keeping our lives from melting into oblivion is a theme to which his work would turn with even more urgency after the death of Chilean president Salvador Allende.

The importance of writing in shaping identity cannot be overemphasized in Dorfman's work. After inaugurating his journal, he confesses, "I think I began, from that moment, to live in order to record life" (*Heading*, 84). For Dorfman, the links among naming, languages, history, cultural geography, and the self are articulated through writing. These connections, for instance, lead Dorfman to be particularly sensitive to the ways that colonial American texts attempted to forge the identity of the New World.[6] As though his own life were forcing him to see the New World through the eyes of an explorer, a conqueror as well as a colonial victim, Dorfman became acutely aware of the ways that writing alternately preserves memory and creates false memories, records and distorts history, registers protest and encourages blind obedience. Dorfman would later develop these theories in his essays and fiction.

Dorfman's decision to change his first name also reveals another motif that persists throughout his literature—the tension between a coherent, unified self at home in a community and a self that is hybrid, fragmented, and solitary. As Dorfman points out, it was fitting that his plan for self-transformation took place aboard a ship, "a site of exile where you can craft your identity any way you want, where you can con everybody into anything because there is no way of confirming or denying your past" (*Heading*, 81). But after the trip, back in Manhattan, Eddie's friends still called him Vlady, and it wasn't until he arrived in Chile in 1954, after his second exile, that he could fully institute his new persona. Dorfman's writing investigates how our own self-perceptions are often out of sync with our public selves, and in his own case this disconnect has taken place at the level of something as basic and as symbolic as his name: "Many of my friends from Chile still call me Ed or Eddie" (81).

After the cruise, Dorfman's efforts at cultural unification were further thwarted when the political tide of McCarthyism reached the Dorfman household and Adolfo Dorfman found himself the subject, again, of political persecution. Always politically active, Adolfo Dorfman refused to succumb to the tyranny of the "red scare." On June 19, 1953, the Dorfman family took part in a vigil outside of Sing Sing Prison the night that Ethel and Julius Rosenberg were executed. This event engendered fear in young Eddie Dorfman because he was forced to recognize the magnitude of U.S. power and the threat that it posed to people like his father. In late November of that same year, the Dorfman family provided refuge to Maurice Halperin and his wife, Edith, who spent the night in the Dorfman's apartment as they fled from investigations by the House Un-American Activities Committee on their way to Mexico. Shortly after this event, Adolfo Dorfman was forced to take a post with the United Nations in Chile, and the family established itself in Santiago in 1954.

Despite his later attacks on the hegemony of U.S. culture, Dorfman spent his first moments in Chile nostalgic for New York. He felt stripped of his cultural identity, uncomfortable in Spanish, and unwelcome in Chile, where enrolling in school proved to be extremely difficult (*Heading*, 101). To counteract these cultural pressures, he desperately tried to maintain his "gringo" self. First, he enrolled in The Grange, a British preparatory school that was exceptionally rigid but that allowed him to conduct most of his coursework in English. Then he clung to the quarterly package deliveries that his father received from the north. Because his father worked for the United Nations, he was able to order U.S. products from catalogs. These "care packages" of U.S. cultural commodities included candy bars, clothes, records, comic books—a veritable treasure trove of products that Dorfman devoured (117). He did everything possible to maintain his cultural ties to the United States, following his favorite sports teams and absorbing any U.S. culture available. He also made friends with other displaced children from the United States. Even after he first embraced Spanish in Chile, he lived a dual identity according to his two languages: "It was as if they inhabited two strictly different, segregated zones in my mind, or perhaps as if there were two Edwards, one for each language, each incommunicado like a split personality, each trying to ignore the other, afraid of contamination" (115).

During these early years in Chile Dorfman wasn't ready to see himself as bilingual; he wasn't ready to acknowledge his "journey towards duality" (*Heading*, 116). Even though he had been able to lead a schizophrenic life, his interaction with Bernie, a buddy whose father worked for a U.S. copper company, drove a palpable wedge between these two aspects of his conception of himself. One day while he was visiting Bernie, his friend showed him an enormous glass jar filled with Chilean pesos made from copper. When Dorfman couldn't guess why Bernie was hoarding the coins, his pal revealed that he planned to go back to the United States, melt them down, and sell them since the value of the metal exceeded their value as currency: "I'm going to get ten times the price. They're Indians, these guys, they like to get fucked" (121). It was in this moment that Dorfman realized that he was not on Bernie's side, that he felt more allegiance to Chile, the "country that, after all, had given [his] family refuge" (121). The conflict with Bernie signaled a transformation in Dorfman's awareness of cultural allegiance that had already begun well before his friend's racism and imperialism disgusted him but which after this event became even more consciously manifest. From that point on, Dorfman recognized that he was undergoing yet another cultural shift that would eventually lead to another name change.

In his final years at The Grange, Dorfman became increasingly active politically. His parents, unrestrained by fears of McCarthy and his cronies, raised Dorfman in a vibrant atmosphere of leftist politics. They hosted dinners for numerous leftists, including current and future heads of state like Guatemalan president Jacobo Arbenz, Argentine president Arturo Frondizi, and Guyanese president Cheddi Jagan. Dorfman became increasingly fluent in his parents' politics, but he also continued to admire the United States and to consider himself an "American." His plan was to graduate from high school and to attend college in the United States: "I dreamed of returning to the Promised Land of New York" (*Heading*, 128). After hearing that he had been accepted with a scholarship to Columbia University, Dorfman excitedly began preparing to return "home." When his parents asked him to consider postponing the trip (he was after all only seventeen years old), Dorfman took a walk to mull it over: "And that is where and when I asked myself, under those mountains, if this country had not become, in some way I had not anticipated, my home. That is where I decided, far from New York and far from Buenos Aires, a different future for my life" (130). It is interesting to note, again, Dorfman's description of this moment in terms that emphasize his self-determination and his decision-making process. At the same time, though, he reveals that this twist of fate also came as a consequence of the way that Chile entered him, almost mystically, changing his destiny. He had become attached to Chile and could not so easily separate himself from its land and its people.

Dorfman's decision to stay in Chile in 1959 coincided with the eruption of revolutionary politics on the continent in the 1960s. He began his studies in 1960 in literature at the University of Chile, and his entrance into a community of young Chileans sparked yet another significant identity crisis for him. With the name "Edward," Dorfman was constantly forced to answer the question "Where are you from?" Up until the age of eighteen the answer had always been "America," and in those instances "America" did not resonate hemispherically but referred specifically to the United States, for it was not until much later that Dorfman would understand his identity as American in a broader sense (*Heading*, 152). During these early days at the university Dorfman had the sense of being an outsider, of straddling Chile and the United States. He continued to write literature in English in the evenings while spending the days discussing politics in Spanish with his friends: "vocal as I might be in support of the Latin American resistance, I kept doggedly writing my most personal work in English" (158–59). A key turning point for him came after an earthquake rocked the south of Chile in June 1960 and Dorfman became actively involved in a relief effort. The experience gave him a profound and intimate connection with Chilean workers, who were hardest hit by the catastrophe.

Shortly thereafter Dorfman began to reframe his identity, and as he describes it, "the change in my name became . . . the first step, the easiest symbolic step" (*Heading*, 159). This time Dorfman did not fabricate a name; instead he recuperated his forgotten middle name, Ariel, which resonated for him on a number of levels and thereby facilitated his multifaceted identity. In Hebrew Ariel means "lion of God" and is used in the Old Testament to refer to the city of Jerusalem, but in Latin America in the 1960s the name more readily evoked Ariel from Shakespeare's *Tempest*. More specifically it referred to José Enrique Rodó's 1900 essay, entitled *Ariel*, which called for the youth of Latin America to use Shakespeare's character as a role model because Ariel reflected the "spirit of air and goodness and magic" and provided an intellectual example for cultural autonomy (159).[7] Consequently in college Dorfman met a number of fellow students with the name Ariel. Their parents, Dorfman's mother included, considered "Ariel" "a symbol of opposition to the United States" (160). For Dorfman, "Ariel" indicated his Jewish legacy, referred to a play by Shakespeare on colonization, and invoked the beauty and spirit of the America to the south. Ironically, in choosing a name that had deep meaning for him and his Chilean friends, Dorfman also chose a name that simultaneously registered close ties to English and to Shakespeare, a writer who has had a tremendous influence on Dorfman's work. As Dorfman has interpreted the event, changing his name to Ariel allowed him to become "Caliban the savage, cannibalizing Ariel, the Hebrew Lion of God, for my own purposes" (160). By renaming himself Ariel, he attempted to merge his own identity with that of Latin America, and the act itself paralleled the rebellious, revolutionary spirit that was overtaking the region: "Latin America, contestatory, insurgent and rebellious, would appeal to an entirely different way of imagining myself, encouraging me to merge my personal crisis of identity with its parallel crisis, my own search with its search, my journey with its journey" (162). Consequently, just as Dorfman used "Eddie" to merge with the "American dream" as exemplified in Mark Twain's *The Prince and the Pauper*, he later used "Ariel" to merge with the Latin American dream of Rodó's *Ariel*. In each case, literary texts served as the basis for his identity; they gave his life structure and meaning, and they bound him, however tenuously, to a community.

Dorfman' resulting change into a rebellious, anti-capitalist, anti-imperialist leftist Latin American would solidify, ironically, when Dorfman, his wife Angélica, and their newborn son Rodrigo spent a year in the United States at Berkeley in 1968 while Dorfman was on a fellowship to write a book on Latin American literature. At this point in his career Dorfman had already cultivated a broad scholarly interest in literature. He had graduated from the University of Chile in 1965 with a *licenciado* (roughly the equivalent of a master's degree) in literature and was an assistant professor of Spanish literature and journalism at the same institution. He wrote his thesis on the pastoral plays of Shakespeare, had published his first book on the theater of Harold Pinter, and was working on a book on the contemporary Latin American novel. While in Berkeley, twists of fate, once again, placed Dorfman in precisely the time and place where history was being made. One of Dorfman's important lessons while at Berkeley concerned the nature of revolutionary struggle. He became acutely aware of the separation between the pleasure-loving hippies and the militant anti-war protesters, and he concluded that it was absolutely essential to bring these two strands of rebellion together. The unabashed quest for pleasure and sexual freedom was something Dorfman had not experienced in the relatively conservative youth culture of Chile: "I was to be permanently affected by those libertarian and anti-authoritarian and hedonistic urges, by the need to see the revolution as a territory of freedom that could not be forever put off" (*Heading*, 227). These concerns prepared him intellectually for postmodern struggles that included feminism, ecology, aboriginal rights, sexuality, and artistic experimentation. The question of how to link the personal with the political, of how to unite various political constituencies while respecting difference, traveled back with him to Chile and became a part of his contribution to debates over the agenda for Allende's party, the Unidad Popular (227–28).

Dorfman's return to the United States in 1968 placed many of his thoughts about inter-American art and politics into relief. On the one hand, both the United States and Latin America were experiencing a heightened explosion of political and revolutionary art and activism. In the United States Dorfman became familiar with the work of Malcolm X, Cesar Chavez, the Beats, Joan Baez, Pete Seeger, the Grateful Dead, and Herbert Marcuse (*Heading*, 198, 217). He was able to see firsthand the influence of Bob Dylan on the hippies (209). He could then experience these cultural icons alongside the writers of the Latin American literary boom, the poetry of Pablo Neruda and César Vallejo, the political writings of José Carlos Mariátegui and Che Guevara, and the music of Victor Jara and Violeta Parra. This comparative inter-American perspective on the region's revolutionary culture further developed his sense of the intersections between culture and social change. Alternatively, Dorfman was reminded of the cultural legacy that had led those in the United States to favor a cult of the hero and that had fostered an individualism contrastive to the collective subjectivity of Latin American political movements. In addition, Dorfman confronted the ways that this individualistic U.S. cultural legacy was also his own; it was what continued to isolate him at a profound level from his Latin American *compañeros*. Dorfman and the Berkeley youth culture shared the same cultural baggage, which included Amos 'n Andy, Esther Williams, Marlon Brando, and James Dean: "[The Berkeley youth] had adored optimistic heroes who always saved the day in the same way and believed in know-how that could solve any dilemma, they had bought into the American dream as kids, just as I had" (212). Even though the youth movements were critical of this ideology, they were often unable to escape it and could not avoid replicating it in their own political practice. With the privileged perspective of an outsider who is also an insider, Dorfman saw these flaws and vowed to try to eradicate them from his own identity, an irony, due to his insistence on an individual act of will, which he recognized but nevertheless could not avoid.

While in the United States, Dorfman lurked; he observed and witnessed the increased politicization of students on campus, but in keeping with his history of being an outsider, he did not become too involved because he was concerned about deportation. At the same time that the rebelliousness of Berkeley youth culture inspired him, it also bothered him in its distance from the immediate working-class struggles that formed the heart of Latin American revolutionary practice (*Heading*, 225). Sitting at a desk in Berkeley, Dorfman made the ultimate move to unite himself with Latin America: he stopped writing in English. In order to be close to Chile he realized that he had to lose the English language and end the game of dividing himself between politics in Spanish and personal writing in English (210). The cyclical nature of this act does not go unnoticed by Dorfman: "Repeating more than twenty years later my childhood gesture in that hospital, reacting in Berkeley just as I had back in New York, I drastically broke off relations with the language in which I had sought refuge from solitude my whole life, I embraced a tongue that would link me to a community that was imagining a different history for itself and for me, and I chose to become a contiguous human being" (220). In phrasing that echoes his recollection of his willful embrace of English as a two-and-a-half year-old boy quarantined in a New York hospital, Dorfman reflects on this moment as an act of agency: he broke off relations; he embraced; he chose. Yet again, coupled with this characterization of subjectivity as an act of free will, he exposes this description as idealistic fantasy and underscores the way that his identity was determined by history. In fact, he indicates that his "decision" was driven by historical circumstance, by the pressures of the moment that called for his identity to be "intact, seamless" rather than "hybrid" (221, 220).

While the reader may be persuaded to believe that a twenty-six-year-old is more capable of enacting a reversal of language and creating his own identity than a two-and-a-half-year-old, Dorfman's description of his transformation while at Berkeley requires skepticism. Both tales of linguistic "control," despite the vast difference in Dorfman's age, read as highly analogous. In each case, Dorfman's will to wholeness mirrored a historical moment that demanded allegiance to a unified, coherent, stable identity. Just as he explains that his immersion into English accompanied the heightened U.S. nationalism of the postwar era, Dorfman explains his quest for unity with Spanish and Latin America as a result of the political climate of the 1960s: "This was the sixties of extreme nationalism, the all-or-nothing, the either-or sixties. It was not a time for shades of difference, for complexity, for soul-searching about the enigma of heterogeneous identity" (*Heading*, 220). Not only does Dorfman depict this "personal" moment as one guided by "public" events, but he also suggests that his current self-presentation as hybrid is indebted to a certain extent to postmodern sensibilities. These descriptions call into question the degree to which critical tides shape our own "self"-understanding.

Upon his return to Chile in 1969, Dorfman (who had previously obtained Chilean citizenship in 1967) became even more actively involved in national politics, and he and his friends began work on Salvador Allende's campaign. Dorfman's experience as the child of leftists, his exposure to radical politics in Chile and Berkeley, and his early life experience of exile and dislocation combined to form the foundation of his dedication to Allendista politics. As an activist, Dorfman recognized early on that his militancy was best served by drawing on his skills as a writer and culture worker. The Allende campaign allowed him to join a community and to struggle in solidarity in a way that he had never experienced. It also allowed him to become a part of one of the few successful socialist revolutions that peacefully came to power. The belief that revolutions can take place through democracy has had a major impact on Dorfman's pacifism and his faith in the transformative experience of gentle solidarity.

The successful election of Salvador Allende on September 4, 1970, had a profound effect on Dorfman's life as well as his writing. He remembers the night of September 4 as utopian, and he describes it in both his memoir and his fiction. In the memoir he writes of that night being "as near to a religious epiphany as I have had in my life" (*Heading*, 243). In his second novel, *La última canción de Manuel Sendero* (1982; *The Last Song of Manuel Sendero*), written in exile, Dorfman narrates the night of September 4 as a singular moment of community: "Estaba por fin en mi propio hogar. . . . La ciudad también estaba satisfecha de que por fin hubiéramos llegado. Después de tantos siglos, que al fin y al cabo sus hijos preferidos, sus reales habitantes nuevos, sus herederos entre los que yo me incluía, que todos ellos hubieran arribado . . . a sus fronteras" (120–21) ("At last I was in my own home. . . . The city was also pleased we had finally come. After so many centuries, at last her favorite children, her true native sons, her heirs, among whom I included myself, had reached her borders"; 148–150). As soon as the experience is over, Dorfman's first inclination is to narrate it, to record it through literature: "I wanted to put every last word of it down on paper" (*Heading*, 45).

Toward the end of the Allende government, Dorfman accepted a position as the administration's communications and media adviser, and he quickly became engaged in advertising campaigns intent on disseminating Allende's message to the people. Throughout the Allende years, he was also involved with publishing, working for the state publishing house, Quimantú, a word that means "sunshine of knowledge" in the native language of the Chilean Mapuche Indians. Dorfman's work with Quimantú included releasing international classics in Spanish in affordable editions. Quimantú released over 5 million books in two and a half years. It also transformed the content of some of the magazines it inherited from before the Allende government and created new ones. In this context of excitement and cultural revolution, Dorfman began work on one of his most internationally read pieces of writing—the critique of North American cultural imperialism *Para leer al pato Donald* (1971; *How to Read Donald Duck*), co-authored with Armand Mattelart. The authors explain in a preface to the English translation that they wrote the book accompanied by "a people on the march to cultural liberation—a process which also meant criticizing the 'mass' cultural merchandise exported so profitably by the U.S. to the Third World" (*Donald Duck*, 10). Dorfman's early affiliation as a young boy with what he termed the ideology of Donald Duck uniquely situated him as a critic of its seductive powers. His attack on Disney bore the weight of his anger over the way that U.S. pop culture had co-opted his identity as a young man (*Heading*, 251). Ironically, it is precisely this U.S.-insider vantage point that sharpened his analysis and facilitated his acceptance into the Chilean intellectual community: "It is paradoxical that it should have been my penetrating and intimate knowledge of the United States that would finally allow most of my compatriots and many other people around the world to identify me as a Chilean writer" (*Heading*, 253).

Prior to publishing this sociological critique of media culture, Dorfman had published two books of literary criticism. His first book, released in 1968 (the year he traveled to Berkeley), was *El absurdo entre cuatro paredes: El teatro de Harold Pinter* (The Absurd within Four Walls: The Theater of Harold Pinter), a close reading of Pinter's work. Dorfman's analysis focused on the violence, conflicts, and lack of communication that run throughout Pinter's theater. The book also investigated the ties between culture and social criticism, especially interrogating the political possibility of the theater of the absurd and Pinter's distinct role in that project. In 1970 he published *Imaginación y violencia en América* (Imagination and Violence in America), the work he developed while at Berkeley. The book has essays on Jorge Luis Borges and a number of boom writers. Each essay bears the historical context of its writing and reveals Dorfman's interest in linking literature with the social conflicts of Latin America. He asks how literature works to promote a fatalistic mentality, how it provides hope, how it assumes violence, and how it fosters rebellion. At the same time, Dorfman completed his first novel, *Moros en la costa* (1973; translated and reedited as *Hard Rain* in 1990), a highly complex meditation on the relationship between art and politics and on the potential disconnect between intellectuals and social struggle. These four books taken together provide the foundation for much of Dorfman's future work, and they underscore the multiple, yet complementary, directions that his writing would later take. The synchronicity of these books reveals much about Dorfman's creative project, which has always been formally diverse in its approach to the underlying issues and themes that nevertheless span his oeuvre. When we read these books in conjunction with Dorfman's university teaching as a professor of literature and journalism, his work for Quimantú, and his other cultural projects in support of Allende's presidency, we see the full range of activities that he has maintained throughout his life. These multiple activities—from writing highly experimental fiction to literary criticism to cultural criticism to political slogans; from teaching to working in the publishing industry to working on ad campaigns and television programs to activism and marches and speeches—reveal the dizzying array of registers within which he operated and continues to operate.

After struggling with exile and displacement early in life, Dorfman felt that he had truly found his home in Chile and the Unidad Popular. Soon, though, Dorfman's personal history of exile repeated itself when Allende was overthrown on September 11, 1973, by Augusto Pinochet's military coup, which sent Dorfman into exile once again. As he recounts in *Heading South, Looking North*, it is because he felt he belonged to the Unidad Popular that the decision to go into exile was especially painful. He could not help but imagine that he should have died with his comrades in Chile. At the beginning of his memoir he refers to September 11, 1973, as the day "when I should have died and did not" (*Heading*, 3). In their study of exile and migration, Leon and Rebeca Grinberg explain that exiles often suffer intense feelings of guilt and anxiety; this was especially true for Dorfman since he was supposed to be at La Moneda, the Chilean presidential palace, the morning that the military invaded. Dorfman spends considerable time in his memoir debating whether he was spared death due to pure chance or for some higher reason. The fact that Claudio Gimeno—the man who replaced him on his shift—died haunts Dorfman and suggests to him the arbitrary unpredictability of life.

Dorfman's survival seems to hinge, in part, on his role as a creative member of Allende's government. He had switched shifts with Gimeno so that he could pitch an idea for a political commercial. Susana la Semilla (Susan the Seed), the lover of Federico el Fertilizante (Fred the Fertilizer), was part of an ad campaign Dorfman concocted to raise public awareness of the politics behind the transportation strike that took place in 1973 and threatened public support for Allende. In order to present his project to Augusto Olivares, the director of national television, he could not be at La Moneda on the morning of the coup. Was this sequence of events an accident, or could Dorfman imagine that his cartoon character had worked to save his life? For many years he would explain his survival as a consequence of Susana—that is, as a consequence of his creativity, because such an explanation "gives me the illusion that somehow I created the conditions whereby I thwarted death" (*Heading*, 30). Yet he also recognizes that it is quite likely that a "series of arbitrary intercessions spared me" (37). The second key intercession came from Fernando Flores, who was responsible for calling Allende supporters to La Moneda the night before the coup and who had purposefully crossed Dorfman's name off the list. Years later, Dorfman confronted Flores and asked him why he hadn't been called. Flores responded: "Well, somebody had to live to tell the story" (39). Dorfman admits that such an explanation is comforting but that to believe it would be to discount all of the other "fortuitous coincidences" that had kept him alive and had buried other young Chilean writers as talented and "as much in love with life" as he was (39). Unsure of whether his survival is logical or a twist of fate, Dorfman hopes that his life, surrounded as it has been by so much death, has grown to have meaning through his work as a writer.

A series of events after the coup led Dorfman to formally seek asylum at the Argentine Embassy. First, he witnessed the burning of his book *How to Read Donald Duck* on television. He imagined that he was "the first author in history to have watched his own work burnt live on TV" (*Heading*, 139). Next, when Dorfman tried to visit a friend to seek his advice, he found that his friend had been abducted by the police. Dorfman was stubborn and procrastinated, hiding out within an underground network until a leader of the underground explicitly told him that as a writer, he was worth more to the party abroad than in Chile (139–49). As he waited to gain entrance to the Argentine Embassy, hiding out in the home of the Israeli ambassador, he watched through a window as his wife was picked up, questioned, and then released by two secret police. It was the experience of seeing Angélica in such a perilous situation that caused Dorfman to realize that he had to get his family out of Chile. That day he reluctantly became reconciled to exile (175–77).

Dorfman would never be reconciled to the fact that Pinochet had tried to rob Allende's supporters of their hopes and dreams, however. He spoke to a fellow passenger in a van shuttling them from the Argentine Embassy to the airport, a worker named Juan who also had sought refuge at the Argentine Embassy; he told Dorfman that he believed the coup had happened because Pinochet wanted to punish the workers for believing in social change, for daring to feel joy. Dorfman realized in that moment that they were "being disciplined for an act of imagination. Pinochet was trying to make [Juan] and millions like him admit that they had been mistaken—not so much in tactics as in their human strategy, the very rebellion itself, the fact that they had dared to dream of an alternative to the life charted out for them since before their birth" (*Heading*, 261). Dorfman now recognized the extent to which Pinochet and his supporters were preparing the world for the mind-numbing consumption of advanced capitalism and neoliberalism (261–62). Everyone close to Dorfman at the time of the coup was either disappeared, tortured, or exiled. Every single friend suffered. It is difficult to convey the extent of Dorfman's loss, especially because his writing, while trying to keep the memory of those who suffered alive, refuses to wallow in the devastations of the coup. Despite living such an extraordinary nightmare, he still maintains hope: "I was not willing then, in the van, and I am not willing now, so many years later, to tell Juan that his joy was unreal" (262).

When he left the Argentine Embassy in Chile, Dorfman fled first to the country of his birth, Argentina, where his recently awarded novel, *Hard Rain*, helped to get him an Argentine passport with which he was able to travel to France. Dorfman's early years in exile were difficult. He was depressed and unable to write fiction for years. "My suffering had been remote before," he says, "but friends were being killed, and we were on the verge of hunger; I was turned into a beggar" (cited in Jaggi, n.p.). He lacked work for a couple of years but eventually found a position teaching at the Sorbonne in 1975. (Dorfman is fluent in French as well as English and Spanish.) Friends credit his wife with helping him to sort through the losses resulting from the coup. Slowly Dorfman was able to turn his pain into language, his sadness into poetry; his first creative writing was a series of poems that were later translated into English and published as *Missing* by Amnesty International in 1982. During this period Dorfman spent considerable time aiding the Chilean resistance to Pinochet, using his bilingual language skills to write letters and petitions. After a few years in Paris the Dorfmans moved to Amsterdam in 1976, where their second son, Joaquín, was born. They then moved to the United States in 1980, when Dorfman was awarded a fellowship at the Wilson Center in Washington, D.C., a move that paralleled his father's refuge in the United States on a Guggenheim fellowship in 1945. Dorfman attempted to gain a visa for Mexico in order to relocate his family there, but when that request was denied and when teaching opportunities became available at Duke University in 1984, he resigned himself to living in the country responsible for Pinochet's dictatorship: "I felt the paradox in Washington; I'm here because this was where Nixon and Kissinger conspired to get rid of my government. . . . But it was also a place where I could make a living" (cited in Jaggi, n.p.). Dorfman used his proximity to U.S. lawmaking to raise awareness of the atrocities of the Pinochet dictatorship. For instance, he delivered copies of *Viudas* (1981; *Widows*) to the entire U.S. Congress, a move that led North Carolina's Republican senator, Jesse Helms, to denounce Dorfman as "one of the prime disinformation agents of the radical Chilean left" (cited in Jaggi, n.p.).

To read Dorfman's work chronologically is to have the uncanny experience of seeing history revealed in fiction before it was enacted in life. Sadly, many of Dorfman's pessimistic literary works have prefigured Latin American history. For example, *Hard Rain* was released at the same time that the warning signs of an impending coup were raining down upon the Chilean people. Dorfman writes in a preface to the 1990 translation that "violence, like a hidden wind, blows through the narrative voices. It would eventually come to the surface in the hard reality of historical Chile. Less than ten months after I completed the text, a military coup brutally ended our experiment" (vi–vii).

Dorfman wrote his next three novels in exile, and each novel progressively reflects his sense of political disempowerment. After experiencing historical agency and political success with the Unidad Popular, the suffering of exile for a third time had a profound effect on Dorfman's writing. Initially exile was particularly difficult for Dorfman because he had strongly believed in Chilean national sovereignty and the Unidad Popular. However, once in exile, it became increasingly clear to him that the socialist experiment of the Unidad Popular was doomed by the requirements of transnational capitalism. He began to see a need to rethink marxist strategy for achieving economic and social change, and he questioned the notion of historical agency. Alice Nelson, commenting on an interview with Dorfman, explains: "After his exile, Dorfman experienced a tremendous difficulty in writing, as all of the structures used to describe reality before the coup seemed to fall along with the Utopian impulse of the Allende years" (245). Still, the literary aesthetics of Dorfman's three exile novels—*Viudas* (1981; *Widows*), *La última canción de Manuel Sendero*, (1982; *The Last Song of Manuel Sendero*), and *Máscaras* (1988; *Mascara*)— are marked not only by a deep sense of loss but also by a persistent hope. Even as these novels describe a seemingly ubiquitous authoritarianism, they tell stories of successful although minor resistance to official history.

Like *Hard Rain*, Dorfman's exile novels also foretell history. *Widows* narrates the experiences of a small village in Greece on the eve of the Second World War. Caught in the grip of a repressive dictatorship, this small village has practically lost its entire adult male population; the men have simply "disappeared." The plot is centered on the claiming of dead bodies that are found in a river. The women of the village fight for the right to bury these bodies, but the government refuses to release information about whether these now decayed corpses are their relatives. Dorfman modeled the tale on historical accounts of human rights abuses, yet it was after its publication that the first unidentifiable bodies were found floating in the rivers of Chile. Dorfman's second exile novel, *The Last Song of Manuel Sendero*, appeared more than a decade after the coup. A far more intricate narrative than *Widows*, it reveals the increasing disillusionment and frustration of the Chilean exile community. Whereas *Widows* has a fairly clear sense of perpetrator and victim, *The Last Song of Manuel Sendero* includes descriptions of political conflict in ethical terms that range from premodern Manichaeism to postmodern relativity.

Dorfman's environment for creative production underwent a number of substantial changes during his exile. *Widows* was written while Dorfman was in exile in Europe, whereas *The Last Song of Manuel Sendero* was funded in part by a grant from the Wilson Center at the Smithsonian. In 1983, as a result of international protests, Dorfman's exile was lifted, and he returned briefly to Chile. In 1986 Chilean news reported that Dorfman was dead, creating quite a scandal. After that, Dorfman visited his country only briefly and with much caution while Pinochet remained in power. This was the atmosphere of Dorfman's third exile novel, *Mascara*, a deeply disturbing narrative about a protagonist totally disconnected from society.

The treatment of exile in Dorfman's work is also related to his Jewish background and his family's legacy of diaspora. As noted above, Jewish themes influence his treatment of exile when he turns to storytelling as a way of preserving history and memory. Dorfman has spoken at various times about the effects of his Jewish heritage on his writing, and over time his thoughts on his Jewish influences have shifted. He explains: "For most of my life I thought I was Jewish merely by accident, that I was Latin American by choice, and that it had befallen on me to be an English-speaking person. . . . If for decades I thought of Jews simply as being very much the observers of a series of religious habits and I observe none of these . . . now I've discovered I might be Jewish in the deepest sense. [So] while I used to answer that I'd be Jewish until the day when there was no more anti-Semitism, today I am more conscious of my background" (cited in Stavans, 310–11). Jewish themes appear in Dorfman's work, especially in *Konfidenz*, which unfolds during the Nazi occupation of France.

In keeping with his conviction that literary activism requires multiple registers of engagement, Dorfman continued while in exile to write journal and newspaper articles, essays, and literary criticism in addition to his short stories, poems, and novels. The eleven nonfiction books Dorfman published during exile can be largely divided between those concerned with cultural criticism and those focusing on literature, although it should be clear that for Dorfman these two projects overlap and intertwine. Some of the key representative works of cultural criticism are the following: *Ensayos quemados en Chile: Inocencia y neocolonialismo* (1974; Essays Burned in Chile: Innocence and Neo-colonialism); *Supermán y sus amigos del alma* (1974; co-authored with Manuel Jofré; Superman and His Soul Mates); *La última aventura del Llanero solitario* (1979; The Last Adventure of the Lone Ranger); *Reader's nuestro que estás en la tierra* (1980; Our Reader's Digest Who Art on Earth); and *The Empire's Old Clothes* (1983). In most cases these works analyze the ideology of neocolonialism and the ideological function of superheroes that originate in the United States and are exported to Latin America. Dorfman's literary criticism in works like *Hacia la liberación del lector latinoamericano* (1984; Toward the Liberation of the Latin American Reader) engages similar issues by focusing on a number of key Latin American literary texts and their relationship with readers from the region. Other works from this period—like *De elefantes, literatura y miedo:*

Ensayos sobre la comunicación americana (1986; *Of Elephants, Literature, and Fear: Essays on American Communication*)—combine literary criticism with media criticism in an argument about the role that culture plays in shaping society. This varied library demonstrates that in addition to publishing novels, poetry, and short stories, Dorfman spent considerable effort during his sixteen years of exile advancing his theories about art, mass media, and politics.

In 1988, shortly after the release of *Mascara*, Chile held a plebiscite to vote "yes" or "no" to Pinochet's continued control of Chile. Dorfman flew to Santiago and was joined by 55 percent of the population to vote against Pinochet's rule. After the official end of the dictatorship, Dorfman began to split his time between teaching at Duke University and traveling to Chile. While he considered relocating permanently to Chile, he came to recognize that he had put down roots in North Carolina. No longer an exile, he began to describe himself as an expatriate. His first significant work after the Chilean plebiscite was *La muerte y la doncella* (1990; *Death and the Maiden*), which he wrote in three weeks while in Chile. As though the fall of Pinochet signified a sort of rebirth, Dorfman worked creatively for the first time with drama, a literary form that allowed him to merge his interest with testimony, public performance, and the written word.[8] *Death and the Maiden* deals with the crisis of a torture victim, Paulina, who believes that her husband, Gerardo, has unwittingly allowed her torturer, Doctor Miranda, to spend the night in their home. Depicting some of the most serious crises facing a nation in transition from a dictatorship infamous for human rights violations to democracy, the play has been an extraordinary success internationally, even though it has been controversial in Chile. Dorfman explains Chile's resistance to confronting the issues revealed in *Death and the Maiden* in an interview with Carlos Reyes and Maggie Paterson:

> In a transition to a democracy as in Chile, Bolivia, South Africa, there are different reasons why people do not want to remember. They say, *Look, if we keep on stirring up the past it's going to destroy us*. This includes many who were themselves repressed, hurt or part of the resistance. Gerardo in *Death and the Maiden* does that, and the Captain in *Widows*. *There's a future ahead, let's turn the page, let's forget this, let's start over again*. This is a desire to reach a consensus about where the country is going, and it means excluding those who continue to remember. But the conflicts are real; you can submerge them but not erase them. (n.p.; emphasis in original)

Set in an unknown location that very closely parallels events in Chile, the play has resonated globally. In 1993 there were fifty simultaneous productions in

Germany alone. Other countries that have suffered dictatorship, authoritarianism, and massive social oppression, like South Africa, have found that the play allows them to confront their trauma.

Death and the Maiden prefigures and dramatizes important events in Chilean history. The play was written after the announcement in 1990 by newly elected moderate president Patricio Aylwin of the formation of the National Commission for Truth and Reconciliation (also known as the Rettig Commission), which was established to investigate both the disappearances that had resulted in death and executions. All tortured victims still alive were completely ignored by this process. Moreover, while the commission provided a lengthy report on atrocities committed during the dictatorship, most of the crimes named in the document were not prosecuted or punished. The atmosphere of immunity that pervaded these crimes is part of the historical landscape within which *Death and the Maiden* was written. But at the time Dorfman was writing the play, he could not have foreseen that Pinochet, having served during the transition as head of the armed forces, would "step down" on March 10, 1998, to assume the position of senator-for-life, which ostensibly ensured his immunity from prosecution. Nor could Dorfman have known that while on a trip to London in October 1998 for medical treatment, Pinochet would be arrested on behalf of the Spanish government and, like Dorfman's character Doctor Miranda, would avoid punishment and would resume his life in Chile.

The ending of Dorfman's play, where Paulina and her torturer, Miranda, are both in the audience of a concert, is a chilling foreshadowing of events in Chile. Pinochet returned to Chile on March 3, 2000, after avoiding prosecution by Spain and after the most significant international acknowledgment of his heinous crimes. Back in Chile, he was prosecuted numerous times, with varying results. He died on December 10, 2006, while under house arrest. In 1991 Dorfman wrote the following in the postscript to the print version of the play: "If the play revealed many of the hidden conflicts that were just under the surface of the nation, and therefore posed a clear threat to people's psychological security, it also could be an instrument through which they explored their identity and the contradictory options available to us in the years to come" (59–60). He could scarcely have known that years later, Pinochet's arrest would send the country into conflict and turmoil yet again. Dorfman admits that "By writing the imaginary, you write the future: what was not happening in Chile, South Africa, the Czech Republic, but was going to happen" (cited in Jaggi, n.p.).

Death and the Maiden, now translated into over thirty languages, continues to be staged across the globe. It premiered in London in 1991 at the Royal Court Theater, where it opened in conjunction with a sketch by Harold Pinter, *The New World Order*, and the play was given the Lawrence Olivier Award. Mike Nichols directed the Broadway show starring Glenn Close, Richard Dreyfus, and Gene Hackman. The success of the play led to a film in 1994 directed by Roman Polanski and starring Sigourney Weaver and Ben Kingsley. Dorfman co-wrote the screenplay. He also was on the set in Boulogne, just outside Paris, where he was able to observe the details of the filming process. The explosive success of *Death and the Maiden* turned Dorfman into an overnight celebrity, and he found himself hanging out with rock stars and famous actors. This instant international visibility, rather than bringing him closer to Chilean society, further alienated him from those who had not gone into exile, and the play came under sharp critique from within Chile. As he describes it, "Many in the cultural elite thought it was time to teach me a lesson, that I had to pay my dues. In a sense they were right: they'd suffered directly while I was running around with Sting and Peter Gabriel" (cited in Jaggi, n.p.).

While Dorfman is quick to rationalize why his Chilean friends did not support the play, it is ironic that his most successful literary work is the one that most signifies the distance between himself and his beloved Chile, the one work of literature that underscores his foreignness, his persistent outsider status. Ilan Stavans has noted that after Dorfman's literary celebrity many came to consider his passion as disingenuous: " 'He's left so he's a traitor; he's successful so he no longer speaks for us.' But by assuming a voice and speaking out, is he stealing it? He's been accused of using causes for self-promotion" (cited in Jaggi, n.p.). Dorfman's many years as a political activist and exile taught him to withstand public disapproval and prepared him for much criticism, but with his increased visibility he had to face such attacks on a much larger scale. The British actor Juliet Stevenson, who won an award for her role as Paulina in the London production of *Death and the Maiden*, notes that Dorfman was able to withstand his success and the attendant criticisms well: "Ariel was over-excited by the world of opportunity laid before him— Hollywood stars vying to do the movie. But he worked through it and came out as himself. He puts himself on the line politically, which you can't do if you're worrying about placating Hollywood" (cited in Jaggi, n.p.). Working with Roman Polanski was one of the ways that Dorfman scoffed at public opinion. For him Polanski was a logical choice to direct, since he too had suffered violence, disappearance, exile, and a ruptured nation: "Roman has spent his life mastering and using the techniques of realism in the service of the unspeakable" (*Other Septembers*, 199).

After the success of *Death and the Maiden,* Dorfman published his memoir, *Heading South, Looking North* (1998; *Rumbo al sur, deseando el norte*), which describes his life prior to the coup of 1973 and is interspersed with eight sections dealing with the events of the coup and his eventual exile. Subtitled *A Bilingual Journey,* his memoir is a meditation on his dual identities in English and Spanish. Dorfman's second novel after the Chilean plebiscite, *The Nanny and the Iceberg* (1999; *La nana y el iceberg*), may be his most Chilean novel in that it engages most directly with Chilean history. In an epilogue to the novel, Dorfman elaborates at length about the bonds between the novel and specific historical events. The one clear connection, he explains, is "the fact that in 1992 the Chilean government did indeed exhibit an iceberg from Antarctica in its pavilion in Sevilla as part of the World's Fair" (355).

Dorfman's work after the plebiscite represents a heightened attention to globalization. Not only was Dorfman responding to the legacy of Pinochet in Chile's transition, but he was also confronting the shape of global culture after the fall of the Berlin Wall (1989), the establishment of the North American Free Trade Agreement (NAFTA; 1994), and the efforts to expand NAFTA in the Free Trade Area of the Americas (FTAA). Heightened attention to *maquiladoras* (sweatshops located in Mexican border regions), to the global labor force, and to the emerging logics of economic and cultural exchange in a world dominated by U.S. capitalism affected Dorfman, who had always been sensitive to the intersections between modes of production and modes of thought. Dorfman's sense of the acceleration of globalization and neoliberalism derives from his observations of Chile, but he then considers Chile within a transnational framework. These interests led him to spend time as a Forum Fellow at the Davos Symposium of the World Economic Forum while he was researching his novel *Blake's Therapy.* Instituted in 1970 by Klaus Schwab, the Davos Symposium gathers together the world's chief executives in order to consider corporate solutions to global, economic, social, and environmental issues. The symposium allowed Dorfman to observe "compassionate" corporate giants, like George Soros, and wonder what role conscientious capitalism might play in the new global order. Even though the World Economic Forum maintains that it is committed "to improving the state of the world" and emphasizes the interdependency of globalized society, in his acknowledgments to the novel Dorfman admits that he did not find a model for his protagonist, Graham Blake, among its members (World Economic Forum, n.p.). Even though Dorfman had written a number of texts that investigated the cultural and social impact of global capitalism, *Blake's Therapy* is the first of his works to tackle the problem head on and through the eyes of a man who is not only inside the system but also has worked to create it.[9]

In addition to drawing Dorfman's attention to globalization, the end of Pinochet's rule signaled further transformations in Dorfman's work. Not only did Dorfman write his first play and most successful work, but he also began to collaborate more formally with his older son, Rodrigo, who helped him envision the ending of the play, where the mirror drops down and faces the audience. Since that moment Dorfman has worked on a number of projects with his sons. He and Rodrigo adapted *Mascara* into a play that was produced in Japan and Germany. Then Rodrigo adapted the play *Lector* (1990; *Reader*, 1995), which itself was an adaptation from a short story, into a screenplay called *Paradise II*. Rodrigo and his father co-wrote the screenplay for the film *Prisoners in Time* (1995), which starred John Hurt as Eddie Lomax, an ex-prisoner of war from the Second World War who confronts his Japanese torturer. Next they worked on the film adaptation of Dorfman's short story "My House Is on Fire," which Dorfman had written originally while in exile in Amsterdam about two children living in fear under Pinochet.[10] The film changed the setting to the United States, where two young illegal Latin American immigrants play "waiting for the enemy" and have to decide what to do when a stranger shows up. Co-directing *My House Is on Fire* in 1997, Rodrigo and his father won awards in the Edinburgh, Toronto, and Telluride film festivals. Vanessa Redgrave described the work as "a tender poem on film" (n.p.). The two collaborated on *Dead Line,* a cinematic adaptation of Dorfman's poetry from *Last Waltz in Santiago*, made to commemorate the fiftieth anniversary of the Universal Declaration of Human Rights. The film was shot in London and produced by Channel 4. Next, father and son co-wrote the play "Who's Who," a murder mystery farce that revolves around five characters from the Hollywood "dream factory": "The play deals with issues of ethnic representation in movies and authoritarian structures of power everywhere" (A. Dorfman and R. Dorfman, "About 'Who's Who,' " n.p.). As of 2007, the play had not yet been produced in the United States. It premiered in Frankfurt in 1998.

Dorfman also co-wrote a novel with his younger son, Joaquín, *The Burning City* (2003), about a young man living in New York City during the summer before the terrorist attacks of September 11, 2001. He is a bicycle messenger who delivers personal messages in an age that has become overrun by the impersonality of the Internet. The book opens with a playful scene that asks the reader to imagine the collaborative process between father and son: "Try to guess which one of us got in the last word." In 2007, the three Dorfmans finished their first team project, *Los Angeles, Open City*, a screenplay about what it means to be an American that delves into issues of immigration and identity. These collaborative efforts with his sons further indicate a new shift since *Death and the Maiden*—Dorfman's increasing work with media and film—which, in fact, signals a return to the work with media that was a part of his life during Allende's presidency.

Following *Death and the Maiden*, Dorfman continued to write a number of plays. First he worked on two adaptations: *Widows*, which was adapted from the novel in collaboration with Tony Kushner, and *Reader* (1995), which he adapted from the short story of the same name. These three plays together formed *The Resistance Trilogy*. In addition to the two plays that Dorfman has co-written with Rodrigo, he has written a second trilogy, which he calls the "Redemption Trilogy." This not yet fully published second trilogy includes *Purgatorio*, "Picasso's Closet," and "The Other Side." *Purgatorio* revises the timeless tale of Medea. The play has only two actors, Man and Woman, and they are confined to a stark white room where each interrogates the other. *Purgatorio* premiered in London in 2001 and had its U.S. premiere in Seattle in 2005.

"Picasso's Closet," which premiered in Washington, D.C., in 2006, opens on a frenzied Pablo Picasso painting *Guernica* and explores the role of the artist during war by delving into an imaginary view of Picasso living in occupied France during the Second World War. "The Other Side" premiered in Tokyo in 2003 and in New York in 2005. As in *Purgatorio*, the play centers on a couple. In this play the couple lives in a zone between two warring nations whose names are fabricated but sound vaguely Balkan. These imaginary nations represent the multifarious border disputes that have plagued human history. The husband and wife make their living by taking care of dead bodies found near their home, collecting identification before burying them. A work that takes a refreshingly original look at the problem of borders and cross-cultural identity, this play investigates the intersection of ideological and physical boundaries.

Consistently advocating human rights, Dorfman's literature turns again and again to themes that illuminate the struggle for human rights. These themes appear in his work beginning with his exile and are found in almost every one of his texts, but they appear with particular force in *Widows*, *Reader*, *Death and the Maiden*, and in his short stories and poetry most recently collected in *My House Is on Fire* and *In Case of Fire in a Foreign Land*. Since his exile Dorfman has also worked extensively with human rights advocacy groups such as Amnesty International, the magazine/organization Index on Censorship, and Human Rights Watch. He regularly writes editorials and articles dedicated to human rights issues and gives public speeches on the topic. These public appearances range from commencement speeches to addresses before the UN General Assembly. This dedication led Kerry Kennedy Cuomo to approach him for help with her project, *Speak Truth to Power*. She interviewed over fifty human rights defenders and used their testimonies to create a book honoring their struggles. Next she asked Dorfman to take those texts and create a theatrical production that would allow these voices to be heard in a public performance. The result was *The Speak Truth to Power Play: Voices from Beyond the Dark*, published by Amnesty International (2000) and released in a later edition as *Manifesto for Another World: Voices from Beyond the Dark* (2004). The play premiered at the Kennedy Center on September 19, 2000, with an all-star cast that included Alec Baldwin, Sigourney Weaver, and John Malkovich.

Since the fall of Pinochet, Dorfman has published a number of nonfiction works that complement and dialogue with his fiction. Three key texts intertwine the personal with the political: *Exorcising Terror: The Incredible Unending Trial of General Augusto Pinochet* (2002); *Desert Memories: Journeys through the Chilean North* (2004); and *Other Septembers, Many Americas* (2004). The first, ostensibly an account of Pinochet's trial, is also a prolonged meditation on the notion of evil. Told with suspense, the text unravels the events of Pinochet's arrest, layering current events with testimony and personal recollection. *Desert Memories* provides a similarly hybrid text that, on the one hand, is a travel memoir of the northern desert of Chile and, on the other hand, is Dorfman's personal quest to find information about his wife Angélica's ancestors and also about the death of a friend, Freddy Taberna, who was murdered in the desert by Pinochet's so-called "Caravan of Death."

Another major turning point in Dorfman's life took place in 2005, when, after becoming a U.S. citizen, he voted for the first time in the local elections in Durham, North Carolina.[11] He used the opportunity to muse on the role of dissent in American identity, creating a multimedia Web site for PBS's POV series that was designed by his son Rodrigo. He describes entering a nearly deserted gym and waiting to see if his name was on the list of eligible voters, vaguely wondering if his name would actually not be on the list. He compares the experience to the experience in Chile, where voting held significant symbolic power and always seemed linked to struggle. The decision to seek U.S. citizenship and to use that transformation as an opportunity to reflect on the meaning of national identity flows from his response to the events of September 11, 2001. *Other Septembers, Many Americas* unites much of Dorfman's political writing since the terrorist attacks of what is now simply called "9/11" on the United States. Beginning with hope for the ways that the attacks might have brought the Americas together by allowing the United States to see that other countries have suffered their own September 11s, Dorfman writes of his dismay over the fact that the moment served to divide the United States even further from the rest of the world.

While on location in Santiago, Chile, in December 2006 to film *A Promise to the Dead: The Exile Journey of Ariel Dorfman*, a documentary based on his memoir and directed by Canadian Peter Raymont, Dorfman again had the uncanny experience of witnessing history when this brief trip coincided with the death of Pinochet. Dorfman and the crew of the film immediately seized on the opportunity to shoot scenes in front of the hospital where Pinochet had recently died of a heart attack. Dorfman spoke directly with a woman who was dramatically mourning Pinochet's passing. In a telling scene that underscores Dorfman's ongoing interest in breaking down barriers of communication, he attempts to connect with this woman, explaining that while he has spent most of his life opposing Pinochet, he understands her feelings and hopes that they can learn to respect one another. As Dorfman reflects on the encounter, he considers it a success, but the viewer may be less convinced.

It is interesting that the film offers similar aesthetics to Dorfman's own work, especially with regard to the complexity of memory and trauma. But it also reveals Dorfman as vulnerable and flawed. Against the image of Dorfman as a public figure and successful writer, in scenes where he movingly describes (for instance) the link between the events of 9/11/2001 and those of 9/11/1973 in Chile, the film captures scenes that reveal another side. We learn, for instance, that he had never visited his grandmother's grave in Buenos Aires; perhaps not doing so was an effort to postpone acknowledging her death, but the consequence is that no one in the family has paid attention to her remains. When Dorfman and Rodrigo finally go to visit her, they find that she has been moved to a common unmarked burial ground. They stand weeping, with flowers in their hands, looking into the general area where she now lies. This detail about Dorfman's life, about his inability to face personal loss, reveals his limits and reminds the audience that the public Dorfman is not necessarily the same as the personal one. For an author who has spent decades memorializing the dead and advocating the importance of public memory in the face of trauma, this scene reveals that he too struggles with these issues.

The film has a series of such scenes, but these moments do not overshadow the larger project of the film, which is to reveal Dorfman's commitment to and compassion for those who suffered under Pinochet. In one especially touching scene Dorfman accompanies Aleida, the daughter of Sergio Leiva, to a Chilean courthouse, where he signs an affidavit confirming that he saw her father shot by a sniper while he was a refugee in the Argentine Embassy. Until Dorfman's words provided a challenge to official history, Aleida had suffered the trauma of not only losing her father but also having his death completely erased from public memory. Another scene presses the point of his outsider status when Dorfman appears on a television talk show with a Pinochet supporter shortly after the general's death. The debate concerns whether Pinochet deserves to have a military burial. Dorfman adamantly opposes the idea, arguing that a man who denies his enemies the ability to bury their dead has violated military codes of conduct. He then directly asks the program's host when he first knew about the torture conducted under Pinochet. The simple truth of Dorfman's words shocks the host, since such bluntness was not common in Chilean discourse. The film was released in 2007 and has won a number of awards, including placement on the short list of fifteen documentaries considered for the 2008 Academy Awards.[12] It was named one of the ten best Canadian films of 2007 and opened the 2008 Human Rights Watch film festival.

Throughout his travels, both forced and voluntary, Dorfman has been a writer, teacher, and activist, and, to the extent possible, he has consistently worked in all three areas since the 1970s. He is committed to a multifaceted intellectual program that involves grassroots activism, scholarly writing, literary writing, journalism, media projects, teaching, and public appearances. He has been a professor of Latin American literature at the University of Chile, in Amsterdam, at the Sorbonne, and at the University of Maryland, and as of 1996 he has held the position of Walter Hines Page Research Professor at Duke University. While at Duke, he has regularly hosted visiting professors from Chile, among them Manuel Jofré, Soledad Bianchi, Willy Thayer, and Raquel Olea—all important intellectuals from Santiago. He regularly publishes in a variety of newspapers and magazines such as the *New York Times*, *Washington Post*, *Los Angeles Times*, *London Observer*, *London Independent*, *The Guardian*, *Pagina Doce*, *Folha de São Paolo*, *Le Monde*, *Die Zeit*, *Time Magazine*, *Harper's*, and *Granta*. His regular commentaries for *El País*, one of the leading newspapers in the Spanish-speaking world, are syndicated around the globe. Dorfman has continued to struggle for what he believes while also paying attention to the demands of history that call for new forms of struggle and protest and new ways of communicating. New communicative strategies were visible in his reaction to the release of photos showing the torture of Iraqi prisoners during the spring and summer of 2004. With unremitting faith in the power of literature he wrote a piece on May 9, 2004, for *The Guardian* on the lessons that humanity could learn about the ethics of torture from *The Brothers Karama-*

zov. He ended his commentary with a question: "Are we so scared that we are willing to knowingly let others perpetrate, in the dark and in our name, acts of terror that will eternally corrode and corrupt us?" (*Other Septembers*, 35). On May 18, 2004, he appeared opposite Chris Matthews on MSNBC's news program, making an impassioned plea to end the torture in Iraq. Responding to the question of whether the torture of one person would be justified if it could save other lives, Dorfman stated, "I insist on this. Humanity has taken thousands of years to reach these agreements. It means that Americans and Iraqis and the terrorists as well have certain human rights, even if they don't respect our rights, even those terrorists, who don't respect our rights. It is fundamental that the rule of law, of international law, be respected" (Matthews, n.p.).

In the span of a few days Dorfman addressed the same problem across registers as distinct as the highly literary and the popular mass media. In the meantime he was hard at work on a novel about Joaquín Murieta, the Chilean-Mexican Robin Hood who lived in California in the 1850s. These varied activities have posed a substantial challenge to scholars of his work, since despite the presence of unifying themes in his many projects, it can be difficult to recognize the links among them. The next two chapters, on Dorfman's literary and cultural influences and aesthetic theory, attempt to begin the process. One of the key arguments I will make is that the lack of obvious ties across these varied projects is one of the most important characteristics of Dorfman's aesthetic strategy.

You don't have anything
if you don't have the stories.
Their evil is mighty
but it can't stand up to our stories.
So they try to destroy the stories
let the stories be confused or forgotten
They would like that
They would be happy
Because we would be defenseless then.

—LESLIE MARMON SILKO, *Ceremony*

2. ON BECOMING A STORYTELLER
Dorfman's Literary and Cultural Influences

Understanding Ariel Dorfman's writing depends on recognizing its affinities
with the tradition of storytelling rather than that of authorship. Dorfman's
sense of himself as a writer is integrally tied to his vision of the writer as a
postmodern storyteller. It is noteworthy, for instance, that Dorfman repeatedly
refers to himself as a storyteller (*Heading*, 6, 10, 39, 40, 204). Following the
legacy of earlier diasporas, Dorfman's sense of himself as a storyteller links him
to a transhistorical tradition of wandering minstrels, who carried their tales
with them and shared their stories with each new community they encountered. As noted in the preface, this vision of the writer as storyteller also ties
Dorfman to both the Jewish and the Native American traditions, cultures that
have been integral to Dorfman's personal identity and depend on the power of
oral communication to maintain customs and preserve history. To conceive of
Dorfman as a storyteller also facilitates an appreciation of the multiple registers in which he works; it underscores the ways that his cultural production
expands beyond the book to include film and other media.

Arriving at this sense of the writer was a long process for Dorfman, and even though he had a close relationship with literature from the time he was a boy, his understanding of the role of the writer went through a number of transformations. From a young age, Dorfman relied on fiction to keep him company. He suffered from insomnia shortly after his hospitalization for pneumonia and began to tell himself stories: "All that I could do to swindle death at that very early age in the City of New York was to make up stories in the night" (*Heading*, 6). His attraction to narrative began as a way to combat his fears and obsession with death: "As a child I had imagined a fictional community as the best answer to death and loneliness" (7). When Dorfman met Thomas Mann aboard ship in 1951, he considered life as a writer for the first time. At this early stage in Dorfman's life literature presented itself to him as a way to transgress limitations of space and time (84). For instance, in his early years in Chile, Dorfman would turn to writing as his "ultimate defense" against a world that he found hostile and foreign (86). Yet even when Dorfman used literature at an intellectual and personal level, he continued to engage in it as a way to connect with his community. He would write solely for himself only to then seek outside approval, especially from his mother. He was "obsessed with contacting others," and his early practice of literature as a private exercise lead him inexorably to seek a broader community, even if those early efforts focused on affirmations of his individuality and creative abilities (84).

As a young man growing up in Santiago and becoming increasingly committed to social struggle, Dorfman discovered that writing could function beyond the realm of the personal. He no longer used stories to keep him company; instead, he used them to build bonds between himself and his Chilean community. During Allende's presidency, Dorfman attempted to create stories that could enhance the revolutionary project. Even though he tells readers of his efforts to learn how to shoot a gun, he remains clear that his primary role in Chile's revolutionary struggle was as a culture worker—a writer, editor, publisher, and teacher. He purposefully ends the first chapter of his memoir by emphasizing his literary calling when he confesses to readers that the night before the coup he was not busily preparing an armed defense of Allende but rather was telling his son Rodrigo a story. Unwilling to focus on the impending death and destruction the next day would bring, Dorfman closes the chapter with "I turn out the light and tell my son a fairytale" (*Heading*, 10). After the coup, his lack of action would haunt him. Could he have done more to protect Allende? Did he selfishly overemphasize his own literary projects at the expense of the revolution?

Once in exile from Pinochet, Dorfman began to doubt the social function

of art even further when he fell into a state of despair and was initially incapable of writing. When he was able to return to writing, his storytelling aspired
to record and reflect the horrors of the coup. Recall, for instance, Dorfman's
encounter with Fernando Flores, who crossed his name off of the list of people
to call to help Allende the night before the coup. Dorfman admits that "it is a
comforting idea that I was spared because I was to be the storyteller" (*Heading*,
39). And while he recognizes that his survival was more arbitrary than logical,
he explains that "if it is not true that this is why I was saved, I have tried to
make it true. In every story I tell" (40). The repetition of words specifically tied
to *storyteller* in these lines underscores the fact that he conceives of his role as a
writer within a broader social project.

It would be a mistake, though, to read Dorfman's writing as merely an
example of premodern storytelling since he clearly is a writer conscious of the
critical debates surrounding authorship and writerly authority. Thus, before
this chapter traces his literary and cultural influences, it will be worth pausing
to consider how he conceptualizes his role as a writer by placing his own theory
of the practice against critical theories about the author. One of the key essays
to put forward the distinction between the storyteller and the author is Walter
Benjamin's "The Storyteller":

> What distinguishes the novel from the story (and from the epic in the nar-
> rower sense) is its essential dependence on the book. . . . The storyteller
> takes what he tells from experience—his own or that reported by others.
> And he in turn makes it the experience of those who are listening to his
> tale. The novelist has isolated himself. The birthplace of the novel is
> the solitary individual, who is no longer able to express himself by giving
> examples of his most important concerns, is himself uncounseled, and
> cannot counsel others. (87)

Benjamin characterizes the rise of the novel, with its "dependence on the
book," as evidence of the decline of storytelling (86). Yet such observations
emanate from Benjamin's European context and are less applicable to Latin
American literary culture.[1] For instance, the notion of the storyteller as witness
is a characteristic of written texts throughout the history of Latin America.
While for Benjamin the novelist focuses on the psychological and the storyteller on the social, such separations are not so easily made in Latin American
literature. However, Benjamin's association of the novelist with the consumer
culture of the book resonates in Latin America. The professionalization of
writing and the conversion of stories into commodities have been, and still are,
major concerns of Latin American writers.

Another critical essay on storytelling, "The Storyteller," by Dorfman's long-time friend John Berger, corresponds more closely with Dorfman's views. Unlike Benjamin, Berger equates writing with storytelling (14).[2] Berger understands writing as a craft that is indebted to the writer's social milieu and that plays a significant role in the shaping of community identity. In keeping with Dorfman's own practices, Berger highlights the ways that storytelling enables memory, functions as witness, and creates social bonds—characteristics that contrast with the modernist vision of the writer as a professional and a solitary artistic genius.

It is worth noting that the idea of the writer as storyteller is also common in human rights discourse, a realm of cultural work that has had an obvious influence on Dorfman's ideas of writing. James Dawes explains in *That the World May Know* that for human rights workers "storytelling is the very nature of their work" since without it, there would be no public attention to atrocity (1). He explains that when literary authors like Michael Ondaatje engage in human rights storytelling, they often emphasize the ethical dilemmas inherent in such projects by avoiding closure, catharsis, and facile moralizing (196). Such writers tend to draw attention to the ways that their ethical responsibility to tell the story conflicts with the "absolute obscenity in the very project of understanding" (Lanzmann cited in Dawes, 195). In this way they blend storytelling with postmodern literary techniques, writing from a double bind: there is an urgency to tell the story even though the author knows that the story can never be properly told.

Such a combination of seemingly contradictory positions, though, has been contentious. In response to modernist notions of the author as a singular creative force, many postmodern theories have argued against authorial autonomy, equating any effort to narrate with an urge to be the dictator of meaning. In his landmark essay, "The Death of the Author," written in the watershed year of 1968, Roland Barthes argued that a writer "can only imitate a gesture that is always anterior, never original. His only power is to mix writings . . . in such a way as never to rest on any one of them" (146). Barthes was interested in liberating the text from a fixed meaning, unlatching the author from his privileged, creative status and thereby placing more power in the reader or the critic. "To give a text an Author is to impose a limit on that text, to furnish it with a final signified, to close the writing" (147). Barthes placed all power in the reader, advocating readerly writing. In addition to Barthes's dismantling of the primacy of the "Author," he suggested that texts be understood intertextually as a web of citations that decentered the text as well as the author.

One year after Barthes's seminal essay, Michel Foucault elaborated a further critique of the author in "What Is an Author?," where he argued against the infinite meaning attributed to the author. He analyzed four major features of the "author function." The fourth was the distinction between the flesh and blood writer and the "I" of the narrator. It is worth noting that this feature likely reminded writers like Dorfman of Jorge Luis Borges's previous dismantling of authorial signifying in "Borges y yo" (1960; "Borges and I"), which describes the gap between the man who writes and the public perception of the author as an immortal creative force.

By the time Dorfman began publishing his writing, he, like most socially committed writers of his generation, would distance his own work as a writer from the idea of the modern, authoritarian author, taking a more anti-institutional stance. Dorfman's theory of the writer depends on a readerly text, and it is equally skeptical of the author system, which connects the writer to regimes of signification. He takes distance from the two essays by Barthes and Foucault, though, in the continued sense that the writer has a social responsibility and thus an urgent calling to narrate, record, and provoke through the text.[3] Writers like Dorfman, who linked the practice of textual production with social change, would inevitably find themselves caught between the urge to liberate the text from repressive systems of signifying and the desire to use the written word to change the way their readers thought. In this sense Dorfman's position on the author is more akin to Mikhail Bakhtin's theory of writing in the 1934–35 essay "Discourse in the Novel." Bakhtin posits that the writer operates as a creative force that mediates heteroglossic voices and seeks a reader/listener who "actively answers and reacts" (280). Sensitive to the fragile connections between historical forces and literary representations, Dorfman, in keeping with Bakhtin's theory, rejects a totalized notion of literature that locates all meaning in the text. Instead, he envisions a collaborative, dialogic process among history, author, text, and reader in which each plays a significant role.

Consequently, Dorfman's notion of the writer is incompatible with a modernist depiction of the author as a solitary creative mind and with an understanding of the text as a reified work of art with only one static interpretation. Despite Dorfman's best intentions, though, his self-presentation as one who was called upon to tell the story of the Chilean coup leads to conflicting responses. On the one hand, his steadfast commitment to be the storyteller of the coup and of Allende has had significant consequences, and Dorfman became the most internationally visible writer to draw attention to the atrocities of Pinochet. On the other hand, his visibility coupled with his unabashed commitment to "speak for the dead" can seem self-aggrandizing (see Jaggi).[4] How can one claim to speak for the dead? Why should Dorfman be the storyteller? In a telling scene in the documentary *A Promise to the Dead* Dorfman faces a room of activist widows, a group of Chilean *madres* who lost loved ones during the dictatorship, and explains that these women were his inspiration and that their actions were what motivated him to write. These women, whose lives were destroyed by the coup, seem both bewildered and a little put off as Dorfman explains that their courage was his muse. In a way this scene reflects the discomfort one feels in the face of a writer who nakedly presents himself as the voice of trauma.

To complicate matters further, Dorfman investigates and encourages these contradictory responses to his sense of himself as a writer. In the scene with the Chilean *madres*, then, one could read his seemingly arrogant emphasis on himself as the writer of these women's strength and suffering to be so blatant as to be purposefully provocative. These moments, when Dorfman lays bare the hubris of narrating such events, can be read either as an example of a prideful writer, made even more troubling because he is a writer of tragedy and loss, or as a critique of one. His incessant questioning of how the writer can represent in a way that is not authoritarian is a persistent feature of his work. He constantly questions how to write, what to write, and whether his writing is itself capable of representing what he hopes to represent.[5] But Dorfman balances these questions with a faith in writing and an admission that his response to trauma, tragedy, and conflict has been to narrate it. It is most significant to note that Dorfman balances four conflicting ideas of himself as a writer: (1) he tries to write in ways that help readers remember the past, especially traumatic events, and attend to social crises; (2) he is not sure that he can achieve such a goal; (3) but he is sure that such issues will be forgotten or overlooked if there is no effort to tell the stories; and (4) if he is able to tell the stories, then perhaps such an act is always connected at some level to authorial conceit or privilege. These contradictory impulses form the crux of Dorfman's theory of the writer as a postmodern storyteller.

For Dorfman, to consider the writer as a postmodern storyteller enables a disintegration of the modernist emphasis on the writer as authority and sole creative force; it also derails the structuralist overdetermination of the text and the poststructuralist insistence on language divorced from context. Dorfman's conception of the writer as storyteller holds a number of concepts in dialectical tension. On the one hand, the writer is the conduit through which timeless and historically specific tales pass in multiple discursive registers. On the other hand, the writer is responsible to history and cultural context, to his stories and characters, to his readers and himself. It should be clear that Dorfman's conception of the writer as storyteller takes into account postmodern theory and that while he is often nostalgic about the social role of storytelling, he recognizes the complexity of representation. It is this combination of Dorfman's almost mystical faith in stories connected with his skepticism of representational structures that can most vex critics of his work since they often key into only one of these two features.

Just as Dorfman's notion of writing shifted as he matured into adulthood from introspection to social activism, Dorfman's literary appetites changed from realism to more complex literary works. At around the age of fifteen he turned to texts that stressed "ambiguity and turbulence," moving "from the Hardy Boys to Hemingway, from Tom Swift to Steinbeck" (*Heading*, 132). At the same time, he expanded his reading beyond authors from the United States by reading British classics, especially Shakespeare and Laurence Sterne; French authors such as Stendhal, Zola, and the existentialists; Russian literature; Kafka; and Thomas Mann (131–32). Reading these authors, he discovered the power of literature: "I knew that literature would be a prayer and a pickax, a way out of the frozen world in which we find ourselves trapped, our only protest against death and loneliness" (132). Ultimately he decided that his literary influences would not be bound by geography but rather would be formed by a "community of like-minded individuals" (132).

THE INFLUENCE OF INFLUENCES

Dorfman's vision of the writer is a consequence of a number of important cultural and literary influences. Almost all writers have a fairly large set of such influences; this fact is not necessarily interesting and certainly not unusual. In Dorfman's case, though, it signals a key part of his aesthetic strategy and one that links him to other Latin American writers from his generation. The practice of intertextual reference and citation is common, especially among writers from the New World, who often have felt uncomfortably shadowed by European literary traditions. In the case of Latin America, this practice became especially intense among the writers of the post-boom, whose work was often a critique of the meta-narratives of their predecessors. For instance, both Reinaldo Arenas (Cuba) and Cristina Peri Rossi (Uruguay), along with Dorfman, have displayed a similarly compulsive habit of citing and referencing the work of others in their novels; examples are especially evident in Arenas's *El color del verano* (*The Color of Summer*) and Peri Rossi's *La nave de los locos* (*The Ship of Fools*). Nevertheless, there are some different features to the influence of influences in Dorfman's work. Unlike Arenas and Peri Rossi, whose nod to other writers and texts tends to be limited to the use of symbolic names and references, Dorfman references other writers and literary traditions by also emulating their style. And while Arenas's references are almost always parodic, Dorfman, like Peri Rossi, combines parody with more serious tones of influence. At the heart of this practice for Dorfman is the complicated question of how writing links to specific historical moments and how earlier forms of writing influence the way that we think today. What happens when a literary mode from the past is translated into the present? Can such a practice encourage a sense of history, or does it destroy the idea of meaningful representation?

From classical tragedy to the Middle Ages to the Renaissance to modernism and postmodernism, Dorfman's cultural influences are vast, both geographically and temporally. During his brief years writing for the Chilean magazine *Ercilla* (1965–67), for example, Dorfman wrote on a plethora of literary topics: from Chinese poetry to Federico García Lorca, from the Beats to Jean-Paul Sartre. My purpose in this chapter is not so much to provide readers with an introduction to this literary heritage per se but rather to provide an introduction to how Dorfman *reads* these texts for his own purposes.[6] While Dorfman's reading practices mirror those of many Chilean intellectuals of his generation, his use of them in his work offers insight into his theories of writing. For clarity, I will trace these influences chronologically, which means that at times they will be presented against Dorfman's own history.

It is safe to say that every major literary movement intertexts at some level with Dorfman's work. From characters like Oriana in *Máscaras* (*Mascara*), named after the wife of Amadis de Gaula, a medieval knight from one of the most famous books of chivalry, to Heller, the protagonist of *The Burning City* named after the famous author of *Catch-22*, Dorfman's intertextual references are quite varied. It is possible, however, to identify characteristics that apply to the majority of Dorfman's literary and cultural influences. He draws insight from artists, writers, critics, and other culture workers who

(1) Investigate the relationship between *art and politics*, especially those who believe that art and politics are inseparable but remain unsure about how that interaction can best take place;
(2) Delve into the *crisis of representation*, experiment with language, and push artistic forms;
(3) Confront major *historical conflict and change*, especially those who respond to the upheavals of colonization, war, authoritarianism, censorship, and exile;

(4) Depict *moral dilemmas and ethical conflicts* in extreme or exaggerated circumstances;

(5) Consider culture as a form of *collaboration* between creator and audience, constructing texts that are open to interpretation and that refuse to infantilize the reader; and

(6) Find *beauty, hope, and inspiration* in the social role of art.

Pressed to contain these myriad influences, I have grouped them roughly into two major cohorts of primarily literary sources—early modern (including the Renaissance, colonial texts, and the baroque) and modern (including modernism, the avant-garde, 1960s culture, and the Latin American literary boom)—and I will briefly survey Dorfman's major influences from each period while also taking some important detours along the way.

Before we turn to the Renaissance, it is important to note that Greek tragedy and its mythical sources have had a major impact on Dorfman's writing, especially his drama. His recent play *Purgatorio*, for instance, is a revision of *Medea*. Likewise, the widowed mothers hoping to bury their dead relatives in *Viudas* (*Widows*) remind readers of the sisters in Sophocles's *Antigone* as well as Euripides's *The Trojan Women*. From classical theater Dorfman takes his concern with the ways that twists of fate often cause calamitous situations and he combines this with his interest in taking the absurdities of modern society to extremes. *La muerte y la doncella* (*Death and the Maiden*), where Paulina finds her torturer asleep on her couch; *Reader*, where the censor must censor his own story; "The Other Side," where the old couple find their home divided by a new national border—all represent extraordinary situations that force characters to make difficult decisions and reveal the catastrophes caused by dictatorship, authoritarianism, and political repression. Dorfman frequently uses stark characters that border on archetypes, and these reveal the influence of Greek tragedy and mythical structure.

EARLY MODERN INFLUENCES

Late Italian Medieval and early Renaissance writers play a role in Dorfman's literary formation. For example, *Blake's Therapy* is structured around Dante's *The Divine Comedy*. Dante's exile, his use of literature to confront a "corrupt" society, his fusion of travel and imagination, and his introduction of vernacular into lyric poetry all interest Dorfman. Medieval tales of chivalry, especially inasmuch as these shape later Renaissance works in Spain, hold special attraction for Dorfman. He draws on stories of allegiance and honor and reads them against the individualism and moral bankruptcy of late capitalism and twentieth-century authoritarianism. Dorfman has described Miguel de Cervantes as a writer who "pushed the limits. He used the genres of the day and split them wide open. . . . What his work suggests if you listen to him hundreds of years later, is that the important genres of the day are the mass media. The popular literary forms of his day were the pastoral novel, the chivalric romances—which he hated and loved—and the picaresque novel. He took all of them and put them into Part One of the *Quijote*" (cited in Incledon, 99). Dorfman attempts a similar move in *La última canción de Manuel Sendero* (*The Last Song of Manuel Sendero*), where the text includes soap opera scripts, comic strips, fairy tales, and academic footnotes (among other things) and again in *The Nanny and the Iceberg*, which similarly combines a panoply of narrative sources that derive from popular culture. Revealing his debt to Cervantes, Dorfman often creates characters whose world visions are out of sync with those around them, as in the case of the protagonists from *The Last Song of Manuel Sendero*. Both the son of Sendero and David are hopeless idealists who refuse to adapt to the practical requirements of their social contexts, characteristics that remind the reader of *Don Quijote*.[7]

In addition to Cervantes, two further Renaissance sources are essential to understanding Dorfman's work. The first is William Shakespeare. Readers of Dorfman's memoir might recall that it is his impromptu recitation of Shakespeare while a refugee in the Argentine Embassy in Santiago that helps him to befriend the ambassador's wife, herself a U.S. citizen. Through Shakespeare and his cultural capital, Dorfman is able to gain access to a telephone, to connect with his family, and to help other refugees make contact with their families (*Heading*, 268–69). Yet before this moment, Shakespeare played a central role in Dorfman's understanding of himself as a writer, and this influence persists: "I continue to think that one of my fundamental influences is Shakespeare" (cited in McClennen in *World Literature Today*, 64). Dorfman is most influenced by Shakespeare's complex use of language, his innovation of the pastoral form, his layering of plot, and his ability to blend social critique with entertainment. Shakespeare was the subject of Dorfman's 1965 thesis at the University of Chile. When Dorfman decided to focus on Shakespeare's pastoral plays for his thesis, he became intimately familiar with Shakespeare's artful use of a variety of discursive registers. Blending puns with parody and using words for comedy and illusion, Shakespeare's innovative rhetoric has a great effect on Dorfman.

Shakespeare's redirection of the pastoral form from its classical sources also provides Dorfman with a model for the ways that writers can adapt traditional models to their own historical contexts. Dorfman firmly believes that the writer's task is to carefully link form and content and that these should organically derive from the writer's circumstances. At the same time, he believes that writers (and readers) should be aware of their literary legacy. Consequently, Dorfman learns an important lesson from Shakespeare on how genres morph over time to reflect changing socio-historical settings. Further, Dorfman, along with generations of other writers, is attracted to the way that Shakespeare treats themes of betrayal, love, deception, political manipulation, injustice, the arbitrary nature of social status, and reason versus folly in a manner that comments on his own historical circumstances and resonates universally.

The picaresque represents the second major Renaissance influence on Dorfman's work. Concerned as he is with investigating the failures of ethical behavior, Dorfman adapts the picaresque protagonist of the Renaissance to his own postmodern moment. If the social upheavals of the Renaissance led to fiction that portrayed characters as rogues and social parasites eager to exploit all who crossed their path, then the massive social alienation of late capitalism, globalization, and neoliberalism led Dorfman to create his own version of an updated picaresque. With greater interest in the cruel and delinquent *pícaros* of Mateo Alemán's *Guzmán de Alfarache* (1599) and especially Francisco de Quevedo's *El buscón* (1626) than in the irreverently witty protagonist of *Lazarillo de Tormes* (1554), Dorfman uses the picaresque as a way to investigate evil and selfishness and to study characters who are disengaged from community identity. Picaresque protagonists are often characterized as rogues who take advantage of their masters, but their stories can also be read as tales of the dehumanizing ways that upper-class Spaniards treated the lower classes. The social dimension of the picaresque plays a central role in Dorfman's adaptations. An early example of Dorfman's creative adaptation of the picaresque is in *Máscaras* (*Mascara*). The novel is not a travel narrative of episodes, but the main character in his almost complete disdain for humanity displays many of the character traits of the *pícaro*. In keeping with the picaresque tradition, the faceless man at the center of the novel is completely disconnected from society, totally outcast and totally forgotten. This extreme isolation leads him to parasitically feed off of others: his almost complete anonymity allows him to take photographs that expose the brutal reality of his subjects' identity, which he later sells or uses for blackmail.

Dorfman's next major work to adapt the picaresque is *The Nanny and the Iceberg*. In this novel his protagonist, Gabriel, is less cruel and more unwitting in his selfish concerns than the protagonist of *Mascara*. An interesting parallel reveals the distinction: the protagonist of *Mascara* has a totally forgettable face, whereas Gabriel has an ageless face. This difference accounts in part for the diverse ways that the characters interact with society. It is the difference between a character who is completely alienated and one who functions in society but lacks history. Even though Gabriel is not cruel and emotionally flat like the faceless man of *Mascara*, he lacks social commitment, he has no sense of politics, and he is mainly interested in getting what he wants. Gabriel, representing the disenfranchised youth of Chile or New York, is concerned only with instant self-gratification, and this social context resonates with the general global decline of community in the face of transnational capitalism. The entire novel is a suicide note, and the reader learns that Gabriel plans to take his life, along with the lives of all those he considers responsible for his unfortunate existence. Here, again, Dorfman has taken a traditional genre and molded it according to his specific cultural context. He has also layered in other major literary influences, since Gabriel's predicament stems from the type of unchecked machismo that has deprived him of a father and has led him to seek fulfillment through sex, similar to that described in José Zorrilla's *Don Juan Tenorio* (1844), a canonical Spanish romanticist play.

Dorfman also takes insight from the texts that represent colonial America. In addition to his fascination with the early testimonial interventions of Bernal Díaz de Castillo, the baroque imagery of Sor Juana Inés de la Cruz, and the representation of indigenous life in the works of El Inca Garcilaso, Dorfman finds Gonzalo Fernández de Oviedo's *Sumario de la historia natural de las indias* (1526) central to understanding colonial literature. He refers to the text in his memoir as "One of the first attempts to transfer into words what the sword had subjugated in a place not yet called America" (*Heading*, 192). Of particular interest to Dorfman is the chapter on the *tigre americano*. According to Oviedo, the name "*tigre*" really doesn't fit this slow beast. Oviedo details how this New World animal escapes what Dorfman calls "his linguistic snares" (*Heading*, 192). And yet he names it anyway. Dorfman uses this passage to exemplify for him the tension between the Old and New Worlds, the violence of colonization, and the role of language in cultural dominance. Oviedo, in conjunction with the imperial project, wanted "to capture that nature [of the New World] and remake it in its own paternal image" (*Heading*, 193). Dorfman recounts in his memoir how the arrogant Spaniards then bring one of these *tigres americanos* to the royal court, only to later kill it when it turns aggressive—what language cannot tame, the sword will. This reading of colonial literature as an early sign of the ties between linguistic appropriation and material control is common to writers from Dorfman's generation. We might think, for example, of Cuban essayist Roberto Fernández Retamar's persuasive call to Latin Americans to adopt the role of Caliban in the *Tempest* to learn the master's language only to then curse him.

Yet Dorfman's interest in Oviedo goes deeper. Dorfman, like many Latin American writers, wants to be that *tigre americano* who can be neither named nor tamed, but he also identifies deeply with Oviedo. Witnessing Latin America as it embraced the social struggles of the 1960s, Dorfman imagined himself in a similar historical juncture to that of Oviedo. "I could see how he had been seduced by his new home and admired even its danger, how he had begun to feel, opening under his feet, an abyss of distance separating him from Europe which made him into something other, wrenchingly like the very *tigre* he wanted to net and carry off" (*Heading*, 193). Dorfman likens his own desire to narrate the region with Oviedo's. This association reveals one of Dorfman's greatest dilemmas and one of his central concerns as a writer because it points to the powerful role played by those who write about history. Is Dorfman, like Oviedo, an outsider who narrates to gain mastery over the region, or is he the conduit through which the region tells its story? This dilemma causes Dorfman to pay particular attention to the ways that Oviedo's text exposes its own shortcomings and its own inability to master the New World landscape. Dorfman further reads in Oviedo an early sign of the ways that language is always "incomplete and incoherent," always incapable of describing a world so "vast and variegated" (193). Similar to Oviedo, Dorfman straddled two cultures, a situation that exacerbated his sense that writing was an inadequate effort at translating, at putting into words that which cannot be expressed (194). The fact that Dorfman's two cultures, like Oviedo's, occupy radically different positions of power in the world order and that one culture endeavors to dominate the other makes the problem of translation even greater. These similarities aside, Dorfman's anti-colonial literary project obviously departs in significant ways from that of Oviedo.

These concerns lead Dorfman to take inspiration from baroque writers like Pedro Calderón de la Barca and their experimentation with fragmentation and multiplicity of meaning. In addition to structuring *Blake's Therapy* with *The Divine Comedy*, to punctuate the opening and closing of the novel, Dorfman uses quotes from Calderón's *La vida es sueño* (1636; *Life Is a Dream*) that ask whether it is "time to wake up." He also finds that the linguistic experimentation of Quevedo's poetry demonstrates the ways that language can powerfully evoke at the same time that it constantly evades interpretation. In keeping with much Latin American literature, Dorfman's writing is often baroque in its descriptive excess, its multilayered plots, and its abundant and plentiful language. Following the legacy of the baroque, the complexity of the narrative project and the difficulty of storytelling are epitomized for Dorfman in Laurence Sterne's *The Life and Opinions of Tristram Shandy, Gentleman* (1759–66), a work he considers seminal to narrative history.[8] In his departure from the "life and adventures" of an autobiographical hero, Sterne's *Tristram Shandy* challenges chronological time and disrupts the construction of the subject. Moreover, Sterne's text foregrounds the writing process over plot and emphasizes the literary text as an object to be scrutinized. He combines humor and wit with formal experimentation and meta-narrative.

These elements all appear in Dorfman's work, especially in *Moros en la costa* (*Hard Rain*), which intertwines humor with meta-commentary on the nature of art, and in *The Last Song of Manuel Sendero*, where there are a number of versions of the story of Manuel Sendero interspersed with comic scenes. A recurrent motif in Dorfman that may derive from Sterne is the notion that birth is an accident and that narrating that accident is humorous and socially critical. In novels like *Mascara*, *The Last Song of Manuel Sendero*, and *The Nanny and the Iceberg* Dorfman refers to his protagonists as accidental births that are caught up in major historical forces, where birth thrusts characters into situations that are not of their choosing. Sterne's readers might recall that Tristram's father, Walter, obsessively worries about the ties between a child's name and his identity, a theme that reappears in Dorfman's work in almost all of his novels. The most interesting parallel between Sterne and Dorfman may be between *Tristram Shandy* and *Heading South, Looking North*. Certainly these are different texts in different genres and with different interests, but the comparisons are worth pursuing. Both texts trouble the notion of autobiography, depart from chronological narrative, and suggest that the subject cannot be isolated from a larger social context. Dorfman's metaphoric association of his birth with falling reminds the reader of Tristram's accidental birth, and the way that Dorfman narrates his own name changes reads interestingly against Tristram's story.

MODERN INFLUENCES

Modernism is the immediate and inescapable legacy of writers, like Dorfman, whose literary careers began in the 1960s. Modernism's extreme exploration of aesthetics; its critique of technology, industry, and the rise of the city; and its attempt to reverse the commodification of art affect subsequent literary generations, who inherited even more advanced versions of modern social structures. Literary investigations of alienation, capitalism, communication, art, and identity, intrinsic to high modernism, experimented with complex aesthetic practices meant to distance modern art and literature from bourgeois culture. Of the writers to confront modernity Dorfman is most influenced by those who refuse to detach literature from broader social concerns. For example, he claims that *Konfidenz*, a psychological novel that investigates vexing questions of morality, is in dialogue with Henry James (McClennen in *World Literature Today*, 64). Other modernist writers like James Joyce, William Faulkner, Thomas Mann, and Marcel Proust influence Dorfman especially inasmuch as they inspired writers from the Latin American boom. A telling example of these layers of influence is Dorfman's essay on the intertexuality between Proust's *À la recherche du temps perdu* (1913–22; *Remembrance of Things Past*) and Alejo Carpentier's *Recurso del método* (1974; *Reasons of State*, 1976) in *Some Write to the Future* (1991).

Many of Dorfman's modernist, avant-garde influences emanate from artists and writers who witnessed the historic upheavals of the Second World War. Three of his texts—*Widows*, *Konfidenz*, and "Picasso's Closet"—take place in the context of that war. The first, in an effort to get by Chile's censors, uses the setting of Greece during the Nazi period as a way to explore the social consequences of dictatorship. The second begins in an unspecified time and place that are made concrete only in the second half of the novel. The third text delves directly into the dilemmas of the Second World War by focusing on Picasso's life during the Nazi occupation of Paris. For Dorfman the larger historic moment of the Second World War, which included the Spanish Civil War (1936–39), Stalin's betrayal of the German Communists, and the betrayal by the French of their own refugees, sets in motion historic precedents that shaped the latter part of the twentieth century; it created the series of events he was forced to confront with his own life and art. Of special concern for Dorfman is the way that these events led to "the destruction of the moral, the destruction of the aesthetic, the destruction of the physical," painful processes he experienced firsthand after Pinochet's coup in Chile (cited in McClennen in *Context*, 8).

The Second World War signaled the rise of fascism and the massive state-sponsored betrayal of enlightenment notions of subjectivity, and it foreshadowed the destructive logic of the Cold War. The cultural response to these events offered by the avant-garde and found in the critical work of theorists associated with the Frankfurt School emphasized the need for culture to directly confront social oppression. If earlier efforts to consider art in a political context remained primarily intellectual exercises, the Second World War radically changed the stakes. For the avant-garde, art and politics were of a piece, inseparable. Avant-garde theorists, like Walter Benjamin and Peter Bürger, understand the movement as a highly innovative effort to link aesthetic experimentation with political intervention. Benjamin stresses the way that the avant-garde was able to deflate the aura of modernist art, and Bürger suggests that "the avant-garde has radically changed the place value of political engagement in art, that the concept of engagement prior to and subsequent to the avant-garde movements is not the same" (83). Across the globe intellectuals and artists participated directly in the conflicts of the era. For example, Ernest Hemingway and George Orwell fought in the Spanish Civil War, and Sartre and Albert Camus participated in the French resistance. This direct, immediate, and insistent merging of art and politics had a tremendous impact on Dorfman, who also saw his work as a consequence of his immediate social context of revolutionary struggle and resistance to authoritarianism.

Key figures from this period for Dorfman are Pablo Picasso, Jean-Paul Sartre, Jean Cocteau, and Bertolt Brecht. The last two Dorfman uses for epigraphs in *Konfidenz*, and, as mentioned, Picasso is the subject of "Picasso's Closet." Unwilling to simply celebrate Picasso's efforts to use art to inspire humanity and to challenge the destruction of war, Dorfman pushes the circumstances of Picasso's life and investigates the "tyranny" of Picasso over reality, over the people who love him, especially over the women, like Dora Maar, who were destroyed by him (Pezzopane and Petruccioli, 51). Dorfman wonders whether that type of egocentrism is essential to artistic excellence. Then the play changes history: What if Picasso had not protected himself? What if he had taken greater risks to help his friends and loved ones? What if Picasso had been murdered by the Nazis during the occupation of Paris?

Dorfman's attraction to avant-garde artists is not limited to the intersections of art and politics; he focuses on these artists' aesthetic experiments, on the original ways that they attempted to use art to comment on reality, and he adapts these practices into his own aesthetic. Describing "Picasso's Closet," he explains: "I was telling the story with the aesthetic of Picasso himself in mind, denying linearity, deriding the surface of things as false, playing with reality so that it reveals its hidden secrets—which all happen, conveniently, to be my own way of understanding art and story-telling. For me art is always an attempt to subvert history while, in my case at least, invariably admitting that we cannot escape it" (cited in Pezzopane and Petruccioli, 51).

In adapting Picasso's own aesthetic, Dorfman reveals his and Picasso's similar artistic concerns while also exposing their divergences. Dorfman's subversion of chronological time and seamless space in this play departs from Picasso's aesthetic because it is a rupture that not only seeks to expose reality by fragmenting it but also hopes to push the artist to be accountable to history.

Rather than creating political art, as Picasso did with *Guernica*, the play centers on the political role of the artist and on the inevitable social concessions artists make in order to work.

The avant-garde was an international phenomenon, and many Spanish and Latin American writers central to Dorfman's formation drew inspiration from and participated in the movement. Writers like Federico García Lorca, Rafael Alberti, César Vallejo, and Pablo Neruda all created avant-garde poetry. Yet in a move that would provide guidance to Dorfman, most of these poets (except Lorca, who died in 1936) altered the symbolism and complex expressionism of their verses during and after the Spanish Civil War in favor of a style that was more accessible to a broad public. These writers' ties to surrealism and the avant-garde shifted toward realism and social realism as a way of confronting more directly the violence of the civil war. It is especially crucial for writers like Dorfman that this transformation yields even greater "literary autonomy" and "creative independence" (G. Dawes, "Realism," par. 4). Greg Dawes explains that Pablo Neruda's experience of historical events and aesthetic innovation resulted in a unique and personal literary form of "guided spontaneity." Neruda's distinctive style was not a compromise between surrealism and realism. Instead it is best understood as an effort to use linguistic complexity to approximate a complex reality. Dorfman and others were inspired by the ways that Neruda was able to compose verse that evoked with equal power political struggle and natural beauty, passion and sorrow, sensuality and revolution. Dorfman considers Neruda to be the best poet of the twentieth century. But for Dorfman he is far more than a poet; he is also the political leader who died days after Pinochet's coup, a writer who passionately combined politics, literature, and a love of life. Neruda's gentle yet intensely confrontational style is foundational to Dorfman's own image of the writer as storyteller and public intellectual. Neruda's influence on Dorfman is most telling in the series of poems published as *Missing* in 1985, many of which were republished in the bilingual volume *In Case of Fire in a Foreign Land*. The first published works of Dorfman's after Pinochet's coup, these poems helped Dorfman express his sorrow and loss, and they represent his first effort to use language in order to bear witness to torture and to the devastations of dictatorship. They also signal the first time that Dorfman departs from his characteristic baroque, multi-perspectival use of language.

Before continuing to trace Dorfman's modern and postmodern influences from Latin America, we must make an important detour through the theater of the absurd and the work of Harold Pinter, a playwright whose work was well known in Chile in the 1950s and '60s. A fact little known among Pinter and

Dorfman scholars alike is that Dorfman's first book was a study of Pinter's early theater.[9] Published in 1968, Dorfman's *El absurdo entre cuatro paredes* (The Absurd within Four Walls) provides an analysis of Pinter's work from *The Room* (1957) to *The Homecoming* (1964). Focusing on Pinter's first play, *The Room*, Dorfman presents the thesis that Pinter's theater encloses humanity in a confined space where the threat of imminent danger promises to erupt violently. According to Dorfman, such situations lead Pinter to create provocative plays that inspire the audience to reject social structures that dictate and contain human identity. This reading of Pinter may strike those familiar with his early plays as slightly embellished since it seems that Dorfman infuses his reading of Pinter with a tighter political edge and a more elaborate progressive method than may be supported by the plays themselves. In his conclusion Dorfman explains that even though Pinter's plays often end in the death and destruction of his characters, there is hope. He suggests that behind these characters and their annihilation there is another figure—that of Pinter himself—and that Pinter's ability to represent the tragedies of human life should give the reader/spectator hope. "Pinter enfrenta las fuerzas desordenadoras (e inevitables) de la material, de la muerte, del tiempo, mediante un acto estético que controla y da expresión a esas fuerzas. Toma en cuenta el caos y lo derrota. En su acto estético está su acto moral" (*Absurdo*, 124); (Pinter confronts the disordering [and inevitable] forces of the material, of death, of time, by means of an aesthetic that controls and gives expression to those forces. He acknowledges chaos and destroys it. His aesthetic act is his moral act.) The hopeful tenor Dorfman attributes to Pinter's work differs from that of other critics like Martin Esslin, who focuses on how Pinter's early plays depict humanity with "cruel accuracy," where violent actions occur without motivation (235).[10] Dorfman's reading of Pinter demonstrates his tendency to read literature as a moral intervention into the violence of human life, and it underscores his belief that any text that is able to expose the violence of society offers hope inasmuch as it provokes the reader/spectator to attempt to change the societal structures.

One of the most important aspects of *El absurdo entre cuatro paredes* for Dorfman's readers is its revelation of many of the main issues that would later shape Dorfman's career as a literary critic and a writer.[11] Even the opening epigraph, written by Dorfman himself, seems to frame all of his later work:

Esta es la historia de una pesadilla.
Y de su comprensión y superación por medio del arte.
Todos hemos vivido, hemos visto vivir, hemos soñado esta pesadilla.
No todos hemos sabido superarla.

(This is the story of a nightmare.
And of its understanding and overcoming through art.
We have all lived, have seen live, have dreamed this nightmare.
Not all of us have known how to overcome it.)

Arguably these lines describe Dorfman's aspirations for his own cultural and literary project more accurately than they do Pinter's. In the opening pages Dorfman explains that much criticism has missed the subtlety of Pinter's plays. He points out that Pinter's work vexes critics because of "la imposibilidad de esquematizarlo, su negativa a dejarse reducir o simplificar" (*Absurdo*, 10); (the impossibility of schematizing it, its resistance to let itself be reduced or simplified). The only alternative according to Dorfman is to turn to the works themselves as "único testigo y juez para una determinada interpretación" (10); (the only judge and jury of a determinant interpretation). This resistance to facile categorization that Dorfman attributes to Pinter would later become characteristic of his own work. Similarly, Dorfman would continue to maintain in his essays and fiction that the first source for understanding a work of art should be the work itself.

Perhaps of greatest interest to Dorfman's readers is recognizing the key themes Dorfman traces in Pinter that are also central to his own writing. In his analysis of Pinter, Dorfman focuses on the threat of violence and the abrupt ways that violence alters life: "las situaciones cambian una sola vez, y en esa única ocasión ocurren *violentamente*" (*Absurdo*, 11); (situations change only once, and on this one occasion they change *violently*). Dorfman further argues that Pinter confronts his audience by challenging it to acknowledge its indifference to the suffering of others (21). In the only article dedicated to the connections between Pinter and Dorfman, Stephen Gregory suggests that Dorfman's study of Pinter "seems to anticipate the condition of being tyrannized by the projection into reality of our worst fears" (339). He points out Dorfman's persistent interest in violence and social responsibility, noting that Dorfman's second book of essays on Latin American literature further develops these themes (340).

In addition to the themes mentioned by Gregory, Dorfman delves into Pinter's multivocal, dialectical use of language, which evades, refuses to signify, and also seeks communication. "Las palabras esconden, semirrevelan y callan una interioridad frustrada que tiene miedo expresarse. . . . En Pinter presenciamos la *búsqueda* de un significado, el *desarrollo* de un proceso, no el previo resultado final" (*Absurdo*, 23; emphasis in original); (Words hide, partially reveal, and silence a frustrated interiority afraid to express itself. . . . In Pinter we see the *search* for a signified, the *development* of a process, not the final result). These observations lead Dorfman to comment on art in general: "El lenguaje—como el arte—ya no tiene . . . la posibilidad de capturar la realidad plenamente: sólo sirve como un instrumento oblicuo, como una llave hacia el otro mundo" (*Absurdo*, 25); (Language—like art—no longer has . . . the possibility of capturing reality fully: it only works as an oblique instrument, like a key to another world). This statement could easily be applied to Dorfman's own use of language in his work, and in some ways *Absurdo* reads as much as a guide to Dorfman's writing as to Pinter's. Dorfman takes special notice of the way that Pinter expresses the inexpressible by *not* speaking to it directly, by recognizing the pitfalls of an imperfect language that remains the writer's only tool. Both authors explore the problems of truth, justice, and human rights by exposing how sources of power attempt to control these notions through their manipulation of language. They both ask how those marginalized and abused by power can learn to speak its truth if language is their only tool of inquiry and if it is inevitably flawed. In addition to focusing on how Pinter's words try to approach the inexpressible, Dorfman analyzes how these cryptic words function as a cipher for reality that the audience is left to figure out (26). Dorfman's study reveals a further point of comparison between the two playwrights: Dorfman describes Pinter's female characters as the eternal center that unites fragmented men (44). Such descriptions also apply to some of Dorfman's own female characters, such as Doralisa from *The Last Song of Manuel Sendero*, Oriana from *Mascara*, and the nanny from *The Nanny and the Iceberg*. Both Pinter and Dorfman have a proclivity for creating female archetypes.[12]

As Gregory has illustrated, the ties between Pinter and Dorfman go well beyond Dorfman's first book of essays. Both writers' lives were radically changed by Pinochet's coup: Dorfman was exiled, and Pinter became more politically active (Gregory, 327).[13] Pinter explains that Pinochet's coup "just froze me with horror, it absolutely knocked me sideways and my disgust was so profound at what I immediately understood to have happened . . . I immediately began following the course of other upheavals in the world" (cited in Schiff, 300). While Dorfman's literature was engaging directly with the tyranny of Pinochet, Pinter wrote a series of plays that dealt with torture and repression: *One for the Road* (1985), *Mountain Language* (1988), and *The New World Order* (1991). Even though Dorfman did not read these later works of Pinter's before writing *Death and the Maiden*, Pinter's influence on Dorfman's first play is clear: "If Harold Pinter hadn't existed, I never would have written *Death and the Maiden*. I never would have written any of my plays" (cited in McClennen in *World Literature Today*, 65).[14] Dorfman acknowledges this debt when he dedicates the play to Pinter (in addition to the Chilean actor María Elena Duvauchelle).

The ties between the two writers took another turn when Pinter lent support to the London opening of *Death and the Maiden* by contributing a short sketch on torturers, *The New World Order*, as an opening for Dorfman's debut. *The New World Order* likely played a part in the London success of *Death and the Maiden*, and it certainly helped the play's production. In Pinter's piece two interrogators/torturers, Des and Lionel, stare at a blindfolded man and speak menacingly about what they plan to do to him. Lionel's words near the end of the piece herald Miranda's confession of the pleasures of torture: "I love it. I love it. I love it" (59). He tells Des that torture makes him feel pure, and Des responds that he's right to feel pure because he's "keeping the world clean for democracy" (60). *The New World Order* creates a chilling, eerie environment where victims are abused physically and mentally by men who are convinced of their righteousness. The cold dialogue of the sketch anticipated Paulina's terror and trauma in *Death and the Maiden*.

Dorfman's book on Pinter reveals how he reads Pinter for his own purposes. This becomes essential to note as we compare how Dorfman adapts a key stylistic trait of Pinter's. Both writers have their characters repeat phrases, but these repetitions resonate differently in each writer's work. The following scene is an example from Pinter's *One for the Road*. Nicolas, the torturer/interrogator, is asking questions of Gila, the wife of Victor, a political prisoner. Gila has been beaten and raped. Nicolas is trying to get information from her about her husband. He asks about the first time that Gila and Victor met:

Gila:	I met him.
Nicolas:	When?
Gila:	When I was eighteen.
Nicolas:	Why?
Gila:	He was in the room.
Nicolas:	Room? *Pause.* Room?
Gila:	The same room.
Nicolas:	As what?
Gila:	As I was.
Nicolas:	As I was?
Gila (*screaming*):	As I was! (62–64).

In an example from the English version of *Death and the Maiden*, Gerardo asks Paulina why she has tied up their houseguest, Doctor Miranda.

Paulina: It's him.
Gerardo: Who?
Paulina: It's the doctor.
Gerardo: What doctor?
Paulina: The doctor who played Schubert.
Gerardo: The doctor who played Schubert.
Paulina: That doctor.

. . .

Gerardo: You're sick.
Paulina: I'm not sick.
Gerardo: You're sick (*Resistance Trilogy*, 107).

In both examples the repetitions of words force the audience to consider what happens when the same words are uttered through different mouths, exposing how words change meaning according to the speakers' distinct subject positions. This technique also often suggests that language is incapable of building a bridge between people, that even speaking the exact same words does not lead to communication. A further common element of such repeated phrases is that they expose how language shifts in communicative force according to how much social power the speaker has. Both Nicolas's and Gerardo's utterances carry more weight than do Gila's or Paulina's. In both cases the women try to wedge linguistic power into their utterances, but they are well aware that these dialogues restrict them and that their interlocutors are trying to control the meaning of the "conversation."

There is a radical difference, though, in how this technique works in Dorfman as opposed to Pinter. Unlike Pinter, Dorfman might point to the limits of language, but ultimately he returns to it as the only viable way to challenge oppression and "speak truth to power." Herein resides the fundamental difference between the two writers: Dorfman is far more optimistic and hopeful than Pinter. In an interview that appears before the text of *One for the Road* Pinter states: "I believe that there's no chance of the world coming to other than a very grisly end in twenty-five years at the outside. . . . Finally it's hopeless" (20). In contrast, Dorfman writes in an epilogue to the British edition of *Death and the Maiden* that the play "appears in English at a moment when humanity is undergoing extraordinary changes, when there is great hope for the future and great confusion about what that future might bring" (61). Repetition in Pinter results in an endless, cruel echo, whereas in Dorfman it incessantly begs for an exchange that can end the lack of communication.

Dorfman's tendency to read more political engagement, more hope, and more social commitment into his favorite writers also occurs with his inter-pretation of Julio Cortázar. Dorfman recognizes that Cortázar has often been characterized as an "escapist" and that his own reading of him may be more politicized than the norm (cited in Incledon, 99). Yet for Dorfman, Cortázar is political precisely because he does not feel compelled to limit himself to narrat-ing Latin American politics. "I think it's political enough to say that we have a right to the whole world" (98). In contrast to critics who suggest that Cor-tázar's turn to political writing is marked by his novel *Libro de Manuel* (1973), Dorfman finds Cortázar to be "political from his very first stories. He is dealing with the liberating force of the imagination all of the time" (98). Parallel to his interest in Pinter, Dorfman is drawn to Cortázar's construction of stories in which "people are shut up in incredibly narrow worlds" (98). The confinement of characters by Pinter and Cortázar allows for a profound investigation into human consciousness and the manner in which an individual's worldviews inevitably conflict with those of others. Even though Dorfman is fascinated by these confined spaces and even though similarly restricted spaces appear in most of his theater and in his novels *Konfidenz* and *Blake's Therapy*, he also narrates a baroque space that is fragmented and overflowing, such as that in *The Last Song of Manuel Sendero* and *The Nanny and the Iceberg*.

Dorfman's work may correlate more directly with that of both Pinter and Cortázar in his explorations of violence and language and in his rejection of realism. Both Pinter and Cortázar refuse the literary style of realism, consider-ing it to be a form that is decidedly *unreal* and that tends to distort and distract from reality. It is noteworthy that both Pinter and Cortázar sense that language has hidden layers of meaning but that it is equally incapable of truly expressing that which it hopes to describe, that there is always something inexpressible about existence. Each of these writers, Dorfman included, rejects the confi-dence of realism, the certainty with which it narrates and names the world. Esslin explains that Pinter feels that his work more accurately describes reality than the social realists who "water down the reality of their picture of the world by presupposing that they have the solutions for problems that have not yet been solved—and that may well be insoluble" (263). Cortázar similarly cri-tiques realism: "In my case, the suspicion of another order, more secret and less communicable [, was one of the principles guiding] my personal search for a literature beyond overly naive forms of realism" (cited in Alazraki and Ivask, n.p.). Dorfman notes that in both Pinter and Cortázar confinement leads to conflict and violence. He explains that the world that emerges in Cortázar's literature is that of the Latin American *bárbaro*, who will not adapt to European existence (cited in Incledon, 98).

Dorfman has stated on more than one occasion that Cortázar may be his greatest literary influence: "If I had to choose the one person who has been my major influence, it's probably Julio Cortázar, because of the way in which he understands the colloquial, the way in which he understands fantasy, and the way in which he dares to experiment. And yet he creates stories in which emotion and intellect are wedded. I think he's probably been the major influence on my literary life" (cited in McClennen in *World Literature Today*, 65; see also Incledon, 98). Dorfman is attentive to Cortázar's experimentation with literary form, especially in his masterpiece, *Rayuela* (*Hopscotch*). Like Cortázar, Dorfman has consistently tried to subvert and renovate the literary forms with which he works. Cortázar also provides a model for Dorfman's use of humor as a subversive technique.

Cortázar formed part of the Latin American literary boom, a generation of writers that included Gabriel García Márquez, Mario Vargas Llosa, Carlos Fuentes, and José Donoso. These writers and their direct predecessors, like Alejo Carpentier, Miguel Ángel Asturias, and Juan Rulfo, exercised significant influence on Dorfman's generation. The writers of the boom reversed forever the notion that Latin American literature was derivative. Even though isolated authors had gained international recognition prior to the boom, the boom established Latin America as a central location for literary innovation. As Dorfman describes in his memoir, "There existed, for the first time in the history of Latin America, a literature that could speak to its own readers while simultaneously appealing to a vast public abroad, and this literary movement asserted that in order to be Latin American you did not have to reject the international" (*Heading*, 196). The success of the boom writers came in the late 1960s, and Dorfman's commitment to Latin American literature and political engagement coincides with the region's literary Renaissance—"a giddy time to be alive for anyone who believed as I did in the power of words" (195). Dorfman noted that the boom writers combined a powerful political narrative that was true to autochthonous forms of storytelling with a smart marketing campaign (196). Writers like Carpentier, García Márquez, and Cortázar revealed the hybrid nature of Latin American identity and represented the conflict and synergy between European and Native American cultural sources.

Dorfman's second published book, *Imaginación y violencia en América* (Imagination and Violence in America), largely written while he was at Berkeley, draws out many of his interests in Latin American literature before and during the boom, and it also reveals how some of the themes of the boom writers would continue to shape his own work. The book has chapters on Borges, Asturias, Carpentier, García Márquez, Rulfo, José María Arguedas, and Vargas Llosa. In each case Dorfman studies how the authors variously depict the violence inherent in Latin American identity. He finds that Borges, for instance, creates a violent world as merely a "juego nihilista intellectual" (*Violencia*, 43); (nihilistic intellectual game). He contrasts Arguedas with Vargas Llosa: describing them both as writers who attempt to challenge Peruvian history, he stresses that the former creates literature that is social, political, and collective while the latter creates literature that appeals to individuals and constructs protagonists who heroically save their country (246–47). Dorfman suggests that these two writers represent two opposing poles of Latin American consciousness.

The writer who best exemplifies for Dorfman the effort to bring these two poles together is Gabriel García Márquez. As Dorfman explains in an essay that appears in *Some Write to the Future*, García Márquez represents two traditions that historically have been oppositional in Latin American history: "one that is the literature of an illustrated minority, elaborated with all of the forms that belong to so-called 'high culture,' basically centered in the cities; while the other, nurtured in popular, oral folk tradition, finds its roots in the countryside" (203). According to Dorfman, García Márquez draws on his Latin American literary heritage and finds a language that is able to bring these dissonant voices together. He unites the cosmopolitan and the local through the use of mythic thinking by narrating in a way that equally captures cultivated traditions and collective memory (204).

Dorfman is particularly drawn to García Márquez's balance between historical determination and hope for change, to his narrative of inevitable doom and destruction versus his description of Latin America as vital, exuberant, and full of possibility. In his analysis of *Crónica de una muerte anunciada* (*Chronicle of a Death Foretold*) Dorfman highlights García Márquez's keen ability to pinpoint the ethical failures of the community of Santiago Nasar, the protagonist who is murdered. Rather than suggest that the destruction of life is inevitable, Dorfman argues that the novel is a "political parable that hints at the ways in which the cyclical wheels of copulation and violence that have determined Latin American history up till now can, in fact, be escaped" (*Some Write*, 220). Dorfman learns from writers like García Márquez how to narrate the extraordinary anguish of Latin American history while simultaneously rescuing collective memories and pointing to the possibility of alternative futures no longer doomed to repeat the past.

Parallel to the rise of the new Latin American novel, writers from Dorfman's generation witnessed the "boom" of the *testimonio*.[15] In conjunction with the totalizing novels of the boom writers, a series of texts emerged beginning in the 1960s that would forever shape literary investigations into narratives of truth, denunciation, and historical witnessing. Even though Bernal Díaz's account of the conquest is often considered the first testimonial text of Latin America, it would be works like Miguel Barnet's *Biografía de un cimarrón* (*Biography of a Runaway Slave*) and the Guatemalan testimonial *Me llamo Rigoberta Menchú* (*I, Rigoberta Menchú*) that set the standard for the literary renovation of narrative as revolutionary political force. Linked as these texts often were with immediate political struggles, the *testimonio* exemplified the use of literature as a powerful and urgent force for bringing public attention to oppression. Dorfman worked directly with Amnesty International while in exile to gather *testimonios*, and his essay on the Chilean *testimonio* that appears in *Some Write to the Future* (written in 1982) is one of the first critical pieces to analyze the literary heritage on which the *testimonio* genre draws.[16] Evidence of the influence of the *testimonio* on Dorfman's writing is clear from the poems in the collection *Missing* to the description of the protests of the women in *Widows* to the rejection of official history in his own memoir. The best examples of his commitment to *testimonio* may be his play *Manifesto for Another World* (which draws on Kerry Kennedy Cuomo's book *Speak Truth to Power* and unites the voices of human rights defenders from across the globe) and his account of the Pinochet trial, *Exorcising Terror*.

Dorfman's generation was left to find a way to dialogue between the boom novel and the *testimonio*, two compatible yet fundamentally different ways of conceiving of the narrative project. Even if the boom novel captured the popular voice, it still remained an elite literary form, whereas the *testimonio* was often taken to be the unembellished voice of the collective. According to John Beverley in a path-breaking study of the genre, the *testimonio* was *Against Literature*. And yet for Dorfman and other writers of his generation like Tomás Eloy Martínez and Elena Poniatowska, the *testimonio* was not opposed to literature; it was, in fact, the most immediate and desperate form of storytelling that already had a long history in Latin America. That the generation of writers after the boom has a more pressing sense of the ties between literature and politics has been observed by Donald Shaw, who characterizes these differences in *Post-Boom in Spanish American Fiction*. He emphasizes that the post-boom writers were more vigorously political than the writers of the boom, that they tended to abandon the meta-narratives of the boom, that they displayed a greater questioning of linguistic authority (especially narrative authority), and that they abandoned the notion of absolute truth and essentialist descriptions of identity (3–50).

Many of the characteristics that Shaw outlines are present in Dorfman's work. Like other post-boom writers, Dorfman was also influenced by 1960s revolutionary culture, which tended to break down the divisions among cultural sources of identity. Their notion of the social role of literature was less reverent and more open, but also more politically interventionist than that of their predecessors. They openly confronted the roles of media culture and popular culture in shaping public consciousness, and their texts often included examples of these cultural referents as well as critiques of them. Dorfman explains this influence in an interview: "Our whole generation was brought up in a mass media world. . . . We may often be critical of these forms, but at the same time [we are] immersed in them" (cited in Boyers and Lectora, 160). The post-boom writers further expected literature to be a viable force in social change. Dorfman writes in his memoir that "I was not alone in being captivated by this illusion that our literature would make us free" (*Heading*, 195). These idealistic aspirations would later face a major shock when the revolutionary movements were crushed by a series of repressive military dictatorships from the 1960s to the 1980s. Dorfman, perhaps more than many of the other writers of his generation, responded to the political repression of dictators like Pinochet by continuing to hope that literature could play a significant role in bearing witness to the atrocities while also inspiring readers to continue to fight for change.

Dorfman self-identifies with other writers considered to be post-boom, like Antonio Skármeta, Eduardo Galeano, Ricardo Piglia, Elena Poniatowska, Rosario Ferré, and Tomás Eloy Martínez (Boyers and Lertora, 160–61). Yet since the end of Pinochet's official rule of Chile he has increasingly come to consider himself part of a global generation of postcolonial (or anti-neocolonial) writers like Salman Rushdie, Nadine Gordimer, Ian McEwan, Peter Carey, Michael Ondaatje, André Brink, Amitav Ghosh, Nayantara Sahgal, and Andrei Codrescu (McClennen in *World Literature Today*, 65).

■ ■ ■

While I have traced the array of Dorfman's literary influences, it is important to note that he is not immune to the "anxiety of influence." He explains that writers "have to kill the fathers. I mean, you have to kill your literary antecedents every time you write. That is very important" (cited in Incledon, 99). At one level this has meant that writers who followed the boom often found themselves trying to destroy the aura surrounding the high-modernist impulses associated with boom novels. It also returns to the question of the way that Dorfman conceives of the writer as storyteller, as both social agent and socially responsible. Yet one of the most difficult issues for Dorfman continues to be the power he places in stories and storytellers and the way that this power seems to resuscitate the writer's aura. In his essays of literary criticism Dorfman repeats the notion that even if the story narrated is utterly devastating— even if, for instance, García Márquez's *Cien años de soledad* (*One Hundred Years of Solitude*) or Pinter's *The Room* end in death and destruction—these texts provide hope. This position is revealed by Dorfman's statement in *El absurdo entre cuatro paredes* (The Absurd within Four Walls) in reference to Pinter's *The Room* that "Frente a Rose, sin embargo, hay otro ser que sí supera la muerte en forma definitiva. Es el artista, Harold Pinter" (124); (Facing Rose, however, there is another being who does overcome death in a definite way. It is the artist, Harold Pinter). This position may seem somewhat romantic and may also seem to place too much power and responsibility on the writer.

Dorfman also attributes great power to literature: "Our literature has an important role, indeed an essential role, to play in the liberation of the people of Latin America" (*Some Write*, xii). The power of the writer and the literary text, though, is realized only through the reader who is active, critical, and engaged: "The violence inscribed like a curse in our literature since its origins can be resolved, through action or compassion or doubt or rage or tenderness, in the lives of the liberated readers of today and tomorrow and beyond" (xiv). Dorfman repeatedly stresses the limitations to these various sources of social power and he consistently questions the liberating role of culture, but his doubts never subsume his belief that literature necessarily plays an essential role in social change.

Even though he conceives of the writer as a being who brings together the many voices of society—past, present, and future—Dorfman continues to place the writer in a position of great responsibility and consequently great power. The writer is the creative force that speaks of and to society and whose work forms the basis for the hopeful potential of literature. Such a stance may reveal the drawback to envisioning the writer in the twentieth and twenty-first centuries as a storyteller. Contemporary storytellers must simultaneously confront the crisis in representation, the globalization of mass media, and the ideology of neoliberalism. They must provide hope without totalizing, they must expose social dilemmas without preaching, and they must inspire despite their very limited ability to reach the public. One of the most complicated features of Dorfman's aesthetic vision is his combined faith in literature and a skepticism of it.

As we look at those writers who have played the greatest role in Dorfman's literary formation, a pattern is revealed: they are writers who in general were able to negotiate the complexities of working as creative individuals, were interested in representing society, and hoped to inspire an audience to think and engage with the world critically. Artist, text, context, and audience all play a role in the creation of meaning. Dorfman's theory of the writer may seem to propose a highly contradictory combination of authorial agency and social determination, but these notions do not function antagonistically for him, nor do they do so for many other Latin American writers who refuse to consider such notions as antithetical. Among Dorfman's generation other writers, like Ricardo Piglia—especially in *Respiración artificial* (1980; *Artificial Respiration*, 1994)—have refused to succumb to Western notions of active reason versus passive existence.

Dorfman's literary quest has caused him to constantly experiment with form. Dorfman speaks of García Márquez's unified, original style, and he notes that his own writing has not achieved such unity: "My style isn't at all unified. I'm full of fragments and contradictions. I haven't been able to find that unity in my work, in my vision. My life had been very fragmented and my vision is as well" (cited in Incledon, 98).[17] In chapter 3, I argue that Dorfman does have a unified aesthetic vision but that it has not resulted in a unified form of writing. His work ranges from baroque excess to the sparse language of the theater of the absurd. Not only has he worked across a wide range of genres, but within these he has also created texts that represent a number of different narrative strategies. His novels, for example, have taken forms as varied as the epic in *The Last Song of Manuel Sendero*, the novel of intrigue in *Konfidenz*, and the picaresque in *The Nanny and the Iceberg*. He has noted two main tendencies in his work, the satirical/critical and the gentle/hopeful, but these appear across multiple forms of expression (Muñoz, 71). On the one hand, these multiple styles speak to the various, rich sources that he draws on in his work, and they show the broad range of his creative work. On the other hand, these multiple styles and their various genres have failed to result in what could be called a characteristic Dorfman literary form. Unlike some of his greatest influences, Dorfman has refused to hone a consistent narrative voice, such as that of Pinter or Cortázar. This multiple style is a consequence of Dorfman's desire to let each story find its best form, and it is also due to his belief that art must consistently seek new structures and new languages with which to reach an audience while also dialoguing with the literary representations of the past. The following chapter argues that what may appear as stylistic chaos is actually a deliberate literary strategy that hopes to surprise the reader and provoke response.

Soy parte de la esencial
mayoría, soy una hoja más
del gran árbol humano. . . .
Es memorable y desgar-
rador para el poeta haber
encarnado para muchos
hombres, durante un minuto,
la esperanza.

(I am part of the essential
majority, I am one leaf more
on the great tree of humanity.
. . . It is memorable and heart-
rending for the poet to have
incarnated for many men, for
a minute, hope.)

—PABLO NERUDA, *Confieso
que he vivido*

This is the bedrock of who I
am: a man who cannot live in
this world unless he believes
there is hope.

—ARIEL DORFMAN, *Heading
South, Looking North*

3. AN AESTHETICS OF HOPE

Many of the men and women Ariel Dorfman worked with during his seventeen years of exile from Chile (1973–90) were torture victims whom he and
others in the Chilean resistance abroad helped to adapt to their banishment.
One day a woman who had been tortured in Chile told Dorfman that what had
saved her in the worst moments was her "unending repetition of some lines by
Neruda or Machado" (*Heading*, 263). Appearing as an anecdote in both his
memoir and in the foreword to his book of essays, *Hacia la liberación del
lector latinoamericano* (Towards the Liberation of the Latin American Reader),
this story symbolizes for Dorfman how literature is able to record history,
incite struggle, and fuel the imagination. Reciting poetry to herself, this unnamed woman carved out a space that could not be touched by her tormen-
tors. "Mientras ella estuviera murmurándose esas palabras, el mundo no podía
ser inagotablemente este dolor, esa humillación; el mundo prometía otras
avenidas, otro tiempo, otro espacio, quizás hasta otro cuerpo" (*Hacia la liberación*, xvii); (While she was murmuring these words to herself, the world could
not be inexhaustibly this pain, that humiliation; the world promised other
avenues, another time, another space, perhaps even another body). She spoke

lines of poetry instead of the names of her colleagues, and it was through verse that she avoided confession and betrayal. This story convinced Dorfman of literature's power to return humanity to those most threatened by its loss. It also reassured him of the essential role of the literary project in imagining a hopeful future. "While there is one person like her in the world, I will find myself defending both her right to struggle and our obligation to remember" (*Heading*, 264).

Dorfman has a myriad of stories that illustrate his belief in the intersections among literature, political struggle, and hope. On the run from Pinochet and his secret police, Dorfman spent a night in a shack in Santiago's slums, worrying about his impending exile. When daylight broke, he discovered a collection of books, mostly published by Quimantú, the state publishing house for which Dorfman had worked. He found a copy of his own *Para leer al pato Donald* (which, incidentally, he had seen burned on television only days before), along with many other Quimantú books—an experience that radically changed his sense of the reach of literature: "If it was true that my words, that books, could not protect me from death and torture, neither could it be denied that those books were here, being read, and tomorrow they would still be here, and what had been read and thought and nursed could not be erased so easily" (*Heading*, 146). Bodies could be destroyed, voices could be silenced, but the stories would persist. They could be sheltered in the mind, uttered during moments of torture, or whispered while putting a child to bed.

These anecdotes begin to illuminate how Dorfman's work exemplifies an aesthetics of hope. Dorfman himself has purposefully shied away from offering readers his own detailed theory of art. In the conclusion to *The Empire's Old Clothes*, for example, he explains that in his analysis of mass-produced literature he has not asked himself "specifically how emotion and intellect come together, and under what circumstances. . . . An examination of culture as an interplay between real readers and real producers was not then, and is not now, my main intention" (178–79). A short piece entitled "The Latin American Aesthetics of Hope" further elaborates his belief in the power of literature and points to a series of elements that Dorfman considers central to an emancipatory literary project. Modeled as a musing on a note in the subway of Buenos Aires announcing the closing of a post office, Dorfman takes this event to be symptomatic of a region that has often resigned itself to the "eternal repetition" of the past (*Other Septembers*, 167). Dorfman explains that he "tentatively" calls literature with an aesthetics of hope that which is "based on the proposition that the dead do not choose for us, but that we choose for them, that we change the past as we forge into the future" (169).

"The Latin American Aesthetics of Hope" unites many of Dorfman's main concerns about literature: literature should be utopian, it should reach out and engage its audience, it should resolve conflicts collectively, it should not simplify the complex problems of life, and it should engage directly with the power of the mass media. As in many of his other essays, though, these thoughts remain sketchy, as much a personal musing as a theory of art. Of course this lack of straightforward structure is a signature trademark of Dorfman's work since he expects the reader to piece together his or her own thoughts and theories, refusing to provide his audience with a careful map of what to think and how to appreciate art. While Dorfman has avoided developing an aesthetic theory per se, careful study of his work, especially of his nonfiction, reveals a number of his essential beliefs regarding the relationship among art, mind, and society. My goal in this chapter is to build on Dorfman's work to make explicit what is often only implicit in his writings and to more fully elaborate on the characteristics of an aesthetics of hope, which applies obviously to Dorfman's own creative production but which also speaks to the work of a number of writers whose literature confronted major political crises in the latter part of the twentieth century and who chose to narrate those conflicts by being simultaneously attentive to the difficulties inherent in literary representation and convinced of the political power of art.

THREE AESTHETIC ELEMENTS OF HOPE

Before delving into aesthetics, into art and its perception, let us consider what it is to hope and why hope might serve as a useful concept for an aesthetic theory. First, hope is a notion that speaks to the ways that art can bear witness to the past, reflect the present, and project a future. To hope is to reach across time because hope unites desire and expectation. If desire springs from experience and expectations are for the future, then to hope is to bridge the past, present, and future. Ernst Bloch develops such a theory of hope and culture in *The Principle of Hope*, where he suggests that hope can bridge the past, present, and future in ways that are critically productive and utopian. He suggests that it is important to know what to flee and what to seek from the past since "we have within us what we could become" (vol. 3, 43). A first step, then, in an aesthetics of hope lies in understanding how the past affects the future. For example, Dorfman has drawn attention to the prevalent Latin American attitude that the "past devours the future" (*Other Septembers*, 167). Places like Comala and Macondo, created by Juan Rulfo and Gabriel García Márquez respectively, are inhabited by people who are literally trapped in a cyclical repetition of the past. For Dorfman, literary representations that exaggerate such attitudes are the first step in provoking the reader to have hope for a different future (*Other Septembers*, 168). Literature can spark desire, and it can inspire different visions for the future, which is why literature with an aesthetics of hope always holds utopian longings, even when these are buried underneath visions that might appear overwhelmingly pessimistic.

Second, to hope is to abolish binary thinking that isolates knowledge from feeling. Hope links reason and emotion; it requires their collaboration to exist. Henry Giroux explains that hope is not blind optimism but is always filled with skepticism and questioning:

> At the heart of politics and political agency is the necessity to imagine the impossible, to see beyond the given, and to propose concrete alternative visions. . . . Without hope, even in the most dire of times, there is no possibility for resistance, dissent, and struggle. Agency is the condition of struggle, and hope is the condition of agency. Hope expands the space of the possible and becomes a way of recognizing and naming the incomplete nature of the present. . . . Hope coupled with skepticism reclaims the possibility of ethics, knowledge, criticism, and social engagement, and democracy. (Cited in Pozo, n.p.)

Giroux emphasizes that hope requires collective agency much in the same way that Dorfman emphasizes that progressive literature requires active readers whose practice of reading leads to social agency. The act of reading itself merges reason and emotion, the mental and the sensual, just as political activism requires both passion and reasoned commitment. An aesthetics of hope depends on a connection between art and audience that is both rational and emotional. Art cannot simply be a mental exercise, nor can it be limited to catharsis; it must find a way to speak to the mind and the body, thereby destroying the false duality between them.

Third, hope is rarely solitary, and an aesthetics of hope speaks to the individual within a collective. Taking place in the mind and fueled by external images, hope often depends on a future with others and on past communal experience. It depends on the intersection of the self, an external reality, and imagination, where art and literature often serve as inspiration for the imagination. Literature with an aesthetics of hope seeks collective responses to social dilemmas and rejects the aesthetic of individualism, where superheroes fix the world. Instead, emancipatory literature reveals the falsehoods of hero worship and happy endings that teach their audiences, according to Dorfman, that "'Tomorrow, tomorrow, tomorrow—is only a day away,' while their real days disappear into a dismal stagnation of today" (*Other Septembers*, 170).

Dorfman witnessed collective hope for the first time when he worked to help lower-class communities recover from a massive earthquake in June 1960. Instead of traveling to the region in the south where the earthquake took place, Dorfman stayed in Santiago, daily raising money and loading trucks with supplies. As he walked Santiago's streets asking people from all classes to aid in the relief effort, he came in close contact with Chilean society. The experience of seeing people from all classes bond together to help others broke open his bourgeois life. What had previously been theoretical now had grounding in the practical experience of seeing very poor people offering all they could to help and the wealthy demonstrating concern and support for those suffering. For the first time, he saw a community's courage and strength in the face of adversity. He uses one word to describe what he saw: "Hope. If I had to choose one word, that would be it. *Esperanza*" (*Heading*, 157). As always Dorfman's attention to language and to the different registers between English and Spanish is revealing: to hope in Spanish is *esperar*, a verb that signifies waiting as well as hoping. It is not surprising, then, that Dorfman tends to favor the Spanish version of the word.[1] When one hopes in Spanish, one is reminded of the need for patience, of the fact that hopes take time and effort to become real. *Esperar* is etymologically linked to Latin's *sperare*, a verb that in addition to signifying hope means to look for, trust, expect, and promise oneself—actions that are all required in order to hope. Unlike dreams, which tend to suggest their own impossibility and to emerge from a state of unconsciousness, hope springs from passionate thinking and wakefulness and depends on a belief in future potential.

The distinction between dreams and hopes is emphasized in yet another anecdote Dorfman uses to illustrate the social role of art. Both *The Empire's Old Clothes* and *Patos, elefantes y héroes* (1985; Ducks, Elephants, and Heroes) begin with the story of another unnamed woman Dorfman met while working on a community project in the slums of Santiago before Allende had been elected president. The woman approached Dorfman and asked him why he was so critical of mass-produced literature since she was especially fond of photo-novels, the comic book romances that have photos instead of drawings. She pled with him: "Don't take my dreams away from me" (*Empire's*, 4). But, in fact, that was precisely what Dorfman wanted to do. For Dorfman, the dreams that emanate from such literature are illusions and fantasies that obscure the real conditions and real possibilities of existence. Some years later, after Allende had won the election and was able to create state support for cultural products that did not infantilize the public, Dorfman saw this woman again. She told him that she now realized that he was right about photo-novels and that she no longer read that "trash" anymore. "Now, *compañero*, we are dreaming reality" (5). To "dream reality" is to hope, and it is literature that enabled this woman to make that transition. Her words would inspire and haunt Dorfman as he wrote about her while he was in exile after the devastations of the coup. What was she reading then? How had her hopes changed?[2]

MATTERS OF STYLE IN THE AESTHETICS OF HOPE

As mentioned in chapter 2, Dorfman's writing varies over a wide range of genres and textual forms. Despite this variety, though, two specific style traits at the level of his sentences appear throughout his work and highlight his unified aesthetic project: fluctuating possessives and subject pronouns and shifting verb forms. Each practice relates directly to an aesthetics of hope since the fluctuating possessives and subjects draw attention to the relationship between literature and identity and the shifting verb forms create a fluid, yet conflicted, notion of time across the past, present, and future.

Fluctuating Possessives and Subject Pronouns. Dorfman's use of fluctuating possessives and subject pronouns foregrounds the problem of the relationship between literature and the self as specific sentences vary in the singular voice from first person (I) to second person (you) to third person (he, she) and from singular forms like "I" to plural forms like "we." How can literature, which has become an increasingly solitary practice, suggest to the reader ways to engage with a larger community? How can it draw attention to the problematic relationship between the self and language that has emerged as a consequence of poststructuralist theory without falling into the trap of eradicating the self all together? Dorfman's interest in breaking the rules of grammar by writing sentences that jump across subject positions also breaks down complacency and forces the reader to think about the connections between the written word and the construction of identity.

Moros en la costa (*Hard Rain*), Dorfman's first novel, written during the presidency of Allende and translated in 1990, demonstrates his early and persistent interest in drawing attention to the relationship between literature and the self. On the first page of the English translation the subject shifts three times, from "All *you* need" to "*we*'ve got" to "the *reader's* doubts" (13). These shifting subjects are especially interesting since they refer to the reader of a book dealing with the murder of a woman in a Nazi concentration camp. The question raised by the reader/reviewer of the book is whether her death is a murder since she was to be sent to the gas chambers two days later. Drawing a parallel between repressive Latin American governments and Nazi Germany, the text turns into a commentary on art and politics. The first chapter ends by asking how literature can participate in revolution, and the shifting subject pronouns draw attention to the difficulty in locating the revolution's social agents.

La última canción de Manuel Sendero (*The Last Song of Manuel Sendero*) may provide the best example of Dorfman's practice of shifting subjects since the narrator constantly switches subject positions. In one case the narrator shifts from first-person plural to singular and back to plural: "¿Cómo podemos ser tan tajantes? Porque nosotros lo supimos, lo supe yo, principalmente por boca suya, de mi abuelo el nuestro" (13); ("How de we all know this? Very Simple. I found out, we all did, largely from the mouth of my grandfather, our old granddaddy himself"; 7). This shifting subject wavers between the individual and the community. In another case Dorfman uses a similar technique to shift from the third person to the first and back to the third: "Ahí fue que comenzó la relación entre Manuel y su hijo, entre mi padre y yo, y que iba a resultar todo lo que el uno iba a conocer jamás del otro, dadas las circunstancias" (30); ("That was the way that the relationship between Manuel and his son began, between my father and me, and, under the circumstances, it was going to be all the one was going to know about the other"; 26). Here the change in voice emphasizes the distance between the intimate language of the first person and the cool distance of the third person. These changes draw the reader's attention to the relationship between language and the self, pointing at the same time to language's fragility and to its power to construct identity. In an example from *Konfidenz* Dorfman equates the betrayals of the Second World War to betrayals of all of humanity: "Alguien nos traicionó, a él, y a mí, alguien en quien confiamos y nos entregó al enemigo" (175); ("Someone sold us out, sold him, sold me, someone we believed in gave our names to the enemy"; 176). Here betrayals resonate and redirect from the collective to the individual and back again so that it becomes difficult to distinguish among them. Dorfman's language mirrors the layered betrayals of the historical moment he is narrating, when the communists betrayed their own comrades in Germany and the French betrayed their own people.

Dorfman often uses the technique of fluctuating possessives and subject pronouns when referring to Chile and to events similar to those that happened as a result of Pinochet's coup. The heightened use of this practice in relation to the narration of the dictatorship is a logical consequence of Dorfman's concern for the ways that the coup attempted to destroy the solidarity fostered by Allende's presidency and the Unidad Popular. For instance, in *Exorcising Terror* he alternates subjects and possessives when he describes the death of Orlando Letelier. He writes that if he were narrating this event as if it were a fairy tale, he would end with the following: "Once upon a time there was a country where three couples danced tango. Once upon a time Orlando Letelier was in our midst. Once upon a time we needed help to keep him and so many others alive. Once upon a time many people inside and outside Chile decided not to let my country die" (163–64). It is important to note that these sentences would mark the *end* of the story and not the beginning, a strategy that reveals Dorfman's commitment to allowing his readers' imaginations to complete the text. These sentences move from third-person to first-person plural to first-person singular. The shifts emphasize both the need for and the lack of a collective with sufficient force and energy to challenge the death and loss caused by Pinochet. Ending with the first-person singular in this case further underscores the movement from community to solitude, from Allende's presidency to Dorfman's exile.

Heading South, Looking North also illustrates the intersections and divergences between the personal and the collective on the opening page, where Dorfman writes that he "always thought this story was meant to start on that morning when the Armed Forces of my country rise against our President" (3). In this case the transition from "my country" to "our President" tries to willfully reverse the movement of exile that disintegrates community and isolates the self. These samplings, while different, indicate a stylistic practice Dorfman consistently employs to force the reader to actively confront the relationship between language and the self, between the self and the community, and between the community and language.

Shifting Verb Forms. The second style trait, perhaps even more prevalent than the first, is Dorfman's play with verb tenses. It is telling that he typically begins teaching Gabriel García Márquez's *One Hundred Years of Solitude* by telling his students to pay careful attention to the use of tenses in the opening sentence and to the way that the novel begins by marking time forward and backward and then further backward from the present. "Muchos años después, frente al pelotón de fusilamiento, el coronel Aureliano Buendía había de recordar aquella tarde remota en que su padre lo llevó a conocer el hielo" (59); ("Many years later, as he faced the firing squad, Colonel Aureliano Buendía was to remember that distant afternoon when his father took him to discover ice"; 11).

The passage starts in the past looking forward with "Muchos años después" (Many years later) and then moves further back to "había de recordar" (he was to remember). Dorfman notes how the present begins in the past of the future. The only way to arrive at the future and not be haunted by the past is to acknowledge this relationship and challenge it. Dorfman explains that this opening sentence offers the reader a choice: "Stay inside the text, like the last Aureliano for whom it is already too late" or "leap outside that ambiguous relationship with death and, deciphering the repression, reading its causes and its loneliness, manage to take that fiction back into reality, make it historical, try to make sure that the next hundred years will not end in the same way" (*Some Write*, 217). When literature shifts verb tenses or unsettles traditional narrative time, Dorfman believes that it creates the conditions for hope because it asks the reader to make a choice. The reader can either learn to recognize the past in order to shape an alternative future or remain a passive subject of history.

Examples of Dorfman's own signature shifting verb tenses appear as early as his first book on the theater of Harold Pinter. In his own epigraph to the book (presented in full in chapter 2) he writes, "We have all lived, have seen live, have dreamed this nightmare. / Not all of us have known how to overcome it." Here all verbs are in the first-person plural present perfect, but the move from "have . . . lived" to "have seen live" to "have dreamed" to "have known" functions to shift narrative time. The first instance refers to the subject's recent past, which may still be in progress; the second, to the subject's witnessing of the recent past; the third, to the subject's recent nightmares of the future; and the fourth speaks to the future by referring to the subject's knowledge of how to overcome the past. These sentences create a blurry line between past, present, and future, and according to the epigraph, the only way to end the cycle of "historical repetition" is through "understanding and overcoming through art." This promiscuously layered time will unravel only through art that denounces this eternal repetition and through a reader who understands history and defies it.

In an essay dedicated to the art of Mozart written well before the *Baby Mozart* craze, Dorfman notes the almost universal appeal of Mozart's music, especially to children. He wishes that Mozart were more available to everyone, but most of all he worries about the next Mozart, the one who instead of composing music is dying of hunger and ignorance, completely forgotten and discarded. The last line of the piece reads as follows: "Y todos cantamos, cantaremos, hemos cantado menos, mucho menos debido a esa muerte que se multiplica y que podríamos evitar" (*Los sueños nucleares*, 236); (And we all sing/sang, we will sing, we have sung less, much less because of this death that multiplies itself and that we could avoid). Here Dorfman moves from the present or the past, depending on how one reads "cantamos," to the future, and then to the present perfect, making time revert back in order to indicate that this cycle of loss will continue until children all over the world are no longer denied a better life. It is noteworthy that in the last two examples Dorfman favors the present perfect (that is, "have sung") over the preterit ("sang") to describe a recently completed event. It is a linguistic practice common in the Spanish of Spain, but in Chile the preterit is more common. By referring to the past with the present perfect rather than the preterit, Dorfman calls attention to the way that he is using language to refer to the past. This linguistic strategy allows him to further emphasize the interplay between the present and the past since the present perfect signifies a moment in the recent past, a past that is still present.

Another telling example of Dorfman's fluctuating verb tenses occurs in the opening of the Spanish version of his memoir, where he writes that he believed that the coup was the moment that "me hace nacer, que me daba comienzo" (*Rumbo*, 9); (gives birth to me, that was giving me a beginning).[3] Not only does he shift from the present to the past, but he also uses the imperfect ("was giving") to describe an act, giving birth, that would typically be described in Spanish using the preterit ("gave"). The use of the imperfect, as in the above examples of the present perfect, stretches a moment that should be defined and closed in time. With the imperfect Dorfman is able to draw attention to the way that the events of September 11, 1973, have spilled beyond the confines of that day. In fact, he suggests that the day was foretold in the history of Latin America and that unless radical efforts are made to change this history of violence, that day will continue to reverberate into the future. Not only must literature confront amnesia so that the past can become history, but it must also honor the dead while at the same time opening the mind to imagine a different future. As in the examples of shifting subjects and possessives above, it would be possible to identify countless examples of Dorfman's fluctuating verb tenses, each of which has a unique register of meaning but all of which ultimately point back to the relationship between art and the representation of time. If an aesthetics of hope writes to the future, then it depends on an audience that will recognize the differences among authoritarian, cyclical time; hegemonic, falsely historical time; and emancipated, progressive time and will understand how literature dialectically resonates both the timelessly universal and the historically specific.

To construct an aesthetic theory characterized by hope is to return to an area of philosophical inquiry that has come under scrutiny by certain strains of postmodern theory that question whether a work of art has intrinsic social value, whether there is any fixed communicability of meaning attributable to art, and whether art should be understood as a totality with its own internal logic. Hal Foster has called this extreme position an "anti-aesthetic." Yet these skeptical, textualist, poststructural positions tend to disregard the long history of aesthetic theory, which itself has often been critical of the notions of art-for-art's-sake, artistic autonomy, and creative genius. Singer and Dunn suggest that it is ironic that in a moment when art is increasingly studied from interdisciplinary perspectives, the theoretical insights of aesthetics, which specifically consider the relationship among art, perception, and society, have been eschewed. In fact, what often passes for cultural criticism is actually aesthetic theory, but it is an aesthetic theory unaware of its own critical history.

Aesthetics is often understood by literary critics as a question of taste, beauty, and/or form, but in a general sense it refers to the philosophy of perception, and the modern usage of the term is attributed to Alexander Baumgarten, whose *Reflections on Poetry* (1735) and *Aesthetica* (1750) went on to later influence the work of Immanuel Kant, especially in *The Critique of Judgment* (1790). Baumgarten's aesthetic theory attempted to merge cognitive thinking and the everyday perceptions of life by positing a theory of perception that brought together the senses and reason, the material and the immaterial. Terry Eagleton points out that Baumgarten's aesthetics led to a discourse of the body and that this discourse represents a "primitive materialism," what might otherwise be described as "the body's long inarticulate rebellion against the tyranny of the theoretical" (13). Eagleton's point is relevant for the purposes of this study since it reminds readers of the fact that the aesthetic has direct ties to the material, physical world as it is mediated through art—questions central to Dorfman's literary project. Aesthetics provides a theoretical ground through which one can consider how historical events can be represented and remembered. Aesthetic theory asks how the material translates into the immaterial or how it is that one can think about an external reality. From its inception aesthetic theory has been opposed to a notion of autonomous art and has been critical of the notion that rational thinking could be divorced from the world of sensory perception and material history.

It is also noteworthy that Baumgarten's call for inquiry into aesthetics coincides with a moment of political absolutism, for it will later be the case that most major aesthetic theories emanate from moments of extreme political rupture. War, revolution, rebellion, authoritarianism, and fascism have all led to reconsiderations of the social role of art. Yet these first forays into aesthetic theory were not oppositional, critical accounts but were instead supportive of the status quo. Eagleton explains that "what germinates in the eighteenth century as the strange new discourse of aesthetics is not a challenge to that political authority; but it can be read as symptomatic of an ideological dilemma inherent in absolutist power. Such power needs for its own purposes to take account of 'sensible' life, for without an understanding of this no dominion can be secure" (15). Some of these same concerns would reappear in marxist analyses of culture, such as Louis Althusser's critique of ideology and Antonio Gramsci's theory of hegemony—theories that took an oppositional stance to the ways that power structures constructed and controlled notions of beauty in their efforts to shape human desire. Some two hundred years after Baumgarten and Kant, Dorfman would conduct his own studies of mass-produced culture, exploring the means by which such culture reinforces existing inequitable power relations through narrative tropes. His aim was to discover how to dismantle the powerful relationship between media culture and society so that he could open a space for emancipatory forms of art.

Dorfman's concerns over the role of art place him within a long tradition of philosophical inquiry into art, the self, and society. Does social context determine the work of art and its reception? Does the artist control interpretations of the work of art? Where does the power of perception reside? Is it found in the artwork, the artist, social norms, or the individual? In addition to concerns over the interpretation and appreciation of art, aesthetic theory has also been especially preoccupied with whether art is able to play a role in developing society's political consciousness. Can art provoke change? Can it push its audience toward social rebellion? Or does it necessarily distract society from material reality? Does it mesmerize or energize?

Following Baumgarten, a number of late-eighteenth- and nineteenth-century European philosophers, such as Kant, Friedrich Schiller, G. W. F. Hegel, and Karl Marx, developed aesthetic theories that were inherently dialectical.[4] But it would be the Frankfurt School and its response to war, revolution, and social crisis in post–Second World War Europe that would radically change the way that European aesthetic theory considered the dialectical and political implications of art. Theodor Adorno, Walter Benjamin, Ernst Bloch, and Herbert Marcuse each constructed aesthetic theories that accounted for the massive mind control associated with fascism and that imagined the characteristics of emancipatory art. Despite differences of opinion, each of these theorists argued that culture had the potential to either affirm existing structures or critique them. Latin American intellectuals like Dorfman, interested in interrogating the political possibilities of art and the mass control of society through media communication, would turn to Frankfurt School theories, along with the work of Antonio Gramsci and Louis Althusser, for insight. Dorfman was especially influenced by Gramsci, whom he quotes in his analysis of the *Lone Ranger*, and also by the aesthetic theories of Jean-Paul Sartre and Michel Foucault.

Even though Latin American intellectuals were well versed in the theories of Europeans, they read these theories within their own long tradition of the social role of art. It is important to bear in mind that the history of aesthetic theory in Latin America is somewhat different from that of Europe and North America. In the nineteenth century, intellectuals such as Simón Bolívar, Andrés Bello, and José Martí tended to approach the study of culture and society in more interdisciplinary terms than their European counterparts. Not only were Latin American intellectuals inclined to simultaneously produce literature, political essays, and philosophy, but they also had a far more fluid notion of the ties between reason and emotion and the interconnectedness of art, politics, and society. George Yúdice explains: "Como precursores de la nueva interdisciplinariedad, los intelectuales abarcaron el espectro completo de la filosofía y de las prácticas culturales estéticas y cotidianas en sus análisis de los procesos sociales" ("Contrapunteo," 339); (As precursors of the new interdisciplinarity, intellectuals covered the whole spectrum of philosophy and aesthetic and quotidian cultural praxes in their analyses of social processes). Following this legacy, in Latin America since the 1960s critics such as Dorfman, Paolo Freire, Augusto Boal, Jesús Martín-Barbero, Néstor García Canclini, and Octavio Getino have assessed the social function of the mass media and have theorized how literature and the arts can raise consciousness, empower society, and lead to political change.[5]

The 1960s were marked by an extraordinary sense of possibility that followed the successes of the Cuban Revolution. Dorfman explains that during this period many Latin American intellectuals "quite consciously set out to explore the possibility of joyful renovation—in life and love, in society and streets, in language and fictional procedures and, above all, in our work" (168). The decade witnessed the literary boom, the first modern testimonial (compiled by Miguel Barnet), and the explosion of the New Latin American Cinema, which held its first regional film festival in Viña del Mar, Chile, in 1967. These cultural revolutions accompanied massive social movements, revolutions, and uprisings, and Dorfman admits that during this time he thought that he and his comrades "would dance forever in the streets of Santiago" (*Other Septembers*, 169). This moment of optimism and confidence would come to an abrupt halt when most of these revolutionary movements would come under extreme attack. Dorfman explains that "repression, terror, exile, and particularly the overriding presence of evil were going to put us and put our hope to the test" (169).

The dictatorships of the 1970s and '80s had a tremendous impact on the intellectual life of Latin America, but this impact was further exacerbated by the fact that such massive political repression converged historically with postmodern theory's growing presence in Latin America. The coincidence of torture, exile, and censorship with postmodern theory's skepticism about the social role of art and the communicability of language described, exemplified, and (some would argue) laid bare the aesthetic optimism of the 1960s.[6] How could artists continue to work and hope without paying attention to their massive failures? How could they register these failures without concluding that their work and their dreams had been a fantasy? In Latin America and elsewhere artists and intellectuals who faced social upheaval during the postmodern period either tended toward pessimism, ambiguity, textualism, and nihilism or found a way to incorporate postmodern notions about the fragile role of art into an aesthetics of hope that remained convinced of art's role in searching for an alternative to dehumanization, suffering, and the alienating effects of global capitalism. Michael McIrvin explains that at a time when "the very notion of 'meaning' is under attack" it has been tempting to retreat from literary projects (47). But to retreat into deconstruction, according to McIrvin, is to cede meaning to the forces that control official discourse—a withdrawal unacceptable to many writers. Consequently, these historical convergences of heightened authoritarianism, capitalism, and a lack of faith in representation led certain writers, Dorfman among them, to work within a political postmodern aesthetic—that is, they confronted directly the critique of representation, master narratives, and authorial agency found in postmodern reassessments of modernism at the same time as they remained committed to the notion that art can contribute to social change. Thus their postmodernism is always resolutely political and opposes ludic or textualist postmodern aesthetics that have abandoned the ideals of modern society and focus solely on the world as text.[7] Intellectuals such as Dorfman who had lived through this transition became acutely aware of what now, after the postmodern turn and the widespread failure of Latin American social revolutions, seemed like artistic arrogance.

They were forced to find a way to incorporate their diminished confidence in their projects within a persistent belief that art is, has been, and will be a primary contributor to the struggle to create a better world.

One way to trace this transition is through Dorfman's work on the mass media both before and after the Pinochet coup. *How to Read Donald Duck*, Dorfman and Mattelart's study of the colonizing impulses in the Disney comics exported to Latin America, had a seminal impact on Latin American theories about art and society. David Kunzle points out that the volume became a best seller on publication and in subsequent editions throughout Latin America (12). There were three printings in Chile during the Allende years, and by the late 1970s the book had sold over five hundred thousand copies in more than ten languages (Lawrence, 115).[8] Written in 1971 as the policies of Allende were rapidly changing Chilean culture, the book marks a moment of political possibility when it seemed that art, politics, and society could work together to imagine a better future. Appearing during the heyday of Latin American social transformation, it provided a blueprint for a critique of cultural imperialism. The attack that it mounted on Disney would be particularly important for later generations since in Chile, according to Kunzle, "it had proved easier to nationalize copper than to free the mass media from U.S. influence" (12). The core concepts of the book, as Dorfman recalls them in his memoir, were that Disney comics "eliminated confrontation, penalized rebellion, ridiculed solidarity, caricatured critical thought, and reduced all social conflicts to easily resolved psychological dilemmas" (*Heading*, 247). John Berger described the study as a "handbook of de-colonisation" ("A Disney World," 478). The ideas developed in *How to Read Donald Duck* would be refined and reconsidered in Dorfman's later nonfiction works on mass media and literature.

Once in exile after the 1973 coup, Dorfman was forced to rethink some of his more optimistic notions about the role of the public in the consumption of mass-media culture. Whereas *How to Read Donald Duck* assumed that a change in government accompanied by cultural support could result in radical social transformation, Dorfman later recognized the difficulty of such changes, a transition especially visible in his later work of cultural criticism, *The Empire's Old Clothes*. Reflecting on those early essays, he confesses, "I don't think my analyses were able to fully appreciate how deeply rooted our myths are in the mind of the common man and woman" (*Empire's*, 10). He also began to wonder about the extent to which mass-media culture reflected basic human tendencies: "These violent undergrowths of imaginary characters are successful because . . . they match and accompany certain deep-seated tendencies and fears" (12). Finally, he came to consider that truly political art needed to resonate beyond the circle of the already convinced. Such dialogue would require "permanent criticism and revision" in the face of constant challenges and would be especially productive because it would force artists to seek more refined and sophisticated means of conveying their message (12).

Thus there is a significant transition in Dorfman's aesthetic theory from the time of Allende to his work in exile and after. Yet all of his essays share a number of common threads and concerns. Taken together, Dorfman's nonfiction texts offer two main theories about culture and society. First, Dorfman argues that the mass-media culture tends to alienate, infantilize, and colonize its audience into accepting the social ideologies of capitalism and neoliberalism. Second, he holds that emancipatory politics depends on certain types of art, especially literature, because such art is able to liberate the reader and inspire social activism.

CORE FEATURES OF AN AESTHETICS OF HOPE

In addition to the three elements of hope that are fundamental to an aesthetics of hope—the bridging of the past, present, and future; the mutual interdependence of reason and emotion; and the association of the individual with the community—three further features are essential to such an aesthetic theory. An aesthetics of hope is dialectical, provocative, and revolutionary. The first characteristic is simultaneously methodological, structural, and metaphysical. It speaks to the way art should be studied, to art's own internal composition, and to art's position in society. The second characteristic describes art's confrontational relationship vis-à-vis its audience and its context. Provocative art is aesthetic, whereas conservative art is an-aesthetic. The third characteristic describes strategies required by an aesthetics of hope that relate to the practices of social rebellion, such as the collective participation of the audience, formal experimentation and variety, and oscillation between representations of a brutal reality and a hopeful future. Even though these concepts intersect and overlap, making a discrete analysis of them difficult, they are described in greater detail below and illuminated through an analysis of the consistent features of Dorfman's work that illustrate his aesthetics of hope.

In keeping with the tradition of aesthetic theories that have investigated the powerful role that culture can play in shaping the way that society thinks and feels, most politically progressive aesthetic theories have been committed to considering art's relationship to society in dialectical terms. Dating as far back as the theories of Lord Shaftesbury in the late eighteenth century, aesthetic theories have emphasized the dialectical function of art and literature. Singer and

Dunn explain that these early theories, especially those of Kant, focused on the dialectic between the concrete particular and the abstract universal. They point out that in political terms this led to a consideration of the way that art mediates the interests of the individual with the good of society as a whole (4–5). Many marxist critics, like Herbert Marcuse, Theodor Adorno, and Fredric Jameson, locate art's mediating function in the determining role played by the society from which art emerges. Marcuse emphasizes the dialectic between the affirmation and negation of social context. According to him, art sublimates reality, reordering, reshaping, and stylizing "data" so that "even the representation of death and destruction invoke[s] the need for hope—a need rooted in the new consciousness embodied in the work of art. . . . The work of art thus re-presents reality while accusing it" (7–8). In Dorfman's work the representation of reality is grounded in the very urgent need to preserve historical memory and expose reality in unsimplistic terms. He explains: "There is an impulse in the activist to convince the other person. . . . But as a writer, the only thing you want to convince people of is that your story is a story worth telling, and that you've been telling the unsimplistic truth of what it means to live in this world" (cited in O'Regan, n.p.). To approach the study of art within an aesthetic of hope is to emphasize the dialectical tensions and the necessary contradictions that arise between the material and its representation.

Dorfman's work is internally dialectical in that he presents oppositional notions in irresolvable tension within the same work.[9] As opposed to one-dimensional art, Dorfman's works are inherently contradictory, and he tends to present a multi-perspectival view of conflicts and their potential resolution. For instance, in *The Last Song of Manuel Sendero*, there are many opposing views as to whether or not Manuel actually had a "last song," and each carries its own interpretation of the consequences of Manuel's singing. The novel's internal tensions are meant to reflect the complexity of material life. For Dorfman, a fundamental difference between liberating versus repressive literature is that "la primera hace preguntas, hace dudar radicalmente, que abre y comunica; que la segunda otorga respuestas, cierra y vuelve a cerrar el mundo, no permite descubrimientos verdaderos" (*Ensayos quemados*, 159); (the first asks questions, prompts radical doubt that opens and communicates; the second gives answers, closes and recloses the world, does not permit true discoveries).

Marcuse explains that "compared with the often one-dimensional optimism of propaganda, art is permeated with pessimism, not seldom intertwined with comedy" (14). Unlike mass-produced media, which script a stable, predictable emotional arc for the spectator, the internal dialectics of art often lead to contradictory emotional responses such as laughter, anger, sadness, pessimism, and inspiration. Most of Dorfman's novels produce this disconcerting array of emotional responses, all of which dialectically interact to incite the reader to reflection, making catharsis impossible. A telling example is in *The Last Song of Manuel Sendero* when the dialogue between David and Felipe wavers between silliness and seriousness, only to end with the disclosure that the two characters are possibly part of a Mexican soap opera. Such emotional shifts are frustrating, and they produce an alienating effect at the same time that they force the reader to consider the ways that art produces visceral responses.

In his essay "Medios masivos de comunicación y enseñanza de la literatura" (Mass Media and the Teaching of Literature) from the collection *Ensayos quemados en Chile* (Essays Burnt in Chile) Dorfman explains the fundamental distinctions between mass-produced culture and literary art.[10] According to Dorfman, only through exposing the relationship between these two forms of culture can students appreciate the process through which literature adapts and confronts the themes of mass literature, or what he terms "subliterature." For example, he suggests that *Don Quijote* is incomprehensible without an understanding of the ways that the novel is responding to the popular tales of chivalry. Side-by-side analysis demonstrates the contrasting ways these cultural forms interact with their audience. He points to a number of fundamental distinctions at the level of language, morality, and representational depth:

> El lenguaje de la literatura tiende a desatar sombras y luces y grises que no han sido elaboradas o reiteradas antes, mientras que en la subliteratura todo está creado en serie para obtener un pasmoso (e idéntico) efecto calculado y limitante, una emocionalidad falsa, una superficial repetición de lugares comunes. Que utilizar un moralismo barato en que bondad y maldad son los únicos términos para enjuiciar a los personajes es diferente que hundir al lector en complejidades ambiguas y profundas, que le hacen cuestionarse y gozarse a sí mismo y a otros. Y la falta de tiempo y muerte y evolución. La literatura que, aunque se inscriba dentro de las co-ordenadas de la ideología dominante, revela las contradicciones del hombre, revela la lucha por la verdad dentro de condiciones enajenantes; y la subliteratura que encubre sus contradicciones. (116–17)

> (The language of literature tends to unleash shadows and lights and grays that have not been elaborated or reiterated before, while in subliterature everything is created in order to produce a numbing, calculated, and limiting effect, a false sense of emotion, a superficial repetition of the commonplace. Subliterature depends on a cheap morality in which good and

bad are the only terms by which to judge the characters, a practice quite different from plunging the reader into ambiguous and profound complexities that make him question both himself and others and rejoice in himself and in others. And the lack of time and death and evolution. Literature that, even though it is inscribed within the coordinates of dominant ideology, reveals the contradictions of mankind, reveals the struggle for the truth within alienating conditions; and subliterature, which hides its contradictions.)

Internally dialectical literature, then, must be open rather than closed; must seek the collaboration and active intervention of the reader; must use a multilayered and fluid language; must avoid simplistic moralizing; and must draw attention to the process of representation itself.

In addition to the dialectical aspects of an aesthetics of hope, such art is provocative. Dorfman used Calderón de la Barca's line that "The time has come to wake up" as an epigraph to *Blake's Therapy*, and it can well be read as a motto for his theory that art should provoke and instigate. Culture is either aesthetic or *an-aesthetic*. Anesthesia tries to block pain and dull the senses much in the same way that mass-produced culture lulls its audience into a stupor of forgetfulness. Dorfman explains in *The Empire's Old Clothes* that mass-produced fictions attempt to provide us with a "secret education" in "how not to rebel" and in "how to forget the past and suppress the future" (9). Following the legacy of the Frankfurt School and mass-media criticism, Dorfman has worked to expose the repressive mechanisms inherent in the mass media at the same time that he has tried to create an alternative art. During the Allende years he collaborated, for instance, on the comic book *Cabro Chico*, which was "designed to drive a wedge of new values into the U.S.-Disnified cultural climate" (Kunzle, 12).

With the colossal onslaught of mass-media culture vastly overtaking literature as a form of entertainment Dorfman worries about the impact of such simplified narrative on literary aesthetics. The media play so tremendous a role in shaping public consciousness, he suggests, that it leads to a temptation to "oversimplify, to subscribe to a falsification of the future, to reduce all ambiguities"—to create, in effect, the sort of literature associated with socialist realism. He proposes instead, half jokingly, that literature should take the form of *socialist irrealism*, a literary mode that has the same political aspirations as socialism but refuses the tyranny of meaning associated with realism (*Other Septembers*, 171). The departure from realism is necessary in order to shock the reader out of complacency. Such an aesthetic, while hopeful, should not be pleasant, at least not always, because it is committed to asking the reader to face unpleasant features of life, to remember horrible moments from history, and, most of all, to recognize each individual's capacity for evil and complicity. *Hacia la liberación del lector latinoamericano* develops these theories, as does *Some Write to the Future*. In these and other texts, most notably *Death and the Maiden*, Dorfman engages with the problem of historical amnesia. In order for literature to confront such amnesia it must go beyond propaganda or denunciation; it must create the conditions of possibility for an "anti-authoritarian reader" (*Some Write*, xiv).

Such a vision of the reader leads directly to the revolutionary aspect of an aesthetics of hope. It is useful to remember Dorfman's interest in the avant-garde and the lessons that he learns from that rebellious cultural movement because some of the characteristics of an aesthetics of hope might be read as signaling a transformation from avant-garde to what I want to call "guerrilla art."[11] The term *avant-garde* derives from the military practice of sending a small, highly skilled advanced troop to plot a future course of attack. In reference to intellectuals and artists the term suggested that their art would blast open new social avenues that the masses would later travel. As Gene Bell-Villada notes, "The military French word 'avant-garde' suggests street revolts and scruffy manifestos; sectarian strife and a taste for scandal; establishment cat-calls and official high dudgeon; Bohemia, buffoonery, and cafes" (126). The avant-garde was militant in its efforts to destroy bourgeois values, and this militancy functioned in a way that often alienated the public as opposed to reaching out to it.[12] According to Eagleton, "The avante garde's response to the cognitive, ethical and aesthetic is unequivocal. Truth is a lie; morality stinks; beauty is shit." But, as he points out, "truth, morality and beauty are too important to be handed over to the enemy" (372). Herein is the difference between the "guerrilla aesthetics" practiced by Dorfman and others in his generation and the avant-garde: those that practice guerrilla aesthetics wish to recuperate "truth, morality, and beauty" in order to return these concepts to those who have been denied the ability to define for themselves what these terms mean. Whereas Dorfman admires the irreverent manipulation of the artistic form and the layered complexity of meaning in avant-garde work, he rejects its disdain for the masses and its elitism.

Similar to the avant-garde, those who practice the guerrilla tactics associated with an aesthetics of hope are part of a small group of cultural and intellectual combatants who engage in asymmetric warfare against a social structure that wields daunting power. And yet a key way that guerrilla artists differentiate their work from the avant-garde's critique of modernism is that they do not have a clearly defined front line. The notion that there is no front line and that those engaged in creating political and emancipatory art must wage many "little battles" or micro-struggles reveals the postmodern influence on this aesthetic over the modernism of the avant-garde. Another key difference that is revealed by using the *guerrillero* as a metaphor for the artist is that such art depends on a broader community for survival and success. Because it is art dedicated to working with society, with readers and listeners and viewers, to construct a better future and to honor the past, it depends on a base of popular support.

This revolutionary aesthetic practice, then, finds utopian potential in complicated, puzzling, unpredictable, layered, open texts that require much of the reader. Thus, unlike Adorno, who when he theorized the possibilities of art after Auschwitz focused on the negative effects of art that facilitate reification and lead to a sublimation of the body, Dorfman did not respond to the devastations of the Pinochet dictatorship with an inherently negative vision. If, according to Eagleton, Adorno suggests that there is a singular global story of humanity, a fable of "permanent catastrophe" (343), then I would argue that Dorfman's corollary fable is one of possibility. This is not to say that Dorfman does not dwell in great measure on the tales of scarcity, oppression, and suffering that have shaped human—and in particular Latin American—history. It is to suggest, rather, that at every moment that Dorfman recounts these tales, he also suggests that humanity has alternatives. To suggest a different course for history is to "write to the future," a literary practice he locates in a number of Latin American writers, such as García Márquez, Neruda, and Carpentier, and Ernesto Cardenal. Dorfman's work always has a utopian longing. Combined with it, Dorfman's texts deeply affirm Eros, which Marcuse describes as "the Life Instincts in their fight against instinctual and social oppression" (11). Not content to simply register loss and suffering, he imagines the world otherwise.

In a similar vein Adrienne Rich writes that she seeks art that is "part of a conversation with the elders and with the future," where "political struggle and spiritual continuity are enmeshed" within art (187). Unlike the avant-garde, which wanted to expose the false consciousness of bourgeois values, the revolutionary aesthetics of hope suggest that art should shape and reflect identity, fight solitude, record life, bridge the creative self and the collective self, delve into the depths of horror, challenge, critique, shock, provoke, and comfort. Ángel Rama points to the need for art to be representative and original, to be independent and responsible, and he emphasizes the Latin American tendency to narrate violence, hope, fratricide, and salvation (see *Transculturación*). Dorfman has also focused on these conflicting gestures and believes that it is only through the narration of these dialectical components of life that literature can contribute to creating an alternative vision of the future. Such attitudes expose Dorfman's mystical, spiritual faith in the power of literature:

> Es algo más profundo: parece haber una relación directa e íntima entre proceso creativo y liberación social. Podría ser, así lo he presentido una y otra vez, que en el altillo de toda literatura, en el baúl de todo ente, hay una tendencia a suponer implícitamente, a soñar, a anticipar, que aquella sociedad es posible o incluso imprescindible. (*Hacia la liberación*, xiii)

> (It is something more profound: there seems to be a direct and intimate relationship between the creative process and social liberation. It could be, as I have felt time and again, that at the very heights of literature, at the core of every being, exists an implicit tendency to suppose, to dream, to anticipate that such a society is possible or even indispensable.)

The relationship among artist, art, and audience is the ideal that drives an aesthetics of hope, and it is one that is not easily achieved. For instance, Dorfman went to a poor, urban community in Santiago to give away free copies of his poetry collection, *Pastel de choclo* (Corn Cake), named after a traditional Chilean dish.[13] The community did not respond as he had anticipated; in fact, people asked why he brought them books when they needed so many other things more urgently.[14] Explaining to them that literature can lead to hope and hope can lead to change would have seemed insensitive in the face of their struggles, and Dorfman left disappointed and disillusioned. Similarly, *Death and the Maiden* was written by Dorfman to help the Chilean public grapple with the extremely difficult issues it faced during the transition from dictatorship, but the play was poorly received in Chile in its first run. Perhaps the public simply was not ready or not interested in being confronted so intensely with the issues the play raises, especially as they were posed by an exiled outsider like Dorfman. And yet these failures to reach his intended public have not led Dorfman to abandon the belief that art is ultimately about communication and community.

AESTHETICS AND FORM:
STRUCTURE, DOUBLING, AND LANGUAGE

In his description of the liberation of the Latin American reader Dorfman details the ways that literature can operate in guerrilla fashion as a force that inspires the reader to participate in social rebellion:

Me parece . . . que la redención del lector como ente estético depende de la estrategia literaria, de las tácticas de construcción de la obra. Nuestra literatura organiza su asalto persuasivo con el deseo de estimular al lector que participe, desgarrándolo para que salga de su pasividad y abulia, invitándolo a recorrer juntos la creación de un continente, de un lenguaje, de una ficción, todavía inacabados. (*Hacia la liberación*, xi–xii)

(It seems to me . . . that the redemption of the reader as an aesthetic entity depends on literary strategy, on the tactics of the work's construction. Our literature begins its persuasive assault on the reader when it attempts to stimulate participation, tearing at the reader so that he/she moves out of passivity and lethargy, inviting him/her to revisit together the creation of a continent, of a language, of a fiction, all still incomplete.)

To stimulate the reader, to provoke a reaction, to actively engage the reader in the construction of a new society requires that literature engage in formal experimentation. Against realism or romanticism or other predictable literary modes, art with an aesthetics of hope engages in constant artistic renovation. This is what Dorfman means by *socialist irrealism*. The literary form must contain surprises and riddles and questions that ask the reader to work to unlock his or her own interpretation. Rather than assume that the ideal form of art is the novel or the theater of the absurd, for example, Dorfman has produced literature across a broad array of textual forms, discursive registers, and genres. In this sense, his consistency resides in his inconsistency, in his never-ending quest to find a new way to narrate a story that can reach the reader.

When asked how he decides the genre in which a story will appear, Dorfman responds that he does not "necessarily subscribe to the idea that there is only one possible perfect way to tell a story" (cited in McClennen in *Context*, 7). In fact many of his stories have appeared in a number of forms. *Widows* began as a poem, became a novel, then a play, and may become a film. "A la escondida" (My House Is on Fire) is a poem, a story, and a film. "Reader" was first a story and then became a play. With each adaptation the stories shift, and they organically interact with the new form that they are taking and with the new social context from which they are emerging. Dorfman explains that he does not "see it as adaptation but as a shifting fluctuation" (cited in McClennen in *Context*, 7). These changes also take place when he is involved with the translation of his texts. When his first novel, *Moros en la costa*, was translated into English as *Hard Rain*, it was substantially shortened and rearranged, and many of the changes reflected Dorfman's thoughts on art and politics after the shock of Pinochet's coup.

These experiments in form and stylistic diversity must be organically linked to the stories that are being told. Marcuse, Adorno, and Jameson argue that form and content should organically complement one another in a work of art. Marcuse writes that "A work of art is authentic or true not by virtue of its content . . . , nor by its 'pure' form, but by the content having become form" (8). Adorno similarly proposes that content "becomes concrete only by virtue of aesthetic form" and that "aesthetics develops its content by rendering forms eloquent" (*Aesthetic*, 290). The form must facilitate the emancipation of sensibility by estranging reality. Singer and Dunn explain that for Jameson form is a direct consequence of the "social and political pressures which shaped the moment in which the text was created" (72). Because mass-media forms detach the story from reality, art must seek to reunite form and content. In his chapter on the Lone Ranger in *The Empire's Old Clothes* Dorfman explains that subliterature needs to create conflicts that will concern the reader in the real world. The battles presented in mass-produced literature between good and evil must have relevance for the reader. "However, that recognition must take place within a carefully circumscribed social reality whose main cause and effect, links with the real world, have been effectively broken" (91). Thus such tales can have happy endings and the problems that they present can be solved by a "masked man." In order to challenge subliterature, which forces content to fit within a prescribed form, artists must conscientiously allow the form of their work to reflect its content, and vice versa.

Dorfman confesses: "I'm obsessed with structure" (cited in McClennen in *World Literature Today*, 66). Dorfman's texts are open; not only do subsequent versions of them change, but each text is also constructed as an open invitation to the reader. This technique, while evident in Dorfman's poetry, essays, short stories, and drama, is most apparent in his novels. *Moros en la costa* and the English translation, *Hard Rain*, are a montage of texts, excerpts, letters, reviews, and short stories. *Widows* has eight chapters, which are divided into thirteen subsections numbered sequentially. The first chapter has three sections, but the second and third have only one, and chapter 4 begins with section 6. The reader is left to determine the correlation between the chapters and the sections. Moreover, section 10 is missing, and the reader is told that "there is no way of knowing what might have happened or what was planned for this section of the novel" (*Hard Rain*, 119). The missing section parallels the missing men of the town and reminds the reader that much of this story has disappeared.

Blake's Therapy is ostensibly organized around Dante's *The Divine Comedy*. The novel has three sections, each consisting of three chapters that open with quotes from the *Inferno*, *Purgatorio*, and *Paradiso*. Nevertheless, this structure already signals a departure from *The Divine Comedy* since the nine chapters could correspond to the nine circles of hell, suggesting that the movement from hell to heaven in Dante does not take place in Dorfman's world. Similar to the hero in Dante's tale, the novel's protagonist—Graham Blake, CEO of Clean Earth, who is suffering from a bout of corporate ethics and is suddenly overwhelmed by what he feels is his lack of morality—has fallen into sin. But unlike the benign sage in *The Divine Comedy*, Blake's guide, Dr. Tolgate, who runs the Corporate Life Therapy Institute and promises to return Blake to the world of corporate success, is no Virgil, and the future of multinational global capital he offers is no heaven. In this way, Dorfman's structure reads against his plot, but it also asks the reader to press further to consider the intertextuality between the themes of this novel and those of *The Divine Comedy*, especially as they relate to the desire to possess an adored woman and to the tension between the self and community that is created by social norms for success.

The Last Song of Manuel Sendero creates a similar disjunction between the novel's structure and plot. The novel is divided into five parts, which correspond to stages of birth from "Incarnations" to "Bearings." The five parts are further divided into nine chapters, which take place "Outside" and "Inside" and correspond to the nine months of gestation. Lois Baer Barr suggests that "the five parts of the novel refer to conception, the three trimesters of pregnancy, and birth" (142). But what is most vexing for the reader is that this structure reads against the plot because the novel suggests that the son of Manuel Sendero may have been aborted, and the fetal rebellion postpones birth and elongates the traditional timetable for pregnancy. In this case Dorfman counteracts the nonspecific time of the narrative with the predictable and stable time of pregnancy, placing the reader in the middle.

Dorfman's memoir may provide one of the best examples of his obsession with structures that are open to the reader's interpretation, that often contradict or put pressure on the themes of the story, and that demand that the reader carefully consider the author's role in constructing a text. *Heading South, Looking North* is organized according to two dualities—that of north and south and that of life and language versus death, while it simultaneously points to the interpenetrations of these oppositions as well as to their supplements. Table 1 maps the text's structure.

In the mirroring effect of the two parts—"North and South" and "South and North"—Dorfman points to a flawed binary, an opposition that is inclu-

Table 1. Text Structure of *Heading South*

Part One: North and South	Part Two: South and North
A chapter dealing with the discovery of death at an early age	A chapter dealing with the discovery of death, sometime in September 1973 in Santiago de Chile
A chapter dealing with the discovery of life and language at an early age	A chapter dealing with the discovery of life and language during the years 1960–64 in Santiago de Chile
A chapter dealing with the discovery of death in the early morning of September 11, 1973, in Santiago de Chile	A chapter dealing with the discovery of death outside an embassy in Santiago de Chile in the year 1973
A chapter dealing with the discovery of life and language in the year 1945 in the United States of America	A chapter dealing with the discovery of life and language during the years 1965–68 in Santiago de Chile
A chapter dealing with the discovery of death in the late morning of September 11, 1973, in Santiago de Chile	A chapter dealing with the discovery of death inside an embassy in October 1973 in Santiago de Chile
A chapter dealing with the discovery of life and language during the years 1945–54 in the United States of America	A chapter dealing with the discovery of life and language during the years 1968–70, in Berkeley, California
A chapter dealing with the discovery of death on September 13 and 14, 1973, in Santiago de Chile	A chapter dealing with the discovery of death inside and outside an embassy in Santiago de Chile in early November 1973
A chapter dealing with the discovery of life and language during the years 1954–59 in Santiago de Chile	A chapter dealing with the discovery of life and language during the years 1970–73 in Santiago de Chile

Epilogue: A final chapter in which we deal with life, language, and death one more time

sive rather than epiphenomenal since what is narrated is not north versus south, but rather north and south, which, in keeping with the title of the book, suggests Dorfman as a Janus face, a being that straddles the north and the south, always to some degree tied to both. This structure gives the reader an early clue into what will be one of the memoir's central dilemmas—the idea that the north and the south are at odds and incompatible and that both of these regions have contributed to his identity. In addition to the combination of these opposing forces in the epilogue, the chapters, while ostensibly setting up a division, do not actually narrate a clear antagonism between life and language versus death since stories of death appear in chapters dedicated to life and language, and vice versa.

In addition to complex and open structures that require the active participation of the reader, who must link form and content, Dorfman's texts also repeatedly include another device that calls attention to formal structure: doubling. Throughout his texts Dorfman doubles characters, locations, language (more will be said on language below), beginnings, and endings. He often has more than one ending, as in the case of *The Last Song of Manuel Sendero*, *The Nanny and the Iceberg*, and *Exorcising Terror*. *Widows* has more than one beginning: a preface by Dorfman, one by the fictitious son of a fictitious author, and the actual beginning of the text. The ending of *Death and the Maiden* mirrors both the audience and the beginning.[15] Not only do the texts themselves have structural doubles, but the characters within them do as well. In *Konfidenz* the narrator is mirrored by another man who also watches the two main characters and will also play a role in their stories. Almost every character in *The Last Song of Manuel Sendero* has a double, and many of the characters in *The Nanny and the Iceberg* have quasi mirror opposites. These doubles and opposites require much active interpretation from the reader since they refuse standard patterns of the doppelganger: they are neither identical nor purely oppositional. In almost every case they overlap and diverge in unpredictable ways. Unraveling their associations is the reader's task.

This technique calls attention to form and representation, but it also links with Dorfman's interest in the ways that literature relates to notions of time and space. Many of his doubles/mirrors ask the reader to wonder whether what is being narrated is unique to a specific time and place or whether it is a conflict that has occurred in many places and many times. Thus the absence of location that begins *Konfidenz* allows Dorfman to suggest that the events of the novel can and have taken place in a variety of contexts. Similarly the frame of *Widows* posits whether the story emerges from a specific context or is more aptly a transhistorical human tragedy. There is a hope that by using literary strategies that reveal how history has repeated itself the reader will learn first how to link these events and then how to intervene to stop them. These dialectical doubles and opposites reflect a number of Dorfman's aesthetic concerns. In each case, though, they call attention to the limits of markers of identity, location, and time. Since the doubles and mirrors both echo and diverge from their other, their representation is always shown to be both lacking and embellished. In this way, Dorfman's use of doubles and mirrors reflects his own ideas about literature itself since literature at one and the same time mirrors, misrepresents, and imagines the world. It is interesting that Dorfman often has difficulty placing boundaries on his writing, finding the place to begin and to end. He begins his memoir, for instance, explaining that he had been mistaken about where to begin. Such a move reveals how literature itself is a double—perhaps fantastic, perhaps accurate—to another world that we can understand only through appreciating the connection between the two.

Dorfman is fond of Jean Cocteau's phrase—"I am a liar who always tells the truth"—because it indicates both the triumph and the limit of language. Given that much of the analysis in the following chapters is dedicated to studying Dorfman's use of language in individual works, here I will sketch only some of the main strategies, in addition to those already outlined, that illustrate Dorfman's practice of an aesthetics of hope. Dorfman likes to layer his words, as though he can pile them up around what he wants to represent and in the hope that at least one word will achieve his goal. This layering of course also draws attention to language itself, to its shortcomings and distractions, as well as to its power and persuasiveness. These layers take many forms, but here is one example from *The Last Song of Manuel Sendero*: "¿Empresa? el niño estalló. ¿Empresa? Emporio. Emporio, imperio, desamparero de menores, laboratorio y ratonera" (33); ("Company? The child burst out. Company? Emporium, you mean. Emporium. Empire. Child abuser. Laboratory. Rat hole"; 30). In these lines the son of Sendero questions the use of the word "empresa" (company) to describe the entity responsible for keeping his mother drugged, and he responds with a plethora of words he considers synonyms. Dorfman's baroque use of language is evidence of his skepticism of the efficacy of language and his simultaneous recognition that language is the only tool available to the writer. The above example also illustrates how Dorfman merges the baroque with the colloquial by placing words like "emporio" (emporium) alongside "ratonera" (rat hole).

Dorfman's baroque language in works like *The Last Song of Manuel Sendero* and *The Nanny and the Iceberg* provides a counterpoint to his use of deceptively simple and stark language in texts like *Death and the Maiden* and

Konfidenz. In the latter cases there are repeated phrases that shift in meaning according to the subject position of the speaker. In *Konfidenz* Barbara and Leon's conversation is narrated almost entirely with dialogue, and Dorfman uses some of the same Pinteresque techniques that appear in *Death and the Maiden*. When Leon explains to Barbara that he knows every intimate detail about her because her lover, Martin, has told him, she doesn't believe it:

> —El no pudo haber—Martín jamás hablaría de mí con un extraño, jamás
> contaría cosas tan íntimas.
> —Martín me contó todo acerca de usted, Barbara.
> —¿Qué le contó?
> —Cosas suyas. De su vida.
> —¿De mi cuerpo?
> —Sí.
> —¿Qué le contó de mi cuerpo? (26–27)

> ("He can't have—Martin would never talk about me with a stranger, telling
> him intimate things."
> "Martin told me everything about you, Barbara."
> "What things?"
> "Things about you. Things only he knew."
> "What things?"
> "About your body."
> "What did he tell you about my body?" [19])

When Barbara says "mi cuerpo" (my body), it is clear that she does not actually possess her intimate secrets, that her body is no longer hers. This eerie exposure of Barbara's private self is heightened by the repetition in the English version of "things"—a word that is at once nonspecific and extremely suggestive—especially as the reader soon learns that the "things" Martin has divulged refer specifically to Barbara's breasts and clitoris. In this example, then, Dorfman uses a bare language of absence and echo to illustrate a breakdown in communication and things left unsaid. Here the use of language also carries a sense of loss. In contrast, the example of his baroque style above uses language to signify a difficulty in communication through humor and irony.

One further style trait of Dorfman's that relates to this last example and links with the practice of doubling described above is the repetition of phrases. *Manifesto for Another World* repeats the phrase "anything else would have tasted like ashes" in an overt and persistent fashion, but Dorfman uses this technique on a more minor scale in most of his works. Near the end of

Exorcising Terror he repeats the phrase "feel fear" in a passage that suggests that Pinochet's arrest will forever make the tyrants of the world afraid (192). In contrast to the "fear" that dictators will now face, Dorfman repeats the word "humanity" four times in a previous section in an effort to counterbalance "the mind of humanity" against the atrocities committed by dictators. But at the end of this section he again casts doubt: "Or am I merely consoling myself with words that try to stir and inspire" (191–92)? He asks whether his writing is able to replace the fear that those under Pinochet felt with a new order in which it is Pinochet who feels fear and the Chilean community who thinks with the "mind of humanity." These repeated phrases function differently in his work, but they all call attention to the links among language, representation, and understanding. When phrases are repeated, do they mean the same thing each time? Are the repetitions disturbing or silly? How does repetition disrupt the reading process?

Dorfman's literature uses a guerrilla strategy of linguistic styles from baroque to colloquial to stark. He repeats phrases; shifts the meaning of words; uses names that are highly symbolic (like "Sofia" in *Widows* and "Gabriel" in *The Nanny and the Iceberg*); and has unnamed protagonists, as in the case of *The Last Song of Manuel Sendero* and *Mascara*. Moreover, as noted, Dorfman is constantly renovating and rewriting his texts, taking translation to literally describe a text in transit, in perpetual motion. When he translated *The Nanny and the Iceberg* into Spanish, for instance, he decided that the epilogue was too long, so the second English edition (published after the Spanish translation) has a shortened epilogue. His texts are also transformed in the process of adaptation from one genre to another. Dorfman explains that his collaboration with Tony Kushner made the drama version of *Widows* more hopeful than the novel: "whenever I work with somebody else I tend to be more hopeful."[16]

■ ■ ■

Despite Dorfman's desire to create art with an aesthetics of hope and despite the multiple elements of his work that combine to construct his aesthetic—fluctuating subjects/possessives, shifting verb tenses, complex structure, doubling, and use of language—such a project is not without challenges and shortcomings. Not only is the idea of creating art that can make a difference fraught with difficulty in an age when people increasingly turn on their television sets or their computers for entertainment, but also the mere idea that art can have a social impact has been questioned more rigorously since the 1960s. Art with an aesthetics of hope, which refuses to prescribe the future, dictate to the reader, or rely on catharsis, is in an especially tenuous position because it depends so thoroughly on readers' reactions. Yet it is precisely this faith in the reader and in humanity that is at the core of this aesthetic.

The potential slippage between the aesthetic ideal and its practical, material reception may plague Dorfman perhaps more than other authors who could be categorized as working within a similar aesthetic—for example, Salman Rushdie or J. M. Coetzee. In addition to the stylistic elements mentioned above, Dorfman's works have tended to include additional elements that have occasionally alienated and frustrated his readers rather than reaching them. These include an incessant self-doubt and self-reflexivity, exceedingly complex narratives, the construction of unpleasant and unattractive protagonists, and highly intellectual narratives that provoke the reader. While I would argue that these elements track closely with his aesthetics of hope and are in fact necessary components of it, they have at times led him to be read as a writer who is overwrought, authoritarian, uneven, and densely complicated.

Dorfman's relentless self-doubt and self-reflexivity represent his desire to create literature that is more a question than an answer. Such literature has led to responses like Joanne Omang's, who in a review of *The Nanny and the Iceberg* writes, "The book could be entertaining if it had any kind of larger point, and one can be dimly discerned at the end. But even so, it feels constructed, a moral tacked on to excuse a prolonged, self-indulgent ramble" (n.p.). Regarding the density of Dorfman's texts, Barr states that "there is a certain authorial arrogance in Dorfman's refusal to be concise" (149). Dorfman of course would respond to the contrary. He would argue that in fact his refusal to be concise is directly related to his desire to avoid authorial arrogance and simplify a story that is inherently complex.

The critique of his complexity also relates to the disapproval of his "unlikable" characters (see Omang). Both the complexity and the characters derive from Dorfman's interest in literary forms, such as the baroque and the picaresque, that have virtually disappeared from the contemporary mainstream literary landscape. These are both forms that are difficult and potentially unpleasant. They require the reader to work to make sense of the text and the story. Discussing the baroque, Umberto Eco has written about the reader's need to play an inventive role because baroque text presents "a world in a fluid state which requires corresponding creativity on his part" (52). Because Dorfman's readers do not always recognize that he is working within his own revised versions of the baroque or the picaresque in novels like *The Last Song of Manuel Sendero* and *The Nanny and the Iceberg*, they have difficulty appreciating the ways that he has renovated these styles in order to use them to comment on contemporary society. Ironically Dorfman's observation that readers have become less sophisticated and more and more programmed by mass literature is reflected in some of the negative reactions to his own work. "Because [the mass-media culture] exists as a major molder of public consciousness, it leads to a major temptation: in order to reach those people we are tempted to oversimplify our literature, to subscribe to a falsification of the future, to reduce all ambiguities" (*Other Septembers*, 171). Dorfman has refused to succumb to this temptation even if it has meant that he has limited his readers.

Producing literature that aims to be irritating, provocative, and self-conscious at the same time that it is moving, beautiful, and utopian reveals Dorfman's interest in striking a balance between appealing to his readers' emotions and their reason. Dorfman and other Latin American artists such as Augusto Boal, who in his work with the theater of the oppressed has cultivated "spect-actors," refuse to use catharsis because they consider it to be manipulative, coercive, and ultimately disrespectful to their audience. Similar to the use of difficult and challenging literary styles, the rejection of catharsis as a means to reach an audience contrasts with most mass cultural production, which depends on it as its principle mode of communication. But such a strategy is easily missed or unappreciated. For example, Deborah Cohn describes *Blake's Therapy* as follows: "Though excessively clinical in tone, machista in its depiction of Blake's treatment of women, and, frankly, formulaic in its structure and presentation of the theme of (un)reality, the novel nevertheless draws its readers in, leading them through a dizzying set of twists and turns" (n.p.). She perceives Dorfman's play between reason and emotion, where the text seems "clinical" while simultaneously drawing "the reader in," but she considers this a flaw rather than a strength of the text. Thus a problem emerges: even if Dorfman means to provoke his readers, if he totally annoys them, his aesthetic project cannot succeed—at least not with those readers. It is noteworthy of his aesthetic project that while certain readers find specific features most extraordinary, others dislike these features intensely. While Cohn dislikes the style of *Blake's Therapy*, Omang, whose negative review of *The Nanny and the Iceberg* was cited above, enjoys it: "Dorfman's universe is absurd and scary, impossible and all too real, just like our own" (n.p.). Dorfman's confrontational and unpredictable relationship with his audience is an inevitable consequence of an aesthetic practice that is purposefully provocative and unsettling.

Dorfman's fiction often seems to turn to the polemic of essay, just as his essays habitually roam into storytelling, and his texts are often hybrid forms that are unfamiliar to his readers. It may be the case that Dorfman's extensive work as a critic of media culture has made it impossible for him to construct fiction without also second-guessing those constructions. This critical perspective combines with his political commitment as an artist. In the foreword to *The Resistance Trilogy* he explains: "My writing has been haunted, ever since I can remember, by twin obsessions, a central paradox that I cannot be rid of: on the one hand, the glorious potential and need of human beings to tell stories; and, on the other, the brutal fact that in today's world, most of the lives that should be telling stories are generally ignored, ravaged, and silenced" (vi). When one writes to the future with an aesthetic of hope, one necessarily writes with a political project in mind and a utopian desire for that future. The next two chapters trace the trajectory of Dorfman's work and explore how his aesthetics of hope have developed over time and as a consequence of historic events.

Anything else would have
tasted like ashes. It would
have been living a lie.

—DESMOND TUTU

Courage begins with one voice.
It's that simple.
I did what I had to do.
Anything else would have tasted like ashes.
That is what we know.

—ARIEL DORFMAN,
Manifesto for Another World

4. ANYTHING ELSE WOULD HAVE TASTED LIKE ASHES *From Popular Unity to Exile (1970–90)*

In Kerry Kennedy Cuomo's tribute to human rights defenders, *Speak Truth to Power*, Desmond Tutu explains that he committed himself so completely to defending human rights because "anything else would have tasted like ashes" (60). Dorfman later turned Tutu's words into a central motif for his theatrical adaptation of Kennedy Cuomo's book: *Manifesto for Another World*. It is telling that Dorfman keys into this particular phrase not only for its meaning to the play, but also for its meaning in his own life. For Tutu, the phrase recalls the prophet Jeremiah, whom he describes as a "very attractive character because he complained: 'God, you cheated me. You said I was going to be a prophet. And all you made me do is speak words of doom and judgment and criticism against the people I love very much. And yet if I try not to speak the words that you want me to speak, they are like a fire in my breast, and I can't hold them in' " (cited in Kennedy Cuomo, 60). Jeremiah's story links with Tutu's vigorous and relentless efforts to mobilize black South Africans to fight for their rights.

He does not regret the fact that his activism led to his imprisonment, for, as he says, "Anything else would have tasted like ashes."

Tutu's identification with Jeremiah resonates with Dorfman's own history. Burdened with prophecy, Jeremiah predicted Jerusalem's destruction during the sixth century BC to an audience uninterested in hearing his tales of impending doom. Villagers in his native town of Anathoth rejected his visions of inevitable disaster and considered him a defeatist. Louis Jacobs explains that "In English a 'Jeremiah' is a person given to woeful complaining but, in fact, for all the denunciations of his people, Jeremiah sounds a note of encouragement and of hope" (n.p.). Jeremiah's message of hope, according to Jacobs, centers on his insistence that the Jewish people would perform their mission to God equally well in exile. Dispersal and diaspora would not destroy them, according to Jeremiah, and some scholars, like Jacobs, suggest that he was the first prophet to understand Judaism as a set of beliefs and not as a territorial affiliation necessarily bonded to Israel. A witness to the destruction of Jerusalem, Jeremiah would become known for his efforts to convince his listeners to remember their history and to be careful to recall their own responsibility in their fate.

As a Jewish man who has suffered multiple exiles and who endeavors to speak the truth even when it is unwelcome, Dorfman must have found Tutu's citation of Jeremiah especially compelling. Dorfman is a confirmed agnostic and it would be a mistake to ascribe too close an affinity between him and Jeremiah. It would equally be a mistake, however, not to notice Dorfman's pantheistic spirituality and its influence on his work. His memoir emphasizes his belief that he has a calling to write in order to record the history of those who died and keep their struggle alive. He tells readers that he writes "haunted by the certainty that he has been keeping a promise to the dead" (*Heading*, 40). So the phrase "anything else would have tasted like ashes" spoke directly to Dorfman and allowed him to combine his own thoughts about his role as a writer with the voices of the human rights defenders that he channeled into his play.

This phrase holds one further layer of meaning for Dorfman, and it is this register that will shape the reading of his work in this chapter from the Allende years to the end of Dorfman's exile. Early in Dorfman's writing career he grappled with a profound tension between literature and politics, imagining a conflict between art and action. Even though he had held a belief in the transformative power of literature and storytelling from a young age, when he began to actively work in politics prior to and during Salvador Allende's presidency, he felt torn between writing and working on political projects. Of course these two activities were not discrete, and he successfully combined them when he wrote political slogans and speeches or engaged in other political cultural activities. Nevertheless, a persistent sense of being torn in two directions haunted Dorfman as he doubted whether literature really mattered and whether his energies were better spent elsewhere.

Dorfman's concern over whether literature is a viable form of social commitment is characteristic of his generation. In contrast to the writers of the Latin American literary boom, the writers of the post-boom were often far less certain of the social role of the writer and simultaneously were far more committed to literature as a vehicle for social change. This conflict regarding the political power of literature shapes many of the cultural products of Dorfman's generation. Donald Shaw explains that as a "consequence of tragic events in Argentina, Chile, Uruguay, and Central America [post-boom writers] tended to return . . . to fiction with greater emphasis on content, directness of impact, denunciation, documentality, or protest" (13). Arguably part of the reason for this generation's concern that literature has an uneasy relationship to social change is due to the practical realities of grassroots resistance movements that appeared throughout Latin America at that time. Sparked by the success of the Cuban Revolution (1959), these movements called on sympathizers to choose between the bourgeois realm of art and direct political action, and debates raged over the bourgeois affinity for theory (and art) over practice. Anxiety over the proper role of the intellectual in social struggle appears in novels like Manuel Puig's *El beso de la mujer araña* (*The Kiss of the Spiderwoman*) and Ricardo Piglia's *Respiración artificial* (*Artificial Respiration*) and in short stories like Cristina Peri Rossi's "La influencia de Edgar Allen Poe en la poesía de Raimundo Arias" (The Influence of Edgar Allen Poe in the Poetry of Raimundo Arias) and Luisa Valenzuela's "Cuarta versión" (Fourth Version). In keeping with these examples, Dorfman's first literary works reflect his profound ambivalence about the validity of literature as a legitimate occupation.

Focusing on this tension between political action and literature, this chapter traces Dorfman's literary career up to (1970–73) and during (1973–90) his years in exile and suggests that the works of this period often revolve around a deep skepticism over the relationship between art and politics that is combined with an urgent need to believe that art plays a central function in shaping a community's politics, values, and identity. In terms of a trajectory, Dorfman begins from a moment of extreme doubt in *Moros en la costa*,[1] moves toward resolution in *Viudas* (*Widows*), only to turn back to ambivalence in *La última canción de Manuel Sendero* (*The Last Song of Manuel Sendero*), and moves toward increasing doubt in *Máscaras* (*Mascara*) and in the revised translation of *Moros en la costa*, *Hard Rain*. Dorfman's treatment of the problem is more circular than linear and reflects his changing thoughts about the ability of literature to challenge dictatorship. These thoughts became progressively more pessimistic as Pinochet's dictatorship continued.

FROM *MOROS EN LA COSTA* TO *HARD RAIN*

It is fitting to begin considering the above-mentioned themes in Dorfman's work through his first novel, *Moros en la costa* (1973), and its translation into English as *Hard Rain* (1990). Because the original Spanish version appeared when Dorfman had little time to dedicate to revisions, the translation is substantially shorter and significantly different. The dates of these two texts provide a neat frame for the period covered in this chapter, and the differences between the original and the translation yield important insights into some key transitions in Dorfman's thoughts about art and politics.

Written during the brief moments Dorfman dedicated to creative writing during the end of 1972, *Moros en la costa* was finished in an atmosphere of fear and anxiety as Allende's government was facing increasing pressures. The text is composed of a number of fragments—of literature dealing with the socialist revolution in Chile; reviews of such literature; film scripts; criticism of the novel itself; and extensive correspondence among authors, publishers, and editors. The fragments are largely disconnected and comment in highly oblique ways on the relationship between aesthetics and politics. They manage to create a whirlwind of artistic and critical voices at the same time that they unite in a meta-commentary on the historical moment Dorfman was narrating in Chile. Dorfman's first novel narrates the complexity of Chile before and during the Allende years while it also more generally debates questions about literary aesthetics and the importance of art.[2] In a section that ostensibly provides a reader's guide to the novel, Dorfman underscores these preoccupations with characteristic wit and irony:

> Tal vez por eso el arte mismo, y la problematización de los medios que utiliza, no ocupa un hueco significativo en la obra. El autor desprecia todo lo que no sea abiertamente político, es incapaz de aceptar que no todo es ideología, tiene que justificar el tiempo que le dedica a las páginas que mancha. Sin embargo, esto se nota. Humildemente, me permito recordarle que el escritor es siempre el verdadero protagonista de su obra, y que las dificultades que enfrenta en la creación y construcción de su fic-

ción se reflejan inevitablemente en el modo en que el personaje central vivirá o destruirá su propia transcurrencia. Poniéndolo de otro modo: no hay que desatender a eso tan inefable que es la forma, estilo, modo narrativo, orden sensorial, palabras, porque esas son las armas del autor, con las que acompaña y refuerza los resultados a los que llegan los habitantes de su mundo. (175)

(It would seem that art itself, and the examination of its methods, do not occupy a significant place in the book. The author may despise anything that is not political; may be unable to accept the fact that everything does not focus on ideology; and yet feels the need to justify the time he devotes to the pages he is filling. He would do well to remember that the writer is always the real protagonist of his work, and that the difficulties he confronts in the creation and construction of his fiction are inevitably reflected in the way in which the central character will live or will destroy his own passage through life. To put it another way: one must not ignore that ineffable factor which is form, style, narrative method, sensory order, words, because these are the author's weapons, the means by which he accompanies and reinforces his vision.) (169)

The unfortunate circumstances of the book's publication—it was released by Editorial Sudamericana in Argentina when the Allende government was facing significant political turmoil—meant that it never reached a Chilean reading public.[3] Even though the year of the novel's release marks the year of Pinochet's coup, by 1971, when Fidel Castro spent a month in Chile supporting Allende, there were indications that the government would soon come under attack. Within a year of Allende's taking office, his supporters lived in an atmosphere of almost constant siege, and they could not help but suspect that their prospects for changing Chilean society were precarious. And yet a sense that they were threatened by forces both within and outside of Chile was counterbalanced by the exhilarating solidarity that emerged as a public force after Allende's election. Dorfman wrote his first novel in a context of hyperinflation, food shortages, daily protests, strikes, and the increasing polarization of Chilean society. He also wrote it as the people who had helped to build the nation were finally, for the first time in history, being given a chance to run the factories, mining companies, farms, and other businesses that were the bases of the Chilean economy. Dorfman watched as lower-income families received steady supplies of milk for their children and as education was reformed to address its historical class bias.

Other novelists would later reflect on this period—for example, Antonio

Skármeta in *Soñé que la nieve ardía* (*I Dreamt the Snow Was Burning*)—but *Moros en la costa* is the one novel written during these years that is dedicated to representing the challenges that faced the Allende government and that tries to narrate the issues that Chilean society faced as a whole. If for no other reason than the extraordinary circumstances of its production, the novel deserves a far more prominent place in literary study than it has received. Because of its publication in Argentina only years before the Argentine junta took power in 1976, however, it would suffer the consequences of censorship (both state-sponsored and self-inflicted) in both Chile and Argentina. Dorfman's flight into exile just as the book was released probably furthered its absence from the literary scene. Another possible explanation for its virtual absence from the Latin American post-boom/postmodern canon may be related to its extremely experimental nature, except this possibility is belied by the fact that many of the writers of this period—among them Ricardo Piglia, Diamela Eltit, and Luisa Valenzuela—wrote highly dense, fragmented texts that are frequently the objects of critical study. To date, the only published works aside from book reviews to mention this novel in any detail are Salvador Oropesa's *La obra de Ariel Dorfman: Ficción y crítica* (The Work of Ariel Dorfman: Fiction and Criticism), which dedicates a chapter to the novel, and an article I wrote on Dorfman in the *Review of Contemporary Fiction*.

Oropesa focuses his reading of *Moros en la costa* on what he calls its "neo-vanguard" style. Disagreeing with Julio Cortázar's categorization of *Moros en la costa* as "crítica revolucionaria" (revolutionary critique), Oropesa characterizes the novel as obsessed with modifying artistic rather than social structures (25–26). Oropesa derives his reading of the novel as neovanguard from a review by Ted Lyon: "The author calls the work a novel, but even in the broadest sense of the new novel it would hardly fit in. Characterization and development, time, space, continuity and various other novelistic elements are weak or nonexistent" (84). Both Oropesa and Lyon read the "unclassifiable assemblage of twenty-seven prose bits and pieces" and the "thirteen narrator-characters" as disconnected, random exercises in literary experimentation (Lyon, 85). Oropesa considers the novel a pastiche of unsystematic elements that create a work where there is no history and no dialogue, where authors take the place of characters, and where readers are displaced from reading.

The problems with these readings of Dorfman's novel are twofold. First, when Oropesa accepts Lyon's literary dismissal of *Moros en la costa* because it is not a novel, he misses the chance to read the text's literary influences.[4] He correctly notes that there is a vanguard influence on the work, but it is also useful to notice the way that the text stems from Renaissance and baroque literature, which emphasized self-consciousness about the process of artistic production. Appreciating *Moros en la costa*'s intertextuality with the vanguard, the Renaissance, the baroque, and also the absurd is necessary in order to recognize the full range of the novel's literary influences. The second problem is a consequence of inattention to the text's historical context. For example, Oropesa states that the majority of the characters in the novel "no dialogan, monologan, que es lo que a fin de cuentas ocurría en Chile en 1972" (29); (don't dialogue, they monologue, which in the end is what happened in Chile in 1972). He is quite right to note the absence of dialogue in the novel, but his interpretation does not account for the fact that there was substantial dialogue in Chile at the time. Dorfman's concern was whether there could be dialogue between those who supported Allende and those who did not, and he was further worried about whether art could play a role in fostering such dialogue. These anxieties were based on the very imminent threats that the Allende government faced. As Dorfman and his comrades watched their government come under ideological and military siege by the United States, they couldn't help but wonder whether collective participation could ever succeed. Hence, *Moros en la costa* asks how literature can play a role in the construction of a social imaginary that aims for solidarity. In this sense it is an homage to the complex narrative worlds of the boom writers and Borges, but Dorfman infuses this intertextuality with an explicitly political angle. At the core of the novel is the question of how to represent the revolution.[5]

Since the text is largely made up of literary and artistic reviews, there are ample moments when the text seems to narrate to the reader how it should be read. For instance, the opening section is a review of a novel by Arístides Ulloa, a fictional author created by Dorfman, that narrates a murder committed in a Nazi concentration camp. Ulloa's novel considers the question of whether one can murder someone who has already been sentenced to die. Shortly after Ulloa's novel begins, it shifts location to a concentration camp of political prisoners in South America, and the geographical relocation produces a change in the murder investigation because now the South American detective, Quiroz, cannot help but identify with the victim. Quiroz does not have the ability to draw a distinction between his existence and that of the victim in the same way that the anti-Semitic Geerhardt can. Interspersed between the concentration camp and South America, Ulloa's novel adds additional fragments that take the same story to other locations, such as Vietnam and Rhodesia. The reviewer, faced with a complex and fragmentary text, stresses the difficult task before the reader.

The end of the review of Ulloa's text further indicates that Dorfman's novel revolves around the tension between political activism and artistic production. In an interview, Ulloa explains that he had conceived of his novel while in jail in Venezuela and wrote it while in exile in Chile. Ulloa decides that writing the novel is the most creative way that he can participate in the revolution. The decision, though, makes him uncomfortable, and he describes the moment as a period of relative inactivity with regard to politics. This explains the "cierto grado de escepticismo, algunas dudas respeto a la muerte, por ejemplo, que de ninguna manera me aquejan cuando vivo en militancia política, pero que parecen infiltrarse cuando me siento frente a una máquina de escribir" (27); ("certain degree of skepticism, some doubts with respect to death, for example, that never bother me when I am living an active political life, but seem to filter through as soon as I face the typewriter"; 29). Ulloa channels Dorfman's own worries that writing a novel is incommensurate with "real" political engage-ment. And yet at the time that Dorfman was writing the novel, he was not Ulloa (although he might have empathized with him) since he was working simultaneously on projects that supported Allende. So it would be a mistake to read too close an identification between Dorfman and his fictional author. Instead, Dorfman uses the review of Ulloa's novel in order to explore one of his main obsessions, which the reviewer aptly identifies: "Las palabras son el campo de batalla en que la confirmación de su propio arte y la duda respeto de él, en que sospecha y cooperación se miran, sin mucho amor" (27–28); ("Words provide the battlefield in which the confirmation of his own art and any doubts with respect to it, in which suspicion and cooperation face each other off, with no love lost between them"; 29). Since this book review opens the novel, its comments on the relationship between art and politics and on the necessarily active role of the reader are crucial indicators of its aesthetics.

Parallel to the opening of the novel, the ending also provides essential clues to its aesthetic goals. The last few pages of both the Spanish and the English versions describe the "último proyecto" (final project)—a play on the Nazi phrase "the final solution"—which stresses the collaborative and ongoing na-ture of a revolutionary project instead of the authoritarian finality of a geno-cidal solution. As further testimony to the fact that this project is taking place in history, midway through the Spanish and two-thirds through the English version, the project, which will be completed at the end, is outlined: One night a group of writers gathers at César Rocafitto's house, is caught by the curfew, and must spend the night. It is October 1972, and Chile has been paralyzed by the U.S.-organized truckers' strike that will eventually result in the coup, a fact that neither the writers described in the novel nor Dorfman yet know about. As the writers muse on the current dire situation, one exclaims, "Si no estuviera tan ocupado políticamente qué lindos cuentos estaría escribiendo" (206); ("If he weren't so busy with politics, what great stories he'd be writing"; 191). This thought leads the group to reflect on the relationship between writing and revolutionary commitment. On the one hand, one writer suggests, "Maldito nos iba a servir renovar la literatura si nos quedábamos sin país" (206); ("A lot of good it'd do us to have a literary renaissance, if we ended up without a country"; 191). On the other hand, another writer suggests trying to combine the revolution with a literary project that would renovate the relationship between literature and social struggle.

This proposal causes the writers to spend the next few hours imagining what such a "final project" might look like, the contours of which appear both at the end of the novel and in the earlier section. The writers would create "un ente colectivo, una sociedad de artistas que podría agotar lo que está sucediendo en el país, que nada se les escape" (207); ("a collective entity, a society of artists that will be able to drain every last drop of what the country is going through, every story, nothing will get away from them"; 192). They would have the collaboration of the people, who would record their every thought and experience. It would be the most extreme example of collaborative writing since all would participate. They would overcome the chasm between reality and representation, creating the first real novel of Chile (373; 265). But then the conflicts arise. Different writers favor different styles. And what of the practical realities of asking all Chileans to write down their every thought and action? One writer suggests that such a task would surely destroy the revolution since it would distract everyone from what was really important. Another points out how foolish they are to think that they can enter the world of the workers like tourists writing a travelogue. Then Inibata (one of Dorfman's fictitious authors) makes the ultimate comparison: Do they want a good novel or a good life? He posits a transcendental choice that they would all have to face soon.

In the end, then, the project is abandoned that night. It has been shown to be futile, impractical, and ultimately counterrevolutionary. It simply cannot be done. The writers conclude that there can be no perfect merging of art with politics, of literature with life. As the conversation turns to other topics, one of the writers "sin que lo vieran empezó a teclear en su cabeza, no pudo evitarlo" (374); ("without anyone seeing him, started to write inside his head; he couldn't help it"; 267). The novel ends with what seems to be the story that the writer is constructing in his head: his own version of the final project. No longer forced to choose between being outside the revolution in order to narrate it or working within it, the writer and his protagonist, thanks to the radically new aesthetic structure of the "final project," become fully integrated into history (375; 267). In a move that demonstrates one of the ways that Dorfman plays with words in order to advance his aesthetic project, the conditional "si" (if) used to describe what might happen tomorrow is replaced by an affirmative "sí" (yes). It is the affirmation used by "el escritor para la palabra, el sí que usa el hombre para la revolución" (375); ("the writer . . . for the written word, the yes that men and women use for the revolution"; 268). Writing and revolution are intertwined, inseparable, mutually compatible, and reciprocally dependent. The last lines of the novel enact the creative process that drives it. What would a *real* novel of Chile during Allende look like? How can a literary text represent society as it progressively changes into a collective?

As can be seen by the opening and closing sections, Dorfman's first novel narrates a moment of change, conflict, and threatening violence alongside revolutionary hope without the benefit of hindsight or reflection. Written "in the moment," the text is raw, jolting, and splintered. For one thing, Dorfman uses the destabilizing tactic of mixing actual authors with fictitious ones. For instance, Arístides Ulloa is Dorfman's creation, but in the review of his novel, the unnamed reviewer refers to Alejo Carpentier and Reynaldo (*sic*) Arenas (both writers from Cuba). But these real writers are mentioned in a list that also including fictitious ones, such as Juan Menguant.[6] This constant combination of actual literary figures and fictional ones produces discomfort in the reader, forcing him or her to continually question whether a figure is "real" or "imaginary." In addition, the novel combines literary reviews, literary fragments, and random sentences or phrases that recall everyday life. One section near the end of the text is an interview with Dorfman about a novel, which may or may not be the novel we are reading. During this fictitious interview he explains that the constant disruption of established norms of discourse means that "Ya no se sabe qué es real, qué es ficción" (311); ("We no longer know what's real, what's fiction"; 248). Eventually the tactic of blending the "real" with the "fictional" and presenting critical comments on both serves to challenge the relationship between fact and fiction since the reader only has representations. This destabilization of the primacy of fact over fiction should not be read as a consequence of ludic postmodern pastiche, but rather as a reflection of Dorfman's interest in the role that fiction plays in the construction of reality. If the reader's perception of the relationship between text and world is unsettled, does that mean that literature can play a more vital role in political praxis by suggesting to the reader alternative ways to think about the world? Or does it mean that literature is always a distraction? On one level the novel seeks to destroy itself: "Existía para ser derrotado como libro" (312); ("The book became its own negation"; 249). But how can the literary text, even with increasingly disruptive interruptions from "reality," ever be more than a text? This question haunts the novel.

Dorfman's mix of real and imagined writers and multiple discursive registers relates to another unusual strategy: almost all of the novel's main characters are authors and artists. Lacking interlocutors, the novel is mainly book reviews, essays, and letters. Most dialogue is about art or is dialogue that lacks sufficient context for the reader to truly understand it. In one section that departs from this pattern a young Argentine doctor enters a bar near the border with Chile and has a conversation with a Chilean exile. Over the course of the conversation the reader learns that the Chilean exile is a conservative, a fascist who has a radio show, and that the young Argentine man is on his way to Chile to be with his Chilean wife. The exiled Chilean tries to convince the doctor that the Chile he has come to know under Allende is false and that what had existed before was nearly paradise. The conversation becomes increasingly menacing, and the Chilean and his friends begin to threaten the Argentine doctor, suggesting that they will not let him leave the bar. Even though the doctor keeps asking for his check and trying to get up, they will not allow it. As the section comes to a close, they ask the doctor for his opinion of Chile, now that he knows what they think. Even though it is clear that they expect the doctor to agree with them or suffer physical consequences, probably murder, they now claim to seek "dialogue": "Es bueno el diálogo—dijo el coronel en retiro—Es bueno tener esto de poder intercambiar ideas" (240); (" 'Dialogue is good,' says the retired colonel. 'It's good to be able to exchange impressions' "; 226).[7] This story allows Dorfman to investigate the fragile possibilities for communication and exchange among social sectors that do not characterize dialogue in similar terms. How can there be dialogue in Chile when the right has historically defined "dialogue" as the freedom for all to agree with its point of view?

The lack of conversation among characters further relates to Dorfman's observation that some of the processes in place for creating social change were not sufficiently dialogic, that too often Allende's supporters gloated in their new-found power and humiliated the right rather than reaching out to it. The key to understanding this problem lies in the role of the critics and reviewers in the novel. Dorfman associates critics and reviewers with social parasites who try to dictate to the public how to read and what to value. (Of course this connection is highly ironic since Dorfman himself wrote cultural criticism and numerous book reviews.) As the novel progresses, the reviews are increasingly interrupted with voices that sabotage their discursive monopoly. In the novel's previously mentioned interview with Dorfman he explains that the interruptions of the reviews were meant to mirror the way that the working class would erupt into the lives of the Chilean bourgeoisie. Ultimately this mix of discourses would lead to the novel's own demise as it slowly evaporated, leaving behind the reader in direct contact with the revolution. Nevertheless Dorfman explains in the interview that this goal was not achieved, that putting the idea into practice was vastly different from conceptualizing it, and that he could not resist a certain affinity for the reviews. He admits that he could not bring himself to destroy the realm of ideas in favor of the realm of the senses, that he could not force himself to choose between the two. So instead of destroying the line between imagination and experience, he tells his readers that he destroyed the novel they are reading. He threw it away and never published it.

> La literatura se iba a liberar de las reseñas. . . . Y el lector iba a entender esa liberación a su propia clausurada existencia. Y con suerte, yo también escapaba de ser crítico y me iba a INACAP o al Perfeccionamiento del Magisterio o a trabajar con periódicos obreros o a hacer fotonovelas con las pobladoras o a escribir guiones para historietas o a dirigir la política de comunicaciones del agro y con ese gesto me destruía como escritor. Fue bonito planearlo. (313)

> (The fact is the literary work never freed itself from the reviews, never succeeded in driving them out of the novel; the reader never extended that model to his own cloistered existence; and on my part, I simply dreamed of escaping my role as a critic, with any luck I'd be participating in working class newspapers, producing comic books, writing soap opera scripts and looking for ways to use images to increase agricultural production in CORA, as well as gathering testimonials from survivors of the nitrate miner's strike. But I didn't. I just went on being a writer. [250])

Comparing these two quotations is a good starting point for analyzing the differences between the original and the translation. In the original Spanish, Dorfman uses the imperfect progressive ("iba a liberar") to describe what the novel should have done but did not do. The English, in contrast, describes the failed goals of the novel in the simple past ("freed").[8] The difference between the two versions is that the Spanish suggests unfulfilled hopes that don't appear in the English, and it explains why the last sentence of the Spanish, "Fue bonito planearlo" (It was nice to plan it), is absent from the English. Perhaps the most important difference for the purposes of understanding the novel's aesthetics is how the two versions reflect Dorfman's changing view of his role as a writer. In the Spanish he writes that the process of breaking down the reviews would eventually destroy him as a writer ("me destruía como escritor"). This idea that Dorfman would cease to be a writer and would dedicate himself entirely to working for the revolution is described in the English quite distinctly. In retrospect he writes that he "dreamed" of escaping his role as a critic and using his writing skills for more practical purposes but that that is not what happened. Instead, he "just went on being a writer"—a phrase absent in the original. Seventeen years after writing his first novel, Dorfman confronted his fantasies about giving up writing to be more practically involved in politics. By 1990, he had realized that his life would be forever dedicated, at least in part, to literature.

Almost one hundred pages shorter, the translation into English both is and is not a different text. As Dorfman admits in the prologue to the English version, "This text is not exactly the one that Spanish-language readers could acquire in December 1973" (viii). On the one hand, the same themes and the same fragmented structures are present in both versions. On the other hand, the Spanish, with its additional sections, larger number of fragments, different epigraphs, and distinct title, is more disjointed, chaotic, and troubled— reflecting perhaps more accurately the time in which it was written. Moreover, on a number of occasions it seems that Dorfman could not help but edit the shortened translation with the aid of hindsight. It was impossible to read this testament to the last moments of Allende's presidency without reflecting the knowledge of what followed. Nevertheless, Dorfman either does not recognize or chooses not to reveal the substantive changes that indicate the historical distance between the original and the translation: "The reader can rest assured . . . that I have avoided the temptation to rewrite the text" (viii).

The differences between the two texts merit a detailed study, but for brevity's sake I would like to point to the changed title and epigraphs as indicators of how the translation reveals Dorfman's perspective on the novel and its historical moment. The original title, *Moros en la costa*, derives from a Spanish colloquial expression that has its origins in the medieval period. In 711 Moors invaded Visigothic Spain and controlled sections of the country until the end of the Christian reconquest in 1492. In reference to this history, "moros en la costa" (Moors on the coast) suggests the threat of invasion. Describing an environment of vigilance and tension, the phrase would have originally been used to sound an alarm about impending attack. It later morphed to signify not only physical attack, but also eavesdropping by someone who represents danger or should not be privy to a particular conversation. At the time Dorfman wrote his novel, the phrase more commonly referred to the idea that interlocutors needed to be wary of what they said because if a hostile third party heard their words, it could be dangerous. (The English equivalent of the phrase would be akin to "the coast is not clear.") Understood in the context of Chile in 1972, the novel's title suggests the threat of foreign invasion, especially by the United States, and the problem of communication, since it was difficult to know who could be trusted with information.

The original Spanish version has four epigraphs, only one of which appears in modified translation in the English. The first, omitted from the translation, is by an acquaintance of Dorfman's, Rodrigo Ambrosio, a leader of the Movimiento de Acción Popular Unitaria, (MAPU; the Unitary Popular Action Movement), a marxist Chilean political party. The party, along with five others, combined to form the Unidad Popular, the political consortium that supported Allende for the presidency. Ambrosio was a vocal and ardent leftist radical who after the 1970 elections traveled to a number of socialist countries, including North Korea and Cuba. In May 1972, shortly before Dorfman wrote his novel, Ambrosio died in a car accident. The quote Dorfman uses from Ambrosio analyzes how the petit-bourgeoisie falls between classes, between the working class and the bourgeoisie. Its comments about the inability of the petit-bourgeoisie to actively participate in revolutionary politics are telling since many of the characters in Dorfman's novel purportedly come from this class. Here is an excerpt of the epigraph, from Ambrosio's *Sobre la construcción del partido*:

> La dispersión de su actividad económica, o su participación indirecta (y no manual) en procesos productivos socializados, explica el individualismo, la inestabilidad y el idealismo de la conducta política pequeño-burguesa. (Carta a Annekov).

> (The dispersion of their economic activity, or their indirect [and not manual] participation in productive socialized processes, explains the individualism, the instability and the idealism of petit-bourgeois political conduct. [Letter to Annekov].)

The second epigraph that is absent from the English comes from the abstract modernist painter Georges Braque, who is famous for collaborating with Picasso and creating Cubism: "No hay que pedir al artista más de lo que pueda dar, ni al crítico más de lo que pueda ver" (Don't ask more from the artist than he can give, nor more from the critic than he can see). This quote adds an artistic aesthetic dimension to Ambrosio's critique of the petit-bourgeoisie and suggests the limitations of both art and its interpretation. It relates to the last epigraph of the Spanish, also absent in the English, which is from Julio García Espinosa, the Cuban filmmaker and critic, who asks, "¿Por qué (el artista) siente la necesidad de tener críticos—mediadores—que lo defiendan, lo justifiquen, lo interpreten?"; (Why does [the artist] feel the need to have critics—mediators—that defend him, justify him, interpret him?) In contrast to Braque, García Espinosa is more overtly negative about the function of the critic. According to him, when artists worry about critics, they change their work to suit the tastes of an alienated bourgeois class that consumes but cannot create art. And *Moros en la costa* asks whether it might be possible to have art overtake its own criticism.

The one epigraph that appears in both texts is "Aquí estamos otra vez, y que fue, y que fue" (Here we are again, we can't be stopped, we can't be stopped). In the Spanish these lines, from a protest chant, are accompanied by two important dates that are not included in the translation. Both versions explain that this chant has been sung for decades by the left in Chile, but the original Spanish mentions that the chant "preferentemente" (preferably) was heard on November 5, 1964, and September 3, 1976. The first date immediately follows Eduardo Frei's presidential inauguration in 1964, when Salvador Allende lost the election. The second date, set four years after the writing of the novel, suggests that the chant would be shouted again on the eve of the first elections held after Allende's presidency, hopefully signaling another win for the Unidad Popular. Dorfman decided to remove these dates in the translation, perhaps because by 1990 he was more interested in using the novel as both a marker for a specific historical moment in Chile and also as a more universal meditation on art and revolutionary change. When he wrote the original version, he would have wanted to signal to his fellow Chilean readers the work that would be required for the next election. By the time of the translation his audience had expanded beyond Chile, and the political resonance of the protest chant had become amplified for Dorfman to include other struggles in other locales and at other times.

The English title and one new epigraph—"A hard rain / is going to fall"— both refer to a song by Bob Dylan. This change is perhaps the most revealing indicator of the time lapse between the two texts. Recall that Dorfman spent time at Berkeley in 1968 and that students across Latin America listened to U.S. rock in the 1960s. Thus Dylan's "A Hard Rain's A-Gonna Fall," composed in 1962, would have certainly been part of his musical culture when he wrote the first version of the novel. What, then, motivated Dorfman to change the translation's title to refer to this famous song?

I propose that there are four main reasons. First, the change in title allows the text's message to expand to a wider realm of social critique. Second, similar to the novel, the song itself is composed of multiple cultural influences and discursive registers. When Dorfman moved away from the concrete, immediate concerns of how the artistic community in Chile could help Allende—concerns evidenced by the epigraphs from Ambrosio and García Espinosa that frame the original—he became more interested in presenting the book as a reflection of a range of voices. Thomas O. Beebee points out in his analysis of "Hard Rain" that the song unites a number of musical and cultural traditions, not only rock and roll, African American, folk, and spiritual music, but also "the ballad tradition, pacifism, scripture, the political lyrics of Bertolt Brecht, and the visionary poetry of Arthur Rimbaud" (23). According to Beebee, the phrase "hard rain" is thematic and incorporates three interrelated areas: "politics, religion, and art" (23). Third, the song provided a useful intertext to the translation because of its own relationship to impending historical catastrophe. Beebee explains that the song was widely considered as "Dylan's response to the Cuban missile crisis of 1962" (23). Referring to a narrowly avoided war, the song, like the novel, is perched at the edge of apocalypse. Even though Dylan's song refers to an apocalypse averted and Dorfman's text prefigures a massive national tragedy, both texts give a similar sense of impending doom and destruction and both consider the role of art in announcing such potential disasters. Finally, I suspect that Dorfman appropriated Dylan's song for his novel's title because of its aesthetic theory. As in Dorfman's aesthetics of hope, Dylan's song is self-conscious and yet passionate about the potential for art to shape society. A "song about singing," just as *Hard Rain* is a novel about writing a novel, Dylan's "Hard Rain" also grapples with "the ability or inability to narrate" (Beebee, 24). Dorfman's translation captured much of the original spirit of his first novel while also suggesting some of the new directions his work had taken since he had been forced into exile in 1973.

WORKS OF EARLY EXILE: POETRY AND SHORT STORIES

It is important to recall that *Moros en la costa* won a literary award that facilitated Dorfman's exile. First, the award convinced the Chilean authorities to grant him safe-conduct to leave Chile for Argentina (*Heading*, 273). Then, it aided him during a crucial interview with a police commissioner in Buenos Aires in which Dorfman offered to dedicate a copy of the book to him. The police commissioner responded that he would read it, and Dorfman admits that for the first time he wished that someone *would not* read it. "I wanted him to have it in his hands and admire it, but not delve into what I was narrating. I didn't want him to read that hymn to the brilliant future of the revolution, and I didn't want him to read the signs of foreboding and silence and death that had crept into the text unawares, that belied its sunny vision of a victory that hadn't happened. I didn't want this man who held my fate in his hands to think I might be dangerous" (274). It is interesting to note that the coup and his exile had already proven to Dorfman that his writing could be considered dangerous. His heart sank even further when, after describing the novel as experimental—"a series of book reviews . . . by non-existent authors about novels that I made up"—the police commissioner responded, "Not like your book on Donald Duck" (274). Dorfman was sure that he would never get a passport to leave Argentina, that his writing had, in fact, had material consequences—in this case that it would send him into exile and brand him as a subversive. But again Dorfman would be surprised by his readers. The police commissioner put the book away, smiled at him, and asked him how he could be of help. One week later, Dorfman had a passport and was on his way to the airport.

Once in exile, as noted, Dorfman suffered a prolonged and intense creative block, and his first literary writing in exile was poetry. These poems are extremely important in terms of his literary evolution because they signal Dorfman's earliest efforts to write in a simple language—a style vastly different from his previous baroque, experimental prose. His state of utter despair led him to seek a new language with which to express himself and his sorrows. Giving voice to the disappeared and to all of those who were suffering the consequences of the coup, the poems forced Dorfman to focus on the bare essentials of literary expression. Inspired by Pablo Neruda and Ernesto Cardenal, Dorfman stripped his writing of any unnecessary adornments and strove to use spare language combined with passion, hope, and desire.

Appearing in print in 1979, Dorfman's first published collection of poems in Spanish is entitled *Pruebas al canto* (Poetic Evidence).[9] Euisuk Kim, John Berger, and I have written critical analyses of these poems. All three analyses attend to the relationship between the poetic word and the representation of torture and violence. Kim's analysis focuses on the way that Dorfman uses the poems to ask the reader to identify with the disappeared and tortured victims of Pinochet (37). John Berger, himself a poet, suggests that Dorfman's words were able to capture the complex problem of how to write about torture. According to Berger, torture is so heinous because it assumes an inability for mutual comprehension, for words instead of blows, for language instead of violence: "Torture smashes language: its purpose is to tear language from the voice and words from the truth" ("The Hour of Poetry," 244). Berger finds in Dorfman's poems an effort to return humanity and dignity to language.

It is noteworthy that *Pruebas al canto* signals two firsts for Dorfman's professional writing career: it is his first writing in exile and his first published poetry. The selection of poetry as the medium through which to narrate torture marks a turning point in Dorfman's aesthetic because these poems represent Dorfman's first effort to bear witness to the agony of torture and the horror of the coup.[10] Dorfman's experience of exile proves for him the power of literature: not only was his own literary writing powerful enough to send him into exile, but literature also serves a prominent role in helping the victims of the coup to mediate and express their trauma.[11] Exile also proves to Dorfman the limits of literature's power because even though it serves a number of essential public and personal functions, it still seems incomplete as a force for social change.

After leaving Chile, Dorfman continued to be politically active—writing letters and editorials, meeting with politicians, and helping the Chilean resistance and Chileans in exile—but he also became more committed to the use of literature as a political weapon, as a way to record history, and as a means to challenge dominant discourses. This dedication to the literary may be a consequence of his experience with the survivors of torture and may explain the several different meanings of the title of his first poetry collection. "Pruebas al canto" is a colloquial expression that has no English equivalent. It literally means "poetic evidence" and was translated by Dorfman and Edith Grossman as "Soft Evidence" in the English translation of the poem that appears in the collection *Missing*. As a colloquial expression used both in everyday speech and in law, especially in the Southern Cone, "pruebas al canto" signifies "here's the evidence" or "to prove the point," but the English fails to capture the polysemic discursive registers that Dorfman's title suggests. "Pruebas," has not only a juridical, but also a medical, rational register and can be translated as "proof," "evidence," "trial," "test," "exam" (medical), or "photographic proof" (among other things). The expression interestingly uses the plural—"pruebas" —a grammatical oddity that highlights a multiplicity to these forms of documentation and proof. "Canto" functions as a foil for the cold rationality of "pruebas" and evokes the poetic, the literary, the oral, and the collective. It can be translated as "song," "poem," or "ballad," and it is also used in Spanish, as in English, to refer to a section of a long epic/heroic poem. "Canto" further refers to the possibility of "singing" in the sense of denouncing or betraying.

This title, *Pruebas al canto*, allowed Dorfman to signal many of his characteristic aesthetic preoccupations. By selecting a colloquial expression that is used in everyday speech and in law and that hints at ties between the poetic and the objective, the passionate and the rational, Dorfman asks readers to consider how words might be used to register—that is, to prove—the atrocities of the coup. At a time when Chilean exiles were giving testimonials to verify their experience of abuse, Dorfman chose to use the literary form typically considered most distant from that of historical documentation. His title, though, belies the supposed incompatability of poetry with proof. On the contrary, he suggests that poetry may very well be the best linguistic form for representing torture, exile, dictatorship, disappearance, and collective anguish. The poems provide evidence by representing that which is left out of testimonials but which remains very real. In the poem that bears the title of the collection a woman reflects on how she *knows* that her husband is still alive even though she has no proof: "Si estuviera muerto, / yo lo sabría. / No me pregunten cómo. / Lo sabría" (42); ("If he were dead / I'd know it. / Don't ask me how. / I'd know"; 43).[12] She knows her husband is alive, but her only proof is what is in her heart, mind, and gut, none of which counts as proof for rational discourse. Dorfman's poems attempt to reflect on the chasm of meaning that is created when victims are forced to provide evidence and when language is forced to favor objectivity over sensuality, a topic to which he returns with even greater intensity in *Death and the Maiden*.

The title additionally suggests what Dorfman refers to as the "trials of poetry," "the trials that poetry must go through," the "proof that poetry is still alive."[13] The collection includes poems that reflect the trauma of the coup—the disappeared, torture, exile, and the pervasive environment of fear—alongside poems about the difficulty of putting such experiences into words. In this sense, the collection has two complementary yet distinct interests: it seeks to render into poetry what Dorfman and his fellow Chileans have witnessed, and it reflects on the writing process itself, on how poetry translates experience. As Kim points out, the discursive backdrop for these musings is the testimonial, a linguistic form that endeavors to denounce crimes, record history, and motivate others to continue their struggles (41). Some of the poems are, in fact, almost direct transcriptions of testimonials, but to these texts Dorfman makes changes, adding rhythm and creating verse.[14] Clearly Dorfman feels that the testimonial is essential in the struggle to bear witness to the coup, but his poetry suggests that once the tape recorder is turned off and the lawyers have left the room, much remains to be said and poetry provides an outlet for that expression.

The poetic, while intimating emotions often ignored in the testimonial, is not, however, a perfect representative vehicle. Kim notes that *Pruebas al canto* begins from the eerie silence of the disappeared (37). Signaling a significant transition between this work and Dorfman's novel *Moros en la costa*, *Pruebas al canto* worries less about the distance between the writer, the people he writes about, and his audience. Instead, the poetry collection's principal struggle is over how to find the right words to convey an experience that is unspeakable. Even though both *Pruebas al canto* and *Moros en la costa* demonstrate Dorfman's interest in using literature to represent Chile, the intellectual musings of the novel are replaced with urgency and desperation in these poems.[15] Much of the desperation comes in the form of anguish over the writer's task, as evidenced by two poems that serve as prologues to the first two sections of the collection: "Traducción simultánea" ("Simultaneous Translation") and "Paracaídas" ("Parachute").

"Traducción simultánea," the first poem of the collection, draws an analogy between the poet and the interpreter, or simultaneous translator.[16]

> No soy tan diferente de los intérpretes
> detrás de sus ventanas de vidrios
> en las interminables conferencias de lo internacional
> traduciendo lo que el campesino de Talca
> recuenta sobre las torturas
> repitiendo en inglés que lo pusieron sobre el catre
> . . . .
> encontrando el equivalente exacto para violación por perros. (2)

> (I'm not so different from the interpreters
> in their glass booths
> at endless international conferences
> translating what the peasant from Talca
> tells about torture
> repeating in English that they put him on a cot
> . . . .
> finding the exact equivalent for rape by dogs. [3])

Here the connection between the two professions stems from the fact that both need to find a way to connect a word with something else. While the interpreter links the words of two different languages, the poet links the word to experience. Each has a difficult task of translation. Shortly, though, the poem breaks the analogy down and indicates that the poet's tasks may be different because of the distinct discursive registers used by the interpreter versus the poet:

> encontrando un lenguaje escueto y conveniente
> para aquello que se siente
> —perdonen la rima y el ritmo—
> cuando la muralla está detrás de las espaldas

y el capitán comienza a decir la palabra fuego,
tratando de sacar el melodrama de las frases
tratando de comunicar la esencia y la emoción
sin entregarse a la corriente oscura y pegajosa
de lo que pronuncien en realidad (2)

(finding a phrase without emotion
that describes exactly the sensation
—please forgive any rhymes or rhythms you may find—
when the wall is at your back
and the captain begins to say the word fire,
trying to take the melodrama out of the sentences
trying to communicate the essence and the feeling
without giving in to the dark cloying current
of what they are really saying [3])

One might imagine that these lines were written after hearing the simultaneous translation of a torture testimonial. Dorfman's depiction of the linguistic control sought by interpreters, who attempt to remove all emotion from the lines that they translate, certainly exaggerates, but the characterization means to push the reader to consider how pain and suffering can be mediated into words. What Dorfman wants to emphasize is the inevitable loss of feeling entailed by such translation. The poem insinuates that the interpreter engages in this dampening of emotion purposefully, but it is clear that the poet's intentions are the opposite.

In either case, both the poet and the interpreter are intermediaries: "un intermediario, ni siquiera un puente" (2); ("an intermediary, not even a bridge," 3). An intermediary comes between, whereas a bridge connects. While it may appear that Dorfman yearns to be a poetic bridge that connects the suffering of torture with words, he recognizes that his linguistic tools are never quite adequate to the task of representation. Try as the poet might, words cannot express the inexpressible. And yet despite this representative gap, something is communicated, as revealed when the poem uses the first person to refer to Dorfman for the first time:

a pesar de mi río de interpretaciones y giros lingüísticos
algo se comunica
una porción del aullido
un matorral de sangre
unas lágrimas imposibles

la humanidad algo ha escuchado
y se emociona. (2)

(in spite of my river of interpretations and turns of phrase
something is communicated
a part of the howl
a thicket of blood
some impossible tears
the human race has heard something
and is moved. [3])

After the poet recognizes the limitations of representing horror and notes that words always sanitize emotion, his response is not silence but resignation to the inevitable imperfection of the writer's task. His hope remains tied to the response potentially provoked in the reader, described in this case as the human race, who the poet hopes will be moved. Without the poet's words there would be no hope of communicating the experience to others. Even though the poet and the interpreter may be intermediaries who frustrate the communication of experience, the imperfect mediation of language, especially when used with an aesthetics of hope, offers the best and only chance to rescue such experiences from oblivion.

These ideas reappear in the collection's second prologue, "Paracaídas" in a section entitled "Poemas que no iba a mostrar a nadie" (Poems I Wasn't Going to Show Anyone). This section laments the pain of the coup and the extreme depression and self-doubt it cast on those who survived. It also signals the fracturing of identity, meaning, and language caused by exile. Both of these themes are highlighted in the poem. The responsibility of the exiled writer to communicate the experience of his nation is countered by his desire to wallow in depression and melancholy. The poem suggests that the poet simply cannot afford the luxury of such self-pity.

En cuanto a él
no puede darse el lujo de una crisis.
Clausura sueños
    y sonríe valientemente
y quedan sus umbrales
quemados entre ruinas (76)

(As for him
he can't afford the luxury of a breakdown.

He locks away his dreams
    and smiles bravely
and his roots
burn among ruins [77])

These lines indicate the split personality required of the writer who suffers loss and anguish while simultaneously trying to maintain hope and energy in support of the Chilean resistance. This split between thought and action is further broken down when the poem shifts from third to first person in lines separated by a parenthetical:

(En cuanto a mí
no voy a darme el lujo de una crisis
Debo seguir como siempre
    funcionando.) (76)

([As for me,
I can't afford the luxury of a breakdown.
I must go on doing what I always do.] [77])

The writer faces a vexing problem, however: in order to face his situation and not recede into selfish depression, characterized by negative and disturbing thoughts, he must write about negative and disturbing images. So at the same time that the writer is forced to overcome his demons, he must write about the horrors that he and his fellow Chileans have witnessed. He tries to reassure his readers that he will find a way to distance himself from these atrocities, that he is a professional, just like a parachuter, who can take risks and survive the dangers implicit in his task.

Si me rodeo sin cesar el pozo más profundo,
si juego a zambullirme en el fuego,
si estos pies tantean el vértigo del barro,
si rugen estrellas negras en el aire,
no se preocupen.
Aquí la llevo, mi cuerda favorita,
un ancla secreta, una brújula
    tatuada,
y agua, agua escondida en la joroba. (76)

(If I endlessly circle the deepest well,
  if I pretend to plunge into fire,

if these feet test the vertigo of mud,
if black stars soar in my air,
don't worry.
Here it is, my favorite rope,
a secret anchor, a tattooed
compass,
and water, water hidden in my hump. [77])

The mythical images used in these lines, along with the metaphor of the poet as traveler who undertakes dangerous adventures, describe the poet's task as transhistorical and transnational. These images also cast doubt on the poet's confidence because it is not clear that the navigational and survival tools he carries will be sufficient to guide him out of the abyss that he must explore; thus the last stanza opens with the caution: "Ten cuidado" (78); ("Be careful"; 79). After the coup and exile, the world of meaning has been shattered and inverted. Now the parachute falls to the sun. Now the poet is called upon to lock away his dreams and write about the nightmares of others. Now writing is no longer a luxury but a matter of life and death.[17]

The relationship between literature and witnessing, highlighted in this poem and a focus of the collection as a whole, remains a constant theme in Dorfman's work after exile, but it is the section entitled "Resaca" ("Undertow") that centers on the dislocation, rupture, and loss of exile. It is interesting that Dorfman chooses the notion of an undertow to describe the devastating effect of exile because the term emphasizes the physical violence of exile as well as the exile's vulnerability. The poems in this section represent Dorfman's first effort to describe the experience of exile, and they are noteworthy for their gentle yet anguished tone. In "Prólogo: Ese ruido ensordecedor es el camión de la basura" ("Prologue: That Deafening Noise Is the Garbage Truck") an exiled man breaks a cup purchased shortly after arrival in his host country, and the loss of something acquired in exile brings home the realities of the experience for the first time. In "Ejército de ocupación" ("Occupation Forces") recalling a moment walking down a street in Santiago reminds the exile that all he has are his memories of Chile and that he cannot physically "occupy" his country but must rather "force" his memory there. These poems show that instead of his moving toward greater fragmentation and doubt, exile helps Dorfman to understand that his commitment to writing does not necessarily detract from his political activism.

Many of these same themes appear in Dorfman's first collection of short stories, *Cría ojos* (Raise Eyes), which appeared in print the same year as his first collection of poems (1979) and which also used a colloquial expression as a metaphor for exploring the relationship between authoritarianism and society. *Cría ojos* is a play on the Spanish expression "Cría cuervos y te sacarán los ojos" (Raise crows and they will take out your eyes), which alludes to the idea that children cannot always be tamed or educated, that they may grow up and turn on their parents.[18] It is a negative view of children that is typically uttered by those who favor strict discipline and obedience to authority. Dorfman's title turns the phrase around and implies that "parents" should raise "eyes." As in much of his exile writing, Dorfman explores the relationship between parent and child as a metaphor for government and society. In this case, the altered colloquial phrase proposes that instead of conceptualizing the relationship between parent and child as one of controlled discipline, parents should raise their children to be socially aware and to think critically rather than to blindly obey. According to Juan Claro-Mayo, "Los ojos que han de criar para mirar e iluminar, habrán de ser una suerte de toma de conciencia de la realidad: la situación del pueblo chileno bajo la dictadura del gobierno militar desde 1973" (339); (The eyes that must be raised in order to see and illuminate will be like raising consciousness of reality: the situation of the Chilean people living under a military government since 1973).

The majority of the stories deal directly with dysfunctional or ruptured families, which mirror a society tormented by dictatorship and tyranny. For Dorfman, young children hold the promise of innocence and hope, and two of the stories, "A la escondida" ("My House Is on Fire") and "Y qué oficio le pondremos" ("Godfather"), cite children's songs, the first as an epigraph and the second as part of the Spanish title, and emphasize the tragedy of children living in a society ruled by fear. Other stories deal with children in adolescence or early adulthood, as in "Putamadre"[19] or "En familia" ("Family Circle"). In these Dorfman explores the turning point into young adulthood when children have to decide whether to follow the example of their seniors or choose their own way. Similarly, adults are described as facing a return to adolescence by the social repression of dictatorship, since authoritarian governments propose to make all decisions for the populace and infantilize the public. Even though the collection's title is optimistic—alluding to the hope that children, understood metaphorically, will be raised to think for themselves—the stories are open-ended and leave the future indefinite. Dorfman also presents another side of childhood, where children or young adults are incapable of human compassion.

Cría ojos has fourteen stories divided into three sections: "Párpados" (Eyelids), "Cuervos" (Crows), and "Ojos" (Eyes).[20] The first two sections have four stories each, and the third has six. As both Claro-Mayo and Kim have noted, each section has a running theme that loosely structures the stories. Nevertheless, even though the sections group stories that share overlapping themes, each story uses a different narrative form.[21] By grouping together stories with similar themes and radically different literary forms, Dorfman asks his readers to consider the relationship between form and content as he playfully experiments with different discursive registers. Again, in keeping with his aesthetics of hope, he emphasizes a conscious engagement with formal experimentation that refuses to privilege one way of telling stories and demonstrates instead how a variety of narrative forms can converge in a shared vision. After all, the collection is organized around the trope of sight as a symbol of social interaction.

The first section, "Párpados" (Eyelids), in keeping with its liminal title, refers to the ambiguous loyalties that often characterize families living under dictatorship. In each story, family members are unsure whom they can trust and what they should do since allegiance to both family and state is often impossible. For instance, in "En familia" ("Family Circle"), the son of a former union leader who is jobless under the dictatorship has been drafted into the military. The father had hoped his son, whose nickname, "Lucho," also means "I struggle," would decline to serve.[22] But if Lucho does not serve, he will likely be imprisoned and tortured, possibly murdered. Lucho feels that he is left with no alternative if he wants to live. At the same time, Lucho's father feels that there is no alternative but to refuse to join the military since it is the military that has caused the family and the community as a whole to suffer. The dilemma leads to an inevitable breakdown in the family, and when Lucho defies his father and enters the service, his father refuses to speak to him. Later, though, after the father learns that Lucho is being transferred to work in the prison where Lucho's uncle is being held, he hopes that maybe his son will use his position to help the prisoners. Again he is disappointed by Lucho, who claims, "si alguno se trata de escapar, le voy a disparar" (34); ("if somebody tries to escape, I'll shoot him"; 20). Recognizing the distance that has grown between him and his son, the father responds with a gentle forgiveness, tenderly guiding his son to put down a burning pot he has in his hands and asking him to come and join the family for dinner.

The story opens with two epigraphs from Aeschylus's and Euripides's versions of the tragedy that befalls Agamemnon's family. Dorfman suggests that dictatorships create circumstances whereby family members are pitted against each other. The question is how individuals should respond in times of conflict. Dorfman's story disrupts the self-perpetuating cycle of violence that plagues Agamemnon's family with the father's simple act of compassion toward his son. In the story "Lector" ("Reader"), it will be the son who has to forgive his father for crimes against his mother. Throughout the collection, but especially in the stories of the first section, Dorfman narrates life after the coup as a tragedy that threatens to destroy the family, the community, and ultimately all of humanity.

The second section, "Cuervos," ("Crows"), takes the viewpoint of those who support the military regime's repressive ideology. Kim explains that the stories in this section are dominated by the point of view of those who "son, en realidad, los títeres de la ideología fascista, de modo que creen fielmente en la eficacia del orden simbólico" (16); (are, in reality, the puppets of fascist ideology, to the extent that they faithfully believe in the efficacy of the symbolic order). In an especially chilling tale, "Putamadre," Dorfman narrates the arrival in San Francisco in 1975 of a group of sailors who serve aboard the *Esmeralda*. Dorfman chooses to highlight the ship because it is famous for its presentation of two radically different views of Chile. The longest tall ship, it travels to ports across the world and has been dubbed "Chile's roving embassy." Yet since it was used after the coup as a site for torture, it is generally greeted at ports with protests by human rights defenders. This vision of a schizophrenic and divided Chile serves as the basis for "Putamadre," a story based on actual events that traces the efforts of three of the *Esmeralda*'s crew as they attempt to have sex on their one night ashore. Expecting to be able to use their dashing uniforms as a way to gain entrance into a brothel, they are shocked to learn that all of the prostitutes in San Francisco have agreed to boycott *Esmeralda*'s crew in protest that the ship had been a site for torture and rape. The sailors wonder: How can women as lowly as prostitutes favor solidarity over money? Can prostitutes refuse sex? In a direct jab at the conservative, reactionary ideology at the core of Pinochet's regime, Dorfman describes a world where prostitutes have greater ethical integrity than the Chilean Navy.

Despite the rejection of the prostitutes, the protagonist, Putamadre, will not abandon his mission to help his shipmate, Chico Valdés, lose his virginity. We later learn that Chico had refused to rape one of the ship's detainees, claiming that it didn't seem right to him to force women to have sex, a position that perplexes both Putamadre and the third sailor, Jorge. After they are turned away at the brothel, Putamadre proposes that they go to the apartment of a blond *gringa*, whom they had earlier seen painting protests against the *Esmeralda*, and rape her. Since she looks a lot like the woman Chico refused to rape earlier, Putamadre feels that violating her will make up for Chico's earlier hesitation. It will be a sign of his allegiance to all that the Chilean Navy represents. The story ends with Putamadre asking Chico if he agrees. Will he succumb to peer pressure? Will he rape in order to prove his masculinity and his allegiance to the state? Told with a tense style of impending doom, "Puta-madre" explores the cruel sadism and violent social logic of Pinochet's military rule.

These tales of the nightmare of Chile after the coup are counterbalanced by the final section, "Ojos" (Eyes), which tells stories of heroic acts and gestures of solidarity. "Titán" ("Titan") narrates the odyssey of a man who flees his captors by simulating the police's incredible version of how they were forced to shoot his brothers as they attempted escape. The far-fetched official version of his brothers' murder provides him with a blueprint for an escape that he could have never imagined. He deviates from the official script exactly in the moment when his brothers were shot and manages to survive. "Y qué oficio le pondremos" ("Godfather") narrates another unanticipated consequence of authoritarianism: A mother is late to register her newborn since this job is usually left to the father, who, it is implied, has been disappeared. The clerk finally agrees to let her register the child late but then balks when she wants to give her son his father's name because her first son is already named after his father. Two sons simply cannot have the same name. When she decides to name the child Salvador instead, the clerk and the mother share a moment of brief solidarity that hints at the subtle ways communities resist tyranny. Absent a godfather for the boy, the clerk states that he will sign the form for her.

Perhaps the story that best reveals Dorfman's concerns over the relationship between art and politics is "Cuestión de tiempo" (A Matter of Time). Narrated in the second person and addressed to Jorge Luis Borges, the story confronts the master storyteller's bourgeois intellectualism and nihilism that lead, in Dorfman's opinion, to an ahistorical and apolitical ideology. For Dorfman, Borges creates a literary world that has no material weight, refuses to connect with everyday life in any meaningful way, and consequently distracts readers and prevents them from raising consciousness or opening their eyes ("ojos"). Attacking the individualistic world of Borges, Dorfman writes: "un compa-ñero, Borges, es algo que no existe en tu filosofía. Pero en la realidad, sí, Borges, en la realidad todo el tiempo nos vamos encontrando con los compañeros" (151); (a *compañero*, Borges, is something that does not exist in your philoso-phy. But in reality, yes, Borges, in reality we are meeting our *compañeros* all the time). As evidenced by these lines, Dorfman appropriates Borges's style, in a cannibalistic fashion, in order to critique him.[23] Claro-Mayo notes that Dorf-man uses the story to confront literature that is mere fiction, nothing more than mental games and socially detached entertainment: "Ante una realidad conflictiva y agobiante la literatura debe ser registro, denuncia y llamado a la participación para el encuentro con los valores y la conducta que han de producir el cambio" (344); (Faced with a conflictive and overwhelming reality literature should register, denounce, and call for participation in shaping the values and conduct that will lead to change). Echoing Dorfman's work in the collection of literary criticism *Imaginación y violencia en América* (1970; Imagination and Violence in America), where he dedicates a chapter to Borges, this story finds Borges's ludic use of time to be complicit with social repression: "Entiéndame, Borges, no se trata de un consuelo ni de un truco intelectual lleno de ríos y tigres ni de un juego de artimañas. Era cuestión de tiempo. Y nosotros también, Borges, tenemos derecho al tiempo, tenemos derecho a multiplicar el tiempo" (152); (Understand me, Borges, this is not about consolation nor intellectual tricks filled with rivers and tigers nor is it a ruse. It is a matter of time. And we too, Borges, have a right to time, we have a right to multiply time). As Oropesa points out, the narrator, who symbolizes those victimized by the coup, engages in a battle over time (126). In Dorfman's story the struggle over time is a struggle for life and death. It is a struggle to see who will narrate the past, present, and future. It is a struggle over who will take charge of history and who will be overcome by it.

Written with the Chilean people as the intended audience, *Cría ojos* was censored in Chile. In 1986, Dorfman was finally able to publish a Chilean edition that included many of the same pieces with the title *Dorando la píldora* (Coating the Pill). In the preface, he underscores his original hopes for these texts: "Desde la lejanía, intenté recorrer las pesadillas de un país remoto, buscando quizás también el modo de compartirlas, de exorcizarlas, de traerlas a la luz del día, aunque era una luz irreconocible y extranjera" (11); (From far away, I tried to tour the nightmares of a remote country, looking perhaps also for the way to share them, to exorcize them, to bring them to the light of day, even if it were an unrecognizable foreign light). Similar to the poems of *Pruebas al canto*, these stories simultaneously inhabit the space of Chile and of exile. They emerge from the rupture of a divided and wounded nation. It is interesting to note, for instance, that the English translations of the poems and stories each use the word "fire" in their titles: *My House Is on Fire* and *In Case of Fire in a Foreign Land*. The use of "fire" suggests both a direct allusion to the apocalyptic space of hell caused by dictatorship and exile and the hopeful "fire" of ongoing struggle and commitment to social justice that characterized resistance to Pinochet's tyranny. The reference also recalls the writer's burning mission to use literature to raise social awareness even when such views are unwelcome.

The next three main texts that comprise Dorfman's exile writing are the novels *Viudas* (1981) (*Widows*), *La última canción de Manuel Sendero* (1983) (*The Last Song of Manuel Sendero*), and *Máscaras* (1988) (*Mascara*). Each of these confronts the consequences of the coup, the anguish of prolonged exile, and the role of art in political struggle. Dorfman's exile literature is marked by traditional themes—alienation, loss, nostalgia—in addition to the problems of belonging, nationalism, language, and identity. At the core of these themes lies the question of whether it is possible to create socially relevant art—a question that was undergoing revision simultaneous to Dorfman's exile. Dorfman's exile coincided with the rise of poststructuralism, with its attendant influence on the literary form, and postmodernism, with its radical suspicion of any systematic way of understanding the world. As I describe in *The Dialectics of Exile*,

> A number of key elements of postmodern theory are particularly compelling for exiled writers. For instance, postmodernism's critique of master-narratives relates to the exile's critique of authoritarian discourse. The privileging of the margins over the center, absence over presence, anarchy over hierarchy, open form over closed, difference over sameness, etc. found in postmodern theory's critique of modernity holds special meaning for the writer who has been forced into exile. These concepts go beyond metaphor and retain particularly painful weight for exiled writers. . . . We find, then, that exiled writers reflect many of the critical concerns associated with postmodern theory. Their historical condition as exiles from repressive dictatorships, though, marks this association as one driven by specific political needs and historical circumstances. (20)

Dorfman's literature in exile is neither freely deterritorial in some Derridean or Deleuze and Guattarian sense, nor is it purely nostalgic, dreaming of a seamless return and employing language as epic, romantic, or transparently realist. Rather it continues and expands upon the issues he explored in *Moros en la costa* regarding the social role of art. Once in exile, he becomes especially attentive to linguistic communication as both triumph and limit, and many of his exile texts directly consider the murky relationship between signifier and signified and between discursive authoritarianism and authorship. Exile furthers his concern about the contested ground of historical memory.

Furthermore, in continuation of the themes raised in Dorfman's exile poetry and short stories, these novels consider the family as a metaphor for society. In *Widows* all of the town's men have been disappeared, rupturing the families. Even though the military attempts to function as the town's surrogate fathers, the women refuse to obey them. In *The Last Song of Manuel Sendero* sons are separated from their fathers as a consequence of exile and tyranny, and in *Mascara* the unnamed protagonist has been completely discarded by his family. Each example suggests that social violence and despotism lead to ruptured families, and vice versa. As noted by Lois Baer Barr, Dorfman is especially interested in patriarchy, and his exile novels pay particular attention to the parallels between authoritarians and authors. How can the author present an alternative version of history without *dictating* to the audience?

The exile novels are also more preoccupied with the problem of evil. After witnessing the contagious corruption of the coup, Dorfman felt compelled to consider the element of evil and the capacity for cruelty that exists within all human beings. The coup and its bloody aftermath further convinced Dorfman that it was impossible to divide the world simply into victims and victimizers. He believed instead that the nightmare of the coup was possible only because the majority of Chileans (and also the world at large) had made Pinochet possible. He explains in *Exorcising Terror* that Pinochet is a mirror of Chile: not only did Pinochet not act alone, but many Chileans also made his rule possible through their silence and inaction (140–41). He considers a number of questions associated with the symbiosis between dictators and ethically bankrupt societies. How can one confront the sadistic pleasures of tyrants? What about those who closed their eyes to the disappearances and refused to hear the screams of torture? Where does evil come from and how can it be stopped? Is silence in the face of tragedy a crime? How can we struggle for justice if we are all guilty?

These themes converge in a concern over the problematic relationship between art and social struggle. For example, each of the texts from this period asks what role storytelling plays in resistance. How can one challenge the falsehoods of official history if we are all implicated to some extent in its perpetuation? Dorfman's attention to the ubiquitous presence of evil might be read in light of postmodern theory and specifically in terms of Foucault's notion of dispersed power. Foucault argues that "there is no binary and all-encompassing opposition between rulers and ruled at the root of power relations" (*History of Sexuality*, vol. 1, 94). Nevertheless, Dorfman departs from Foucault on the issue of resistance. In contrast to postmodernism's seemingly pessimistic position on the possibilities for rebellion, Dorfman, owing to his experience of collective struggle, disagrees with Foucault's argument that there is "no single locus of great Refusal, no soul of revolt, source of rebellions" (96). For Dorfman, acknowledging the capacity for evil within is the only way to build an even stronger collective opposition to tyranny. In his first two exile novels, he specifically explores the scope and limit of collective refusal, revolt, and rebellion. *Widows* ends with a community of women challenging the military, and *The Last Song of Manuel Sendero* mourns the loss of social collaboration experienced by a world ruled by fear. In *Mascara*, rebellion takes place in the realm of memory. The vulnerable Oriana, a perpetual amnesiac, collects the memories of the dead, but her fragile existence holds only minimal hope for the survival of these alternative histories. In these novels, Dorfman explores the role that art plays in the recovery of truth. He questions the relationship among discursive representation, historical event, personal identity, and collective struggle. For him, these issues turn on material, concrete questions of justice, responsibility, and social commitment. In a statement that illustrates his departure from poststructural theory, he writes: "The mind of humanity is not something mystical, a mere utopian illusion, but a battleground of ideas and emotions in constant dispute" (*Exorcising Terror*, 191).

Widows. Dorfman's first novel in exile, *Widows*, begins with the problem of authorship, authority, and the battle over who has the power to narrate history.[24] Because his work was censored during the time he wrote the novel, Dorfman tried to create a ruse whereby *Widows* could gain entrance into Chile. He created a fictitious author for the novel, Eric Lohmann, who purportedly was a Danish resistance fighter murdered in a concentration camp by the Nazis. Then he relocated the novel outside of South America to a small Greek town and set it during the Second World War. Decades later Eric Lohmann's son, Sirgud, supposedly finds the manuscript in a trunk and decides to publish it. This artifice was created in order to make it possible to present the novel as a translation into Spanish from the "original" Danish. The "translation" would be issued in Argentina by a publishing house that could distribute it in Chile. Despite all of Dorfman's efforts, the publishing house that had originally agreed to the project decided not to risk it. Rather than rewrite it without the ruses of author and context, Dorfman chose to publish the novel in Mexico under his own name but keeping the false frame.

Dorfman explains in the preface that after he no longer required the authorial, temporal, and geographic dislocation of the novel, he was reluctant to recast it into his own immediate context. The shift from his experience in Chile to that of a Danish author working during the Second World War had given the novel far greater resonance: "No era possible aludir a la circunstancia inmediata, fui explorando un lenguaje diferente que nadie debía reconocer, quise encontrar un público más vasto, e intenté una inevitable universalización" (8); ("By forcing myself to choose my words with caution, by forcing myself to witness such a traumatic and immediate experience from a distance . . . it seemed to me that I had managed to make the plight of the missing people into something more universal"; ii). The changed particulars of the story reinforce the common and persistent struggles at the novel's core, allowing the text to delve into the pernicious problem of repetitive historical cycles of violence. In addition, the multiple layers of authors and storytellers illustrate the conflict over who has the power to narrate history.

In a mirroring effect, the cyclical nature of history is emphasized when the preface by Dorfman mimics the preface by the fictitious son of the fictitious author. Sirgud Lohmann explains that his father had distanced the events of the novel from his own context much in the way that Dorfman explains his own writing process. Instead of using his own location, Eric Lohmann situates the novel in the town of Longa, which, along with the characters' names, appears to situate the novel in Greece, although it is never specifically named as such.[25] Even still, as the fictitious author's son explains in his preface, the details of the novel do not correspond exactly to Greek history. Instead, the author uses the location of Greece in order to create distance between his own context as a Jewish Dane during the Second World War and the events of the novel. According to the son:

> El país que él creó no es Grecia, sino que un lugar imaginario, equivalente de toda la Europa de su época. Escrita entre 1941 y 1942, la novela presagia lo que ha de ocurrir en su propio país, en Holanda, en Francia, en Italia, en Polonia en los años que sobrevendrán. . . . Y más aún, presiente, con una exactitud alucinante, lo que sigue sucediendo hoy, décadas más tarde, en tantas regiones del Tercer Mundo. (16)

> (The country he created is not Greece but an imaginary place equivalent to all Europe of the epoch. Written between 1941 and 1942, the novel presages what was to occur in his own country, in Holland, in France, in Italy, in Poland, in the years to come. . . . Beyond that, it prefigures what is still happening now, decades later, in so many Third World countries. [5])

The Greece imagined by Eric Lohmann doubles with his own context in the same way that it then doubles again with Dorfman's experiences in the Southern Cone, thereby creating an ahistorical spiraling of events that intersect and overlap. As Kim points out, "Dorfman denomina 'doble distanciamiento' la tendencia de incluir en sus novelas otros tiempos históricos y espacios geográficos que no se refieren al hemisferio de Hispanoamérica" (58); (Dorfman's "double distanciation" describes a tendency in his novels to include other historical times and geographic spaces that do not refer to the Spanish American hemisphere). The telling of this story is meant to change the future and stop the cycle of violence described in this Greek tragedy—understood in both the classical and modern sense—that has been repeated endlessly throughout human existence. Echoing Dorfman's own voice as a writer dedicated to socially relevant literature, Sirgud Lohmann explains that he has decided to publish the book because he hopes that "la publicación de este libro pueda contribuir, aunque fuera de una manera infinitesimal, para que lo que aquí se narra y pronostica nunca más tenga que acaecer" (16); ("this book may contribute, even in the smallest way, toward the prevention of what is told here ever happening again"; 5). Not only does Dorfman display his aesthetics of hope through his belief that telling difficult stories is essential to social justice, but also the doubling and mirroring of authors and stories emphasizes the necessary role of the active reader, who must work to recognize and challenge the connection between these stories and societies that are burdened by unequal relations of power.[26]

Despite the atemporal, repetitive nature of the novel's plot, *Widows* investigates many of the issues that were to plague the Southern Cone during the period of the Dirty Wars, and it performs an important recuperative gesture toward recovering local memory. One day, a dead body in an advanced state of decay appears in a river. Its face is totally unrecognizable. Shortly thereafter an old woman, Sofia, asks the captain in charge of the military base in Longa if she can bury the body since she is convinced that the body is that of her missing son. Thus the battle over who has the power to define the dead body begins. As in the case of the Argentine Mothers of la Plaza de Mayo and similar women's resistance movements in Chile and elsewhere, the women of the village, because of the profound absence of men, are forced to take charge. Using their roles as mothers, wives, and daughters, they argue that they must have the right to give their loved ones a Christian burial, while the authorities argue that the women cannot prove the identity of the dead men.

The novel turns on the issues of identity, memory, power, and loss. Its central conflict revolves around who has the right, and the authority, to explain the existence and identity of the first unidentifiable body and those that chillingly continue to appear. Dorfman had firsthand knowledge of similar atrocities in Chile and other parts of Latin America. As Jennifer Wallace explains, even though Dorfman's novel is set in Greece, "implicitly the exiled Dorfman is describing Chile under Pinochet" (106), and she points out, "Naming the men, showing that they are not merely bodies but had a history, constitutes a vital act of resistance to the indifferent military regime" (107). The power to choose a name for the dead is not merely a rhetorical game; it is a matter of life and death that allows Dorfman to illustrate the extreme connections between language and life. The women of the village challenge the authorities, but the captain and the military have more power. In the same way that they have erased the existence of the town's men, they threaten to erase any traces of the women's rebellion. They can even erase their very existence. That they are women provides only limited protection, as evidenced by the fact that the captain eventually orders the arrest of Sofía and her grandson, Alexis. His plan is to end the women's struggle by removing their leaders and all memory of what they said and did: "Y esta conversación jamás existió. La borro así. No va a quedar ni su recuerdo porque ustedes, ustedes no cuentan para nada. Para nada, ¿entiende? Mire a lo que han llevado sus esfuerzos. Mire. A esto. Mire" (190); ("And this conversation, this conversation never took place. I'm erasing it like that. Nobody's going to remember it. Because you people, you people don't count. You don't count, understand? Look at what your efforts have accomplished. Look at this. Look"; 136). The captain's words, inasmuch as they are represented in a novel that does record the women's rebellions, are revealed as vulnerable. They are not as vulnerable as the bodies that he and his men destroy, but they are still susceptible to attack. In the precise moment that the novel suggests that the women's refusal to be narrated by the military will end in tragedy, the narrative itself emerges as a tremendous voice of hope because, in fact, it is the voice that rescues the loss of Longa, which ultimately has the last word.

The complex and multiple voices that make up the novel are the best example of how it exemplifies an aesthetics of hope. In addition to the double, echoing prefaces, which suggest layers of authors writing texts under extreme contexts of authoritarian repression, the main plot is also told with a variety of shifting subject positions. These shifts, as I described in chapter 3, indicate Dorfman's interest in the relationship between language and the self. As seen in the poem "Simultaneous Translation" (analyzed above), where Dorfman breaks down the assumed distinctions between literary language and the language of denunciation and between objective and subjective versions of the truth, *Widows* similarly provides the reader with varied perspectives on the same event in order to expose the connections between language and power. The novel is narrated in a shifting narrative voice that strategically alternates among the first, second, and third persons. These shifting subject positions also ask the reader to constantly reassess the relationship between language and community, language and authority, and language and identity.

The first chapter sets the stage for the conflict in traditional third-person narration, and this voice dominates the majority of the novel. A number of key sections break from this pattern, and it is important that they all correspond to the younger generation: Emmanuel, the young orderly who works for the captain, and Fidelia and Alexis (the twin children of Dimitriou [Sofía's disappeared elder son] and Alejandra). The voices of this younger generation represent a far more nuanced and complex view of the events than that provided by their seniors. Sofía and the captain, for instance, are clear about their views on how to handle the dead bodies: the captain wants to deny their existence, and Sofía wants to claim the bodies as family members and bury them; each is intransigent. But the younger members of the town are not as certain as to how to proceed. Fidelia, Alexis, and their mother worry that if they follow Sofía's plan and claim these bodies as those of family members, it may be a death sentence to the men who could be living in prison. In contrast, Emmanuel represents the voice of the youth on the path to indoctrination by the military and the power elite (like Chico in "Putamadre"). He works for the captain now, but he had worked before for the town's wealthy landowner. Each of these characters faces major ethical decisions, which Dorfman presents as symbolic of the types of challenges that face the youth living in moments of historical crisis and conflict. More important, in the chapters that he dedicates to them, he uses an experimental and shifting narrative voice that illustrates the difficult decisions they must make regarding their role in society.

There are three major examples of the shifting narrative voice. The first correlates to three sections (4, 8, and 13) narrated in part in the collective "we." In sections 4 and 8 the "we" is identified as emanating from the perspective of Fidelia, whereas in section 13 the "we" alternates only with the third person. In each of these examples Dorfman oscillates between the first and the third person, a strategy that highlights the tensions between the personal voices of rebellion and the cold, "objective" voices of official history. The unusual style of the first example from section 4 is highlighted by its opening lines: "Algo tenía que pasar. Eso lo sabíamos todas, desde el día del funeral, desde que Fidelia le había visto la cara a su hermano dentro de los dos soldados y mamá me apretó más todavía las manos pero a él no le preguntó nada" (65); ("Something was going to happen. All the women knew that much, since the day of the funeral we had known it, since the day Fidelia had seen her brother's face between the two soldiers and Mama had squeezed her hand. Mama squeezed my hand even harder when they brought Alexis back, but she didn't ask my brother a thing"; 43). Employing a dizzying style, the opening lines switch from third person to first-person plural, and, assuming that Fidelia is the source of the narration, she refers to herself both in the third and first person, setting the tone for a chapter that investigates the cracks in the family's rebellion and Fidelia's doubts about her grandmother's plans. Even vaguer in the original Spanish, the style in these first sentences suggests the fragile subjectivities of the women, who worry that their efforts to recover the bodies will backfire and cause more death and loss. In one scene from the section, Alejandra confronts Sofía and questions her decision to challenge the military: " 'Nos estamos equivocando, abuela. . . . Usted se está equivocando.' Y pronunció la palabra abuela como se pronuncia la palabra suegra, la palabra vieja. Así" (68); (" 'We're killing our own men, Grandma. . . . You're killing them.' And she pronounced the word 'Grandma' as one pronounces the words 'old woman.' Like that"; 45).[27]

Alejandra's anger at Sofía undercuts the idea that the novel presents an idyllic and utopian collective where all of the women peacefully coalesce into one unified force of resistance.[28] The division among the women explains in part why the chapter has a number of narrative voices. In addition, because the chapter includes the first-person perspective of Fidelia, the shifting voice corresponds to her own growing assessment of her role in the collective. For the bulk of the chapter Fidelia is a passive observer of events. Like her brother, she is mainly guided by her elders. Near the end of the section, she literally finds her own voice when she asks her mother if she has learned anything about her father at the market. The novel narrates this coming into being as the merging of her voice with that of her absent father: "me sorprendió mi propia voz saliendo de adentro mío como un pájaro desprevenido. . . . me extrañó . . . que no se notara la presencia de papá como una piel que lo cubre todo, su ausencia, en mi voz" (77); ("my own voice surprised me flying out of my insides like a bird escaping. . . . It was strange that . . . no one could hear Papa's presence, Papa's absence, covering everything, beating in my voice"; 51). This example illustrates a sense of social agency, where individual identity attains its most meaningful and enriching existence through association with a collective.[29] In this case, it is Fidelia's merging of her voice with that of her father that allows her to intervene for the first time in the family's deliberations. She grows as an individual precisely in the moment when she actively participates as a member of a group.

Sections 8 and 13, which present the collective perspective of "we" to the reader, continue to illustrate central moments in the women's rebellion. In section 8, the narrative wavers between third and first person as the family prepares for the return of Sofía's younger son, Serguei, from detention. In this section the divisions of the family intensify when Sofía assumes that Serguei has been returned to the family because he signed a confession. She does not greet him or welcome him but instead accuses him of weakness and then leaves to go to the river to await the next body. The family is shocked at her coldness. Fidelia, again largely an observer, does not end this chapter with her voice but rather with her silence. She refuses to listen to her grandmother as she pronounces the imminent return of Fidelia's father's dead body. In a style very similar to section 4, the voice of Fidelia shifts, emphasizing her fragile identity. The youngest woman in the family, she continues to struggle with her sense of self and its relationship to her family. Then section 13, in which all of the women converge on the river to welcome the last body, begins with the first-person plural, continues in the third person, and concludes with a final collective sentence. While there are no personal markers to prove that the voice of the women corresponds to the voice of Fidelia, in all of the preceding examples she was the medium for the group, thereby suggesting that this last section may very well emanate from her perspective as well. It is most noteworthy in this last example that the collective "we" has a tone of confidence and unity that had previously been absent. The text no longer shifts between "I" and "we" because a collective voice has been found. Even more telling is that the novel's last sentence is that of the women, giving them the last word as it were: "Mientras el muerto se mecía entre nuestros brazos como un recién nacido" (202); ("While the body was rocked in our arms like a newborn child"; 146). If Fidelia's voice can be read as the conduit for that of the group, then the beauty and strength of the women coming together to embrace and welcome the lifeless body of the dead man hold considerable hope for the future.

The second example of Dorfman's unusual style occurs in section 9, which focuses on the orderly, Emmanuel. This style is evident in the scene when Emmanuel and his girlfriend, Cecilia, stop by the river. The section is in an odd form of third person because it has the characteristics of intimate first-person narration: "Era el río. El mismo. . . . Cuando se ha lavado todo la vida, desde que se tiene conciencia, cuando se ha descendido en busca de cabra descarriada, cuando se han iniciado los primeros juegos, cuando se tejen leyendas, ese río, ése, es inconfundible" (144–45); ("It was the river. The same one. . . . Since he'd washed in it all his life, as far back as he could remember, since he'd come down here in search of the stray nanny goat, since he'd played his first games, since the first tales were spun, that river, that one, it was unmistakable"; 101–2). Even though these lines are written in the third person, they reveal Emmanuel's inner thoughts. The style suggests that his allegiance to the power elite has caused him to be alienated from his own self. He has lost his ability to articulate his own identity and instead defers in most of the chapter to providing the captain with the information he seeks.

In this section the reader learns that Emmanuel betrayed his father to work for the influential landowner, Philip Kastoria. Now he works for the military. He exemplifies the next generation, who will continue to support the power elite. Dorfman does not romanticize youth, assuming that all of the young are innocent and full of hope. Instead, he contrasts Emmanuel with Fidelia and Alexis and shows that all three grapple with their role in the future. Unlike Fidelia, who strives to find her voice and to learn to speak with the other women, Emmanuel endeavors to merge his voice with that of those in power. In the section Emmanuel recounts to the captain his trip to deliver a message to Kastoria, and it is interspersed with elements from the trip that he does not reveal. Emmanuel excludes details that correspond to what he and Cecilia discuss and do since she has been allowed to accompany him on the excursion. Nevertheless, even though the unspoken moments hint at his own doubts about his future, the narrative voice never wavers from presenting his thoughts in a distant and alienating third person. The reader learns that he does not want his children born in Longa, a sign that he may recognize that the town lives under constant threat. Moreover, the reader knows that he does not reveal to the captain everything that happened on the trip because he neglects to mention that he and Cecilia thought that they had discovered yet another dead body. Nevertheless, the chapter holds little hope that Emmanuel will develop his own voice and assert his own identity. Like Lucho from "En familia," he is selfish and incapable of incorporating himself into the larger social fabric. He believes that he is serving the military because he has no other options and because he is convinced that the resistance suggested by his father is futile and suicidal.

The last example of a shifting narrative voice appears in section 11. Corresponding to the third member of the novel's youth, Alexis, it provides a third perspective on the role of the self in society. Fidelia finds her own voice and then actively merges with the women's resistance, Emmanuel remains alienated and isolated. Alexis exemplifies the heroic voice of rebellion. This section, which recounts the incarceration of Sofía and Alexis, is narrated in the first, second, and third persons. The section also utilizes another common Dorfman strategy: shifting verb tenses. Both strategies are established in the opening lines: "Antes de que le sacaran el capuchón, bastante antes de eso, Alexis ya sabe dónde se encuentra, recordó este lugar. Conoces esas escaleras donde uno se tropieza, este aire húmedo y con olor a excremento, el sonido áspero de los pasos por este corredor interminable de piedras" (171); ("Before they take the hood off, well before that, Alexis already knows where he is, he remembered this place. You know those stairs where you stumble, this damp air that smells of shit, the harsh sound of footsteps along this endless stone corridor"; 123). Emphasizing the fact that Alexis has already been in this horrific jail, the verbs shift from the present to the past. These temporal slips also signify that history repeats itself. Just as Dorfman's writing process mirrors that of Eric Lohmann, Alexis must listen, as have countless other political detainees, for the harsh footsteps of his torturers as they approach his cell. Dorfman uses the echoing sound of footsteps throughout the section as a metaphor for historical repetition. In order to stop this cycle of violence, Dorfman merges Alexis with the reader, using the second person.

The section uses different indentation to signify communication between Alexis and his grandmother, Sofía. Sofía bargains with the captain to have a few final hours with Alexis before what is certain to be her execution. Sofía recognizes in those brief moments that Alexis represents the next generation of the Angelos family and that it will be up to him and Fidelia to lead the family's resistance in the future. She asks his opinion about how she handled the rebellion, and like his sister, he criticizes her decision to assume that his father was one of the dead bodies found. Then she tells him a secret that will help him survive. She tells him that in the worst moments he needs to focus on one person that he loves and that the presence of love and joy will help him find a way back home. As the jailers pull his grandmother out of the cell where she and Alexis have been talking, the rebellion's leadership transfers to Alexis. Her fingertips cease to touch him, and he begins to transform. "La abuela ya no te está tocando" (190); ("Grandma's not touching you now"; 136). Here the use of the second person again seeks to draw a bond between the reader and Alexis precisely in the moment of Alexis's epiphany. When Sofía leaves the cell, Alexis suddenly recognizes her wisdom, and the reader appreciates the symbolism of her name. She will surely die, as have many of the Angelos family, but the rebellion will never end. Not only will Alexis tell the story of his grandmother to his children, but he will also find a way to rebel against the tyrannical forces that threaten his family's survival. When he assumes his new identity as an active force of resistance, the first person appears for the first and only time in the chapter. After his grandmother has been taken away, Alexis experiences increasing confidence and self-assuredness. He nods his head at Sofía in a parting gesture, even though he knows that she can't see him. And rather than be blindly guided by the soldiers, he moves decisively with "voluntad" (192); ("free will"; 137). Instead of conceding that he is going to the capital to be taken to prison, he converts his imprisonment into a quest to find his father: "Me iba a la capital a encontrar a mi papa" (192); ("I was going to the capital to find my father"; 137). After the shifts between the third and second person, the first-person voice of Alexis now asserts its individual identity and serves as a model for rebellion and heroism.

The voices of Alexis, Fidelia, and Emmanuel combine to present readers with varied responses to life under dictatorship. Dorfman's first exile novel asks readers to recognize the extraordinary strength of the members of the Angelos family. Despite their vulnerability, they refuse to succumb to tyranny because to do so would be to live a lifeless life, to become like "them," to be "huecos" (189); ("empty"; 135). Written literally far away from Chile, *Widows* is a story of extraordinary will and rebellion that attempts to capture the spirit of the Chilean resistance.

The Last Song of Manuel Sendero. Dorfman's second novel in exile, *The Last Song of Manuel Sendero*, is significantly more complex than *Widows* and re-mains Dorfman's most ambitious novel to date.[30] In addition to its complex structure, it also has an extremely wide range of narrative concerns.[31] The novel can be read as a sequel to *Moros en la costa*, which has a similarly dense style and is equally concerned with how storytelling and art can affect social life. Whereas the first novel was a meditation on the relationship between art and revolution, *The Last Song* depicts a society living under dictatorship and wonders about the role of art in resistance.

The novel is not a linear narrative but rather a series of six narrative lines that intertwine and circle one another. The major plot lines share overlapping themes and are divided into two categories, which correspond to "Adentro" (Inside) and "Afuera" (Outside), sections that alternate in the first three of the five parts of the novel. Two of the narrative lines appear in the parts that correspond to "Adentro": (1) the story of Manuel Sendero (a legendary singer committed to social activism), his pregnant wife (Doralisa), and the rebellion staged by fetuses who refuse to be born until the adults rid the world of tyranny; and (2) the story of Manuel Sendero's son, who returns to his native land to lead the second fetal rebellion and confront his father's tormentor, the Caballero. "Afuera" includes the remaining four narrative lines: (1) the dia-logue between the Chilean exiles David and Felipe, who meet in Mexico City on New Year's Eve to work on a comic strip project along with another fellow exile, Paula; (2) the story of the comic strip, which narrates the adventures of Carl and Sarah Barks, who travel to a dystopian country, Chilex, where Carl (a famous cartoonist for Disney) has been asked to help develop the image of the ideal man for the nation's repressive government and where Sarah has been promised the possibility of finally becoming pregnant at the age of eighty; (3) a series of critical footnotes from scholars analyzing the dialogue between David and Felipe thirty thousand years later; and (4) the legend of David and the Dragon Pinchot, also told far in the future. Each of the narrative lines relates in some way to the notion of exile, internal or national, and each comments on the problems of being socially outcast. They also all engage the problems of trust, social commitment, and the tensions between seeking personal gain and being loyal to collective struggle—problems that are highly difficult to solve because in the repressive world of the novel there is no absolute division between good and evil, between the innocent and the guilty.

In addition to the two categories with six plot lines, the novel has what Barr calls a "gestational structure" that relates to the stages of pregnancy (142). She notes that the five parts of the novel correspond to the five stages of pregnancy and delivery: inception ("Encarnaciones"; "Incarnations"); three trimesters ("Maduraciones"; "Maturations"); labor pains ("Dolores"; "Pangs"); the passage through the birth canal ("Pasajes"; "Passages"); and birth ("Alumbramientos"; "Bearings").[32] Given that *The Last Song* narrates frustrated reproduction, the use of a birth metaphor to structure the novel serves to further complicate an interpretation of the text. At one level the structure suggests that the process of writing the novel is similar to the act of giving birth.[33] In addition, the novel likens the development of social struggle to that of childbirth. The birth of a just society, Dorfman suggests, requires similar acts of love, patience, strength, and courage to that of giving birth. This connection is highlighted by Dorfman's choice of the novel's epigraphs. The first, from César Vallejo, reads: "Pues de resultas / del dolor, hay algunos / que nacen, otros crecen, otros mueren, / y otros que nacen y no mueren, y otros / que no nacen ni mueren (son los más)"; ("Well, as a result / of pain, there are some / who are born, others grow, still others die, / and there are others who are born and do not die, and others / who are not born nor do they die [they are the majority]"). The second, from Hermann Hesse, adds to Vallejo: "El que quiere nacer, tiene que romper un mundo"; ("He who would be born must break a world"). Vallejo plays on the word "dolor," which can mean labor pain but here also means the pain of revolution as well as the pain of tyranny. Vallejo suggests that the majority of people never live life fully because they are trapped in a painful world that represses them. Similarly Hesse argues that in order to really live one must be prepared to vigorously struggle to break down unjust social structures.

Taking guidance from these two quotes, Dorfman correspondingly links social struggle to the painful process of birth, but because of his experiences, he also narrates the reverse circumstances that take place in a society that has turned away from popular participation and toward authoritarianism. As I noted in *The Dialectics of Exile*, Dorfman creates a dialectic vision of the family, which functions as both a positive model for building a collective and a negative example of the root sources of authoritarian behavior (180–81). Similarly, the novel's representation of sexual reproduction is ambivalent. On the one hand, it mirrors that of a society that is on the verge of extinction: David's girlfriend, Gringa, gets an abortion; David gets a vasectomy; his son probably commits suicide; Sarah Barks is infertile; it is suggested that the son of Sendero was aborted; and the fetuses refuse to be born in two massive rebellions. On the other hand, the female body, and the womb in particular, are depicted as utopian places of sanctuary and refuge, and the children born from it are a source of hope. Consequently, even though Dorfman structures the novel as though it were a birth, his experience of exile and dictatorship indicates that the type of collective regeneration experienced by Chileans under Allende is not a "natural" process but rather one that requires extraordinary effort. He suggests that the birth of a new society as a result of revolutionary struggle suffers constant threat from those that would abort it or those that would make its leaders politically sterile.

The effort to radically change social power structures depends, according to the novel, on finding a way to motivate people to struggle for hope, and such struggle relies on cultural stimulus. Similar to *Moros en la costa*, *The Last Song* combines Dorfman's critique of the media culture's infantilization of the public with his commitment to producing complex literature that requires the reader's active participation. Dorfman has consistently maintained in his essays and fiction that there are stories that inspire and there are stories that numb, and *The Last Song* pits these two discourses against one another. Therefore, in addition to linking childbirth with revolution, the novel connects reproduction to the writer's craft. The classic literary metaphor of linking storytelling and human reproduction, though, is frustrated by Dorfman since, even though the writer has been able to produce a novel, the novel itself implies that what has been produced has only a very tentative chance of survival. Or, to push the birth metaphor, Dorfman may have produced a "son," but he may be stillborn. This fragile view of the future of the novel is apparent in the novel's series of father-son relationships, all of which are seriously damaged. Kim has noticed that this tentative future is reinforced by the use of the future perfect and is thus predicated on hypothetical possibility (77).

At the center of the novel are some of Dorfman's major obsessions: What role do stories play in shaping collective memory, inspiring resistance to oppression, and rescuing human dignity? What happens when heroes and villains are no longer abstract but real and concrete? Dorfman explores these questions via a broad spectrum of cultural discourse: myth, legend, fairy tale, comic strip, academic writing, narrative, media culture, folklore, gossip, confession, and more. In an essay that predated the release of the novel by one year, Dorfman, writing under the pseudonym P. Donald, provided readers with the author's own "book review" and offered clues to interpreting the novel:[34] "In his newest novel, Ariel Dorfman continues to examine the subjects that have obsessed him in his previous fiction and poetry, but more than that, it seems to be an illustration, as well as a tentative exploration, of certain themes of Latin American culture that he has been expounding recently in essays, articles and interviews: the idea that the major challenge that literature in Latin America must face today is the unpeaceful coexistence of three main strands of cultural traditions which give that continent its fragmented, distorted, glorious flavor" (19).

The three cultural strands to which the "review" refers are the art of literature, the mass-media culture, and the popular counterculture. Dorfman/P. Donald considers the first strand to be minor but influential, and he reminds us that it is this elite form, which caters to only a small sector of the population, that the author has chosen as the vehicle for his message. The mass-media culture, in contrast, exerts tremendous social influence even though it is largely imported from abroad. The third strand represents forms of cultural resistance that have allowed populations to weave stories of rebellion and hope for centuries in Latin America. The novel forces these "trilateral trends" into intense conflict, creating a "laboratory test of literature" that attempts to "break down the barriers which artificially divide the popular, the pop, and the elite, or realism, myth, and mass media" (22–23).

Along with the multiple discursive registers, the novel reveals an intricate array of cultural influences, which range from Greek tragedy to the Bible, from Julio Cortázar's *Rayuela* (*Hopscotch*) to Günter Grass's *The Tin Drum*. It references folk culture through the likenesses between Manuel Sendero and Víctor Jara.[35] It also intexts with media culture, most notably through the comic strip character Carl Barks, based on a Disney cartoonist, but also through the TV program *Busca, Busca* (Search, Search), on which the son of Sendero appears hoping to bait the evil Caballero. The program parodies Hollywood shows like *Queen for a Day* or *The Millionaire* from the 1950s, when television game shows and "reality" programs first began to hit mass audiences, distracting viewers from their problems by immersing them in the difficult stories of others, whose lives were quickly and easily transformed by the acquisition of material goods. It is also likely that *Busca, Busca* parodies the Chilean variety show *Sábado Gigante* (Giant Saturday), especially via *Busca, Busca*'s emcee, who may remind readers of *Sábado Gigante*'s legendary Don Francisco.

Clearly Dorfman places his greatest hope in popular counterculture, which is why the main focus of the novel is the story of Manuel Sendero. Manuel, a popular folk singer, loses his voice after he is jailed by a repressive military government. When he is released after two and a half years, he returns home to find that his wife remains pregnant with his son and that his son has organized a rebellion and refuses to be born until the adults make society safe for the defenseless. Manuel is faced with a dilemma: should he sing? On the one hand, his song might help motivate social change, allowing his son to be born. On the other hand, the Caballero, the military leader who represents absolute power, is threatening to abort his son if he doesn't sing, and Manuel worries that his song might be used by the government to pacify the public.

The reader never learns with any certainty what Manuel decides to do, and his story is narrated years into the future by his descendants. Similar to the different legends about the deaths of Víctor Jara and Salvador Allende, the facts about Manuel's song are fuzzy, allowing his story to be adapted according to the narrator and audience. Indicating Dorfman's concern for the future of such tales, Manuel's legendary history is mixed with that of his son, who may or may not be alive and who never receives a name. When the son returns to help with a second fetal rebellion, he finds various competing versions of his father's story. For instance, the Caballero tries to project his own version of the story of Manuel, one where he doesn't sing and his son is never born (322, 409). Pamela, the woman that Manuel's son loves, remembers Manuel differently, and she repeats his story to give her comfort and strength: "Pamela había repetido esa leyenda como culaquier otro niño, para darse fuerzas cuando las cosas andaban mal y nadie le comprendía" (343); ("Pamela had repeated that legend like any other child, to give her strength when things were going badly and nobody understood her"; 435). So even though this narrative line represents the rebellious spirit of popular counterculture, it does not provide an easy solution.

Parallel to the tale of Manuel and his son, the novel presents another discursive register, which corresponds to concrete history and novelistic narrative; in it two Chilean friends, David and Felipe, debate about how to handle Pinochet's dictatorship and the experience of exile. Dorfman/P. Donald describes their dilemmas as a sort of "echo to the problems that Manuel Sendero is dealing with in the legendary realm" (21). David is a writer and Felipe is an economist, and they characterize two opposing personalities. Felipe has invited David to Mexico in order to collaborate with him on a comic strip that will be published by a journal he manages, and they dialogue during a traffic jam in Mexico City on New Year's Eve. Felipe represents Chilean exiles who remain true to the party line and firm in their convictions. Like Eduardo, from the narrative line that corresponds to Manuel Sendero, Felipe does not question the past, and he has little patience for David's emotional messiness. Felipe remains a member of the party and has made a number of clandestine trips to Chile to aid the resistance. David, in contrast, after being told that he was a danger to the resistance and needed to go into exile, has been forced out of the party. Madly in love with Chile, David was unable to remain true to the exiles' boycott of Chilean products, and he has also granted an interview with a conservative Chilean newspaper in an effort to lift his exile. His love makes him reckless and unreliable, whereas Felipe's cold, calculating presence saps the joy from social struggle. The novel asks whether it is possible to combine the best of David and Felipe or whether any political struggle will have to learn to reconcile these two tendencies.

In addition to the Felipe-David "dialogue" as a discursive counterpoint to the legend of Manuel Sendero, one of the main themes of this section is the power of cultural representation. Similar to the question of whether or not Manuel Sendero sang, this narrative line recognizes that the power to narrate the past and to connect with an audience is an essential political tool that affects the future. Barr notes that "David's story is a deprecating and somewhat ironic view of the power of art to defeat a dictatorship" (144). In combination with David's fictional work, like that of the comic strip, his letters and journalism have been influential in gaining the release of prisoners, like Felipe. These minor efforts have made a big difference, and they reveal the power of the written word. In contrast, though, the comic strip, which is intended as a satirical criticism of Pinochet, suggests the limits of counter-discourse. Felipe, ever the skeptic and pragmatist, listens to David's description of the comic strip and critiques it. He thinks it is too complicated and that no one will understand all of the references, especially not a Mexican audience, but most of all he doubts the power of art as a form of resistance. "Yo no sé si sacarle la cresta a ellos en una historieta no será finalmente una confesión de impotencia. Ellos nos cagan en la historia. Nosotros los cagamos a ellos en la historieta" (184); ("I don't know if poking fun at the rulers in the comic strip isn't the ultimate confession of our own impotence. They shit on us in history. We shit on them in a comic strip"; 231–32). Felipe's word play between "historia" (history) and "historieta" (comic strip) is lost in the English translation, but

Felipe's question is whether a comic strip can play a role in historical struggle. Pinochet's critics poke fun at him while he murders his critics. How can art ever compete with brute violence as a form of social influence?

The answer to this question comes in part via the comic strip itself, which narrates the story of Chilex, which, as noted, has hired a retired Disney cartoonist, Carl Barks, to fashion the ideal man. The goal is to create a man who has the urge to work but not to work for rights. Everything that the exiles know about Pinochet's Chile is magnified into the exaggerated realm of cartoons. David's vision inverts the mind-numbing cartoons created by Disney by satirizing the process of creating a mass-media culture designed to pacify the public into accepting life in a hyper-capitalist authoritarian society. Emphasizing the propagandistic role of the mass media, he depicts the collaboration between pop culture and consumer society in supporting authoritarianism and capitalism. But according to Felipe, this strategy of challenging Pinochet is doomed to fail. "Este tipo de sátiras está muy encima de los hechos inmediatos. Se leen un día y al otro se olvidan" (215); ("This kind of satire is too topical. You read them one day and forget them the next"; 272). But Felipe misses the point. As the comic strip makes clear, culture is powerful, but it is not all equally powerful. The pop culture of the mass media, like that created by Carl Barks, depicts worlds where problems are easily solved by purchasing goods, where individual gain trumps collective community building, and where every story has a happy ending. Such stories minimize the possibilities of civic engagement, and they exert great social power. The comic strip stories are so easily "forgotten" not because they are too "topical," but rather because such stories have to compete with those of media culture to attract the public's attention.

Dorfman makes this point in a different section of the novel when the son of Sendero appears on the television program *Search, Search*. The son asks why what is seen on television holds so much more power than that of a human being. Later, as he recounts his tale to his grandchildren, he laments that they believe what they see on television more than they believe what he tells them. His grandchildren believe that it is possible to take a pill that will allow one to lose weight the more one eats, but they don't believe that it is impossible to silence the dead, that the dead send back words to inspire and comfort the living. "A mí no me creen, está bien, gruñía, pero al animador ese le creían todo" (238); ("Me you don't believe. OK, he would growl. But you believed everything that damned emcee said"; 299). This power of media culture to affect the public's imagination is taken to great extremes in David's comic strip, where Carl Barks is expected to create a way to colonize the minds of all the people of Chilex so that they lose their will to struggle.

In a certain sense the comic strip and the legend of Manuel Sendero are twin cultural responses to life under extreme authoritarianism. By presenting both of these views, Dorfman contrasts two types of counterculture: that of the intellectual elite and that of the "people." But unclear about its trajectory of storytelling and the various ways that events are narrated, the novel creates a chorus of heteroglossic voices that recount competing versions of events. For these reasons, Mikhail Bakhtin's notions of the "dialogic imagination" and "dialogized heteroglossia" apply to *The Last Song*. Bakhtin explains that "no living word relates to an object in a singular way: between the word and its object, between the word and the speaking subject, there exists an elastic environment of other, alien words about the same object, the same theme, and this is an environment that it is often difficult to penetrate" (276). Each important historical moment holds within it a panoply of representative potential. According to Bakhtin, though, this signifying elasticity places great stress on the language of the novel since to a certain extent the novel creates the words that will be available to the future: "The word in living conversation is directly, blatantly, oriented toward a future answer-word: it provokes an answer, anticipates it and structures itself in the answer's direction" (280). Rather than script this future, Dorfman chooses to narrate the process, hoping, at some level, that the novel will serve to reveal the extraordinarily complex ways that counter-discourse and hegemonic discourse are generated. Most important, he shows that these two modes are not mutually exclusive, as evidenced by Felipe's efforts to censor/edit David's ideas so that they conform more closely to Felipe's idea of political satire.

The counter-discourse of the people is also varied and fluid, as indicated by the multiple versions of Manuel's story. In addition to the Caballero's efforts to present his own version of Manuel's past, those that make up the resistance have a variety of views. Dorfman explores this point when the son of Sendero meets his father's friend, Flaquísimo (Skinny) and tries to use his version of his father's story as a way to enlist Flaquísimo's help. But Flaquísimo doesn't believe him: "La gente inventa muchas cosas, especialmente cuando se trata de Manuel Sendero" (25); ("People make up a lot, especially about Manuel Sendero"; 20). The multiple versions of Manuel's last song have concrete consequences, and the battle over which version will have the most representative power is intense, especially for the son of Sendero, who stands to be obliterated by the versions that disallow his own birth. According to Flaquísimo, Manuel never sang and his son was never born. Of course such a version conflicts with that of the son of Sendero, who, years into the future, when he has become a grandfather, narrates his experiences to his grandchildren. The essential question the son of Sendero asks his grandchildren to ponder is not why Manuel's last song has multiple variations but how to convince people like Flaquísimo that their version is lacking because it denies the inspirational power of stories of hope. The son of Sendero asks his grandchildren: "¿Cómo convencerlo? ¿Cómo convencerlo de la saciedad de mis testigos? Cómo traer ante él a papá que me lo había transmitido con sus manos en el vientre sur de Doralisa esa misma noche? ¿Cómo llenar su casa de las voces aquéllas que Manuel oyó, y que eran nuestras?" (26); ("How could I convince him? How could I march all my witnesses in front of his itchy eyes? How could I conjure up Papa, who had told me the whole thing with his hands resting on Doralisa's southern belly that same night? How could I fill his house with the voices Manuel heard, our voices?"; 21).

How these stories will be told in the future is one of the main preoccupations of the novel, and it explains why three narrative lines take place in the distant future: the narrative of the son of Sendero, who tells his story to his grandchildren; the legend of David and the Dragon Pinchot, which is also told to children in the future; and a series of scholarly footnotes that comment on the dialogue of David and Felipe thirty thousand years later. The last two narrative lines represent two different cultural responses to the same events since they both represent interpretations of the dialogue between David and Felipe. Dorfman complicates our understanding of these different interpretations even further when the reader learns that the dialogue of David and Felipe is not an exchange between "real" Chilean exiles but that instead the two characters are from a Mexican soap opera. To an extreme extent, every important event in the novel is told in various ways, from various perspectives, and according to different cultural registers. The reader's efforts to determine what happened to Manuel, to his son, to David, and to David's son, for instance, are constantly thwarted. Eventually the novel attempts to force the reader to stop searching for answers and to begin paying attention to the process of cultural production, or at least to mix the need to know how the story ends with attention to how stories are created, transmitted, and adapted.

The best example of this attempt is found in the four epilogues, all of which focus on the process of cultural production by asking how stories circulate into the future, what role the dead play in the minds of the living, and how the past, present, and future coexist. The first three epilogues represent five of the narrative lines. The first narrates the end of the comic strip, when Carl Barks dies or, to be more precise, stops living. The second blends the legend of the Dragon Pinchot and David with the end of the dialogue between David and Felipe. The third recounts yet another rendition of Manuel's last song, interspersed with the story of the son of Sendero's death and Pamela's possible pregnancy with his child. The fourth, which is entitled the "epílogo último y primer prólogo" (last epilogue and first prologue), returns to the narrative lines of Manuel Sendero and his son. The layering of these four epilogues points to Dorfman's interest in suggesting that Latin America has three main divergent cultural registers—pop culture, the popular, and the elite—which coexist in constant interplay.

The use of four epilogues points in obvious ways to Dorfman's desire to leave the novel's ending open, and as mentioned in chapter 3, complex structures and doubles are a key component of Dorfman's aesthetic strategy. Even the last lines of the last epilogue are written in the future tense, a technique that allows Dorfman to underscore his belief that Latin American history is caught in a cycle that will end only when the future represents a genuine beginning and not simply a variation of the past. In addition to the open ending created via the four epilogues, each epilogue is open-ended, thereby eluding any totalizing interpretation or final summary. All of the lines, moreover, investigate death and its impact on the future. In the first epilogue, Carl Barks is on his deathbed. He wants to confess to his wife that he has had a child by another woman, and he wants to die in peace. But the officials in Chilex do not want him to die. They want to put his brain on life support so that they can use his mind to control the public. In the last moments of his life, they explain that they do not want him to join the dead because the dead are involved in organizing an uprising: "desde la tumba joden, infectos, corrompidos, virulentos, hirviendo de actividad siglos más tarde, sin darse por vencidos. Susurrando rebellion en los oídos de los enterrados anteriores" (332); ("from the tomb they screw everything up, all of them, infectious, corrupt, virulent, still crawling with activity even centuries later, never giving up. Whispering rebellion to everyone who preceded them into the grave"; 421). The Chilex authorities clearly worry that if Carl decides to repent for his past and joins the uprising, he might use his considerable power as a storyteller to help the dead inspire the living.

The power of the dead to inspire the living is also a central theme in the next two epilogues. In the second, David learns that his son is hurt, probably dead, at the same time that a group of children hears the legend of David and the Dragon Pinchot. As the children's father recounts the legend, he refuses to end the story, telling the children that if they want a happy ending, they will have to send air from the future back to help David in his battle. In the third epilogue, Pamela asks to hear the story of Manuel Sendero one more time, and, as always, the facts of the story remain blurry. As the section ends, her own story becomes unclear since her life seems to mirror or blend into that of Doralisa. The reader further gets conflicting information that suggests, on the one hand, that the women are shot to death or, on the other hand, that they give birth. Logically it would seem that these versions are contradictory, but in fact Dorfman portrays a world where death is a form of giving birth. In the last epilogue, Eduardo is left to care for Manuel's descendants because their parents are dead. In each case, death leads to life, and those who have been silenced and disappeared return to whisper, sing, and comfort the living. Underscoring the etymological roots of the term "epilogue," each epilogue adds another layer of language, each ending is a beginning, and each death affects the future.

Mascara. While *The Last Song* displays far greater doubt and despair than *Widows*, Dorfman's third novel in exile, *Mascara*, is the most dystopian of the three.[36] The questions Dorfman raises in *The Last Song* about the possibility of narrating in a way that can counteract oppression, authoritarianism, and imperialism now take an even darker turn. In the acknowledgments that appear in the English version Dorfman describes *Mascara* as a novel of "deception and betrayal" (iii). The increased pessimism of the novel may be a result of Dorfman's prolonged exile since by the time *Mascara* appeared in print, he had been in exile for fifteen years and Pinochet's rule seemed interminable. It is important to recall, however, that the novel appeared at a crucial turning point in Chilean politics. The novel was released in Spanish via the Argentine publishing house Editorial Sudamericana in May 1988, the same year that a vote was scheduled (in October) to allow the Chilean people to decide whether Pinochet should continue as head of state. Rather than use the novel as a revolutionary rallying cry, Dorfman wrote a text that described what could happen if Pinochet won. Instead of emphasizing the beauty and strength that comes from solidarity, *Mascara* is populated by arrogant, selfish, narcissistic, and sadistic characters. Even though Dorfman has stated that he does not consider the work to be overtly political, *Mascara* takes a highly critical, and consequently political, view of societies ruled by extreme hierarchies.[37] Its world is governed by those who sadistically wield power over others, and even the characters who resist the dominant order lack passion and loyalty, with the notable exception of the childlike Oriana. In contrast to *The Last Song*, the novel does not compare competing world views; instead it delves deeply into human psychology and asks what motivates human beings to inflict pain and suffering on others. The sheer pleasure with which characters force others to submit to their will is testimony to the novel's intense curiosity about the ways that human beings participate in the abuse of others.

In *Mascara* Dorfman continues to work on many of the themes that were present in *The Last Song*, but these themes take on a far more intimate and less epic scope. For instance, *Mascara* also struggles with the problem of how stories survive and how history is recorded, and the novel structures these issues according to trilateral cultural trends that parallel those in *The Last Song*, but in *Mascara* these trilateral trends are represented by the inner thoughts and obsessions of the three main characters. The novel is divided into three sections, each of which has a different narrator and each of which represents a different segment of society, a different way of seeing the world, and a different vision for the future. The first section is told from the perspective of an unnamed narrator who has a face no one remembers and who has the uncanny ability to capture the most awful truths about people on film. These two characteristics combine to give him significant power since he is able to photograph people unawares and then use those photographs to take advantage of his subjects. Egotistical and politically apathetic, for some years he has been taking photographs for the state with no real interest in the consequences. It has never occurred to him to ask why certain people are targeted. "Algo habrían hecho, supuse, aquellos hombres, esas mujeres, para que los buscaran" (96); ("They must have done something, I supposed, those men, those women, if the police were after them"; 92). The son of a television makeup artist and a medical supply salesman, the faceless man has been abandoned by his family and is socially outcast. He has no history and no place in society.

The second section is also told from the perspective of a social outcast, Oriana, but her story is vastly different from that of the faceless man. At the age of four, Oriana witnessed her father's murder at the hands of the secret police, who then raped her. From that point on she suffers extreme psychological distress, and part of her is incapable of growing up. She lives divided between her body, which continues to age, and her inner self, which remains stuck in the moment before she lost her innocence. This need to stay innocent means that each day she awakens anew with no memory of the day before. She has constant, recurring amnesia (technically anterograde amnesia), which does not allow short-term memory to become long-term memory. Similar to the protagonist from the movie *Memento*, she builds no new lasting memories from the moment when she experienced extreme trauma. In a parallel to the fetuses that refuse to be born in *The Last Song*, this innocent girl rejects the evil society created by adults. She lives in an alternate reality, roaming the city in advance of the secret police, helping those persecuted by them to die in peace rather than agony. The secret police want to harvest the hands of the dead so that they can bleach them white and recycle them, thereby annihilating their history and memory, but Oriana arrives first and takes the hands for herself, preserving their memories and leaving the dead with a smile on their faces. Consequently, like the faceless man, she is also a character that comprises two extremes. On the one hand, she has no memory and no history, but on the other hand, she protects the memories and histories of others. The faceless man is unrecognizable to others but has an uncanny ability to remember and record faces. Both characters have a highly tenuous connection with society, but Oriana records the beautiful memories of the dying while the faceless man captures the ugliness of the living. As J. M. Coetzee explains in an afterword to a recent edition of the novel, "He has no identity, she has no past. They are like twins" (133).

One day a woman knocks on the faceless man's door and asks if he can give Oriana refuge for the night since the police are after her. He reluctantly agrees. One night turns into many, and the faceless man realizes that Oriana will allow him to play out any fantasy he wants. Each day he tells her to be his lover, his sister, his mother, etc., and she willingly complies. Angry at society, the faceless man uses Oriana to satisfy his need to dominate others. But there is one problem. At times the adult Oriana seems to hint at her existence, and the faceless man desperately wants to preserve the childlike Oriana forever. He fears that the adult Oriana would not be a willing participant in his fantasies. To secure his future and that of Oriana he needs to destroy Oriana's adult self. He looks for a photo of her in the state archives, but his access has been blocked by the evil Doctor Mavirelli, a plastic surgeon who helps the powerful stay powerful by transforming their faces.[38]

Doctor Mavirelli helps the authoritarian state stay in power. Like the doctors from *The Last Song*, he practices medicine that does not help his patients; rather, it ensures that they will conform to the system, that they will not resist, and that they will believe that the government protects them. He can put the face of a dying politician onto a young body, or he can take a politician whose face reveals his authoritarian tendencies and change him so that he looks benevolent and kind. The faceless man knows of the doctor because Alicia, an unattractive political militant who spent a week with the faceless man as his lover, had been exposed to the police by the doctor when she went to him for surgery. After the faceless man has a traffic accident with the doctor, he decides to try to sue him, use the press to bring him public shame, and get revenge for Alicia, but the doctor seems to always be one step ahead of him. The faceless man knows that the doctor is able to change people's faces because he has observed his surgeries. He has also observed the doctor putting a strange device into the faces of his patients that helps him control them after the surgery is complete. Now the doctor has been caught on film, and the faceless man wants to exchange the photo for the doctor's help with Oriana. He has abandoned his quest for revenge and simply wants the doctor to help him fulfill his dream of an eternally childlike Oriana. Doctor Mavirelli agrees to meet the faceless man because he too wants something: he wants to steal the faceless man's chameleon-like appearance because anonymity would give him even more power. In fact, he explains to the faceless man that he has been waiting for this day since he first saw the faceless man as a newborn and recognized his uncanny abilities. But Doctor Mavirelli needed the baby to grow into a man before he could harvest his skin.

The third section ends with the doctor referring to the faceless man as his "son," and the two men seem poised for a literal "face-off." In the "sort of epilogue," the men confront each other and Oriana flees. Afterwards one man with an unrecognizable face leaves the operating room. Is it the doctor or the faceless man? It is likely that it is the doctor since the man who leaves no longer limps the way the faceless man did. To add to the confusion, the dead man, whose body is now missing, died with a smile on his face. In a typical Dorfman move, the epilogue is not an ending, and the reader simply is told that the story will be continued.

Not only does the novel exhibit a number of Dorfman's favorite themes, allowing it to be read comparatively against his other works, but it also has a number of important intertextual connections. Oropesa notes that the faceless man has been compared to Woody Allen's *Zelig* but that a comparison with *The Last Tango in Paris* is more apt because the faceless man rapes both Oriana and his photographic subjects in a state of emotional detachment and angst that compares to that of Marlon Brando's character (98). Oropesa also notes that the name of the secretary in the epilogue, Maya Lynch, most likely is an adaptation of the name of the Argentine writer Marta Lynch, whose *Informe bajo llave* (Information under Lock and Key) narrates a relationship between a woman and a member of the junta as an allegory for the way that authoritarian governments violate their citizens (99). Barr analyzes at great length the intertextuality between the novel and the story of Moses. She reads the faceless man as a reverse image of Moses. The faceless man is abandoned by his family; Moses receives special care. The narrator's face is virtually invisible; Moses's face was radiant after he received the Ten Commandments. She notes that the opening of the novel echoes Moses's encounter with God ("And the Lord spoke unto Moses face to face"; Exodus 23:11) (154). The novel begins: "Así que por fin nos vamos a encontrar, doctor. Cara a cara, si me permite la ironía" (11); ("So, we're finally going to meet, Doctor. Face to face, so to speak"; 3). Barr points out that the saga of Moses is one of redemption and liberation and that that of the faceless man is one of increased enslavement and impunity (154–55). Coetzee sees links between the novel and the work of William Burroughs and Jacques Lacan. He also compares the faceless man with Dr. Frankenstein's creature and the hunchback of Notre Dame (135).

The style of the novel eludes typical generic constructions, and it combines the confession and memoir with the thriller. The first section, narrated by the faceless man, invokes the style of the confession and is reminiscent of the defensive tone taken by the *Confessions* of Jean-Jacques Rousseau, who imagined that he was the victim of a sinister plot. But the section, even though it is directed at the doctor, also appears like an aggressive monologue that allows its narrator to vent his anger and frustration at a society that has abandoned him. The cold, calculating voice of the faceless man creates a chilling atmosphere. The tone of the second section is quite different. Oriana's narrative is split between a first-person voice that corresponds to the part of her that is still a four-and-a-half-year-old girl and a third-person voice that describes the actions of her adult body. Most striking about the section is the fact that Oriana's narrative seems like an intercalated supplement. The first section is directed at the doctor and even ends when the faceless man asks the doctor if he is ready to take off Oriana's clothes and begin the operation. The faceless man offers Doctor Mavirelli the next word: "Usted tiene la palabra" (106); ("What do you say?"; 102). After this, Oriana's section seems like an aside or an interruption, especially because the two men address each other and Oriana's voice is directed outside to a different audience. Her section recalls the tone of the legend of Manuel Sendero but is more melancholy: "En cuanto a mí, sigo en este reino que yo misma me construí" (109); ("As for me, I am still enclosed in this kingdom that I built for myself"; 105). The third section, narrated by Doctor Mavirelli, continues the monologic macho exchange between the doctor and the faceless man, but in contrast to the faceless man's hostility, the doctor's tone is paternalistic.

The disjunction between the discourse of the men and of Oriana is at the heart of the novel. Even though they are members of the same society, none has much potential for interaction. This communicative disconnection is emphasized by the fact that the faceless man's entire monologue aims at convincing the doctor to help him with Oriana although he has no knowledge of her whatsoever, as we learn after reading the section by Oriana. The faceless man is simply interested in her body, her lack of identity, and her lack of history. The doctor is equally selfish and sadistic. Oriana, the only one that signals hope, is a voice that no one can hear because her thoughts remain in her head. The novel's title, *Mascara*, thus emphasizes social relations as makeup, and its Spanish title, *Máscaras*, or masks, emphasizes identity as superficiality. As Coetzee explains, "One of the targets of *Mascara* is the intrinsic superficiality of a political culture based on television images. In such a culture, a creator and manager of images like Doctor Mavirelli becomes the power behind the throne" (134).

As a novel that emerges in the wake of the massive torture, disappearance, and exile of Chileans, *Mascara* further delves into questions about the relationship between the body and identity, history, and society. In the world of *Mascara* the physical self is totally vulnerable to manipulation, mutilation, destruction, and disappearance. The secret police harvest the hands of the dead, Mavirelli's surgeries change the looks and destinies of his patients, Oriana's body and mind are out of sync, and society suffers constant violence. The government has almost absolute control over physical space, which has allowed it to control interior, mental space. Dorfman's return to the symbolism of hands, which appeared in *The Last Song*, takes an even more intense turn in *Mascara* because memory is lodged in the hands rather than the minds of the dead. This connection between memory and body is reiterated in the story of Oriana, who abandons her memory after her physical body has been violated.

If the body and memory are so integrally connected and if the body is so fragile, then what hope is there for social change, and what chance is there that history will be remembered? At first glance, the future looks grim, especially since both the faceless man and the doctor seem to be the narrators of history. They both attempt to aggressively impose their worldviews on their readers, and they both presume to be able to determine the future, even though their desires are at odds: the faceless man wants to live happily with his childlike Oriana, and the doctor wants to occupy the skin of the faceless man. Oriana appears to be merely the innocent victim to their macho posturing, aggressive rhetoric, and violent acts. They further give the impression, through their confident recounting of events, that they control the narrative flow, leaving Oriana's voice unheard and unheeded. Or so it seems. But even though the men appear to occupy the focus of the novel, the novel's questions all ultimately turn on Oriana.

With the male characters Dorfman delves into anger, alienation, sadism, betrayal, megalomania, and apathy. Oriana, in contrast, remains the novel's biggest enigma. She is the only source of hope, but her audience is unclear and may possibly be nonexistent. On the one hand, she is driven by a strong passion to preserve memory, but on the other hand, she retreats into amnesia. Her rape by the secret police leads her to be the vulnerable victim of the faceless man, and he is able to rape her repeatedly. She is so powerful that the secret police are tirelessly searching for her, and yet she is so weak that she depends on the faceless man to survive. She allows the faceless man to script her identity each day, yet she holds the memories of the dead within her. Even though the men appear to control the word and the world, ultimately it is Oriana who holds the key to the novel's meaning. Understanding Oriana, though, is no easy feat since the Oriana known by the faceless man seems to have little in common with the Oriana who narrates the second section. The fragile, vulnerable body of Oriana contrasts with the strong, passionate, tender voice of the second section.

The reader's need to understand Oriana becomes even more vital when we recognize that within the world of *Mascara* she is the only one left who can tell the stories of the dead; she is the only one who has dared to collect them, and she is on the verge of total destruction. From the time that she watched her father's murder, she has been a defiant and passionate protector of memory and history. Near the end of her section she fiercely explains that she will continue with her work even if no one cares or listens.

> Voy hasta el perímetro de mi reino y llamo. Como un lobo que quiere hacer aparecer una luna muerta con sus aullidos. ¿Pero quién me va a oír? ¿Y si me oyen, quién me va a contestar? ¿Quién me va a recoger estas palabras como yo recogí las de quienes se estaban murieron [*sic*] sin una luna para sus manos?
>
> Aunque nadie me responda, no me arrepiento.
>
> Hice lo que tuve que hacer. (124)

> (I go to the outskirts of my kingdom and I call from there. Like a wolf that wants to make the sky give birth to the dead moon with its screams. But who will hear me? And, if they hear me, who will answer? Who will gather my words as I gathered those who were dying without a moon for their hands in the night?
>
> Even if no one answers, I do not repent.
>
> I did what I had to do. [120])

With this last line *Mascara* brings us full circle to the phrase from *Manifesto for Another World* that opened this chapter: "I did what I had to do. Anything else would have tasted like ashes" (27). It is likely that Dorfman was unaware that he was citing Oriana when he later included these lines in his play dedicated to human rights defenders. As explained in the introduction to this chapter, the line emphasizes the theme of the storyteller who must do what no one else will do: tell stories that disturb and tell stories that those in power want silenced. Both Oriana and the faceless man are horribly damaged as children. The faceless man responds with anger and destruction, whereas Oriana responds with tenderness and compassion. *Mascara* asks why pain can cause such different reactions. Why does Oriana risk her life to record the memories of the dead while the faceless man helps the state track down dissidents? Why is Oriana so alone? Why doesn't she have more help? On the eve of the election to decide Pinochet's future, Dorfman told a story that would be difficult for Chileans to read. He told a story of a lone woman who had been victimized by her country and her lover and whose story had no audience. In these ways Oriana's story anticipates the character of Paulina from *Death and the Maiden*. Most important, Oriana's voice allows Dorfman to return to the haunting tenderness of his poetry and to recapture the raw emotions of his first exile writing.

Through Oriana Dorfman continues to explore the idea of the storyteller who has a mission to record history against insurmountable odds. Oriana confesses: "Apenas había nacido supe cosas que otros tardan toda la vida en saber, que algunos nunca llegan a saber" (124); ("As soon as I was born I knew things that others take a lifetime to learn, that some never know at all"; 120). Oriana cannot avoid this role. Even though she is at tremendous personal risk, she must continue to help those who are about to die. Her only form of protection is the complete annihilation of her own identity, a move that is reminiscent of Dorfman's poem "Paracaídas," which describes how the poet has to suppress his own feelings in order to write. In order for Oriana to listen to the dead, she cannot grow, remember, or feel. Even such a fragile existence is a threat to the repressive state in which she lives. As her section ends, she pleads with her audience for help: "Quiero que sepan que la que ahora se está muriendo soy yo. Quiero que se pregunten si no tengo derecho a un milagro. Si a mí no me pueden rescatar, una sola vez, una sola vez, una sola vez como ocurría en los cuentos de hadas que me contaba mi papá" (125); ("I want you to know that the one who is dying now is me. I want you to ask yourselves if I do not have the right to a miracle. If I cannot be rescued just once, just once, just one single time, the way it came to pass in the fairytales my father told me"; 121).

On October 5, 1988, Dorfman joined the majority of Chileans and voted against another eight-year term for Pinochet. A horrible epoch in Chilean history and in Dorfman's life came to an end that day, but Dorfman's questions lingered and his doubts persisted. What circumstances made it possible for Pinochet to take power and keep it for so long? Who was responsible for Pinochet's atrocities? Even though the vote signaled a break in his work, the next chapter, on Dorfman's writing after exile, will demonstrate that he continued to grapple with many of the same issues. While this chapter has focused on Dorfman's interest in the relationship between art and politics and the difficulties that face the writer who is committed to telling stories that will engage and trouble his audience, the next chapter takes a more detailed view of Dorfman's vision of the intersections among literary representation, truth, and the imagination.

I am a liar who always
tells the truth.

—JEAN COCTEAU

There are no hard distinctions
between what is real and what is
unreal, nor between what is true
and what is false. A thing is not
necessarily either true or false; it
can be both true and false.

—HAROLD PINTER

Literature reveals the truth
that lies behind the fiction
of everyday life.

—SALMAN RUSHDIE

5. I AM A LIAR WHO ALWAYS TELLS THE TRUTH *From Exile to Diaspora (1990–2005)*

After the votes to oust Pinochet in 1988 and to elect Patricio Aylwin in 1989, Ariel Dorfman suffered yet another strange twist of fate when his personal life intertwined with historical events and intellectual developments. These intersections revolve around three often overlapping social and critical shifts. First, Dorfman's move from exile to diaspora, from outcast to global citizen, occurred contemporaneously with the fall of the Berlin Wall (1989) and the end of the Cold War. Dorfman's official exile ended as the era of globalization began, causing him to reassess his relationship to the nation-state at a time when some scholars were heralding "the end of history" (Francis Fukuyama) and predicting the end of the nation (Homi Bhabha).[1] Second, the establishment of truth commissions in Argentina (1983), Chile (1990), and South Africa (1995), coupled with Rigoberta Menchú's receipt of the Nobel Peace Prize in 1992 and the opening of the U.S. Holocaust Museum in 1993, focused attention on the relationship among historical memory, trauma, testimonial, and justice —themes central to Dorfman's first play and first post-exile work, *La muerte y la doncella* (1990; *Death and the Maiden*). Third, with the U.S. invasion of Iraq in 1991 simulcast on CNN globally, the 1990s signaled what might be called the moment of *high* postmodernism. Delving into questions about representation in a global society that appeared increasingly incapable of discerning truth from fantasy, this critical turn is epitomized by Jean Baudrillard's exposé on media and war, *The Gulf War Did Not Take Place* (1995) and works like Fredric Jameson's *Postmodernism, or, The Cultural Logic of Late Capitalism* (1992). Taken together, these three social and critical developments coalesced into a series of questions Dorfman would ask about the role of literary representation in the struggle for social change. Dorfman's writing during this period examines a triangulated set of concerns about representing the local and the global; the role of literature in the representation of truth, trauma, and memory; and the challenges posed by global media that depict suffering as spectacle and translate news into infotainment. While these questions have been present throughout his literary career, after the official end of Pinochet's rule they took on a heightened urgency and intensity.

The period covered in this chapter was one of widespread political, economic, and cultural changes, accompanied by a number of important critical approaches dedicated to understanding these changes. After describing this social and critical panorama, the following analysis considers how these developments took center stage in Dorfman's work beginning in the 1990s. I argue that Dorfman's consideration of these themes reveals that there is a certain logic to the confluence of theories about globalization, trauma/justice/memory, and representability. For Dorfman the nexus of these questions revolves around the problem of truth and its representation. He explains: "Artists have a way of telling truths. And the truths are often . . . full of lies. But they're good lies, you know? Not lies that hurt people. Lies that ask questions. Jean Cocteau says that art is a lie that tells the truth" (cited in Morgan, n.p).[2] The sense that meaningful representation requires artistic intervention and innovation led Dorfman to ask a series of questions about the social role of literature: Why does truth need fiction to be recognized as true? What happens when novels reveal more truth than the news? And why does historical memory have an uncomfortable relationship with the truth?

These questions took a particular form in considerations of globalization, both as event and as theory. If the nation-state was diminishing as a marker of identity and a source of economic and political power, what would be the principal geographic source of meaning? When the nation weakened as the primary representative concept for peoples, economies, and political policies, it led to a massive rethinking of how best to represent global flows of power and local realities. The vote that determined the end of Pinochet's rule on October 5, 1988 took place amidst a series of worldwide transformations that came to be known as the era of globalization. Added to the fall of the Berlin Wall in 1989 and the collapse of the Soviet Union in 1991, which signaled the end of the Cold War and marked the waning of the age of three worlds, free trade agreements and transnational alliances developed—for example, the Southern Common Market (MERCOSUR, founded in 1991); the European Union (1992); NAFTA (implemented in 1994); the FTAA (initiated in 1994); and the World Trade Organization (WTO; founded in 1995). Furthermore, the 1990s witnessed unprecedented growth in multinational corporations that frustrated a clear-cut association between capital and national economies. These changes called into question the legitimacy of the nation-state as the primary motor of economic and political power. When "global" replaced "international" as the preferred term to describe the post-1989, post–Cold War geopolitical landscape, it led to an outcrop of critical terms, such as "transnational," "postnational," and "multinational," and it signaled the need to radically reassess the space of the nation within the larger global context.[3]

The synchronicity of Dorfman's end of exile with the era of globalization logically led him to reconsider his ideas about the ties between the self and geographical space. Exile is a state of being that always necessarily depends on national identity, even if that identity exists merely in opposition to the identity of the exile.[4] When Dorfman's exile ended, he could have defined himself without regard to the limits of the nation-state, thereby epitomizing Deleuze and Guattari's notion of the deterritorialized nomad in *Nomadology*: "If the nomad can be called the Deterritorialized *par excellence*, it is precisely because there is no reterritorialization *afterwards* as with the migrant. . . . With the nomad, on the contrary, it is deterritorialization that constitutes the relation to the earth" (52). But Dorfman was not to become a deterritorialized nomad after the end of his exile. Even though he found that the end of exile did not result in a permanent return to Chile, he would be unable to consider himself unbound by geographic identity. If anything, the end of exile meant that Dorfman found himself alternately more and less Chilean.

Thus while Dorfman's own identity entered a new, post-exile phase, his acceptance of theories about the free flow of global identities would be measured by his continuing commitment to specific national contexts, particularly that of Chile. At the same time, however, the official end of Pinochet's rule freed Dorfman to place his writing and critical interventions into a broader global context. Consequently Dorfman's engagement with globalization is best characterized by a set of dialectic tensions between the local and the global.

Eschewing abstract theories about postmodern globalization, Dorfman retains clear-cut ties to history and place in his version of multiculturalism, border crossings, and the global flow of identities. It is most apparent in Dorfman's engagement with theories about identity in the era of globalization that he is neither wholly a skeptic nor a convert. While he remained skeptical of abstract high theory, he remained keenly aware of the ways that globalization was affecting personal identities and the nation-state.

Dorfman's first work of this period, *Death and the Maiden*, also addresses the problems of memory, history, justice, and trauma and thereby bridges two sets of critical ideas that came to the fore in the 1990s. It is hardly a coincidence that concomitant to theories about the ways that globalization and postmodernism were flattening out social awareness of space, other theories began to reconsider the relationship between historical memory and social trauma. Andreas Huyssen emphasizes the link between globalization and the destabilization of history: "If the historical past once used to give coherence and legitimacy to family, community, nation, and state, . . . then those formerly stable links have weakened today to the extent that national traditions and historical pasts are increasingly deprived of their geographic and political groundings, which are reorganized in the process of cultural globalization" (4). Huyssen points out that when history "as a canonical form" was delegitimized as a "pedagogical and philosophical mission," it was accompanied by an upsurge of narratives of the past that favored "memory" over "history" (5). Theories by Paul Ricouer, Peter Burke, and Pierre Nora engaged with the supposed disjunction between memory, understood as personal or popular appreciations of the past, versus history, understood as an official, intellectual account of the past.

History was often described in these theories as a vehicle for the ruling class, and memory became the counter-discourse of the past. In one example Nora claims that history and memory are fundamentally oppositional categories: "Memory is life . . . always subject to a dialectic of remembering and forgetting . . . vulnerable in various ways to appropriation and manipulation. . . . History, on the other hand, is the reconstruction, always problematic and incomplete, of what is no longer" (3). Dorfman, however, would be unwilling to separate history from memory, as a number of his works from this period indicate. Since 1990, for instance, Dorfman has written three texts—*Heading South, Looking North*; *Exorcising Terror*; and *Desert Memories*—that intertwine personal memory and public history and suggest the impossibility of understanding these ways of recording the past epiphenomenally.[5] Dorfman's postdictatorial experience, in fact, suggested that any effort to adjust public history to collective memory would require artistic projects dedicated to bringing these forms of representing the past into dialogue and productive confrontation. For Dorfman, this exchange is exemplified by the way that the voices of Paulina, Gerardo, and Doctor Miranda from *Death and the Maiden* speak to the public form of accounting for the trauma of the coup that took place via the Chilean truth commission. As Dorfman explains in the afterword to the play, "I found the characters trying to figure out the sort of questions that so many Chileans were asking themselves privately, but that hardly anyone seemed interested in posing in public. . . . How do we keep the past alive without becoming its prisoner? How do we forget it without risking its repetition in the future?" (*Resistance Trilogy*, 146).

A number of events from this period indicate that, along with the sense of the disintegration of history, societies across the globe found it necessary to commemorate, reflect, record, and honor the past. The establishment of truth commissions in fourteen nations by 2001; the wave of monuments to memory, both erected and planned, in the 1990s (such as Memory Park in Buenos Aires and the Chilean Wall of Memory in Santiago's general cemetery); and a growth industry of films, books, and other cultural products dedicated to rescuing memory—all are evidence of the widespread international urge to attend to painful historical events.[6] At the center of many of these projects was the Holocaust: "Most retrospective views of twentieth-century history assign the Holocaust a privileged place as the paradigmatic event of unspeakable human suffering" (Miller and Tougaw, 3). According to Ricoeur, "Events like the Holocaust and the great crimes of the twentieth century, situated at the limits of representation, stand in the name of all of the events that have left their traumatic imprint on hearts and bodies" (498).

Dorfman is one of the few writers who has narrated across the traumas of the Second World War and the Southern Cone, and his work presents an opportunity to consider how these events share similar characteristics.[7] The first examples of his efforts to do so, which probably stem in part from his Jewish heritage, can be found in much of his early work, but they reach greater intensity in the post-exile phase. From the brief mention of a novel that connects Holocaust concentration camps to those in South America in *Hard Rain* to the frame of the novel *Widows* to David's Jewish background in *The Last Song*, Dorfman moved on to write works like *Konfidenz* and "Picasso's Closet," which were entirely situated in the conflicts of the Second World War. The screenplay that Dorfman co-wrote with his son Rodrigo for the BBC movie *Prisoners in Time* (1995), for instance, depicts a British ex-prisoner of war who is confronted with his Japanese torturer fifty years after the end of the war. The woman who helps the protagonist confront his trauma has had earlier experience helping victims of torture from Latin America. Dorfman observed an astonishing point of connection between the Second World War and contemporary human rights violations when Secretary of State Colin Powell announced the U.S. decision to go to war in Iraq before a shrouded replica of *Guernica* on February 5, 2003. That event coincided with the first U.S. readings of "Picasso's Closet." The episode led Dorfman to write a poem that imagines Picasso directly confronting Powell: "Were you afraid of my art / what I am still saying / more than sixty five years later / the story still being told / the vision still dangerous?" ("Pablo Picasso Has Words for Colin Powell," n.p.). Central to the poem is Dorfman's interest in the way that Picasso's art was able to make Powell uncomfortable, testifying to a truth that Powell wanted to censor. From Dorfman's view Picasso's art is able to speak about the horrors of the past and the horrors of the present: "'Guernica' continues to stick its finger in the wound of reality and make us scream, and reveal to us the truth merely by its presence in the world" (cited in Morgan, n.p.). These interests reveal another important link between Dorfman's post-dictatorial work and broader scholarly trends that were dedicated to understanding the relationship among truth, testimony, and witnessing.

Research by scholars of the trauma of the Holocaust intersected with a wave of research dedicated to understanding testimony and reconsidering the role of truth in historical memory. As Dori Laub and Shoshana Felman claim in the introduction to their highly influential study, *Testimony*, "Our era can precisely be defined as the age of testimony" (6). The desire and need for testimony, they suggest, is due to a "crisis of truth" and a profound questioning of the evidence that has been used to define the past (6). Added to the crisis of truth was one of representation, concerns exacerbated by postmodern theories about the incommunicability of experience and the rupture between signifier and signified. Jameson makes this point in *The Political Unconscious* when he argues that "any doctrine of figurality must necessarily be ambiguous: a symbolic expression of a truth is also, at the same time, a distorted and disguised expression" (70). All theories of the postmodern dedicated considerable attention to the crisis of truth and its representation; while some theorists rejoiced in being liberated by the confines of truth regimes, for many this crisis led to a profound reconsideration of how to rescue political engagement in an era that called for major rethinking of all of the traditional structures of thought that had previously supported political vision.

The postmodern trouble with truth claims would become one of the defining features of Latin Americanist literary criticism in this period, as evidenced by Raymond Leslie Williams's work on the postmodern novel, where he claims that "Latin American writers such as Eltit and Piglia share with North Atlantic postmoderns a generalized mistrust of the capacity of any language to render truths about the world" (19). And just as Latin American novels were coming under scrutiny for their relationship to truth regimes and history via works like Ángel Rama's *La ciudad letrada* (*The Lettered City*), a "boom" of research took up the *testimonio* as an antidote to literature, most notably in John Beverley's *Against Literature*. The *testimonio*, which consistently eluded an exact definition, was generally defined as the true, urgent account of a witness to history whose voice had been silenced in official versions. The study of the *testimonio*, especially in response to David Stoll's critique of the veracity of Rigoberta Menchú's account, highlighted the complex ways in which literary forms represent truth and engage in politics.[8] Abril Trigo highlights the ambiguous nature of the *testimonio*: "What provides *testimonio* with this political and epistemological counter-hegemonic potential is its dual status as a truthful account of sociohistorical events (its ethical value and epistemological veracity) and as a literary artifact (its aesthetic value and narrative verisimilitude)" (353). But in fact, as evidenced by the myriad debates over the *testimonio*, this dual status would lead to conflicted notions about the role of writing in revealing or complicating the truth.[9]

Again, as with globalization, Dorfman's literary texts and critical essays both place him within and set him apart from many of the critical trends that analyze the relationship between testimonial writing and the representation of truth.[10] On the one hand, he advocates testimonial writing as a textual form that challenges the grand narratives of western society and provides alternative versions of the truth from the perspective of the historically voiceless. But unlike scholars who position the *testimonio* "against literature," Dorfman believes that what makes the *testimonio* a powerful textual form is precisely its combination of the literary and the truthful.[11] For instance, he suggests that the most compelling Chilean testimonial texts are those by authors who are conscious of the storyteller's craft and who thereby seek to find an aesthetically poignant form and structure for their stories. A paradigmatic example of the blending of truth telling and literary art, according to Dorfman, is Hernán Valdés's account of his experience in a Chilean concentration camp, *Tejas Verdes*, which Dorfman describes as "a cross between the fictive and the real, between literature and testimony, between an elaborate treatment of great inventiveness and a crude and realistic recording of events" (*Some Write*, 166–67).

The desire to blend documentary fact with the art of storytelling has also been characteristic of much of Dorfman's work, but he draws a distinction—

albeit a soft distinction—between works whose primary purpose is the denunciation of the present and those that explore the tragedy of a particular moment through a wide creative lens that allows the artist to address a broader audience. Accordingly, he condemns some of the Chilean testimonials for their inattention to the complexity of language: "They consider it as a mere vehicle for a truth that is already established" (159). For Dorfman, this failure to grasp the ambiguities of communication and representation limits such texts. On the one hand, he believes that there is a distinction between the testimonial as an urgent and local form of bearing witness and an artistic recreation of historical events. But on the other hand, he feels that the most powerful testimonial texts are indistinguishable from the greatest works of art. Works like *Guernica*, for instance, manage to speak to a particular, local moment with urgency and force while continuing to comment on the "wound of reality and make us scream" (cited in Morgan, n.p.). Many of Dorfman's works from this period explore the relationship between testimonial urgency and artistic production, especially *Manifesto for Another World*, which brings together testimonial segments of fifty-one human rights defenders in a dramatic work.

Alongside the interest in understanding the relationship among artistic representation, truth, and testimonial, another wave of research interested in truth and representation studied new media and technological change. While the study of testimonial writing focused on the voice, the tape recorder, and the transcribed text, another branch of research considered the host of new technologies that were both frustrating and liberating the possibilities for subversive communication. Highlighted by work by Baudrillard on the role of the news media in converting the events of the first Iraq war into infotainment, this research considered the ways that the global flow of information technology was disrupting meaningful communication. In this sense the 1990s could be described as a moment of *high* postmodernism where theories like those of Marshall McLuhan and Roland Barthes about the role of technology in shaping public perception, which had begun to circulate in the mid-1960s, were intensified by the age of cable television and the Internet. Work by Jameson, Baudrillard, Michael Hardt and Antonio Negri, and also Douglas Kellner (among others) asked how postmodern theories could help explain the social impact of these technological shifts, and, as with theories of globalization, the changes were alternately celebrated and mourned. Dorfman, who was well known as a cultural theorist owing to his work on the imperialism of Donald Duck comics, continued in this period to write media criticism that built on his work from the 1960s and '70s.[12] His literary work during this period directly confronts the role of these new media in shaping public consciousness, especially in texts like *The Nanny and the Iceberg* and *Blake's Therapy*. Dorfman was most troubled by the fact that these changes seemed to exacerbate the already superficial ways that most media represented social conflict. His attention to the flattening of the truth common in media culture connects his interest in mass media to his interest in literature in the era of globalization and testimony.

Against this backdrop of critical innovations and historical shifts Dorfman's literary works from the 1990s to the first decade of the twenty-first century address a triad of concerns that revolve around globalization, truth/testimonial/trauma, and representation. While these three clusters do not appear in equal measure in all of Dorfman's works from this period, the following analysis will show that they consistently flow throughout the post-exile texts in a combined quest to interrogate the relationship between art and truth. To appreciate the complexity of this quest it is essential to recognize that Dorfman's work intertwines two competing aesthetic approaches to representing the truth: the testimonial and the surreal. Not only does Dorfman bridge the moment of the Holocaust, the Spanish Civil War, and the Second World War with that of the dictatorships of Latin America from a historical perspective, but he also brings these components into an aesthetic dialogue. This combined approach to understanding the relationship between truth and representation explains the ways that he alternates the playfulness of surrealism with the urgency of *testimonio*. Dorfman borrows from the surrealists' efforts to make the real seem strange so that neglected associations and concrete materialities become visible. Similarly, he appeals to the stark, bare, and raw aesthetics of witnessing and denunciation. To these aesthetic trends he adds the absurd, the picaresque, the baroque, the postmodern, and other styles in combinations that attempt to put different ways of representing the world into dialogue and intellectually provocative conflict via an aesthetics of hope. Following the chronological trajectory of Dorfman's post-exile writing, this chapter traces the themes of representation and truth in Dorfman's literature and highlights the way that his work engages in many of the critical and social debates that shaped the turn of the twentieth century.

TRUST, BETRAYAL, AND STORYTELLING IN *THE RESISTANCE TRILOGY* AND *KONFIDENZ*

Death and the Maiden. *Death and the Maiden* represents a watershed moment in Dorfman's literary career for a number of reasons. It is his most internationally successful work, his first post-exile work, and his first published play. It is also an example of the way that his post-exile writing bridges the local and the global. Even though Dorfman has grappled throughout his career with the ways that art alternately speaks to the specific and the universal, *Death and the Maiden* pushes this tension to a new level.[13] On the one hand, it is a text that grows out of a concrete, local event: the establishment of the Chilean truth commission (the Rettig Commission), which investigated only the crimes of the dictatorship that ended in death or a presumption of death.[14] On the other hand, it spoke to a far broader global need to ask questions about the ways that communities can emerge from a state of enormous pain and horror, especially when the state itself has been responsible for inflicting atrocities. So at the time of its writing, the play was alternately Dorfman's most specifically local and most universal text.[15]

The description of the setting for the play emphasizes its local/global dialectic: "El tiempo es el presente; y el lugar, un país que es probablemente Chile, aunque puede tratarse de cualquier país que acaba de salir de una dictadura" (14); ("The time is the present and the place, a country that is probably Chile, but could be any country that has given itself a democratic government after a long period of dictatorship"; 88).[16] As the description makes clear, the events may parallel those in Chile, but they also reflect a common condition suffered by nations recovering from state-sponsored violence. It is noteworthy that the setting asserts the national context of Chile while also speaking to a global audience. Arguably the most internationally significant play by a Latin American writer, *Death and the Maiden* has been staged in more than thirty countries; in 1993 there were more than fifty different productions running at the same time in Germany alone.[17] Bhila Blum studies how *Death and the Maiden* plays in Israel, how it mixes the context of Chile with that of an Israeli audience in a way that leads the audience to reflect on its particular social circumstances (156). The play represents the local and the global simultaneously as a way of delving into the deepest psychological and social crises faced by a nation in the post-dictatorial healing process. What happens when one has to sit down to dinner with a man that could have tortured a neighbor? How does a nation heal from years of psychological and physical torture when the perpetrators remain unnamed and unpunished?

Death and the Maiden has a deceptively simple plot line, beneath which lie layers upon layers of questions and dilemmas. It takes place in a country that has recently emerged from a long dictatorship. Paulina, a torture survivor, is married to Gerardo, who has just agreed to serve on a truth commission that will investigate the disappearances that resulted in death during the dictatorship. Experiencing car trouble on his way to his house in the country, Gerardo is aided by Doctor Miranda. Later, when Miranda stops by the house, Paulina recognizes his voice and is sure that this man who has befriended her husband raped and tortured her while she was held in detention. She decides to make this man confess, since her husband's truth commission will ignore her needs for justice. Gerardo is stunned and unsure whether to believe her. Miranda continues to profess his innocence, and Paulina has no way to prove her story. If Paulina was blindfolded and never saw her torturers, how will she be able to provide proof of their identity? The only evidence she has is the fact that she recognizes Miranda's voice and remembers his verbal tics and his smell; also, he used to play Schubert for her before he raped her, and she has found a tape of Schubert in this man's car.

For some it seems that Paulina has incontrovertible evidence, but for others, it appears that Doctor Miranda is being treated in exactly the same way that Paulina was treated. If Paulina uses the methods of her torturers to exact a confession from Miranda, then is she any better? Gerardo reluctantly acquiesces to Paulina's plan, but it is unclear if he genuinely supports her since when he listens to her story, he ostensibly does so in order to provide Miranda with details that he can use to fabricate a confession. After recording Miranda's confession, Gerardo goes to retrieve Miranda's car, believing that they will now set him free. Meanwhile, Paulina confronts Miranda. She explains that she made a few errors in her account to Gerardo in order to see if Miranda would correct them, which he did. She then tells him that she is going to kill him. The lights go down, a mirror is placed in front of the audience, and Paulina and Gerardo appear at a concert accompanied by Doctor Miranda, who may or may not be a phantom.

Ambiguous, provocative, and driven by questions that have no easy answers, the play lends itself to numerous avenues of inquiry that relate to the social role of truth commissions; the representation of a nation in crisis; and themes of betrayal, trust, deceit, and redemption. Dorfman's most studied text, it has been analyzed from a variety of critical angles—legal-juridical, psychological, symbolic, and poststructural. Different aspects have drawn the attention of scholars: violence and torture (Kim, Castro, Avelar); truth (Maree); politics (Gregory); trauma (Morello); memory (Jofré; Hildebrand, Sotomayor, Valdés); law (Barsky); Schubert (Schroeder); gender (Pinet); theater and crisis (Glickman); voice (Munro); and staging (Blum, Morace).[18] Many essays take up several themes, and it is well beyond the scope of my analysis here to provide an exhaustive survey. Consequently, in the analysis that follows I will attempt to fill in some of the gaps not thoroughly addressed by already existing studies. It is interesting that few studies of the play center on the role of art in seeking the truth, and none ask why Dorfman's first post-exile project was a theatrical work. While many studies of the play inquire about the intertextuality between the play and Schubert's quartet, none ask about the importance of Doctor Miranda's citation of Nietzsche and how that reference might relate to larger questions about the role of art in representing the truth in a time of terror. Nor do they wonder about the play's other references to art, such as Mozart's "Dissonant Quartet" in the third act. Despite the fact that a number of studies approach the play from a postmodern perspective, relatively little attention has been paid to the way that the text uses language to ask questions about how words can simultaneously reveal and hide the truth. Most important, in order to understand Dorfman's literary project it is necessary to ask why he chose to focus on these themes in a play—a public work of art that requires collective engagement—rather than in a novel, the genre that he had originally imagined for the story (*Resistance Trilogy*, 144). To that end, the following analysis situates the play within Dorfman's aesthetics of hope, focusing on the critical questions of the relationship among art, truth, and representation that have shaped Dorfman's post-exile work.

First, let us begin with what may be the most important question to ask about how this work fits into Dorfman's overall literary project: Why a play? And why does Dorfman write his first play as his exile officially ends?[19] In Dorfman's afterword to the text he explains that he had had the kernel of *Death and the Maiden* in mind for eight or nine years but that every time he sat down to write what he imagined would be a novel, he could not get past the first few pages. After the announcement of the Rettig Commission the story resurfaced in his mind. He now had the right context. To have the tension he sought, it would be placed during a transition to democracy, and in order for the husband to have a "tremendous stake in the outcome of that kidnapping" he would have to be a "member of a commission similar to the one headed by Rettig" (145). The events taking place in Chile as Patricio Aylwin became the first elected president after Pinochet, loaded as they were with extraordinary tension, helped Dorfman refine the conflicts at the core of his story. The key information Dorfman reveals in his afterword is that "It did not take me long to conclude that, rather than a novel, what needed to be written was a play" (145).

It is worth remembering that Dorfman's exile began with a similar shift in genre. Grieving for the losses of the coup, Dorfman published his first poetry. The poetry was intimate and tender and allowed Dorfman to write in a form that was simple and intense, unlike the complex baroque language of his first novel.[20] Parallel to Dorfman's turn to poetry in exile, he moves to theater post-exile. Clearly, as evidenced by his thesis on Shakespeare and his book on the theater of Harold Pinter, Dorfman has been interested in the theater throughout his literary career. But he did not choose to work in this form during the exile years. According to Dorfman, he had been working on a play in 1973 as part of his community-oriented artistic projects during the Allende presidency, but because of the coup the play was never completed. Once in exile, he lost his sense of community and therefore his ability to write theater since he lacked an imagined audience. And even though he had begun working on the theatrical version of *Widows* before the end of his exile, it was only when he could return to Chile that he felt he could fully commit to writing theater.[21] In his afterword to the Spanish version of the text, he makes it clear that he conceived of the play as a form of public intervention and a way to symbolically end his exile: "No era justo que, después de tantos años de ausencia y tantos años luchando por la democracia, estrenara la obra primero en el extranjero. *La Muerte y la Doncella* fue el regalo de retorno que yo quise brindarle a la transición" (97); (It was not fair that, after so many years of absence and so many years of struggling for democracy, the play would be staged first outside Chile. *Death and the Maiden* was the gift I offered to the transition). The first sentence in the above quotation displays an interesting twist of subject as Dorfman merges his own experience of exile, his years of struggle for democracy in Chile, and his desire to return with that of the staging of the play since clearly the play had not been absent and had not struggled for democracy; rather it was its author who had. The play, then, was not simply Dorfman's gift to Chile; it also was a way to publicly acknowledge his return and his desire to be a part of the reconstruction. It is significant that this play about the silences and absences of the Rettig Commission was written by an exile who, like the thousands of exiles who had been forced to flee Chile during the Pinochet years, also had suffered from the dictatorship but whose traumas were even less likely to receive official recognition than those of torture survivors like Paulina. That this effort to publicly stage the inner turmoil of the nation was the product of an exile explains for Dorfman its lack of success when it premiered in Chile (98).[22] The nation had grown suspicious of exiles, who were often portrayed as having abandoned the nation to enjoy the easy life abroad. Many had come to believe the myth that exile had been a matter of choice and not a painful tragedy, a belief that likely hindered the play's reception as well, and one that ironically complicates the play's investigation of betrayal even further, for the same two social sectors that refused to listen to Paulina—the Pinochet supporters and the left-center members of the transition government (some of whom were Dorfman's friends)—also could not tolerate watching the play.[23]

While *Death and the Maiden* may have been a symbolic way to end his exile and perform an act of public dialogue with Chile, fraught as such dialogue may have been, these were not Dorfman's conscious reasons for choosing to tell this story in the form of a play. Dorfman explains that he was convinced that the play would serve an important public function because it would allow the nation to collectively address the contradictory and complicated process of recovering from dictatorship. The theater had long been used in the Southern Cone to stage the conflicts of dictatorship. In Chile an active group of play-wrights and artists was dedicated to using theater and performance as a form of critical intervention in public consciousness—for example, Marco Antonio De la Parra, David Benavente and the theater collectives ICTUS and TIT, and Diamela Eltit and the Colectivo de Acciones de Arte (CADA; Collective of Artistic Actions).[24] Many of the plays and performances served to counter-balance the censorship, self-censorship, and constant sense of vigilance under which the Chilean public was forced to live during the Pinochet years. As Alice A. Nelson notes, these works often depended on an indirect language that served to establish an intimacy between the actors and the audience, thereby "joining other precarious local struggles for representational power taking place in pockets scattered throughout postcoup society" (90). Diana Taylor, in a study of theater during the military regime in Argentina, emphasizes that such regimes commit "percepticide" because they blind and pervert the public gaze. Daily violence is visible and ubiquitous, a fact that leads the public to distort its ways of looking: "Percepticide blinds, maims, kills through the senses" (123).

In such an environment any effort to publicly attend to the traumas of authoritarianism is bound to be complex, difficult, and incomplete. Henry James Morello describes this type of theater as "post-traumatic" since it bears the symptoms of psychological devastation. Morello focuses on how theater about national crises alternates between the personal and the public, between witnessing and avoidance, and between recording the past and repeating it in an effort to function as an aesthetic intervention that shocks and disturbs the audience. In analyzing a spectrum of post-traumatic plays, he situates *Death and the Maiden* on one end, as an example of one of the least fractured and most direct efforts to publicly stage social damage—an aesthetic that may further account for why the play was not as well received by the Chilean theatergoing public as (for example) De la Parra's *Lo crudo, lo cocido, y lo podrido* (*The Raw, the Cooked, and the Rotten*), a play that translates a dic-tatorial atmosphere to the confined space of a restaurant. In contrast with De la Parra's highly metaphorical play, Dorfman's commented in very direct, albeit complex, ways about the process of transition, much in the same way that Griselda Gambaro's *Información para extranjeros* (*Information for Foreigners*), an Argentine play that had very limited public acclaim, provided a raw representation of torture and state violence.[25] This point is emphasized by the young actor Paula Sharim in a scene from the documentary *A Promise to the Dead: The Exile Journey of Ariel Dorfman*. In a conversation with the actor who first played Paulina in Chile, Maria Elena Duvauchelle, and with Dorfman, Sharim describes Dorfman's play as "sticking a finger in a wound" when discussing why it did not attract a large audience in Chile. Perhaps the lack of local success for the play was a consequence of its relative directness and local specificity. In fact, as James Dawes explains in relation to human rights storytelling, it is often ironically the case that internationally successful texts that represent human rights violations are intolerable to the local audiences that they purportedly represent (182).

Despite the degree to which plays about social trauma are well received by the public, it is clear that their authors, in choosing the genre of theater, intended to use an artistic work as a form of communal intervention. Plays are the most public form of literature, and they require collaboration and collective reception even in the most alternative venues, a fact of the genre that makes it well suited to addressing collective crises. Taylor explains that theater serves an important public function in moments of political contestation: "Plays, performances, and theatrical spaces themselves are very much part of wider social struggles. 'Theater,' in its traditional use as the sum total of the above, participates in the shaping, transmitting, and at times challenging of group fantasies and desires. Therein lies the danger and the hope" (226–27).

As Chile began to transition to democracy, asking as a nation deep questions about the possibility for dialogue and a public accounting of the traumas of the coup, Dorfman decided to stage a play about three characters who were struggling to find a way to speak to each other and be heard. It is no coincidence, for instance, that the three characters almost never engage in dialogue together while on stage. In scenes where all three characters are visible to the audience, one character is typically set apart, listening to the conversation between the other two, an effect that highlights the ways that segments of society were marginalized from debates about reconstruction.[26] There are only two times when all three characters speak. First, in the first scene of the second act, Miranda addresses Gerardo and essentially refuses to speak to Paulina. He looks at her and tells her he has never seen her before in his life, but he knows that she is sick. Then he appeals to Gerardo's sense of justice to free him. After that plea, while they prepare to take him to the bathroom, Paulina forces him to speak to her, but their "dialogue" is limited to his telling her that he can use the toilet standing. The second time takes place as Miranda is signing his confession. Miranda's voice echoes because we hear him speak and we also hear his voice on the tape recorder. When Paulina tries to describe her feelings, Gerardo tells her to be quiet. Even though all three characters' voices are heard in this scene, it is clear that there is no dialogue among them. Again Dorfman's choice of genre is significant. There is no better genre to emphasize the difficulties of dialogue than the theater.

Not only is the dialogue of *Death and the Maiden* fractured and thwarted, but the actual words and phrases of the characters also suffer ruptures in signification. Dorfman's interest in the limits of linguistic representation began well before the coup, but the extreme misapplication and censoring of language that took place during the Pinochet years exacerbated these concerns. As Chile moved to transition, Dorfman questioned whether the massive linguistic abuse of the Pinochet years could be reconciled, whether Chileans could dismantle what Marguerite Feitlowitz describes in her analysis of the dictatorship in Argentina as a "lexicon of terror." In this sense the play suggests that not only were bodies physically abused during the dictatorship, but the words used to speak about the damage were hurt as well. This preoccupation with words links the play to other moments of extraordinary social violence; George Steiner's thoughts about the Holocaust could easily be applied to Chile: "Use a language to conceive, organize, and justify Belsen; use it to make out specifications for gas ovens; use it to dehumanize man during twelve years of calculated bestiality. Something will happen to it. . . . Something will happen to the words. Something of the lies and sadism will settle into the marrow of the language" (101). Dawes explains that at the heart of human rights literature is the "idea that language has been ruined, that it must be rescued" (219). Dorfman frames the linguistic question at the center of *Death and the Maiden* this way: "How do you reach the truth if lying has become a habit?" (*Resistance Trilogy*, 146).

The play asks questions about the relationship between language and truth in a number of ways. The most salient methods Dorfman uses to question the representational limits of language are repetition, linguistic slippage and word play, silences, lies, evasions, and forced utterances. In effect the entire play is organized around the expression of words, many of which do not function in a way that can meaningfully lead to dialogue, healing, or human contact. This linguistic disconnect is to be expected in exchanges between Miranda and Paulina, but it is made even more tragic in those between Paulina and Gerardo. The opening dialogue emphasizes that well before Paulina recognizes Miranda, the relationship she has with Gerardo is terribly wounded. When Gerardo enters the house to find Paulina hiding, he addresses her with words of affection —"m'hijita," "linda," "mi amor"—calling her his "gatita amorosa" (*La muerte y la doncella*, 16, 17); (my dear; pretty; my love; my loving pussycat).[27] At the same time, he is visibly angry with her for not fixing the spare tire and for loaning out the car jack. The use of these phrases of affection alongside Gerardo's angry tone serves to deflate their meaning, preparing the audience to understand that the confrontation between them is a ruse for the real conflict, the real conversation that cannot happen openly. Behind Gerardo's anger at Paulina for letting him down—a reasonable disappointment but one that is common to all relationships—is a deeper, more anguished conflict. He has agreed to serve on the commission without asking her. Even worse, he lies about his decision, making it seem that he won't serve if she does not agree. The following exchange is an example of almost all of the ways that Dorfman suggests that the language they share has become radically ruptured:

Gerardo:	¿A . . . ? Pero si no lo conozco. Es la primera vez en mi. . . . Además todavía no dicidí [*sic*] si voy a. . . .
Paulina:	Ya decidiste.
Gerardo:	Dije que le contestaría mañana, que me sentía extraordinariamente honrado pero que necesitaba. . . .
Paulina:	¿Al presidente?
Gerardo:	Al presidente. Que lo tenía que pensar.
Paulina:	No veo qué tienes que pensar. Ya lo decidiste, Gerardo, sabes que lo decidiste, es para esto que llevas años trabajando, por qué te haces el que. . . .
Gerardo:	Porque primero tengo que . . . tú tienes que decirme que sí.
Paulina:	Entonces: sí.
Gerardo:	No es el sí que necesito.
Paulina:	Es el único que tengo.
Gerardo:	Yo te he escuchado otros. (20)
(Gerardo:	You mean Roberto Miranda? I hardly know the man. Besides, I haven't decided yet if I should. . . .
Paulina:	You've decided.
Gerardo:	I said I'd answer tomorrow, that I felt extremely honored but that I needed. . . .
Paulina:	The president? You said that to the president?
Gerardo:	To the president. That I needed time to think it over.

Paulina:	I don't see what you have to think over. You've made your decision, Gerardo, you know you have. It's what you have been working on for years, why pretend that. . . .
Gerardo:	Because first—first you have to say yes.
Paulina:	Well then: yes.
Gerardo:	That's not the yes I need.
Paulina:	It's the only yes I've got.
Gerardo:	I've heard others. [93])

These lines are filled with ellipses that mark the heavy silences between Gerardo and Paulina. Paulina's torture was not limited to the violence of the state. When she sought out Gerardo after being released, she found him in bed with another woman; as a result, she was unable to tell him about her experience. Then she never officially denounced her torture and arrest. Not even her own mother knows. She has kept silent about her experiences, only revealing bits to Gerardo. They have internalized that silence behind a rhetoric of deception. Layers of betrayal and years of silence have seeped into the words they supposedly share.

Dorfman emphasizes this point by making the characters repeat each other's words on multiple occasions. In this exchange they repeat forms of the verb "decidir" (to decide) and "pensar" (to think). Most painful about this repetition is the fact that Gerardo suggests that his thinking and deciding are contingent on Paulina's thoughts and decisions. That of course is a lie because he has already decided. What is contingent on Paulina is whether she will be emotionally stable enough for him. That is why he forces her to say "yes," a "yes" that can be uttered only under duress and that does not satisfy Gerardo. When he mentions that he has heard other forms of "yes," ones that are intimate and sexual, Gerardo attempts to elicit not only the words but also the feelings behind the words that will validate his decision to listen to the stories of all the victims except those who suffered like Paulina. Later, though, as the scene climaxes, the words take a turn. They begin to signify more meaningfully. Gerardo tells Paulina that the commission will be limited to hearing the cases that are "irreparable" (21; 95). But before he can do that, he warmly asks her to tell him her story while he holds her. At this point Paulina connects affectionately with him and gives him the "yes" that he had been hoping to hear, that signals they will do this together (21; 95). This connection does not last, though, and the end of the scene oscillates between damaged language and the language of healing. After Paulina and Gerardo enjoy a brief moment of intense collaboration, Paulina asks if the criminals will be punished. As she realizes that the work of the commission will be more of a public sham than a real investigation, she becomes more agitated. In the final lines of the scene Gerardo confesses his lie, uttering "yes" repeatedly (23; 97). Now "yes" is not forced, and it is not a sign of camaraderie; it is an affirmation of Gerardo's betrayal, and while anguished, it reveals the painful chasm that lies between them. Not only have the words of pain and violence been shattered by the dictatorship; the scene shows that years of linguistic abuse have damaged the words of love, reconciliation, and hope. The question is whether that damage is "irreparable."

Many critics have noticed that the characters shift position, from victim to victimizer, from dominant to submissive (Jofré, 94–95; Vidal, 291–93). They also all twist language in similar ways. All of the characters lie. All of them attempt to censor and silence. All self-censor. All attempt to force (sometimes violently, sometimes subtly) the others to speak, to articulate words that they want to hear. Characters parallel each other: Gerardo betrays Paulina while Miranda (supposedly) rapes her; Paulina lies to her husband and he lies to her; Miranda (supposedly) violates Paulina and she later kidnaps him; and they all punish each other.[28] Paulina adopts a masculine voice on more than one occasion; in the Spanish version of the play when Gerardo describes Miranda as his good Samaritan, he says that they are "almas gemelas" (twin souls) (23).[29] All of these parallels seem to suggest an impossibility of arriving at the truth; a fact made all the more noteworthy since each of the characters uses the word "verdad" (truth) on various occasions, but they almost never mean the same thing. To underscore this problem one of Miranda's linguistic tics is the phrase "la verdad la verdad" (the real real truth). He has two other linguistic "tells": he often says "pocón" (teensy-weensy), and he quotes Nietzsche.

It is likely that Dorfman gave Miranda these three linguistic tics for a reason because, considered together, they offer important clues to the play's major themes about language and truth. First, these tics form the cornerstone of Paulina's proof of his guilt. What may appear as random utterances and casual expressions serve as the foundation for her belief in his culpability. Second, the three tics form an interesting commentary on language and truth. The repetition of the phrase "la verdad la verdad" playfully and disturbingly suggests the absence of truth. It is uttered in moments when Miranda suspects that he will not be believed or when he seems to be confessing an intimacy. "Pocón" is a similarly strange linguistic term for a grown man to use, one that again performs linguistic deception since in his word play Miranda uses an augmentative (-ón) instead of a diminutive (-ito or -illo) to exaggerate the idea of smallness.[30] In effect, he twists the word, much in the way that the dictatorship twisted words, by deforming it to signify strangely. Most important, these two linguistic tics are not common; they are not part of a larger collective lexicon used in Chile. They sound odd. Consequently, they suggest Miranda as one who manipulates language and one whose words themselves indicate his distance from the community.

An essential clue to Miranda's use of language comes from his misquoting of Nietzsche, who uttered many misogynistic statements but not the one that Miranda ascribes to him: "Jamás podemos poseer esa alma femenina" (28); ("we can never entirely possess that female soul"; 99).[31] Miranda is actually referring here to Freud, who spent considerable time wondering about the soul and femininity.[32] Nietzsche, in contrast, was not concerned with women's souls. When Dorfman decided to have Miranda misquote Freud and instead attribute the statement to Nietzsche, he was able to link, albeit obliquely, Miranda's use of language with Nietzsche's critique of the truth. There is no question that Dorfman uses Nietzsche strategically. At the time of the play's writing, as noted, poststructural theories skeptical about the relationship between language and meaning were widespread, and it was common for intellectuals in Chile and elsewhere to question the idea of truth and the foundation of ethical commitment. One of the forefathers of these anti-foundational postmodern theories was Nietzsche, who critiques, for instance, in *Beyond Good and Evil* what he calls the "Will to Truth" (1) and who describes truth in *On Truth and Lies in a Nonmoral Sense* as a "movable host of metaphors, metonymies, and anthropomorphisms" (3).[33] An enigmatic figure who appealed to both the Nazis and the poststructuralists, Nietzsche's claims that there were no universally true facts and that all ethical statements were relative combined to form a fundamentally nihilistic philosophy. Dorfman's insertion in his play of words purported to be Nietzsche's, uttered by the accused torturer of Paulina, is highly significant and attests to an important distinction between Dorfman's views about the difficulties of uncovering the truth and those of the nihilist postmodernists.

By the late 1990s, with the era of globalization and the era of testimony coinciding with what I have described as *high* postmodernism's questions of all forms of signification, it was common to wonder whether it was possible to represent the truth. These questions tended to take two forms. On the one side were the nihilists, who considered that any effort at uncovering the truth was essentially identical to the construction of a dangerous master narrative. On the other side was a branch of postmodern thinkers who recognized that binary divisions between truth and lies, good and evil, meaningful language and deceptive language had grown increasingly blurred, but they believed that the lack of a clear foundation should not lead to nihilism but rather to more nuanced, more dialogical and dialectical ways of approaching these problems. These issues are absolutely essential to the play. When a nation has been ruled by violence and deception and when the people have grown complicit through their submission to terror, how is it possible to construct an ethical system? Dorfman asks, "How can you tell the truth if the mask you have adopted is identical to your face?" (*Resistance Trilogy*, 147).

Death and the Maiden begins from the starting point that there is no universal truth. That is not the dilemma. Rather the problem is that if all of the characters in the play have violated one another to some degree, if they have all lied and all deceived, then how can justice be possible? If there is no foundation and no clear line dividing good and evil, how will a new society be formed? That is the challenge because clear guidelines do not exist and there are no easy paths to justice. The most important lesson of the play is that all lies are not equal, all deceptions and transgressions are not identical. Just because all of the characters lie does not make them equally deceptive, and just because they all hurt one another does not make them equally guilty of crimes against humanity. They intersect and overlap and occupy parallel places, but they are not the same, nor are they entirely different. Thus the audience is left with the difficult task of determining how to arrive at justice when all are relatively guilty.

It is important to remember that Paulina was tortured, at least in part, to discover the truth. Page DuBois explains that torture is also about breaking the spirit, terrifying the public, and creating a global spectacle (157). Every way that the Pinochet regime defined and crafted and coerced the truth was violent and deceptive. Then the Rettig Commission came forward as a gesture toward the truth, but it was such a weak attempt, so small in the face of so much suffering, that its efforts to correct the truths of the regime were almost more painful because they denied the truths of so many. Rather than relegate the idea of the truth to the realm of hegemonic master narratives, Dorfman's play refuses nihilism as much as it refuses certainty. This is evidenced by the fact that even though Paulina's testimonial to Gerardo is not absolutely true and even though the audience never learns the details of her torture, the audience does not question whether or not she was detained, tortured, and raped. Similarly, even though Miranda's confession may be coerced and may not be entirely factual, there is no question that the words he speaks are true in the sense that if he had not been the torturer, then it had been someone like him. DuBois claims that it is false to assume a binary between violently imposed truths and relinquishing the "will to truth": "there are other ways of describing the truth—as the correspondence between words and things, between knowledge and reality, as a multiple, polyvalent assembly of voices. Truth can be understood as a process, a dialectic, less recovery of something hidden or lost, rather a creation in democratic dialogue" (147).

This struggle for truth is the core dilemma that concerns the play, and it is a dilemma that is never fully resolved. The clearest indication of this ambiguity lies in the ending, which mirrors both the audience (when a mirror is placed in front of the stage) and the beginning of the play. Critics are as divided on what to make of the ending as they are on whether or not Miranda is guilty. One of the keys to the ending is that the first lines of the play are repeated at the end, when Gerardo speaks first to Miranda and later to the audience about Paulina's ability to mix a strong drink. He says she "hace un piscosour que es de miedo" (16; 83); ("makes a margarita that will make your hair stand on end"; 89; 143). It is a repetition that could suggest that there has been no change, that Gerardo has learned nothing, and that he is still the same man, bragging about the domestic skills of his wife. But what is most important about this repetition is that the phrase "de miedo" translated into English as "make your hair stand on end" doubly signifies because it can refer to a strong drink as well as to torture. Are both of Gerardo's utterances the same? Do they mean the same thing to the audience, and does he mean the same thing when he says them? It is my reading that they do not mean the same thing and that the play has slowly turned language into one of its main characters. Over the course of the three acts, the audience has gone from being able to casually listen to Gerardo say that his wife can make a drink that will make one's hair stand on end to hearing such phrases carry an entirely different weight. No matter what the audience thinks about Paulina's sanity or Miranda's guilt, those words will not sound the same, and therein lies Dorfman's final message about language and truth: their connection may be unstable, shifty, aporetic, and imprecise, but the ongoing project of critically considering such communicative disruptions constitutes the hopeful challenge of life rather than the nihilism of despair.

The last words of the play are not its last sounds, however; those are left to Schubert and the quartet that lends its title to the play. In tandem to the play's interest in the relationship between language and truth is its interest in the role that art can play in mediating terror, offering inspiration, and representing tragedy. Carolyn Pinet points out that Gerardo's role on the commission will be to create a new text (95). By the end of the play that text has been completed, even though it was "censored in advance" (95). The play produces two additional texts: Paulina's testimonial, which remains unwritten and unheard, and Miranda's coerced confession, which he both records and writes. These texts and their incomplete, frustrating ambiguity connect directly to another set of texts—those that are artistic. The play wonders how these different types of representation relate to one another. For just as Paulina's testimonial is tied to Miranda's confession, the two characters share another bond: they both listen to and take pleasure in the music of Schubert. While Miranda has enjoyed Schubert and led a privileged life, Paulina's story has gone unheard, and she has been unable to listen to Schubert since her torture. The Schubert connection allows Dorfman to pursue another set of urgent questions about art and social trauma. How can victims and perpetrators share the same art? Given the fact that Paulina and Miranda both love the same art, what role can art play in attending to the truth and trauma of the past?

These questions are aptly channeled through Dorfman's choice of musical interlocutor, Franz Schubert. Many scholars have pursued the ties between Schubert's quartet and the play, tracing the connections among a poem by M. Claudius; a song by Schubert; and the quartet, which only later came to be known as *Der Tod und Das Madchen*. The themes of the song, where a maiden is frightened by death, who responds that she need not be afraid because he is her friend, have obvious connections to the drama of the play. David Schroeder provides the most thorough analysis of the intertextuality between the play and the quartet, and he suggests that Dorfman chooses Schubert because of the links between Schubert's aesthetic project and his own: "In struggling with a society unable to find its way after a period of brutality, questioning its capability of returning to civility and decency or even recognizing hope, Dorfman could not have found a spirit more resonant to the same probing than Schubert" (n.p.). Schroeder identifies a number of crucial aesthetic links between the play and the quartet: both works shrink the space between the performance and the audience; both are profoundly ambiguous; and both refuse to satisfy the desire for beauty, nostalgia, and reconciliation after a moment of destruction. Similar to Dorfman's aesthetics of hope, where the absence of easy answers leads to a form of hope that requires active recognition of pain and violence, Schubert's music, according to Schroeder, "allows for the possibility of hope, as its beauty can transcend the devastation" (n.p.).

A key part of the interplay between Schubert's quartet and the play is the form of the quartet. Often referred to as a conversation among equals, the quartet is one of the most intimate musical forms, and it was common for the composer to play one of the instruments. The pairing of a quartet that uses four instruments over four movements with a play in three acts with three characters allows Dorfman to push on the relationship between art and form. On one level the play revolves around a series of triangulations—among characters; among acts; among the three moments when Schubert's music appears in the play; and, most important, among the three views of the truth that each character represents. Against these triangulations Dorfman's intertextuality with Schubert's quartet inserts a fourth element that repeatedly intervenes to disrupt this structure. For instance, the three sources of sound that come from the characters' voices are interrupted by a fourth source, which alternates between the music of a quartet (by either Schubert or Mozart) and the voice of Miranda on the tape recorder. During the first scene of the third act, when Paulina explains how listening to Schubert while being tortured allowed her to briefly reclaim her humanity, the audience hears the music itself. Paulina's voice fades, to be replaced by Miranda, who confesses that he used the music to manipulate his victims. For her, the music was a salvation, but it was a false and ultimately destructive one because its beauty is precisely what lured her to suffer her most excruciating terror. Like the false words of death in Schubert's song that tell the maiden not to worry and that she should not be afraid, the music provided a brief respite from the horrors of torture. As Paulina explains, Miranda was her most devastating torturer because in contrast with the barbarity of the others, he "ponía Schubert" (54); ("would play Schubert"; 121). Miranda confirms this in his confession: "Ponía música porque eso ayudaba al rol que me tocaba hacer, el rol del bueno, que le dicen, ponía Schubert para que me tomaran confianza" (70); ("I would put on the music because it helped me in my role, the role of good guy, as they call it, I would put on Schubert because it was a way of gaining the prisoners' trust"; 134–35). He uses Schubert because it reminds his prisoners of the civilized world, making it easier for them to withstand the darkness of terror. Eventually, though, the music's association with torture contaminates the idea of civilization for Paulina entirely. After confronting Miranda with her certainty of his guilt, Paulina claims that she will now kill him. With this act she believes she will be able to recover her sense of civilization and, by association, her country and her husband (75; 139). But the solution is not that simple because the work of art and its meaning cannot be controlled so simply. If she kills him, her Schubert may become even more disturbing.

Dorfman illustrates this point by breaking the fourth wall of the stage and implicating the audience as the fourth instrument as a mirror descends in a Brechtian move of distanciation. In the background the audience hears the fourth movement of a different quartet, Mozart's Dissonant Quartet. The choice of music is again quite telling. There is a prior link to Miranda, who earlier in the play had said "También me gusta Vivaldi, y Mozart, y Telemann" (59); ("I also like Vivaldi and Mozart and Telemann"; 125). The last movement of Mozart's quartet is often thought of as a lighter ending to the disturbing first movement, but as Schroeder explains, the last movement "initially creates an illusion that all is well, but through its procedures quickly undermines that sense of stability."[34] The reference to dissonance is yet another clue to the intersections between the play and the music: art may help to build a bridge, but it may also be a way to destroy everything. As Pinet explains, "One of the most enticing qualities of music is that it is no one's and everyone's" (97). Dorfman pushes this notion by suggesting that art can create community just as surely as it can annihilate it. If Schubert's quartet has become irremediably tainted for the characters and the audience, what are the hopes that the play, *Death and the Maiden*, can highlight the social function of art?

Pinet proposes that *Death and the Maiden* forces the audience to consider whether art can be "fatally polluted by history" (97). It is a question that resonates with research on art and the Holocaust in a series of projects that asked how a supposedly civilized society was capable of such barbarity. Implicating Schubert in this history, Steiner writes: "We know that a man can read Goethe or Rilke in the evening, that he can play Bach and Schubert, and go to his day's work at Auschwitz in the morning" (ix). Of course, the composer most tainted by the Holocaust is Wagner, but Schroeder contends that Schubert plays a similar function in the drama of *Death and the Maiden*. How can victims and victimizers share the same art, and if they can, what does that say about the social function of art? Theodor Adorno's famous comment about the possibility of poetry after Auschwitz adds another layer of doubts about society, art, and trauma: "To write poetry after Auschwitz is barbaric" (*Prisms*, 34). Often misread as a statement about the end of art, Adorno's words speak to the intractable limitations of art in the face of horror and to the absolute necessity for it. When artistic discourse has been thoroughly implicated as an accomplice to the massive abuse of human life, how can art serve the process of reconstruction and reconciliation? Adorno argues that art after Auschwitz must move past "self-satisfied contemplation" (34). Similarly, Dorfman's aesthetics of hope requires an art that is neither complacent nor complicit; that exposes its own failures; and that recognizes the slow, painful, imperfect process of recovery.

Konfidenz. Many of the same questions posed in *Death and the Maiden* appear in amplified form in Dorfman's next work, the novel *Konfidenz* (1994).[35] *Konfidenz* mirrors a number of the play's central themes, but these themes are reflected in ways that are more distorted and more fractured. Similar to *Death* *and the Maiden*, *Konfidenz* ponders the difficulties of trust and love in a world full of treachery, deception, and violence. But in a reverse move from *Death and the Maiden*, where Dorfman makes the correlative context of Chile clear from the outset only to slowly broaden the reference, *Konfidenz* begins in a historical and geographical vacuum and the reader remains unaware of the plot's historical specifics until the middle of the text. In *Death and the Maiden* the core conflicts are largely visible to the audience in the first act; the drama is in watching the characters attempt to dialogue and express their versions of the past. In contrast, *Konfidenz* withholds everything from the reader. And where Gerardo and Paulina in *Death and the Maiden* are seeking a way to end a painful chapter in their lives so as to find a way to continue their love, *Konfidenz* is about beginnings, about whether love can begin amid war and betrayal.

We eventually discover that *Konfidenz* is set in Paris on the day that Germany invades Poland, causing France and Great Britain to begin the Second World War. The location allowed Dorfman to pursue his interest in drawing ties across parallel historical contexts. Even though he had made references in prior works to the war, this text is significant because it is the first one that attempts a departure from Latin America. In the case of *Widows*, for instance, Dorfman manipulated the context in order for the book to pass by the Chilean censors. The Greek setting and the Danish frame were literary maneuvers meant to enable him to write a novel about Chile for Chile. In *Konfidenz* the setting is also a consequence of personal and political events, but this time the movement is away from Chile. Dorfman explains that "the work on *Konfidenz* is a very major moment for me because it also coincides with the moment when I decide that I will not return to Chile" (cited in McClennen in *Context*, 7). After years of participating in the struggle to end the dictatorship and restore democracy to Chile, Dorfman wrote *Death and the Maiden*, his most internationally successful work; he imagined it as a gift to Chilean reconstruction, but it was resoundingly rejected by the center-left elites. After *Death and the Maiden*, Dorfman's plans to return to live permanently in Chile changed, and he began to conceive of himself as a global citizen who belonged nowhere. Added to his transition from exile to expatriate, Dorfman wrote *Konfidenz* literally while shuttling between France and the United States to work on the French set for the film version of *Death and the Maiden*; being in France likely contributed to his interest in returning to the conflicts of the Second World War. Dorfman describes the fundamental conflict of *Konfidenz* as one that he could not have imagined during the years of struggling against Pinochet:

So the next step, in *Konfidenz*, was to do something I had not yet ever attempted, which was to look at a revolutionary movement that might be
willing to betray one of its own, which is a terrible thing to conceive for
somebody like myself who has participated in a revolution and who would
never have thought that possible in the Allende years. It seems almost in-
conceivable, in spite of the whole sorry story of socialism and of human
beings, right? Let me just say that it was almost impossible for me to express that directly or openly while I was engaged with a collective that was
trying to overthrow a dictator. In other words you bring in certain doubts,
but those doubts cannot be the focus, they cannot be in the center of what
you are writing, because he who doubts to the degree that I do in *Konfidenz* is unable finally to engage in immediate political action. (Cited in
McClennen in *Context*, 7)

The novel's suspicions that even the most politically progressive projects are
contaminated by betrayal and manipulation were likely fueled not only by the
fact that Dorfman was no longer part of an active political struggle, but also by
his own sense of betrayal by the Chilean community, which he had envisioned
as his home. This sense of disappointment may explain why the novel doubts
everything, including the writer's ability to tell a story.

Framed as a novel of suspense, *Konfidenz* begins when a woman who has
recently arrived in a hotel in Paris receives an anonymous phone call from a
man who knows her every intimate detail. The man tells her that he is calling
on behalf of her lover, Martin, who can't come to the phone because he is
working for the anti-Nazi resistance. They speak in a series of conversations
over nine hours, during which time the man, who is eventually named as Leon
(and later as Max), attempts to seduce the woman, Barbara (whom he also calls
Susanna). According to Leon, since he was twelve he has dreamed of a woman
named Susanna who has guided him and loved him. It has been his goal in life
to find her. When he met Martin while he was training him for the resistance,
he saw a photo of Barbara and recognized her as his Susanna. Barbara does not
believe him.

Throughout the text the conversation between Barbara and Leon is interrupted by short sections in which the author/narrator provides meta-
commentary on the act of writing, on his lack of control over the story, and on
an ominous other man who is also observing the two characters. Every time
the novel reveals details to the reader, these are quickly destabilized, but eventually historical circumstances overtake the conversation, even if these events
create more confusion than clarity. It is September 1, 1939, and a maid at

the Parisian hotel where Barbara is staying has been eavesdropping on the phone conversation, her curiosity piqued by Barbara's speaking German. Unbeknown to Barbara, Germany has invaded Poland, making the French very tense and very suspicious of Germans, whom they imagine to all be enemy spies, disregarding the many Germans who had taken refuge in France to form the resistance. Knocks on the door lead to Barbara's detention, and Leon, who comes to her rescue, is detained as well. The only way for Leon to arrange for her release is to agree to return to Germany to spy for the French; there he will likely be arrested by the Gestapo. He also negotiates with the police inspector, who may or may not be the ominous male presence that has been observing them, to have one night with Barbara. Later Barbara is taken by the inspector to Leon's wife, Claudia, and entrusted to her care. The inspector then, in a move that mirrors that of Leon, tries to seduce Claudia. Barbara is deceptively introduced as Leon's daughter, not his lover, and Barbara is pregnant, later giving birth to a daughter named Victoria. Is the child Martin's or Leon's? The novel ends the night before Leon and Martin are set to be executed. They are in prison together. Leon has learned of the baby and hopes it is his; he also hopes that Barbara will tell his story to the child.

Konfidenz proposes a similar ethical dilemma to that of *Death and the Maiden* because both stories take place in a world where there are no universal truths and where all are guilty of deception, betrayal, and falsehood. But where *Death and the Maiden* staged this conflict publicly, *Konfidenz* is painfully intimate. Narrated almost entirely in dialogue, the novel simulates the theater of the absurd, especially that of Pinter. Characters confuse each other, dialogue is vague and unspecified, words repeat, and silences abound. Despite these literary elements, the novel's self-consciousness and the author/narrator's frequent interruptions force the reader into the uncomfortable position of a reader/voyeur. As Andrei Codrescu writes of *Konfidenz*, "We could be in a play rather than a novel, if it were not for the author (or someone like him), supremely self-conscious of both his inventions and his inability to control them" (v–vi). Whereas *Death and the Maiden* situates the audience as the quartet's fourth instrument, *Konfidenz* make no similar gesture toward a collective resolution. Not only does the novel refuse to glorify collective resistance, but it also seriously questions an exalted, pristine notion of love as a human emotion capable of building solidarity and solace. As Codrescu points out, two of the novel's causalities are abstract ideas of "the people" and "love" since neither "can be found apart from the contexts in which they are thought" (vi).

In keeping with the novel's postmodern noir aesthetic, the unforgiving and alienating world in which the characters live is morally ambiguous. For every glimpse of light, there is a shadow, and for every gesture of beauty, there is betrayal. Dorfman constructs this world using a simple yet confounding technique of doubling and mirrors.[36] For each character and each gesture there is a twin. Sometimes that twin is a double, other times it is a mirror opposite, and most times it is a combination. Every significant feature of the novel is doubled, reflected, and layered over other traces that may or may not be similar. To mention only a few examples: The two main characters each have two names, as does Martin, who is also called Hans; the author/narrator is mirrored by an ominous male presence who may be the inspector whose actions with Leon's wife mirror Leon's actions with Barbara; Barbara contemplates the telephone and her camera as similar yet distinct modes of communication; she looks at herself in the mirror twice; Barbara has been deceived by Martin and also by Leon; both Martin and Leon may have been betrayed by the resistance, and they will both die, each believing that Victoria is his daughter.

In a complex example of this technique the reader learns that Leon began to dream Susanna on his twelfth birthday. On the same day that he crossed the threshold of adult masculinity, his father and brother were arrested by the Gestapo. Later his father is released, but his brother is forced to fight in the war and dies. His father is consumed by his pain and unable to care for Leon, and since his mother died when he was three, he is left without parental support. Like Oriana from *Mascara*, Leon has been radically traumatized, but instead of losing his memory and collecting those of others, he is rescued by Susanna, who visits him every night in his dreams, acting as both mother and lover, giving him advice, sensual pleasure, and comfort. He considers the night she first visited him as the night that he was born. Susanna has helped Leon develop his two most powerful skills: first, he is an excellent forger, not only because he can copy text perfectly, but also because he is able to totally immerse himself in the minds of others so that the words he forges are identical to those they would have written. Once he forges a letter from his father that his father later reads and believes that he wrote. Second, Leon is a master storyteller, but like the stories of Scheherazade, his stories do not reveal anything. All they do is entangle the listener in stories within stories. In a mirroring of these experiences, the reader learns that Barbara works with twelve-year-old boys in Berlin. She gives them cameras, and they photograph their dreams for the future. She helps boys to become men just as Susanna helped Leon to manhood. But Barbara helps these young men place their dreams in the form of an external representation—a photograph—whereas Susanna has cautioned Leon to keep everything inside, only appearing to him while he is sleeping.

The mirrors between Barbara and Leon are refracted through the various forms of representation they produce. They represent stories about themselves, about others, and about history. In almost every case these representations are layered with many often contradictory versions. As Marcelo Coddou explains in his analysis of the novel, "Opera en la novela de Dorfman . . . un concepto de negación dialéctica, en que la mimesis del orden establecido va simultáneamente acompañada por la negación de ella" (111); (A concept of negative dialectics operates in Dorfman's novel in which the mimesis of the established order is simultaneously accompanied by its negation). This literary strategy drives toward a fundamental epistemological question at the core of the novel. Dorfman explains that the novel asks, "How do we trust language? How do we trust fiction as such? Can fiction tell the story? And I question the difference between the dream and reality, or between what we dream and what we desire, and what we see. So there is an epistemological questioning at the very basic level of storytelling itself" (cited in McClennen in *Context*, 7).

These intertwined questions are mirrored by the eight sections interspersed through the text in which the author/narrator provides meta-commentary on the novel and his role in writing or discovering or shaping it.[37] During the first break in the narrative the narrator informs the reader that this story is not invented but discovered. According to the narrator himself, he functions as a conduit for a timeless yet historical tale of desire and deceit, politics and love. This simple notion of the narrator as an objective instrument of the facts becomes complicated when the narrator explains that he knows that he has a double, a man with sinister intent who also wants to take charge of the lives of the characters (19–20; 11–12).[38] This twin/double/other to the narrator is presented as having more power to control the characters' destinies; Coddou reads this character as a double for the reader, who has the power to control the destiny of the text (109). Another reading of these two characters is that the author/narrator is the loving, gentle recorder of the lives of his characters, selflessly transcribing their story so that it will live on forever, and the sinister man is the fascist state that wants to eradicate their bodies and their history. Then there is the possibility that the ominous man is the inspector, who is a more sinister version of Leon. It seems that the text has set up a binary between a passive conduit for the lives of the characters, the author/narrator, and the sinister man who wants to control their destiny, but even this division is shown to be false, and the novel denies such nostalgic notions about the emancipatory power of literature.

The deception of this binary is made clear when the author/narrator insists repeatedly on his lack of control over the story, only to later claim that he is responsible for it, which means that he also has narrative power. This control is highlighted when he decides to muse about his own failures as a writer while his main character, Leon/Max, is left alone, unheard and forgotten: "Claro que mientras medito sobre estos dilemas, y empiezo a lamentar mi propia impotencia, y conjuro estrategias literarias, y juzgo la moralidad de un mundo que produce tanta falacia y sufrimiento, lo único que realmente importa es que he dejado solo a Max. Y que este hombre que sí tienes planes se acerca más y más. Si es que ese hombre existe" (137); ("While you mull all this over and feel sorry for yourself and conjure up literary strategies and moralize about the suffering of the world, the only truth that really matters is that nobody is with Max. You have left him alone"; 137). As these two passages demonstrate, there are significant differences between the Spanish and English versions. In the original Spanish this passage is written primarily in the first person, while the English translation narrates it primarily in the second person, merging more directly the author/narrator with the reader.[39] Moreover, the last lines of the Spanish, which allude to the sinister man approaching Leon/Max and then wonder if he exists at all, are completely absent from the English, a version that is in general far sparser than the original.

These layers within the texts and across them create a fun house of mirrors that is disturbing and confusing, a tactic that eventually forces the reader to confront the relationship among representation, discursive structures, and power. Dorfman makes this point most clearly in the last meta-commentary section, where he shifts the subject of the author/narrator again in a final comment on whether or not the text is capable of reflection, representation, and recognition. In the Spanish the shift is from the first-person singular to the first-person plural, and in the English it is from the second-person to the first-person singular and plural: "¿O existe una manera en que yo pueda mantenerme leal a él, ahora que estamos llegando al desenlace? . . . ¿Pero quién puede asegurar que Max, tal como lo oímos ahora, más allá del tiempo y de la muerte y del lenguaje, no nos llamó desde un momento anterior a nuestro propio nacimiento? ¿Quién puede afirmar a ciencia cierta que Max no haya existido tal como nosotros lo soñamos?" (166); ("Many will think that you are also making all this up, again compensating for not having been able to help him, again looking for a way to write one story that has a good, decent man at its core. But who is to say that Max, as I hear him now, across time and death and language, did not call to me from a moment before my birth, who is to say he did not exist as we have dreamt him?"; 166).[40] In an example of the poetics of his aesthetics of hope, Dorfman shifts the subject position of these sections, calling attention to the way that language and subjectivity are intertwined. Language can force, reinforce, and resist identities. It can rescue them, and it can annihilate them. At one point the author/narrator wonders why the focus of the story wasn't Susanna, but such questions are asked too late. By then Susanna/Barbara is gone. The author/narrator has chosen to focus on Leon/Max, and Susanna/Barbara's story will be forgotten.

The twists and turns taken by the author/narrator, who alternately shapes, discovers, mediates, and forgets key components of the story, are mirrored by both the other man and by the storytelling of Leon/Max. The narrator, who wants to reveal the story of his characters, must contend with the other man, who wants to silence them, but then there is the problem of whether or not Leon/Max is a con man. Even if the author/narrator wants to directly transmit the story, what happens if that story has been manipulated and fabricated by his main character? "¿Y si Max me ha estado engañando, tal como todo este tiempo ha estado engañando a la mujer que él llama Susana? ¿Haciéndome creer que es inocente, cuando quizás ha sido él quien traicionó a sus compañeros de organización para inculpar a Martin, para quedarse con esa mujer?" (135); ("The question can no longer be avoided. Has Max been conning you? Has Max been fooling you all this time just as he has been fooling the woman he calls Susanna? Making you believe he's innocent, when all along he's been the one who betrayed his own men back home in order to blame Martin, in order to keep the girl?"; 135). Who can be trusted? And how can we tell the difference between a con game and a love story? This tension also exposes Dorfman's concern with the liberating possibilities of storytelling: even though his literature depends on its liberating potential, after exile the painful realities of Chile's past were still being silenced. Now, though, it was not only the figures like Pinochet that wanted to keep history quiet, but it was also members of the moderate center—like Gerardo from *Death and the Maiden*—who were willing to sacrifice the truth for a false peace. *Konfidenz* explores the ways that power controls the forces of historical memory, except now the division between those with power and those without it is far less clear.

One of the central ways that Dorfman explores this problem in *Konfidenz* is through the protagonist, Leon, who remains an enigma. He forms part of a collective resistance but keeps many secrets and manipulates others. He censors and forges. He tells stories that may or may not be true but are always captivating. He seduces Barbara by trying to convince her that she is the woman of his dreams. Is she the woman of his dreams, or is she a girl that he became obsessed with years earlier when he worked as a journalist in Berlin, or is she his daughter? Barbara travels to Paris to visit Martin, her lover, but upon arrival at her hotel the phone rings, and the caller is a man she has never met. This man knows an extraordinary amount of personal information about her.

She stays on the phone in the hope of finding out about Martin, but Leon/Max weaves a web of stories around her. Even though she is suspicious of him, he slowly gains her confidence—or does he? He believes that it is his right to enter her private world. When she becomes angry, he responds that under the current government in Germany there is no privacy. Like a fascist government that takes away the rights of its citizens at will, Leon believes that his violation of Barbara's rights is justified (40; 44). Leon, then, is not just a member of the resistance; he is also a threat to Barbara—or is he a man desperately in love with her? Similarly, the narrator of the novel is not simply a man who is afraid of his evil other; he is a combination of representational forces: one that wants to transcribe the story meticulously, recording each character's words; one that wants to bend the story to his will; and one that wants to silence the story. Each effort at representation is highly ambiguous, contaminated by desire and power, death and love, hope and despair.

Because of the novel's insistence on the ambiguities of representation, the reader does not learn the national origin of Barbara and Leon until the middle of the novel, when the narrator also discovers their identity. At a deep level the novel pushes the reader, in conjunction with the author/narrator, to struggle over what can and cannot be narrated and known. If literature is epistemologically fractured and flawed, if there is no way to know a text, then what is the purpose of literature, especially literature that struggles to be socially relevant? Modernist obsessions over evil and nationality are disrupted by the postmodern, post-exile aesthetic that preoccupies Dorfman. Nevertheless, the postmodern aesthetic of dispersion does not mean that evil does not exist or that it is not important to fight it. Therefore as the phone conversation progresses between Barbara and Leon, the narrator slowly reveals certain orienting features of the story. The nationality of the characters (74; 77), the year the novel takes place (94; 94), and other local referents are revealed only after the global reach of the story has been established. And when these details are finally revealed, they are exposed along with the author/narrator's own confession that he had hoped the story would be more about him, about Latin America. But, no, he writes, no one cares about his country, that "país perdido" (lost country) "con un pasado que nadie quiere recordar" (76); ("with a past that no one seems to remember"; 76). The author/narrator is an eternal exile; the story he wants to write cannot be written. Instead he is stuck with this story, which is so much like the one he nostalgically wants to write yet so different. He describes the differences as though they were the differences between the memory of a loved one and someone seen from afar who seems almost identical, but when that person approaches, the mind procrastinates the recognition of their differences: "rehusa minuciosamente fijarse en los rasgos que no encajan" (77); ("you painstakingly refuse to notice the little traces that don't match"; 75).

The novel asks how these layers relate and connect. Do they unravel one another or reinforce one another or both? The effect of constructing all of these layers and traces within a larger aesthetic project that desperately seeks to have faith in the social role of literature underscores some of the central questions about representation. Not surprisingly, such a tactic has led scholars like Euisik Kim to consider Dorfman in Lacanian terms: Kim reads *Konfidenz* as a study in transference. *Konfidenz* aims straight at Derridean traces and Lacanian mirrors, but just as the reader thinks that Dorfman is situating his work in a nihilistic world of self-perpetuating uncertainty, he takes a turn back toward the political postmodern and unmasks what Codrescu calls "a stubbornly poetic faith in something the ambiguous narrator calls 'the future'" (vi).

Behind all the novel's reflecting layers and mirrors there remains a tremendous wound of historical terror and human betrayal. From Susanna, Max/Leon learns that he has carried this wound since he was born, an enormous crack in the center of his being that allows the pain of the world to enter him. This wound, though, she tells him, is not a lack, not an absence or a flaw; it is what makes him beautiful because it is what connects him to the world: "mi grieta era parte de una grieta mucho más ancha y profunda" (72); ("the crack inside you is part of a more serious and wider and deeper crack"; 70). In this way, the novel's relentless deconstruction of identity, certainty, trust, and representation is more aptly understood within the ethical debates about recognition of difference and the tensions between pluralism and consensus than the poststructural psychoanalytic obsession with the fractured self. Reading the novel through the ethical philosophy of Emmanuel Levinas, for instance, brings Dorfman's preoccupations about the possibility of representing the other into conversation with Levinas's concerns about how these communicative gaps affect social justice. Such a pairing also takes into account the novel's setting of the horrors and betrayals of the Holocaust and Second World War. It also facilitates an appreciation of the novel's last line: "¿O vas a permitir que nuestra historia muera conmigo?" (175); ("Or will you allow our history to die with me?"; 177). Here Dorfman toys with the precarious relationship between a plurality, "our history," and the single self, "me," which are both separated and united, mutually dependent and independent, and never perfectly understood. They are identities that can survive only through storytelling.

Widows: The Play. The last line of *Konfidenz* closes the novel with a recurring theme that flows throughout Dorfman's work: storytelling as a recuperative and restorative act that has the power to challenge domination and oppression. The theme appears in many of Dorfman's works, including the two theatrical adaptations that followed the publication of *Konfidenz*: *Lector* (1995; *Reader*), based on the short story "Lector" ("Reader"), and *Widows* (1997), adapted from the novel *Viudas* (*Widows*) with the collaboration of Tony Kushner. These two plays and *Death and the Maiden* were then published as *The Resistance Trilogy* (1998). All three plays had been previously published in separate volumes, but this collection provides readers with definitive versions.

As with *Moros en la costa* and *Hard Rain* the multiple versions of these texts provide extraordinarily rich opportunities for scholars interested in the transformations of texts over time, across languages, and through genres. *Widows* began as a poem, became a novel, and was transformed into a play. Dorfman's afterword to the version in *The Resistance Trilogy* describes how the play itself underwent a variety of incarnations: "The poem had taken a night to compose and the novel, a year. The play was to bedevil me for almost a decade" (81). Dorfman drafted a first and second version of the play but remained unsatisfied with the result. Then in 1989 Bob Egan and Gordon Davidson from the Taper Theater suggested that Dorfman seek another writer to collaborate with him on the text. They recommended that he work with Tony Kushner, a playwright who at the time was relatively unknown but later went on to become incredibly successful with *Angels in America*. The two writers worked on the text for two years, and Dorfman credits Kushner with helping him in many ways: "Tony became in effect the bridge I had been looking for to enter the world of theater and reach the U.S. audience which I had found trouble in connecting to this particular story so removed politically and aesthetically from the typical American tradition" (82). The premiere of *Widows* took place in 1991, ten days after the opening of *Death and the Maiden* at the Royal Court in London, but the play still was not what Dorfman had envisioned, and he began to rework the script again, this time alone because Kushner, who was busy with the success of *Angels in America*, felt that the play would benefit most if Dorfman did the final rewrites on his own. The play opened again in 1996 with the addition of a new character, a narrator who, like the play's author, was an exile. When Dorfman watched the play, though, he found that the narrator failed to create the bridge he had sought, and instead of bringing the audience closer to the drama, the narrator functioned as an unwelcome intermediary. So for the definitive English version of the play Dorfman decided to eliminate the narrator, but he tells readers that the narrator may very well reappear in the story's next transformation into cinema (84).[41]

In addition to the differences among the various versions of the play, there are a number of significant distinctions between the novel and the play.[42] The novel's Greek setting and Danish frame have been replaced by a hybrid setting that is more overtly Latin American. Certain characters have been altered. For instance, Emmanuel's girlfriend, Cecilia, is now older and married to a man who has been disappeared. In essence, though, the play retains the substance of the novel. It narrates the fate of a small village where all of the adult men have been disappeared by a totalitarian regime. When the play begins, a new captain has come to the military post to head the transition away from extreme repression and toward economic recovery. Instead of violence there will now be investment. As a sign of these changes the captain plans to build a fertilizer factory, but the place on the riverbank where the factory is to be constructed is precisely the place where the women of the village begin to discover dead bodies floating in the river. One of the most significant signs of the historical shifts that mark the novel and the play is that the play emphasizes divisions among the men in the military, especially between the captain and the lieutenant, as a way of indicating the difficulties that face nations attempting to steer totalitarian regimes toward economic progress. Some of the dilemmas depicted in the play are also reminiscent of the challenges that face transitions to democracy.

Another important change, especially for the purpose of tracing the themes of storytelling, truth claims, and resistance, is the play's development of the mute baby's relationship to Fidelia, the youngest of the women in the Fuentes family. Whereas the plot of the novel opens with the family's matriarch, Sofía, showing up at the captain's office asking to bury a dead body found in the river, the play opens with women washing clothes in the river and speaking about Yanina's baby, who has yet to utter a word.[43] In a certain sense the key to the play is this mute male baby, whose silence is alternately perceived as a wise way to avoid the violence of the state and a tragedy because silence is a form of death. The hope for the baby's entrance into the verbal is placed in the character of Fidelia (again in a way more overt than in the novel), who, we learn in the first scene, whispers stories to the baby. This relationship returns to close the play, as Fidelia is left caring for the baby when all of the women return to wait and probably to be massacred by the river. The baby's father, who has been released from prison, cannot take care of him since he has been thoroughly damaged by his experience of torture and imprisonment. It is Fidelia who will be required to represent the future of the family, not only by caring for the baby, but also by literally being its only surviving female. As the final scene of the play opens, Fidelia addresses the nameless, silent baby she holds in her arms:

> You must learn to talk. You'll need to talk. There are things you'll have to tell.
> But if you decide never to speak, your stories will get told anyway. There are stories that cry out to be told and if the words aren't there they will seep through the skin.
> The wind carries them, the smoke does, the river does, the words of the story will find their way, from the farthest, loneliest places, to places where there are people willing to hear. . . .
> I can wait, I can wait for you to speak. I'm patient. I can wait a long time.
> (73–74)

These lines, which echo the last line of *Konfidenz*, express the notion that the future depends on stories: which stories get told, who tells them, and who listens.

These lines from the last scene also demonstrate the way that the play intertexts more directly than does the novel with classical Greek tragedy. Dorfman's use of the mute, nameless baby as a metaphor for a human society that has consistently refused to name and narrate the atrocities of the past reveals how he takes an aesthetic practice common to tragedy and adapts it to a contemporary situation. Across his works Dorfman has repeatedly used babies —unborn (*The Last Song*), mute (*Widows*), or maimed ("In the Dark")—as symbols for social ills.[44] Alongside these classical literary techniques, Dorfman employs modern and postmodern strategies as well. In conjunction with the play's silent baby, for instance, Dorfman stages a modern conflict between the captain and the lieutenant.

Reader. A similar strategy of aesthetic promiscuity takes place in *Reader*. The play revolves around a censor who, in the course of vetting texts for state approval, finds himself reading a novel about his own life. As the censor plans to prohibit the novel, he realizes that his own life requires that the subversive novel exist. In the tradition of plays like *Death of a Salesman*, *Reader* explores how the structuring narratives of modernity asphyxiate identity. Like Willy Loman, Daniel Lucas, the censor, is a man trapped in his job who has grown estranged from his son because his son has rejected the assimilating tendencies of his father. Both plays present the audience with layered views of the main characters, and in both cases the protagonists die as a consequence of their stifling societies. Where Loman is a symbol for the salesman, though, Lucas is a censor, a profession that allows Dorfman to reflect on the relationship between art and its reception. Parallel to Loman's role as a seller and buyer in a capitalist society that eventually destroys him, Lucas is a censor and reader in a society that controls all forms of media. Lucas finds that in order to really read, which means allowing society and especially his son to read as well, he has to sacrifice himself to the state.

Lucas represents a departure from Dorfman's characteristic protagonists, who tend to be already engaged in a struggle for survival. As Dorfman explains in the afterword, "I wanted to focus on somebody different, someone who, instead of being the captive of terror, is one of the many wheels in the machinery of established power that creates victims, that crushes and forbids the words of others" (212). Dorfman wanted to force his character to face a nightmare in which he would be compelled to recognize the power of literature since the novel that he wanted to censor would be about his own life. To censor it would be to destroy himself and his son, but to allow it to come to life would lead to his death as well. The difference would be that he would die alive rather than live dead. In order for the censor to be the author of his own life, which means that he can read the novel of his own life, he has to take responsibility for the damage he has done to his wife, his lover, his son, and also his community, because in each of these relationships he has been a censor; he has forbidden expression, including his own. When he takes that responsibility, he will die as have many others before him, leaving the "reader" of the play to wonder how such a cycle can end.

These multiple layers and twists reveal the ways that Dorfman's play intertwines a modern dilemma with a postmodern view. Lucas is in many respects a quintessentially modern character, filled with anguish over the way that his life has been scripted by modern society, but he is also postmodern in the sense that he is layered with other versions of himself. Dorfman structures the modern dilemma at the core of *Reader* with postmodern techniques that self-reflexively call attention to the process of representation itself. In two major ways Dorfman adds a postmodern twist to the modern anguish of Lucas. First is a strategy of fragmentation, repetition, and doubling, common features of his aesthetic practice. Doubling reinforces the idea that authors, censors, and readers often overlap. The play begins with Don Alfonso, a censor, reading a novel about the future. With no change of scene but merely a change of lights, the audience then sees Daniel Lucas, a censor, read a novel about the past. *Reader* employs a similar tactic to that in *Konfidenz*, where all of the characters have doubles and where the doubles both are and are not mirrors of each other.

Even though the tendency is to consider Lucas the protagonist, the "primary" character could be either Lucas or Alfonso. One lives in a South American dictatorship in the past. The other lives in a repressive yet liberal society of the future. Each character, each act, and each idea has a double in another time and another place, allowing Dorfman to draw attention to historical repetition via a postmodern questioning of the "original" source of the story.[45]

The second hallmark of a postmodern aesthetic is the play's self-reflexive questioning of representation and art. In a reverse on the postmodern tendency to write about writing, this is a play about writing and reading. In the shift from the past to the future, the censor works for the Director of Moral Resources, who controls both print and screen materials, meaning that the theater is visibly absent from the cultural world of the future. Because Lucas is not working in a dictatorship, Dorfman uses the play to comment on the subtle forms of censorship that affect even the most ostensibly open societies. The Director explains the delicate balance that the cultural arm of this government faces: "We're being watched. We've got to authorize more, so our enemies can't accuse us of not being liberal enough. And we've got to authorize less, so that they can't accuse us of not being conservative enough" (166). By drawing a parallel between the overt censorship of an "ecofascist dictatorship" and the covert censorship of democratic authoritarianism—the government of Lucas's world is referred to as a "democracy" even though there is nothing democratic about it—Reader hints at the insidious ways that control of expression affects all forms of social organization (161).

The central theme of the play is that art that speaks the truth will emerge despite the most egregious forms of censorship and state repression. Daniel Lucas assumes that the novel he is reading has been written by someone who knows him and is mocking him, but he later learns that is not the case. Similar to Fidelia's comment that even if the mute baby chooses not to tell the story of his family, it will be told anyway, Lucas learns that his story has surfaced in the form of a novel because stories like his demand to be told, and it is this knowledge that eventually teaches him to come to terms with his past and take responsibility for his life. These two plays from The Resistance Trilogy, then, present a different perspective on art, representation, and truth than that found in Death and the Maiden and Konfidenz. In these two plays Dorfman suggests that the author simply is a conduit for a story that will inevitably materialize. Regardless of the degree to which power structures attempt to control all social narratives, the "true" stories cannot be silenced. In contrast, Death and the Maiden and Konfidenz suggested that the fate of society depended on a storyteller/witness and a receptive audience capable of attending to the traumas of the past. Rather than understand these differences as indicative of a shift in Dorfman's views on the artistic process, though, these variations on the theme of art and truth should be read as a consequence of Dorfman's interest in approaching the question from a number of angles.

HEADING SOUTH, LOOKING NORTH AND
THE DIASPORIC SUBJECT

One of the interesting features of *Reader* is the way that it tangentially touches on Latino culture. Since the book read by Lucas is set in South America, his assistant, Irene, encourages him to find a way to edit it for publication: "Because sponsors have been demanding more dramas with Latino themes—and if we can get a crippled actor to do the role of this Morales guy, then . . ." (163).[46] These references allow Dorfman to critique an essentialist, quota-oriented notion of cross-culturalism. It would be his next work, his memoir, *Heading South, Looking North* (1998), though, that would give Dorfman an opportunity to explore his ideas about biculturalism, bilingualism, and cultural crossings. Contrary to depictions of ethnic identity in quantitative terms, in the memoir Dorfman points to the conflicts that distinguish identity from identity markers. *Heading South, Looking North* tests the limits of the traditional critical categories used to understand ethnic, diasporic life writing at the same time that it reconsiders the structure and shape of the memoir.[47]

Academic studies of U.S. ethnic literature, exemplified by the early work of Werner Sollers, were originally organized around a dominant critical paradigm that understood the ethnic self as bicultural—divided across two cultures, two languages, two identities; struggling between assimilation and dissimilation; caught between dominant and minority culture. This focus on the bifurcated subject receded when ethnic studies increasingly considered the self as hybrid, multiple, and plentiful. With the work of writers like Gloria Anzaldúa and Cherríe Moraga, axes of identity registered a number of markers that exceeded traditional ethnic categories and included gender, sexuality, and class. Globalization theory has expanded on this sense of self even further by considering the subject in relation to local and transnational spaces (Mendieta; de la Campa).

In a parallel vein, the theoretical bases for autobiography studies have shifted. Sidonie Smith and Julia Watson provide a periodization of critical approaches to life writing, and they single out three phases: (1) studies that focused on the way that autobiographies recorded the life of a great man; (2) studies that problematized the representation of the subject; and (3) contemporary studies, which focus on the "referentiality and relationality of life narrative" (139). The first phase stressed the agency and autonomy of the autobiographer, whereas the second performed a complete critical reversal. The third strikes a balance between the extremes of the first two positions while also highlighting the craft of life writing. Most current life-writing criticism engages at some level with the dualist representation of the self as agent or as socially determined.

Heading South, Looking North challenges many of the critical trends in studies of ethnic, diasporic life writing and reveals that many of the major theoretical approaches employed to understand this type of writing miss the complex interaction of competing ontologies. Dorfman's text has two intersecting and overlapping critical frameworks that shape the way that he narrates his life. The first is a strategy of duality, where the self is described as interacting with two oppositional social forces, and the second is a strategy of polyvalence, where the self is described as a hybrid that cannot be represented through dualisms. These gestures combine to form what I call the *diasporic subject* found in the life writing of exiles and the displaced. The notion of the diasporic engages with Dorfman's experience of triple dispersal—thrice exiled, his attachment to space is constantly in question—and also reflects his Jewish heritage since, well before his birth, his parents' families had experienced a number of forced migrations. My understanding of the diasporic, however, resonates beyond these historical particularities, and the word's etymology suggests the intricate ways that Dorfman's text layers subjectivity. "Diaspora" comes from the Greek "diaspeirein," "to spread about," where "dia" means "apart" and "speirein" means "to sow or scatter." On the one hand, scattering suggests the polyvalent self, and, on the other hand, sowing suggests the binary tension between the attributes found in the seed and those found in the land. These two notions inseparably traverse Dorfman's memoir.

To trace this theory in terms of ethnic studies Dorfman's memoir, at first reading, seems to describe a bicultural self that straddles the borders of a North American, individualistic, materialist subjectivity and one that is Latin American, collective, telluric, and political. From a U.S. source of identity Dorfman's text stresses a sense of autonomy, agency, and responsibility, and the confessional mode he uses reflects an ontology that emanates from an Anglo-European tradition. Alternatively the text has a nonlinear, circular structure typical of Latin American personal storytelling that functions as a counterpoint.[48] This division of the self between the north and the south, especially between English and Spanish, locates Dorfman's text within Latino life writing, and *Heading South, Looking North* could be comparatively read against texts that also perform similar divisions—for example, Richard Rodríguez's *Days of Obligation*, Cherríe Moraga's *Loving in the War Years*, and Reinaldo Arenas's *Antes que anochezca* (*Before Night Falls*). Yet on closer reading, these two competing visions of identity are shown to be porous and are accompanied by further *mestizajes*: Dorfman represents himself as caught not only between the north and the south, but he reveals that his identity is also a product of his European Jewish heritage: "part Yankee, part Chilean, a pinch of Jew, a mestizo in search of a center" (220).

In addition to this being the story of a man raised in an atmosphere of border crossings, Dorfman's memoir is the story of a global writer. Knowing Dorfman's love of Renaissance literature, for instance, is essential to under-standing how his memoir's chapter titles intertext with Spanish Golden Age literature, in particular *Don Quijote*. The memoir titles all begin with the phrase "A Chapter Dealing with . . ." in English and "En el que . . ." in Spanish, paralleling the chapter titles from *Don Quijote*, many of which begin with the phrase "Que trata de . . ." and "De lo que . . ." (Which Deals with . . .). Similar to Cervantes's text, Dorfman's chapter titles are a ruse, and what they signal is not always what the reader encounters. If *Don Quijote* is the story of a frustrated but stubborn reader who refuses to have the forces of history thwart his worldview, then Dorfman's memoir is the story of an equally tenacious, if quirky, writer, an identity that also links his memoir to another Golden Age genre he admires, the picaresque.[49] In many respects his memoir, in the tradition of Jean-Paul Sartre's autobiography, *Les mots* (*The Words*), recounts the formation of a writer. So while it may seem that *Heading South, Looking North* suggests a bicultural identity, a binary between north and south, culturally Dorfman is far more hybrid: he is North and South American, Jewish, thrice exiled, a survivor of trauma, and a writer well versed in world literature. Most vexing for the scholar of his work, though, is that he draws on these multiple cultural influences throughout his text while also still reinforcing the notion that dualities (especially that of north versus south, English versus Spanish) hold particular identitarian purchase.

In considering how *Heading South, Looking North* relates to scholarship on life writing, it is revealing that Dorfman's life narrative is consistently referred to as a memoir and not an autobiography.[50] While the two terms are often used interchangeably, there are key differences. "Autobiography" resonates more closely with the narration of a singular life; it suggests an autonomy and agency inappropriate for describing Dorfman's text and is difficult to sustain in terms of recent critical reflection on the construction of subjectivity. Situated between the collective narrative of *testimonio* and the personal presentation of autobiography, memoir—in Spanish *memoria*, with its allusion to memory and its etymological links to the creation of official records—situates the text between historical document and personal reflection; recalling and recording; musing and witnessing; the self and the collective. Dorfman functions as history's scribe and as historical actor as he narrates his life and his life's inextricable ties to his social context. Nancy K. Miller states that memoir "hesitates to define the binaries between public and private, subject and object" (43). Yet as Dorfman creates a diasporic subject, it is not so much a hesitation to define these binaries but rather a revelation of these binaries and a departure from them. Ostensibly Dorfman consciously creates the tension between the agency of autobiography and the collective subjectivity of *testimonio*.

A telling example of this conflict comes during an early trauma in Dorfman's life, when he is hospitalized and quarantined for three weeks with pneumonia in a New York hospital shortly after his arrival in the United States. This event leads him to English, since his sickness forces him to use English to communicate with the hospital staff, and denies him the ability to talk with his parents, whom he sees soundlessly mouthing words from the other side of a window, and it abruptly forces a split in his identity between Spanish and English unusual in most cases of exile and immigration. In describing the duality that emerges from this harrowing incident, Dorfman wavers between emphasizing agency and choice in his use of language and admitting his submission and passivity to the circumstances of his cultural displacement. The reader must make an effort to recall that at the time of his illness Dorfman had not yet turned three years of age because from the confident tone of the narrative one would imagine a much older child. Despite his young age and budding linguistic skills, Dorfman maintains that he "instinctively chose" English and that he "refused" hybridity. Adding further confusion, he admits that the event led to his "quick and complete surrender to English" (42, 41). This antagonism between understanding his identity as composed of choices exercised by free will or determined by social and historical forces persists throughout the text. Dorfman's description of this moment further reveals his layered, multiple, and yet also binary diasporic sense of self: "I instinctively chose to refuse the multiple, complex, in-between person I would someday become, this man who is shared by two equal languages and who has come to believe that to tolerate differences and indeed embody them personally and collectively might be our only salvation as a species" (42). The description of himself at the moment of writing as "multiple, complex, in-between" suggests the self as pastiche, as a product of *mestizaje*, and his reference to simultaneously being shared equally by two languages portrays the self as dual and double.

Added to the dialectic between autobiographical agency and the subjectivity of *testimonio*, Dorfman constructs a text that oscillates among the modalities of the confession, the apology, and the memoir. Francis R. Hart points out that each of these forms has its own "principles of memory selection and narrative perspective" and that each author discovers his or her own "fluctuating mixture" (508). The autobiographical registers intertwine in Dorfman's text in response to the excruciating difficulty he has narrating the trauma of Pinochet's coup. Trauma, which derives from the Greek for "wound," characteristically results in a lack of language, an inability on the part of the traumatized to name their experience, and *Heading South, Looking North* can be productively categorized as trauma narrative. Leigh Gilmore explains that "the subject of trauma refers to both a person struggling to make sense of an overwhelming experience in a particular context and the unspeakability of trauma itself, its resistance to representation" (47). Here it might be useful to appropriate Paul de Man's notion of autobiography as *prosopopeia*—the act of linguistically constructing a life that is imaginary or absent—within the concrete context of a writer who is attempting to bear witness to the lives lost during Pinochet's dictatorship. The text balances the weight of Dorfman's presence against all of those who are absent, disappeared, and unable to tell their side of the story. Consequently, Dorfman's text is autobiographical in that it endeavors to highlight the active way in which he has constructed his life; it is testimonial in that it is the story of a collective; it is memoir as it wavers between recalling and recording; and its evidence of apology and confession designate it as trauma narrative.

To unpack these multiple modalities it might be useful to focus on the opening lines of the text:

> I should not be here to tell this story.
>
> It's that simple: there is a day in my past, a day many years ago in Santiago de Chile, when I should have died and did not.
>
> That's where I always thought this story would start, at that moment when history turned me, against my will, into the man who could someday sit down and write these words, who now writes them. I always thought this story was meant to start on that morning when the Armed Forces of my country rise against our President, Salvador Allende, on the 11th of September of 1973, to be exact, and the death I have been fearing since I was a child enters my life and, instead of taking it, leaves me to survive:

I am left here on this side of reality to remember what ends forever that day in me and in the world, still wondering why I was spared.

And yet I cannot bring myself to begin there, that day I should have died. (3–4)

The passage has a confessional, apologetic tone that is counterbalanced with the vision of the writer, the storyteller, who exercises a certain degree of control over his text. Dorfman suggests that he was the victim of history but that he answered that victimization with the agency of writing. He is certain that he cheated death. This is not egotistical hubris but is grounded in the fact that he was meant to be with Salvador Allende on that fateful morning but had arranged with a friend to switch shifts—a fact made even more obvious in the Spanish version's phrase "alguien . . . murió en mi lugar" that closes the first sentence (9); (someone . . . died in my place).[51] This twist of fate, over which he feels no control, leads him to respond with writing, and over the course of the memoir it becomes clear that Dorfman's identity as a writer is what saves him from despair and structures his life. Freighted with guilt over his survival, Dorfman makes it his mission, his calling, to act as a medium for those who died in his place. To underscore this tension between artistic agency and lack of free will, Dorfman artfully refuses to use contractions after the subject pronoun "I," a technique made all the more noteworthy by the two contractions ("It's" and "That's") that begin the second and third paragraphs. This refusal to blend the words, to shorten the phrases describing the subject and its actions, highlights the separation between his coincidental survival and the tragic loss of so many of his friends and so many Chileans. The "I" stands alone, isolating him, while the verbs are separated, stilted, an effect that also calls attention to the performance of writing. In the Spanish version, which Dorfman translated from the English, this practice necessarily changes since Spanish does not allow flexibility in the use of contractions—there are two required forms that are prepositional phrases ("al" ["a" plus "el"] and "del" ["de" plus "el"]). Consequently, Dorfman employs a parallel strategy in Spanish by repeating phrases in the first person that underscore his solitary identity. In the first and last lines that correspond to the English passages noted above, the lack of contractions is replaced by a repetition of phrases that similarly suggest a search for the proper link between subject and action: "Si estoy contando esta historia, si la puedo contar" and "No puedo, no quiero, comenzar ahí" (9); (If I am telling this story, if I can tell it; I cannot, I will not, begin there). The last phrases in Spanish also draw attention to the distinction between subjective reality ("no puedo") and desire ("no quiero").

These lines illustrate how the text departs from trauma and from the unspeakability of trauma, and they call attention to the writer's craft, to Dorfman's dialogue between what he wants to write and what he feels that history has compelled him to write. The phrase "the man who could someday sit down and write these words, who now writes them" emphasizes the traumatic warping of history where the past occupies the present. Dorfman opens his memoir by stating that he will not begin at what he thought was the beginning but instead will rewrite himself: by altering his own version of events and his own privileging of the coup as a marker for his identity, he recreates himself. This gesture, which emphasizes the fragile and subjective ways that history is recorded, immediately makes the reader suspicious of Dorfman's historical memory and his self-presentation. The memoir repeatedly suggests that the reader should not trust Dorfman's account of events. In relaying his time in the hospital, he reveals that his memory may not even be his own: "My parents have told me the story so often that sometimes I have the illusion that I am the one remembering" (28). These asides to the reader reinforce the notion that Dorfman's memory is a construct. Indeed, Dorfman's goal is to challenge the reader to take an active role in attending to history, and his consistent references to faulty memories are meant to distance the reader while simultaneously building a sense of fraternity, for by admitting his inaccuracies, he lets the reader in on a shared secret and makes the reader his accomplice. Dorfman's authorial strategy is clear: the memories of the dead will not be honored by a passive reading; they require collaboration between the reader and the writer.

In addition, the opening lines of the memoir establish Dorfman's writing as a form of resistance. This memoir is his, not Pinochet's, and he cannot allow his life story to begin on a day that marks an end rather than a beginning. In the Spanish this reversal of opinion over the importance of September 11, 1973, is made even more obvious when Dorfman admits that he had always thought of that date as the moment that "me hace nacer, que me daba comienzo" (9); (gives birth to me, that gave me a beginning). To start with the coup would be to start in the historical moment that destroyed the collective of which Dorfman was an active member. As opposed to beginning with the coup, the disappeared, and exile, Dorfman narrates his way in; he recollects all that brought him to Santiago on September 11, 1973, and he does it in order to make sense of his own life autobiographically, as well as to honor his memory of the dead. That this memoir is both personal and collective is made all the more noticeable by the shifting possessive in the same sentence from "my country" to "our President."[52] To stress this exchange between self and collective, the rest of the first chapter reveals Dorfman's early obsession with death and what he envisioned as its unbearable solitude. He imagines that in death "you'll be so alone that not even you will be able to accompany yourself" (5). This preoccupation is answered for him by a vision of "a brotherhood of the dead," which functions also as a metaphor for all of the lives lost under Pinochet who cannot speak but are not alone and are kept company by Dorfman and those like him who are committed to keeping their stories alive (5).

This text's complex structure provides another key to how Dorfman represents a diasporic subject. The memoir is organized according to two main dualities—that of north and south and that of life and language versus death—while simultaneously pointing to the interpenetrations of these oppositions as well as to their supplements. Since the English version of the book provides the reader with no table of contents, no easy reference to this structure, it is necessary to delve into the book, flip the pages, and scan the titles to discover the memoir's pattern—an act that reinforces the complicity and collaboration between Dorfman and his readers.[53] In the two parts—"North and South" and "South and North"—Dorfman creates a division that is false because what follows is not north *versus* south but rather north *and* south. This structure gives the reader an early clue into what will be one of the central dilemmas for Dorfman: his early exile from Argentina to the United States, timed as it was during an intense moment of U.S. nation building from 1945 to 1954, left him desiring complete assimilation to U.S. culture: "I wanted to melt and dissolve . . . into the gigantic melting pot of America" (78). Then, during his second exile, when his father was threatened by McCarthyism and the family relocated to Chile in 1954, Dorfman rejected all things Chilean by engaging in a defiant act of dissimilation that he later reversed when he sought complete assimilation into Chilean culture in the 1960s. He comes to learn over the course of the memoir and in the process of writing the text that he is American in the hemispheric sense of the term, that he is of both the south and the north, and that complete assimilation to either is not possible.

If we return to the dualist structure, we note that there are eight chapters in the two sections that alternate between the "Discovery of Death" and the "Discovery of Life and Language." Apart from the first two chapters, which ostensibly take place "at an early age," the "Discovery of Death" chapters are dated from September 11, 1973, and end as Dorfman is about to go into exile. All of the chapters on the "Discovery of Life and Language" precede the coup. Once again Dorfman appears to set up a binary between life and language versus death, only to then expose its limits and explode its boundaries, for the epilogue merges life and language and death, suggesting that after the coup it would no longer be possible for him to conceive of life and language apart from death since with every breath of life he takes he remembers those who no longer share the air with him. Moreover, the chapters do not narrate a clear antagonism between life and language versus death. The chapters on the discovery of life and language include discoveries about death—for example, Dorfman describes the executions of Ethel and Julius Rosenberg in a chapter on "life and language" (73). Similarly, the chapters reveal specifics of time and place that are not entirely accurate, and the limits of chronology and geography are constantly tested by the text. While the first chapter ostensibly tells us about Dorfman at "an early age," in fact it wavers temporally in narrating his obsessions as a child; marking the key moment of September 11, 1973; describing his actions the night before the coup; and describing the author in the present moment of writing. The text's play with time might hint at the tension between European and Native American *kronos*, but it also points to the incommensurability of the subjective time of memory and historical time. Spatially the chapter moves from Santiago, Chile, to New York City, and in the Spanish, Dorfman makes a point of highlighting that he works on the translation in North Carolina (9). In the last chapter of the first section, supposedly recounting Dorfman's "Discovery of Life and Language during the Years 1954–1959 in Santiago de Chile," Dorfman opens by describing the moment when he decided that he would write creatively only in Spanish.[54] This event takes place in Berkeley in 1968. He uses the event to introduce a corollary moment of isolationism in his life: his arrival in Chile in 1954 as an exile who could think only of returning to his beloved United States and who hated speaking in Spanish. So structurally Dorfman decides in this chapter to emphasize the theme of the "discovery of life and language" and neglects the markers of time and space that ostensibly code the chapter title. Such a move tests the structure he has established and demonstrates the way that he narrates his identity in terms that are both binary and polyvalent.

The text's structure, like other trauma narratives, circles around the event that is unspeakable in a way similar to Toni Morrison's *Beloved*, rocking the reader back and forth between Chile in 1973 and the trajectory of Dorfman's life. Dorfman has subtitled the memoir "A Bilingual Journey," perhaps because a journey signals, as revealed more overtly in the Spanish *jornada*, both the events of one day and a trip that knows no limits.[55] On one level, the subtitle indicates that it is only at the end of this journey that Dorfman finally comes to accept himself as bilingual, to reconcile himself to the two forces of his two languages, and to more comfortably inhabit a world where both English and Spanish function compatibly. At another level, though, "journey" suggests that his travels in bilingualism and cross-culturalism persist, that they began well before his exile from Pinochet, and that they have not ended.

Both of these examples—the opening lines and the complex structure—indicate that this is the memoir of a writer. In fact, Dorfman's confidence in his ability to write may be one of the few elements of his life that he does not endlessly question. When he tells readers that he may have been spared by the coup in order to be its storyteller, he admits to his doubts: "If it is not true that this was why I was saved, I have tried to make it true" (40). But these doubts do not persist in the same way that he worries over other aspects of his identity. Philippe Lejeune has pointed out that the life writing by writers of fiction might be more elaborately constructed than the life writing of nonprofessionals, and Dorfman's memoir certainly opens itself up to such a reading.

Mikhail Bakhtin, in his analysis of discourse in the novel, makes a further argument for such special consideration when he describes the ways that heteroglossic voices converge in the mind of the writer. He explains that these opposing world views "encounter one another and co-exist in the consciousness of real people—first and foremost in the creative consciousness of people who write novels. . . . They may all be drawn in by the novelist for the orchestration of his themes and to the refracted (indirect) expression of his intentions and values" (292). Bakhtin's emphasis on the writer as the medium for heteroglossia resonates well with the multiple, dialogic ways that Dorfman describes identity and with the complex layering of competing subjectivities in the text. Much in the same way that Bakhtin argues that literature reflects and refracts reality through myriad voices in tension that come together in the space of a novel, Dorfman's text captures a polyphony of voices that resound contrapuntally and emerge through his identity. A telling example of the way that Dorfman works as a social echo takes place in Chile as Spanish and Latin American culture take a more active role in shaping his identity. "That Spanish out there contained my future. It contained the words of García Lorca I would say to Angélica one day, *Verde que te quiero verde*, the lover-like green of desire, and the words of Quevedo I would say to my country, *Miré los muros de la patria mía*, watching the walls of my fatherland crumble, and the words of Neruda I would say to the revolution, *Sube a nacer conmigo, hermano*, rise and be born with me, my brother" (114). When Spanish starts to guide his identity —or, as he puts it, when "Spanish was beginning to speak me"—he repeats the words of famous lines of poetry that he shares with a community of Spanish speakers who have drawn on these verses to represent their thoughts (114). Then when he unwittingly begins to live bilingually, he still functions as a medium for the voices of others. He describes his "schizophrenic, adulterous existence, writing in English and speaking in Spanish, singing American songs at sunrise and being lullabied into sleep by the Chilean mountains in the evening, crazy about Conrad and crazy about Cervantes, suspended vulnerably between two nations and two languages" (132).

After the coup, Dorfman's literature attempts to capture the voices of the dead and disappeared, and their stories resonate throughout his memoir. When he tells of the suicide of Taty Allende, Salvador's daughter, who shot herself while in exile, he reiterates that his survival has left him with the responsibility of telling these stories, of letting the dead speak through him. "I will have to carry her and her father and all the other dead of Chile like an orphan until the day I die" (59). In each of these instances Dorfman's identity is shaped through the voices of others. The discursive registers of popular culture, poetry, and historical trauma dialogue and contradict, further frustrating the dialectic between Dorfman as medium for others and as author of himself.

By creating a diasporic subject that at one and the same time attends to the binaries that structure identity and moves beyond a dualist ontology, Dorfman creates a multilayered self that remains true to the complexities of subjectivity, especially for those who have experienced violent dislocation. To present the self as a hybrid pastiche would eradicate the material history that separates north from south, English from Spanish, life from death, agency from victimization, the individual from the collective, life before from life after September 11, 1973. Similarly, to focus solely on the binary would invariably lead to Manichean oppositions that fail to register the ways that these forces interpenetrate and would miss subtle details of life that refuse to be easily designated as good or evil. Worst of all, structuring the life of diaspora dualistically would allow these oppositions and the official histories that depend on them to have too much power over identity and would grant them too great a capacity to dictate mutually exclusive categories of existence. Dorfman is far too interested in seeing himself as part of humanity to succumb to such pressures. Through his memoir Dorfman explores the intersections between writing, identity, and representation, and he describes his identity as indelibly marked by Chilean history and global culture.

NEOLIBERALISM, TECHNOLOGY, AND THE GLOBAL AGE

Dorfman's next two novels turn away from issues of human rights and memory in order to focus on the relationship among neoliberal economics, global social structures, and changing technologies. *The Nanny and the Iceberg* takes up these issues within the context of a post-Pinochet Chile interested in becoming a player in the global market. *Blake's Therapy* traces similar conflicts through the character of a powerful U.S. CEO who is suffering a crisis of conscience. Both novels make direct links between the ways that technology has altered human contact and the heightened individualism and narcissism of neoliberal ideology.

The Nanny and the Iceberg. *The Nanny and the Iceberg* (1999) toys with a Chilean locale and its global context.[56] Unlike *Death and the Maiden* and *Konfidenz*, both of which deal with the difficulty of dialogue and the relationship between power and communication, *The Nanny and the Iceberg* discards dialogue in favor of a modified version of the epistolary novel. In this case, though, it is not a series of letters but one very long suicide note sent to a woman, Janice Worth, his *gringa* girlfriend with whom the protagonist communicates via the Internet. The epistolary genre has often been associated with an investigation into the construction of the self, and the protagonist of *The Nanny and the Iceberg*, Gabriel McKenzie, is unquestionably in search of his identity. Returning to Chile at the age of twenty-three after having spent over fifteen years in exile with his mother in New York, Gabriel hopes that a reencounter with his father will help him lose his virginity and find his sense of self.

The novel was inspired by an actual event—Chile's decision to send an iceberg to the World Expo in Seville in 1992. As Dorfman explains in the novel's acknowledgments, "It was this bizarre way of celebrating the five hundred years since Columbus's voyage across the Atlantic that allowed me to first conceive the idea behind *The Nanny and the Iceberg*" (361). The event served as a springboard for Dorfman's imagination and allowed him to delve into a different side of post-Pinochet Chile from that seen in *Death and the Maiden*. In this novel his focus is on the version of Chile characterized as an economic miracle and a nation reborn. While many had begun to debate by the late 1990s the successes and failures of the Chilean government's efforts to deal with the traumas of the coup, less debate surrounded the efforts of the Chilean elite to fully enter the global marketplace. Dorfman describes the moment as one "accompanied by a process of euphoric and accelerated modernization as well as by bouts of collective and selective amnesia" (*Nanny*, 362). The legacy of Pinochet's economic model resulted in an entrenched neoliberalism that turned all social relations into commodities and deflated any sense of the public good. In addition, Dorfman noted that globalization and the rise of the technology age, rather than building a sense of a global community, had tended to isolate and alienate. Face-to-face contact was increasingly diminished in the age of e-mail, cell phones, and Internet chatting.

In keeping with Dorfman's tendency to adapt literary genres, the novel plays not only with the epistolary genre, but also intertexts with a variety of other literary forms. These multiple literary associations, not the least of which include a dense postmodern baroque style, make it exceedingly difficult to summarize the novel. The story centers on Gabriel, who lacks a sense of self owing to his separation from his father while in exile in New York. After years of not seeing one another, Gabriel's parents met again the night after Che Guevara's assassination (October 9, 1967), conceived Gabriel, and later got married. When Pinochet takes power, Gabriel and his mother go into exile, but Gabriel's father, Cristóbal (Cris), stays behind and runs a detective agency that searches for runaway boys. Gabriel later learns that his father did not go with his family into exile because of a bet he had made with his brother, Pancho, and his best friend, Pablo Barón, the day after Gabriel was conceived, during a lunch to celebrate his father's and Barón's twenty-fifth birthdays on October 11, 1967 (the day before Columbus Day). His father bet he would have sex every day, his uncle bet he would see socialism rule Latin America, and Barón bet he would be the most powerful man in Chile. The bet is due to be settled on their fiftieth birthdays. The consequences of this bet have been haunting Gabriel his whole life.

When Gabriel returns to Chile, he hopes to be reunited with his father, but the legacy of the bet continues to frustrate him. In preparation for the World Expo in Seville in 1992, on the quincentennial of Columbus's encounter with the New World, Chile has decided to display an iceberg as a sign of its technological skill and natural resources. The government believes that the iceberg can help Chile shed its image as a backward nation led by a despot, allowing it to fully enter the global economy as the New Zealand of South America. Barón, who is now a minister and the "power behind the throne" in the transition government, is in charge of the project and has received threats that the iceberg would be destroyed. He has called on Cris for help since if the iceberg is destroyed, Barón will lose the bet. While Gabriel and his father investigate the threats, the plot only becomes more twisted and complex. Who is sending the threatening notes? Is it the nanny who has cared for Gabriel's family for years? Is it Barón's daughter, Amanda Camila? Is it Gabriel's mother, Milagros? Or is it any number of enemies of the transition government? Over the course of the novel, Gabriel falls in love with Amanda Camila, and even though he has promised Barón not to sleep with her, he does, and in keeping with the way that the narrative layers and overlaps events, on that night the nanny dies. Forty days later, when Barón finds out that Amanda Camila is pregnant with Gabriel's child, he goes berserk: they cannot have a child because they are siblings. He explains that the night before Milagros and Cris had sex, he had slept with Gabriel's mother. After hearing this news, Gabriel and Amanda Camila decide to abort the baby, and Gabriel, disillusioned and confused, does not even accompany her to the doctor's office. Instead he talks to his uncle, who reveals that they are probably not siblings because Cris, in an effort to ensure that he would win the bet, slept with Amanda Camila's mother. In anger and frustration over the layers of deceit that have structured his life and over his inability to stop the abortion, Gabriel plots his revenge. He will blow up the iceberg along with his entire "extended" family. Writing from his hostel, located symbolically on Rodrigo de Triana Street, he tells Janice that he plans to cook a *cazuela*, a traditional Chilean soup, to celebrate Barón's and his father's birthdays. Then he will kill the whole party and destroy the iceberg. Looking on from the other side of death, the nanny, accompanied by Che Guevara, attempts to convince him not to do it. Will they succeed? The reader never knows.

In the tradition of *The Last Song of Manuel Sendero*, this text is an intricate, multilayered narrative that uses family relationships, especially those between father and son, as a metaphor for Chile.[57] For each significant narrative line there are a number of parallel or corollary stories. Cris's assistant, Polo, who has effectively replaced Gabriel as his father's son, was rescued by Cris on the same night that Gabriel was supposedly conceived. Polo's close relationship with Gabriel's father and his sexual prowess contrast with Gabriel's impotence and alienation. In addition, there is Max, who, in a reverse of Gabriel's travels, came to Chile as Gabriel left for New York. A filmmaker, Max knows more about Chilean history than does Gabriel. Furthermore, Gabriel's generation parallels that of his and Amanda Camila's parents in numerous ways, and almost every main character is missing one if not both parents. The novel has numerous examples of these sorts of connections.

Overlapping these doubles, mirrors, and parallels are frequent historical dates and events that connect with the narrative. But the references to Columbus, Che, Pinochet, Allende, and the massacre of the Native Americans (especially the Onas of Chile), among others, are shown to be both meaningful and meaningless. On the one hand, the link among the characters is driven by their ties (or lack of ties) to history. On the other hand, the baroque surplus of historical facts overflows the possibility of linking the past directly to the present. Dates, places, and figures abound in ways that are alternately overdetermined and empty. Mixed within the historical references are literary links; these serve in a similar fashion as both signposts and detours to understanding the text. Thus the text, in typical neo-baroque fashion, refuses to be exhausted by traditional modes of reading. As commentary on Chile in the era of globalization and on writing in the era of high postmodernism, *The Nanny and the Iceberg* situates itself in a critical crossroads. It forces the reader to find a new way to attend to the onslaught of information common in the age of the Internet and to decide how to remember and engage with history in a moment when history and memory have become commodities for sale on the global market.

In keeping with the almost frenetic referencing of historical material in the novel, there is an equally dizzying array of literary references and connections. In fact, it is possible to link the text chronologically with representative works from the classics to the present. The novel nods to tragedy, chivalry, quixotic blunders, and baroque word play. It also parodies epic, epistolary, picaresque, and romantic texts. It can additionally be read in the tradition of nineteenth-century national novels that link the future of the nation to healthy young love and sexual reproduction. There are, however, three main literary lines that play a central role in the construction of the narrative: the epistolary, the theme of Don Juan/Don Giovanni, and the picaresque. Dorfman uses postmodern versions of these literary trends to consider the possibilities of communication (the epistolary); the intersections of sex, deceit, and society (Don Juan); and the relations between the self and the community (the picaresque).

It is noteworthy that Dorfman decided to narrate the disjointed social landscape of Chile post-Pinochet with a variation on the epistolary form. The text in the form of a letter underscores not only the protagonist's problem with his own identity but also the problem of the addressee since Janice is clearly an inadequate recipient of the text. They spent one night together when they were fifteen but never had sex, and later they reconnected via the Internet. Gabriel really knows nothing about Janice (they haven't seen each other in years), and she only knows what he wants to tell her. For instance, he has neglected to tell her that he has not aged since the night they were together. When he came home late after a date with her, his mother assumed that he had had sex with Janice, that he had entered manhood, and that he was ready to hear about his father's bet; and when Gabriel learned of his father's bet, he became paralyzed, physically and emotionally: "He jinxed me, Mom jinxed me by prematurely telling me the story, fucking Che Guevara jinxed me by dying" (51). Since that time he has not been able to have sex, and his face has not aged. He has a "baby-face," a face with no history or experience. It is as if his father's self-centered and abundantly passionate way of living has sapped him of the ability to live for himself. So not only does Janice not really know the writer of the letter, who repeatedly falls back on the lies that he has previously told her, but he himself also lacks a stable identity. Even though Gabriel creates a version of his identity through writing a letter, he is a fragment; his life has been fractured, and his community is largely uninterested in his problems. This situation contrasts with the typical setting of the epistolary novel. Indeed the use of the epistolary form serves to totally disrupt the concept of communication because it emphasizes that a unified subject is *not* writing the text, nor is a unified subject who will learn from the adventures of the writer going to receive it. Most important, in a dramatic rupture of the epistolary form, there are no other letters, and there is no exchange of words. In this sense, *The Nanny and the Iceberg* frustrates the traditional epistolary genre.

Similar to Manuel Puig's *Boquitas Pintadas* (*Heartbreak Tango*), which also modified the epistolary genre, *The Nanny and the Iceberg* intimately links questions about the possibility of communication to the theme of Don Juan in its many varieties. Is Cris, as the consummate male seducer, a source of social devastation and sexual violence, or is he simply a man who is obsessively in love with women? Is his desire driven by homosocial machismo, or is he a hopeless romantic? The novel presents Cris as a hybrid, thereby frustrating the reader's ability to place his actions within a particular ethical code. In addition, Cris's promiscuity is counterbalanced both by Gabriel's virginity and by the fact that Cris himself was almost twenty-five before he lost his virginity to Gabriel's mother. To complicate matters further, Milagros, Gabriel's mother, was not a virgin when she first slept with Cris. The fact that she had been sexually active before Cris twists the traditional gender dynamics of the Don Juan tale, a point made even more obvious by the fact that she openly discusses sex with her son. She tells Gabriel that she fell in love with Cris when she was twelve but had to wait for years to see him again. All the years that she waited for him, though, she was sexually active so she didn't mind that the bet he had made with Barón and Pancho meant that he would sleep with other women. She explains to Gabriel: "Remember, I already knew you could screw around and still be deeply faithful to one person. I knew because that's how I had lived my life since Cris took me back to my father's home. That day, when I was a twelve-year-old girl hugging my Papá first and then my Nanny, I became acutely aware that that was not enough. I needed a man, I needed something physical and deep that neither of them could give me. That something was sex and I began to take it where I could" (47). While the different traditional variations on the Don Juan theme tend to hold to a clear division between active and passive gender roles, Dorfman's version deconstructs this binary, a move that not only suggests a postmodern view of gender as a social construction but one that also complicates the Don Juan theme as a vehicle for exploring the connections among ethics, sex, and society.

The Don Juan theme is most often associated with the archetypal interest in the ways that individual passion conflicts with social structures, and it is a theme that originated in Spain. Its preferred form is the theater, a fitting place to explore the performative nature of machismo and sexual prowess. One of the most interesting features of *The Nanny and the Iceberg*'s exploration of the Don Juan theme in Latin America is that Dorfman brings the literary trope of Don Juan into conversation with the New World tradition of the national novel of romance. Similar to the way that the nanny's famous *cazuela*, the dish that Gabriel prepares before his intended act of destruction, blends the food and flavors of the Old World with the New, Dorfman's exploration of sex, ethics, and social structure combines the Old World concerns with Don Juan's morality with the New World worries about sexual reproduction and nation building.[58] These transatlantic connections mean that Cris's Don Juanesque sex life must be measured against that of his son, whose inability to form a sexual union is symptomatic of the future of the nation. Gabriel's potentially incestuous relationship with Amanda Camila and its concurrence with the extinction of the last living member of the Ona tribe, the nanny, reveals how the novel revises the themes of nineteenth-century Latin American novels like Clorinda Matto de Turner's *Aves sin nido* (*Torn from the Nest*) that suggested that the legacies of colonial social structures would inevitably lead to incest and social decay. Novels in this tradition often worried that the nations of the New World would be forever plagued by the founding violence of colonialism, and Dorfman's text points to many of the ways that Spanish colonial structures and ideologies continue to shape Chile's future.

In a nod to one of Dorfman's favorite works of literature, *The Nanny and the Iceberg* intertexts with García Márquez's *One Hundred Years of Solitude*, which coincidentally was first published the year that Gabriel McKenzie was conceived. In one interesting connection, the Chilean iceberg project allows Dorfman a serendipitous link to García Márquez's description of how the "discovery" of ice in Macondo led the town to have a frustrated and complex relationship with science, technology, and social progress. The iceberg project represents a postmodern, neoliberal version of the same conflicts. Both novels also use incest as a metaphor for the ways that personal passions can destroy the future, a theme that has a long and rich literary history, especially in Latin America.[59] These literary links explain how Dorfman constructs a text that has as many layers as the pages of the novel itself. What is most important to note is that these layers are in tension, often violent tension, as well as in complementary collaboration. The novel pits the personal against the social, the theatricality of Don Juan against the national novel, father against son, and so on as a strategy to tease out a web of interconnected links. The task of the reader, as a detective who follows in the footsteps of the novel's multiple detectives (including its protagonist, Gabriel), is to sort out which leads are dead ends and which are "hot."

Gabriel's function as a detective, though, must be balanced against his role as a rogue, a postmodern *pícaro* who lacks an ethical commitment to society and is interested only in personal gain.[60] Abandoned by society and angry in return, picaresque characters are disruptive and violent in ways that mirror the social devastation caused by Don Juan figures. The novel draws these two social problems into tight orbit when, before going into exile, the young Gabriel takes a shower with his father. Gabriel points at his father's penis, which, while not erect, shows the signs of recent sex with another woman, and he begins practicing the variety of words he has learned to describe this part of the body. His father tells him not to use those words except around men. For women, he should call it *pene*, but Gabriel mispronounces it as *pena*: " 'No,' the great McKenzie said. '*Pena* is sadness, when you feel like you want to cry. *Pene*, Gaby, is the opposite. One tiny letter difference. But if you know how to use your *pene*, believe me you'll have less *pena* in the world" (252). That advice, it turns out, is not quite true since it is his *pene* that causes Cris to spend much of his life away from the woman he loves, and it also keeps Gabriel from growing up and claiming an identity.

The violations of Don Juan and of the *pícaro* are ultimately more similar than different, and Gabriel's actions reveal both the macho need to conquer women associated with Don Juan and the disdain for humanity and self-interest of the *pícaro*. But where these figures have tended to herald a generational rupture, Gabriel has inherited these qualities from his parents' generation. Gabriel is amoral and self-absorbed, but his social alienation is also the result of a neoliberal consumer society that has sacrificed community in favor of individualism and materialism. This extraordinary sense of alienation is explained as the consequence of post-Pinochet Chile, where community has been so thoroughly fragmented that the youth react by social withdrawal.[61] An epigraph in the novel by Deena Metzger is referenced to show that young men and women become paranoid, violent, and anti-social in the face of war or the disintegration of community. In this way, *The Nanny and the Iceberg* must be read as an investigation of the problems facing Chile almost ten years into the transition from dictatorship: practically none of the necessary healing work had been done by the nation, and the most common tactic for handling the past was amnesia.[62]

Gabriel, who symbolizes the disenfranchised youth of Santiago or New York, is concerned only with instant self-gratification, and this social context resonates with the general global decline of community in the face of transnational capitalism. The fragmentation of society has become so complete that Gabriel's letter is not the most important letter of the text. The protagonist's story has to vie with a number of other narrative threads for novelistic centrality. Shortly after Gabriel arrives, his father is called to meet with his friend Barón, and the story of the bet overshadows Gabriel's. The vanity and egocentrism of the bet is shown to be symptomatic of Chilean machos, who are too concerned with male honor to be able to function as social agents: Gabriel's father would have sex every day (like Don Juan), Pablo Barón would become the most powerful man in Chile (a desire for power similar to Columbus's), and Gabriel's uncle would see socialism rule the continent (like Che Guevara). In addition to competing with the megalomania of the bet, Gabriel's story must compete with that of the threatened iceberg. Tagging along with his father, Gabriel sees the first of many letters written on blue paper with a hostile message about the iceberg. Wanting to impress his father, he agrees to investigate the matter. As a consequence, while he is writing his suicide letter, he is also writing about the other letters. The possible suspects for the threatening letters, many of whom are also disenfranchised members of Chilean society, displace the primacy of Gabriel's story. These literary tactics also disrupt the typical protagonist so thoroughly that the novel ends with another narrative voice that takes up where Gabriel's monologue has left off. The final epilogue includes two voices, which, significantly, are not exactly in dialogue: those of the nanny and her afterlife companion, Che Guevara.

These various literary twists and textual references, as I have pointed out, create an exceedingly difficult interpretive task for the reader. Just as there are three main literary genres that the text parodies and rewrites, there are three fathers to Gabriel—Cris, Pancho, and Barón—and each of these men relate to three historical/literary figures that guide the text—Don Juan, Che, and Columbus.[63] But such linkages are not quite right, and the connections as well as the divisions among these triplets are not perfectly neat. In fact, the interpretive clue to the novel is to be found in a word that is repeated endlessly, almost gratingly, from the mouth of practically every significant character (except the nanny). It is a word that can be a noun, an adjective, or a verb. It can refer to sex, to failure, to destruction, to idiocy, to apathy, to everything, and to nothing. In fact it is its linguistic and signifying fluidity that makes it an appropriate interpretive cornerstone to the novel because despite its flexibility it is a powerful word that can signify a lot. It is the word "fuck."

We are first exposed to its use when Gabriel tells Janice about the circumstances of his birth. According to his mother, the night after Che died, "we were fucking you into existence" (18). Shortly thereafter Gabriel makes a point of explaining to Janice that that choice of language was his mother's: "She had no problem using that sort of language around me" (20). The text provides a number of meta-commentaries on the use of "fuck" or one of its variations, and many of these comments call attention to how it must be used in order to translate other similar expletives from Chilean Spanish. In one case Gabriel explains that he has chosen "fucking clue" as his translation of "puta idea," but then he thinks maybe "motherfucking" would have been a better choice (65). The text clearly plays with the links between the way this idea is expressed in Chilean Spanish and in English. For instance, the first letter threatening the iceberg uses the verb "culear," which gets translated as "fuck" (74). Such linguistic games run throughout the text, adding to its humor and sense of play. But beyond these games is a far more serious questioning about why this society has found itself expressing itself this way so often.

Apart from the many ways "fuck" appears as a way to add color and to mirror the colloquial expressions of the Chilean lexicon, the novel uses the word strategically to refer to a series of contexts in which it is often used. The use of "fuck" and its linguistic kin, like "screw," to signify these different contexts allows Dorfman to draw a linguistic link between them that he hopes will lead his readers to understanding their deeper connections. First is the use of the word to describe sex. Of interest is the way that "fuck" is used to refer to sexual acts that ostensibly should be referred to more gently, such as the above example of Milagros's description of Gabriel's conception. In another crucial example, Barón notices that Gabriel is attentive to Amanda Camila and wants him to swear not to touch her:

"Swear what?"
"You'll never try and fuck my little girl."
"Tío," I said, "this really isn't necessary."
"It's necessary. Believe me it is."
He had me cornered. I lied my head off, crossed every mental finger in my
    brain, swore I would never try and make love to his little girl.
"Fuck. Use the word. Never fuck her."
"I'll never fuck her."

"If you do, may all hell break loose. Say it."

"May all hell break loose."

Heaven and hell did break loose when I finally fucked her, Janice. (198)

The fact that all sex, even that between people who purportedly love each other, is referred to as "fucking" is the first warning sign that this is a society that has become radically alienated, deeply angry, and constantly violent. No matter the context in which the word is spoken, in English or Spanish, by young or old, by men or women, when it refers to sex, it rarely, if ever, refers to sex as an act between two willing partners who care about one another. At best it refers to casual sex for fun, and at worst it refers to sex as a conquest, a violation, and a physical possession.[64]

The second most common context for the use of this word and its linguistic cousins is to equate "fucking" with taking advantage of others, betraying, cheating, or victimizing, and Dorfman shows how the word represents the anti-ethics of neoliberal ideology. He contrasts the two main uses of the word in a conversation between Cris and Barón, when they are discussing the threats to the iceberg. Barón asks:

"Have you had your fuck of the day?"

"You know I have. . . . This morning. Only once. So I haven't fucked as many people as you have today."

Pablo Barón laughed at this and took it as praise. "That's what this business is about. Fucking others for the greater good, for their own ultimate happiness. And some people end up loving it and claim they're your friends and others hate it and they think they're your enemies forever, that you've done it for personal reasons. Big mistake. Nothing personal." (75)

There are a couple of important observations to make about this exchange. First of all is the fact that Cris acknowledges that what he is doing to the women with whom he has sex daily is a violation, but he quickly justifies it by suggesting that Barón's manipulation of the public for his own desire and pleasure is far worse. Second is the fact that Dorfman places these two men side by side to allow the reader to decide which version of "fucking" is worse. Or are they intimately tied to one another as evidenced by the bet?

In addition to the use of "fuck" to describe sex or the taking advantage of others, the word signifies a society of damaged individuals who have become radically disconnected. This linguistic register describes someone who is damaged—"fucked up"—and consequently does not "give a fuck" about anything. Obsessed with the iceberg and its potential to raise interest in investment in Chile, Barón angrily accuses Cris of not helping to find out who is threatening the iceberg: "McKenzie you haven't been doing fuckall" (104). Of course, Barón is right; he has not. Trapped as these men are in the bet they made almost twenty-five years ago, they are incapable of seeing past the need to win and are unable to commit to anything else. Inheriting the sins of their fathers, Gabriel and Amanda Camila echo their parents, deploying the same word as a sign of their apathy and frustration. Amanda Camila explains to Gabriel that since Pinochet is no longer head of state, everything has become gray. She yearns for something, anything, to happen, and when life does not bring the apocalypse, "You make your own earthquake. . . . You try to fuck things up real bad. I've done some things" (131). This desire to be an agent leads Amanda Camila to write the first letter threatening the iceberg. Then the hope that the threat to the·iceberg can reunite Cris and Milagros causes Milagros, with the help of the nanny, to write the rest.

Layered over the use of "fuck" to describe people who are psychologically devastated and misguided is its use to signal violence, anger, and destruction. From the first letter threatening the iceberg to the last, it functions as a sign for an extreme act of damage. Here again Dorfman shows that such acts cannot retaliate for social violence because they are waged by isolated individuals who simply seek revenge. Gabriel explains why he decided to bomb the iceberg and those he loves: "Wasn't it Che who said that only violence can set the world right, put things back on course? I'd fuck the iceberg, just like the letters said. . . . Violence Janice. Che knew what he was talking about. Nothing like violence for people to realize you matter" (336–37). Certainly the violence contemplated by Gabriel is not the same as that espoused by Che, but Dorfman makes an important point that acts of violence share commonalities regardless of who stands to gain or lose. The connection is the will to destroy as a means of gaining what one desires. It is a tactic that will never produce peace. As the nanny looks on at Gabriel's final preparations, she tries to convince him not to do it: "You want guarantees, that everything will turn out all right, that if you allow yourself this reprieve, if you go back on your vow to blow everything up, you won't find your life full of grief. I can't give you that guarantee, that those who keep hope will be rewarded" (357).

Practically everyone in the novel has been violated in some way to some extent. The question is: how do they respond? In post-Pinochet, neoliberal Chile it seems that most respond by seeking personal gain, a practice that promises to yield more alienation, frustration, anger, and destruction. In an artful nod to poststructural suggestions that words had become detached from meaning, Dorfman keyed the theme of his novel to a word that has historically held a fluid signifying field. What is more, it is a word that is extreme, taboo, rarely written.[65] Dorfman shows, though, that it is a word that symbolizes both the extent and the limits of linguistic playfulness because even though it is used in myriad ways in the novel, its signifying power still circles around violence, anger, and betrayal. Almost all of the characters "fuck" and "are fucked" in one way or another. All except for the nanny.[66] And the iceberg.

Blake's Therapy. After completing *The Nanny and the Iceberg*, Dorfman continued to work on themes related to globalization and social alienation, and there is a clear trajectory between the central concerns of *The Nanny and the Iceberg* and those of his next novel, *Blake's Therapy*, which was released simultaneously in English and Spanish in 2001 and which is set in the United States.[67] Both *The Nanny and the Iceberg* and *Blake's Therapy* focus on the social impact of globalization, but where the first concentrated on the impact for Chile post-Pinochet, the second delves into the world of the U.S. corporate power elite. The novel follows a corporate success, Graham Blake, whose company, Clean Earth Inc., sells herbs, health supplements, and other products that are "environmentally friendly." A "socially responsible" businessman, he pioneered a plan that called on hotel guests not to have their towels washed daily, a move that saved hotels billions in costs and also helped the environment. He begins to have problems, though, when his company faces a series of takeover threats that force him to shut down some plants and outsource others. The situation worsens when Blake refuses to shut down an old plant in Philadelphia founded by his father, and even though he tries to package it as downsizing with a heart, his ex-wife and business partner, Jessica Owen, sees through the charade and accuses him of saving the plant for sentimental reasons. When the novel opens, Blake has suffered from headaches, insomnia, and impotence for the past ninety-five days. To cure himself he decides to enroll in the Corporate Life Therapy Institute, where Dr. Tolgate, the main therapist, will help him through this crisis. For $3 million and a month of Dr. Tolgate's time, Blake will receive the latest in therapy treatments to cure corporate executives of "Immorality Syndrome," a condition that Tolgate hopes will one day be named after him.

When Blake arrives at the institute, Tolgate explains the therapy. While screens come to life in a large control room, images of an apartment come into view: " 'There she is, Graham,' he said, 'the woman who will cure you of your mental sickness. Do with her, with all of them, what you will' " (24). Blake, bewildered, learns from Tolgate that his therapy is to monitor every aspect of the lives of a Latino family, some of whom work for Clean Earth, including the beautiful Roxanna, who is a nurse at the plant. He can control any aspect of their lives—kill them, make them rich, make them suffer—anything except have contact with them. He has thirty days to find out if he is immoral, amoral, or ethical. Tolgate explains: "If you don't hurt her at all after having her at your fingertips, then you are confirming how truly ethical you are" (24). Her every movement is recorded for Blake's viewing pleasure. He can watch her use the bathroom, pray, have sex, sleep. He can view her at her most intimate and vulnerable.

The novel delves into the ethics of the socially responsible business movement that emerged as a consequence of globalization. As the power of nation-states declined and as social services were increasingly privatized, corporations vied to present themselves to the public as ethical and committed to the social good. Often these efforts to promote an eco-friendly, socially committed corporate profile were merely rhetorical, and they obscured two major social shifts: the waning decline of the state as the source of social support and the rise of the individualism of neoliberal ideology. As Henry Giroux explains, "Wedded to the belief that the market should be the organizing principle for all political, social, and economic decisions, neoliberalism wages an incessant attack on democracy, public goods, and noncommodified values. Under neoliberalism everything is either for sale or is plundered for profit" (*Terror*, xiii). Dorfman's novel, though, is not about the corporate executives of a fictitious Enron or Halliburton. Instead he selects a far more ambiguous protagonist in Graham Blake, a man who likes to think of himself as good: "He cares, perhaps excessively, about how the world perceives him, what others say about him" (13).

Through Blake, Dorfman is able to expose the inconsistencies inherent in the notion of socially responsible capitalism. For instance, Tolgate explains to his financial backer: "As to the future, with four million multimillionaires in this country alone and more pressure than ever on them to both rack up profits and at the same time appear more and more ethical, well, there should be a good number of mental breakdowns, and we expect a healthy growth in revenue" (81). More akin to the principles of figures like George Soros, who lends an epigraph to the book, and the Swiss-based World Economic Forum (where Dorfman went to do research for the novel), which is committed to forming business alliances that can improve the world, than to the leaders of the WTO, the business practices of Blake and his company allow Dorfman to ask the following about philanthropy, business, ethics, and capitalism: "If he did not have the chance to fill the void around him and inside him by easily spreading his charitable wings, doing good, solving the food crisis, answering the energy crisis, brilliantly intervening in the towel crisis, what would happen if he could not think the world of himself as he is saving the world and the Amazon Indians. Just something for you all to chew on" (21). The novel suggests that such acts of charity and social awareness assuage the attacks of guilt suffered by some of the extremely wealthy.

Thus the novel yokes together two key features of globalization: the ethical dilemmas of global economics and the distorted perceptions of humanity offered by media culture. When wars are simulcast and when viewers can spend hours watching the simulated identities of reality television, a profound dehumanization takes place between viewer and viewed. The essential difference for Graham Blake in his therapy is that rather than passively watch the intimate moments of a family, he can control them. At first, though, Blake refuses to take part in the therapy. It is clearly immoral, he cries, and he will not be a part of it. Then luscious, peaceful Roxanna enters, and he is entranced with her tranquility, her sensuality and spirituality, and especially her calm, slow sense of time—all attributes that contrast with the fast-paced world of big business. Would it be possible to change her worldview? Blake would like to find out. Watching her begin to make love to her boyfriend, Johnny, he becomes jealous and makes his first wish: Send Johnny to jail; get him away from Roxanna. After that first move, Blake is hooked.

Over the thirty days of his treatment, Blake toys with the family, attempting to find Roxanna's breaking point. Then on the last night of his treatment she comes into the apartment hysterical. Johnny has just died in prison. Distraught, she swallows pills in a suicide attempt. Blake suffers an attack of conscience and is shocked that his therapy has cost Johnny his life. He convinces his assistant to let him into the apartment to save Roxanna, to beg her forgiveness, and to confess his sins. As he cradles her in his arms, Tolgate appears. It suddenly dawns on Blake that this has all been a show to determine how he would handle the consequences of his decisions. Tolgate congratulates him. He has now learned his true character. He is good; he is ethical. He may have done some awful things to Roxanna and her family, but he was prepared to give up everything, confess, and repent.

After he leaves the Corporate Life Therapy Institute, Blake is able to sleep, but he remains haunted by his experience. He has become excessively paranoid and addicted to watching the people in his life on video. After sex one night with his girlfriend Natasha, he videotapes her sleeping and then spends the rest of the night watching the tape of her sleeping. The obsession intensifies, and he has video surveillance installed not only in his house and office, but also in the homes of his friends and ex-wife. In an interior monologue with Roxanna, Blake describes his new problem: "What's wrong is that if I want to sleep, if I want to rest . . . there's a price to pay. . . . I am forced to secretly film the secret world that threatens me. . . . Now I spend the day devouring images or thinking about how I can witness what people near me do, everything they do" (86). And he has found a way to absolve himself of these acts of intrusion: "As long as you don't hurt anybody permanently, why should it matter what you do, how you enjoy yourself. A good man can ultimately do no harm" (88).

These developments allow Dorfman to link the excessive power of global corporations to the increasing dissolution of privacy brought on by the Internet age and the era of reality television. When the intimate lives of others are constantly offered up for public consumption, the notion that there are thresholds to the self that should not be crossed or violated disappears. Daily life is so full of simulacra, virtual reality, screens of images that may or may not be staged, that it has become increasingly difficult to find the borders between life and its representation. As these multiple layers of images have distanced viewers from a sense of what is potentially "really" behind them, the advent of a screen society has made the lines between viewer and viewed exceedingly difficult to determine and has dispersed the power of the voyeur since the power of looking is so pervasively accessible. Nevertheless, *Blake's Therapy* exposes the fact that power hierarchies, however muddy, remain.

Blake fails to fully grasp that his benevolent turn at the end of his therapy still depends on a world where he has disproportionate control over the lives of others. He refuses to understand that the economic system of which he is a part creates vast power imbalances. At one point he differentiates his company from Tolgate's practice, stating that he affects "millions of people around the world," whereas Tolgate deals with only "just a few." Blake means that his products are consumed by millions, but Tolgate denies him the illusion: "The few I deal with determine what happens to those millions" (171). But Blake continues to avoid facing this reality. There are hints that Blake is unconsciously aware of his power, though, as evidenced by his need to tape those who he thinks have power over him. If he acknowledges the injustice of his ability to affect the lives of those who work for him, then he must acknowledge his own lack of control in the larger scheme. He may control much of the world of those who work for Clean Earth and his money may make it possible for him to manipulate much of society, but others, like the board of Clean Earth, Hank Granger, the man trying to launch a hostile takeover of Clean Earth, and the global market exercise control over him. Similarly, his place in the hierarchy of global power affords him the opportunity to spy, observe, and conduct surveillance on many others, but he is not the panoptical source. The more information he acquires about others, the more paranoid he becomes. Each intrusion only furthers his suspicion that he is being watched as well. The novel's readers know that, in fact, he is being watched. Tolgate has given the tapes of his therapy to another anonymous source.

Blake's Therapy layers voyeurs over voyeurs, creating a fun house of mirrors and images. Blake watches tapes of his friends and employers, while others watch tapes of him. Everyone is spying, and everyone is being spied on. Jessica shows Blake video surveillance of the Philadelphia plant in order to convince him to close it down. It appears that the workers there may be planning a strike. While watching the video, Blake sees a woman that reminds him of Roxanna. The woman is Rose, and her life mirrors almost exactly the fabricated family that Blake observed during his therapy. Blake then leaves for Philadelphia, contacts Rose, sets up surveillance equipment in her apartment, and deceptively inserts himself into her family. Saving them will be a way to save himself. When Rose learns that she is about to lose her job because the plant will be shut down, she attempts suicide. Blake is watching and calls for help. In the hospital he tries to lift her spirits by revealing his true identity and promising that he will not allow the plant to close. He turns on all of his charm, sure that he will win her adoration. But her response shocks him as she looks at him with pure, unadulterated hatred: "That's what Rose is feeling towards her savior: a rancor that threatens to twist her face beyond recognition" (147). Blake is in shock, in denial. His view of himself as a benevolent savior is shattered by this woman he has grown to respect and care for: "She told me to get the fuck out of that room and the fuck out of her life and the fuck off this planet. She said I was off my rocker, a pervert, a voyeur, a heartless monster. She said my greed had almost destroyed her family, had caused her more pain than I could ever imagine" (148). Finally, Blake allows her words to surface in his narrative: "I'd have to wash for twenty years, soak for twenty years, submerge myself in water for twenty years, rub myself for a million years, and I still wouldn't be rid of your stench, the smell of your lies. It clings to me, fills me, fills me. And the worst thing is that you think you are Mother Teresa. You think I need Mother Teresa?" (149).

Blake never really understands Rose. The next day, as he delivers a speech at the plant promising to save it, even if it means his own financial ruin, he stares at Rose, hoping for the look "telling me I am a wonderful man, a good man. Telling me that I can sleep at night because I am doing what is right, no matter what the consequences" (152). His ego betrays his neoliberal sensibilities and capitalist circumstances. He is incapable of understanding the world as a community that belongs equally to everyone, where success depends on everyone and not on a benevolent savior. Blake also fails to grasp that the global market does not afford him such power. Even though he promises to go to the board meeting in Houston to save the plant, he may not be able to, and the reader never learns the outcome of the meeting or the fate of the plant.

Taut and suspenseful, *Blake's Therapy* presents readers with a psychological thriller that continues many of the themes from *The Nanny and the Iceberg*. Both novels are populated by characters who have lost their ability to form a community and who are trapped in the paranoid delusions that accompany neoliberal ideology. Similarly both novels construct a web of layers within their plots and across literary texts and historical references. As mentioned, *Blake's Therapy* joins the global economic scene of the WTO, NAFTA, and the General Agreement on Tariffs and Trade (GATT) with references to corporate icons like Aristotle Onassis, J. P. Morgan, and George Soros.[68] It also comments on the reality television boom, which erupted in 2000 with a number of programs that followed "real" characters in contrived settings. At one point, Blake compares the fabricated "reality" TV of Tolgate's therapy with the boring practice of watching Rose and her family: "That's what happens in real life, when nobody is pre-selecting the juiciest scenes, when there's no Dr. Tolgate who wants to make sure that his patient is hooked and anxious to get involved" (130). What is most significant about the structure of the novel's narrative is the way that it shows these two trends as inextricably linked to one another.

These two links are only part of the web of connections that *Blake's Therapy* builds, and the novel is full of literary references for the reader to pursue.[69] The most obvious links are to two texts cited in its epigraphs: Dante's *The Divine Comedy* (1308–21) and Pedro Calderón de la Barca's baroque play *Life is a Dream*.[70] Dante is quoted at the start of each of the novel's three sections, each of which has three chapters, and it thus mirrors the medieval poem's use of the number three as an organizing structure. Beyond these quotes, *Blake's Therapy* holds a number of connections to Dante's seminal work. First, just as Dante attempted to provide a map of the physical space of fourteenth-century Italy, Dorfman attempts to provide readers with a view of the way that physical space and virtual space have become intertwined under globalization. Second, much in the same way that Dante critiqued the relationship between church and state, Dorfman critiques the transformation of big business into a religion, where corporate leaders become society's spiritual guides. This similarity leads to the most profound connection between the texts: the search for a new moral compass. Blake is guided by Tolgate and then by Rose, just as Dante is guided by Virgil and Beatrice, but rather than arrive at a place where man's journey leads him to understand his place in the world and his moral responsibility, the outcome of Blake's journey is far less clear. In *Blake's Therapy* the questions outweigh the answers, and the hope for any ethical resolution lies in the reader. In this way, the ascent of the epigraphs reads against the plot of the novel since Blake seems to grow little as a result of his journey.

Dorfman's refusal to make Blake's journey one of redemption relates to the book's intertextual connection to Calderón de la Barca's *Life Is a Dream.* The play alludes to the difficulty of determining whether life is illusion or reality, whether one is controlled by external forces or has free will, and whether wealth and power inevitably lead to ethical abuse. Dorfman takes these baroque themes and recasts them in light of the postmodern world of simulated identities, thereby creating links to recent films that have explored this topic— for example, *The Matrix* (1999) and *The Truman Show* (1998). Even though Blake is at the center of the story, the novel presents this dilemma as one that plagues society in general. Blake's moral crisis is analogous to the destabilized realities of all of the characters.

In order to construct a narrative world where it is difficult not only to determine reality from illusion but also to disentangle the life of one character from another, Dorfman structures the narrative as a series of nonparallel parallels. This structure hints at the way that Dorfman blends the intertextual influences of Dante and Calderón de la Barca. On the one hand, the structure is organized around the number three, as was *The Divine Comedy*, but rather than have this tripartite structure suggest the holy trinity, Dorfman instead suggests it as a form of baroque supplement where meaning is displaced by a constant shift in perspective and point of view. To appreciate this strategy it is important to break down the narrative voices of the chapters because these follow a pattern that shifts and twists. Divided into three sections with an epilogue, each section starts with a chapter narrated by Tolgate (he also narrates the epilogue), followed by one narrated by Blake, then one that centers on Roxanna/Rose's voice. These parallels, though, are fluid, and in each case the voices vary.

Each time Dr. Tolgate narrates, his audience changes. In chapter 1 he speaks to a collective audience, to "us," an anonymous group that will observe Blake's therapy. The first line of the first chapter places the reader in the role of meta-voyeur: "I want you to take a good look at him. I want you to take a good lazy look at Graham Blake" (11). The last line of the same chapter suggests the reader as one of Blake's therapists: "We're going to save Graham Blake in spite of himself" (21). So the members of the audience in a sense shift from being passive voyeurs to active therapists. These twists are only the beginning; Tolgate then narrates chapter 4 to his unknown, anonymous superior, who wants a report on the Blake case and who receives a copy of all of Blake's therapy tapes (including the surveillance tapes of his life before therapy). The anonymity and power of Tolgate's superior link with his desire to watch over every move that Blake makes. This presence reinforces the idea that Blake is merely part of a larger scheme. As Tolgate explains in this section, despite the complex web of viewers and viewed, there is still a hierarchy of power. Either we are the "eye that watches the microbe" or we are "fated to become the microbe that is watched by some superior eye" (81). Then Tolgate narrates chapter 7 to his secretary, the anonymous inferior who watches her boss watch others but lacks any power. In each of these chapters Tolgate's audience has been vague and unspecified, but in each case the intended audience has a different place in the social hierarchy. In chapter 1, the collective "we" to whom Tolgate speaks is like a group of fellow therapists, a peer group to a master therapist. In chapter 4 he speaks to a superior and in chapter 7 to an inferior. In the epilogue, which Tolgate narrates to Jessica, we get the only hint that after the speech in the plant in Philadelphia Blake may have arrived at some epiphany and surprised everyone. Or else why would Jessica want more information from Tolgate about Blake's state of mind? What did Blake do in Houston? The last line of the novel reads: "What he did next you already know" (172). But the reader does not know.

Chapters 2, 5, and 8 are narrated by Blake. Each of these is narrated to Roxanna. Blake makes it clear from the first chapter he narrates, however, that his intended recipient cannot hear him and that he is speaking to her only in his mind. These chapters present a major clue to the way that Dorfman intersects baroque excess with noir voyeurism. Blake imagines a Roxanna who will listen to his story and offer him redemption, yet he knows that she does not really exist. On the contrary, he knows that Roxanna represents a dream that depends on his power to watch her. But this power is tempered by his inability to possess her. At the heart of his narrative is a fundamental contradiction that often drives the psychological anguish of the voyeur: he needs the object of the voyeurism to be passive, and he needs that object to actively absolve him. These tensions are made manifest in the novel through a linguistic tic that Blake uses when he addresses Roxanna. He repeatedly calls her variations of Roxanna "mine, not mine" in a word play between possession and its denial. Then, after he begins to tell Roxanna about Rose, he constantly confuses them, alternating between separating them and overlapping them. For instance, when Rose attempts suicide and Blake is rushing to her, he claims, "I won't ever make it to where she is, Roxanna, where you were waiting for me" (142). Not only are their identities overlapping, but also the mixed use of the present and past tenses creates a displaced sense of time.

Rose's story is told to different men. Rose, a Latina originally from Colombia, has a mystical, spiritual quality that functions as a counter to the cold, rational world of Tolgate and Blake. The first two chapters she narrates (3 and 6) are told to anonymous men who videotape her during interviews. The reader never learns their identities, but it seems likely that she is under surveillance by someone interested in learning if she or her family pose a strike risk to the company. It is the third chapter she narrates, chapter 9, that is the most moving and the most devastating. Here she speaks to Gus, Blake's pseudonym while he is stalking her. The chapter is a flashback to before her suicide attempt and to before Blake's unmasking, and it comes at a moment when he has gained her confidence and admiration for all of the ways that he has helped her family. She begins by asking him if she can trust him because she wants to tell him a story she has never told anyone. She tells him about the day she was born, when her father left town before holding her. The story itself is complex and layered, but according to her father, he had received a call from Aristotle Onassis asking for orchids for his wedding to Jackie Kennedy. Her father struck a deal that would make the small Colombian town rich. But when they harvested the flowers and waited by the landing strip, no one ever came to get them and the townspeople sought her father for revenge, causing him to flee. So Rose suffers because a "millionaire who was playing around with my father betrayed him" (162). She has her doubts about her father's version but prefers not to search for the real answers. When Blake asks why she has decided to tell him this, she explains: "This story is the one thing that belongs to me, only to me. The story of how I was made, why I am the way I am. It's my gift to you" (164). The novel asks whether Blake will know what to do with his gift.

Each time Rose narrates, she speaks to men who are deceiving her. The first two men pose as detectives, probably linked to the police, and she is clearly suspicious of them from the beginning. But it is her story to her trusted friend, Gus, that is the most disturbing. There she speaks with hope and intimacy to a man who has lied to her about his identity. This simulated listener contrasts with the anonymous men, who are also deceiving Rose but whom she does not trust.

In a parallel yet shifted way, Tolgate's voice changes in an artful effort to present a constructed image of himself according to his intended, yet always anonymous, audience. Then Roxanna, while always incapable of hearing Blake, changes as she moves from a potentially real woman to a simulation to a simulacrum of another real woman (Rose) and finally to a composite of the simulacrum and the "real" woman. Not only do the voices of Tolgate, Blake, and Rose parallel one another in their anonymous (that is, virtual) audiences, but their own voices also become traces of themselves. These shifting subjectivities represent the consequences of a society that depends on destroying many for the benefit of the few. Eventually all identities are contaminated and fractured.

Here again Dorfman pushes on the limits of postmodern theory by creating a world of simulated identities and shifting realities that coalesce around a clear indictment of the ethical failures of global capitalism. Both *The Nanny and the Iceberg* and *Blake's Therapy* describe the era of globalization and neoliberalism as social devastations that whittle away at historical memory and ethical commitment. These values are replaced by identity as commodity and object to be purchased, manipulated, and consumed. Both Gabriel and Blake wrestle with an imbedded desire to "wake up" from these altered realities, but Dorfman refuses to make their journey easy. Each novel offers the reader only the most tentative hope for resolution. Gabriel receives whispers from the nanny and Che, who try to convince him not to commit suicide and murder, but it is unclear whether he will listen. Blake promises to save his factory but seems incapable of relinquishing his narcissism or appreciating the reality of the market economy. Both characters seem far too damaged to learn from the stories they have been told. The real hope, then, lies in Dorfman's prodding of his readers, who have been asked to actively engage in reading these highly layered, complicated narratives.

SPEAKING TRUTH, WRITING MEMORY

Dorfman's next three literary works all take up complementary themes about speaking truth and representing memory. The novel *The Burning City* (2003), co-written in English with Dorfman's son Joaquín; the play *Manifesto for Another World* (2004); and the travel memoir *Desert Memories: Journeys through the Chilean North* (2004) represent a range of literary genres that converge in a constellation of shared interests. These three texts, in addition to *Exorcising Terror* (2002), Dorfman's coverage of the Pinochet arrest, all present different yet complementary approaches to questions about the role of the written word in speaking truth, recording history, and preserving memory.[71] As described in the introduction to this chapter, the end of the twentieth century and the early twenty-first ushered in an era of intense concern about how to adequately attend to public memory when societies seemed increasingly emptied of a sense of history. In addition, many of the projects dedicated to preserving public history often seemed inextricably contaminated by the commodity-driven logic of globalization. Was it possible to represent historical memory without turning memory into an object for consumption? Each of the texts analyzed in this section provides a distinct literary approach to these questions: *The Burning City* mixes the personal quest of an adolescent boy living in New York City with the difficult truths he delivers as a messenger; *Manifesto for Another World* creates a dramatic work out of the testimonials of fifty-one human rights defenders; and *Desert Memories* crosses a number of borders by combining Chilean history with personal history and natural history with politics.

The Burning City. *The Burning City* is a fast-paced tour of New York City as viewed through the eyes of the novel's protagonist, Heller Highland, a bike messenger during the summer before the 2001 terrorist attacks. Heller is sixteen years old and on the verge of adult masculinity. He works for Soft Tidings, a company that delivers "news with a personal touch" by verbally delivering face-to-face messages of babies born, relatives dead, and marriages celebrated. Soft Tidings has become a successful business because it counteracts the impersonal communication that dominates contemporary life by providing its clients—mainly ethnic immigrants to New York—with a human connection to personal news. Not only is Heller the company's youngest employee entrusted with the most difficult messages, but he also refuses to wear the mandatory roller blades, traveling the city by bicycle instead and dreaming of being the youngest winner of the Tour de France. Like most adolescent men, he is a jumble of opposites, such as raging hormones combined with awkward shyness and macho bravado mixed with introversion. But Heller's contradictions, like those of the city in which he lives, go beyond those of a typical adolescent. He combines macho competitiveness and extraordinary empathy, extreme sensitivity and daredevil antics. Most important, he vacillates between self-interest and camaraderie. He wavers between solitude, because his parents have left him with his grandparents to conduct mission work abroad, and community, because his job has created an extended family for him.

Heller's life takes a turn when he delivers a message to Salim Adasi, a Turkish Kurd illegally living in the United States and hoping one day to be joined by the woman he loves, Nazima. Heller arrives at Salim's apartment with the message that Nazima has married someone else. Salim immediately reaches out to Heller, inviting him to a bar, introducing him to his friends, and sharing with him his wisdom. Heller, who is in love with Silvia, a Chilean-American who works in a coffee shop, is hungry for advice since he visits Silvia every day at work but has yet to find the nerve to speak to her. Heller and Salim quickly become friends. Meanwhile, Heller's nemesis at work, Rich Phillips, has tracked down Heller's "girlfriend," Silvia, and begun to court her. When Heller sees them together, he decides to blame Salim, but Salim is not so easily rebuffed. Later, when Heller's frustration prods him to pick a fight with an overly violent cop named Bruno, Salim comes to his rescue and is beaten to within an inch of his life.

Salim's beating marks another turning point for Heller. He visits Salim in the hospital, finally aware of the depth of his friend's affection. When he leaves Salim to rest, he is given a new message to deliver, a welcome diversion from his worries over Salim's health. But as the door opens to the apartment where he will deliver a message of death, he is greeted by Silvia. Suddenly the flowers of condolence he is carrying transform into those of a young beau, and Heller stuffs the message of her father's death deeply into his pocket and invites Silvia out. They spend the entire night together, walking the streets of New York and falling in love. Walking back to Silvia's apartment, Heller's first bad omen is his missing bike, a sign that his future dreams have been shattered. Then in Silvia's apartment Heller finds his irate boss, Dimitri, who has come to do Heller's job. Once Silvia learns of Heller's deception, she lashes out at him. Back at home, he receives a phone call: Salim is missing from the hospital.

Heller has lost everything. Or has he? Recounting his woes to a Nigerian friend, Benjamin, whom he met delivering a message, he gets his first sign of hope. Benjamin suggests that he call on all of his former clients to ask them for help, and all willingly come to join the search for Salim. Heller transforms from a solitary adolescent to a young man with a community of friends, all of whom are happy to help him. After a night of fruitless searching, Heller falls asleep, only to wake up to Silvia. She is not there to forgive him, though. Instead she comes with a Soft Tidings message from Benjamin: Salim has been found dead. After the funeral Heller sees Silvia again, but the novel refuses the reader a happy ending with lovers strolling hand in hand. Instead the final scene is of Heller helping Silvia learn how to ride a bike—away from him—while he holds Salim's ashes.

The novel blends a quick, choppy style that simulates the fast pace of bicycle wheels with slower more lyrical passages of reflection and warmth. Time slows down when Heller delivers his messages. He takes time to notice details of his surroundings and to carefully attend to his clients. As soon as he leaves their apartments, though, he is back on his bike and flying through the streets of Manhattan. His ability to connect warmly with his clients contrasts with his own inability to interact with his family and Silvia. It is only after he meets Salim that he begins to try to connect with the people he cares about. While they are eating at a Turkish restaurant, Salim gives Heller advice: "If you wake up to find your house burning down, do you try to escape as fast as you can, rush out of the house in a frenzy? Or do you slowly make your way out, even through the flames?" (136). Heller, as expected, responds that he would run. Salim explains that running is not the answer, even though it is everyone's impulse: "What should be done is simple; and that is to slowly walk through the fire. Take your time. Slow down, because the smoke will char your lungs, your skin will burn, and the flames will devour your house either way, . . . Slow down" (136). If he does not slow down, Silvia will not even notice him. Heller is sure to face conflict, pain, and, sorrow. If he is always running, he will never have a chance to experience love, beauty, joy, and tenderness.

The novel links Heller's struggles to those of the city in which he lives. It further creates a web of links between the characters and other literary works and historical events in typical Dorfman fashion. There is the obvious connection between Heller and Joseph Heller, author of the infamous anti-war novel *Catch-22*. Then, as revealed in the novel's opening vignette, which describes the collaboration between Dorfman and his son, the reader learns that Salim's bookselling boss, Velu, is named after a famous rebel from Kerala, India. Heller's Nigerian friend refers to Heller as the Yoruba god Eshu, who plays tricks in order to teach how choices have consequences. In other literary links, Salim quotes poetry from Nazim Hikmet, known as the first modern Turkish poet, and Silvia reads *El Quijote*. These links point to the novel's themes of the human struggle to build community while avoiding the insanity of modernity, but the novel's most significant literary link is to Virgil's *Aeneid*, which recounts the events of another *burning city*, Troy.

It is through this tie that the novel bridges the city of Heller to the city that will suffer terrorist attacks on September 11. The multiple references to the "burning" city allow the authors to playfully allude to the way that urban spaces morph under the summer heat, sending people outside and building community connections often invisible in the cooler months. The burning motif, though, has a far deeper resonance, thereby allowing the authors to subtly link the novel to the devastation that awaits the city only a couple of months into the future. Heller, who celebrates his birthday on the Fourth of July—a clearly symbolic date—faces questions about his identity that foreshadow the questions that would plague New York after the terrorist attacks. Is it possible to forgive in the face of violent loss? Can new communities be created by the displaced? Can there be hope for the future built on a past of horror? Many of these questions are filtered through the nostalgic, philosophical, and sensitive voice of Salim, a character whose combination of Muslim religion, sensitivity, and nonviolence counterbalances the post-9/11 stereotypes of violent Muslim terrorists. He tells Heller, "You can never call a place home until you have buried someone there. . . . The Prophet Muhammad never said he was coming back from the dead. He knew it wasn't necessary. . . . So what comes next? . . . You wander. Keep wandering until you find the place you can call home" (70).[72] Salim also has a poetic view of the battle of Troy. Rather than remember the violence, rape, and destruction, he prefers to remember the ten years that Paris was able to make love to Helen. Delirious after his beating, Salim tells Heller, "My father was from Troy. . . . First, I escaped the burning city. . . . I crossed the sea . . . they all wanted to stop me, but the gods said . . . no. You were waiting for me. . . . Now the city is burning again. The city is always burning. . . . If I cannot escape the burning city this time . . . it will be your turn. This time, you must stay" (186). Linking the empires of New York and Troy, the authors suggest that such historical catastrophes are inevitable. Where humanity is challenged is in its response to them.

The choice of Troy as the historical link to New York prior to 9/11 provides the novel with a global connection that moves beyond the obvious ties the Dorfmans have to Chile's own 9/11. Reflecting the authors' interest in globalization, the novel alternates between concrete specifics and timeless archetype. The best example of this practice is the way that the novel's multiethnic community suggests an alternate view of globalization. Through the lives of Heller's clients, all of whom have traveled to New York to seek a better life and all of whom flee various forms of persecution, the reader glimpses a truly global community. But their lives in New York are complicated. For each opportunity, there is loss, and that loss is always the loss of a loved one. Suffering displacement, these immigrants come together to form a multiethnic community that eventually becomes like a family to Heller.

The novel's questions about how such a global community will survive and what hopes it has for building meaningful connections revolve around the ability or inclination of people to receive the world's messages. Although Heller is a messenger, he has not yet learned how to deliver messages to his loved ones. The novel makes a clear critique of the alienating effects of the mass media and the impersonal communications of the digital age. For example, Heller's boss, Dimitri, first met Heller's father when the latter came to find him in Siberia to deliver the message that his mother had died. Later, as a refugee in New York, Dimitri knew that others, like him, would need to hear certain news personally, even when time and space made physical contact with loved ones impossible. But Dimitri is a world of contradictions himself, playing with his television remote, drinking vodka, and sending others to make human contact that he desperately needs. In a subtle indictment of pre-9/11 New York, the

Dorfmans suggest that this breakdown in human contact may be partly responsible for the terrorist disaster. Beyond posing the question of what it means when a society needs a company like Soft Tidings, the novel then asks a deeper question about why Heller is so successful at consoling his clients.

Heller isn't entirely sure himself why he is so successful. He listens, he takes his time, but some intangible quality unknown to him guides him and makes him able to provide clients with a sense of connection and comfort. This intangible quality to Heller's messages intersects with Salim's quoting of poetry by Hikmet, whose words provide Salim with extraordinary solace and joy. The novel asks why certain words are able to move humanity, build bonds among people, and inspire hope in the face of despair. If Heller can figure out the answer to this question, the reader assumes, he will find a way back into Silvia's heart. If he can find the answer, he can stop running from himself.

In the background of the novel is an ongoing theme about the need to remember loss, pain, and death, especially when these are tied to human rights violations. During the novel's first description of one of Heller's deliveries, he goes to the home of a Chinese woman to tell her that her son is dead. Her son had been in a Chinese reeducation camp, a *lao gai*. When his client asks Heller if he knows what that means, he nods that he does, and she responds with surprise. Heller has learned about these camps from his parents, who are human rights activists. The client goes on to tell a moving story about how she collects small wooden objects made in China that have a broken butterfly engraved on the bottom. These, she believes, are made by her son, and the butterflies are his way of sending her messages. In words of consolation for her loss, Heller tells her, "I don't think he ever stopped speaking to you" (34). The Dorfmans suggest that messages can take many forms. They can be verbal, symbolic, or imaginary. The task facing humanity in an era of globalization is to find a way to be open to receive them.

Manifesto for Another World. The scene between Heller and the Chinese immigrant from *The Burning City* reveals the novel's theme that certain messages have the ability to bring hope and build bridges across humanity. The scene also links *The Burning City* and Dorfman's play *Manifesto for Another World*, which was completed in 2000 and appeared in a new edition in 2004.[73] The play is based on Kerry Kennedy Cuomo's book, *Speak Truth to Power*, an anthology of the voices of fifty-one human rights defenders. Among the voices in the book is that of Harry Wu, himself a victim of a *lao gai*. Wu says, "The victims of the *laogai* number more than those of the Soviet gulag plus the concentration camps. . . . Why doesn't Steven Spielberg film the *laogai* the way he did the concentration camps? I want to see *laogai* become a word in every dictionary" (Kennedy Cuomo, 245). In a gesture of solidarity with Wu, the Dorfmans built his mission into their novel, layering his message and his struggle for human rights with the novel's depiction of a city on fire and an adolescent man in crisis.

The link between the novel and the play indicates the extent to which Dorfman continued to pursue the relationship between culture and human rights struggles well after the official end of Pinochet's rule. These interests stemmed in part from the specific context of Chile—as evidenced by his 2002 book on the arrest of Pinochet, *Exorcising Terror*—but they also began to take an increasingly transnational view. Even though *The Burning City* and *Manifesto for Another World* have brief references to Chile, these texts continue the global trajectory in Dorfman's writing that began with *Konfidenz*. The two later projects, however, are not only physically distant from Chile, but they are also populated by a chorus of characters and voices that hail from across the globe. In *The Burning City* Dorfman and his son collaborated on a novelistic technique that would allow them to provide readers with a view of the multi-cultural context of pre-9/11 Manhattan, and as the prologue to the novel jokingly suggests, the collaboration required father and son to balance their different styles and worldviews: " 'You've done a great job on Chapter One. Chapter Three is too dark.' 'Dark is how I write, old man,' retaliates Joaquín." They end the prologue with the challenge: "Try to guess which one of us got in the last word" (i).

This banter between father and son provides an interesting parallel to the challenge that faced Dorfman with *Manifesto for Another World* since he was given the difficult task of condensing fifty-one voices into a short play. To construct the play he had to engage in a complex writing process that would at one and the same time let these voices emerge as a dramatic work while simultaneously allowing Dorfman to practice his craft as a storyteller. As he writes in the introduction, when Kerry Kennedy Cuomo approached him about the project, he felt ambivalent. On the one hand, he explains, "I felt I had been preparing all my life to become a bridge for those voices" (14). In many respects the project was a logical result of Dorfman's lifelong commitment to find a way to use artistic expression to advance social struggle. On the other hand, he worried that the project, if not handled carefully, could result in a heavy-handed production that seemed to simply harangue the audience with tales of heroes (15). In an extreme amplification of the challenges that face those who compile testimonials, this project asked him to compile, edit, and shape not one but fifty-one voices. Dorfman explains that he accepted the task because the voices themselves whispered to him "ways in which the stories could be staged as a sort of spoken oratorio which interwove testimonials and poetry and narrative" (15). Of note in this passage is Dorfman's description of his role as a medium, a conduit, a carrier for the voices.

It may very well have been the novelty of the project, alongside the obvious honor of working with the words and stories of such an extraordinary group of people, that ultimately convinced Dorfman to accept Kennedy Cuomo's offer. It is important to remember that one of the central characteristics of Dorfman's career has been his constant innovation and experimentation. The paradox that a constant feature of Dorfman's work is innovation provides one of the most vexing challenges for scholars of his work since his consistency as a writer is aesthetic rather than stylistic.[74] While Dorfman does not openly acknowledge the fact that the writing of this play would offer him a rare opportunity to challenge his writing in a new way, the following lines from the play's introduction suggest that he found the idea of bringing his practice of constructing morally flawed characters (who engage in constant questioning) into dialogue with human rights defenders (who require a degree of confidence in order to do their work) to be a particularly intriguing proposition: "Could I find a dramatic form that remained true to the valor, the purity, the righteousness, of these champions of human values, while at the same time taking into account the frailty and darkness of our contemporary condition? Can the hope and inspiration necessary, indeed crucial, for social activism be married to the mistrust and transgression, the linguistic experimentation and playfulness, that nurtures the most significant literature of our times? What, if anything, do the Dalai Lama and Samuel Beckett have in common?" (15).

Dorfman adds that the fact that only a handful of the defenders were well known internationally further attracted him to the project (16). It is likely that another appealing factor was the type of questions that Kennedy Cuomo asked the defenders. Her book centers less on the details of the human rights projects of the defenders than on their character, their fears, and their courage. As she explains in the introduction to her book, her questions touched on a number of common themes: "Why do people who face imprisonment, torture, and death, continue to pursue their work when the chance of success is so remote and the personal consequences are so grave? . . . Where do they derive their strength and inspiration? How do they overcome their fear?" (6). All the defenders speak in detail about their particular, concrete struggles, but the nature of Kennedy Cuomo's questions also leads them to discuss at length topics that were far more muddy and intangible and that were far more likely to have piqued Dorfman's interest. The original text, then, is not a series of passages that describe the battles of the defenders. Instead, it allows the defenders to speak about how they cope with fear, indifference, and loss, as well as where they find their courage, hope, and strength.

As Dorfman read the texts compiled by Kennedy Cuomo, he recognized that they needed to be staged as a "collage of verses and phrases and incantations" that would allow him to blend the testimonial with the lyrical (16). This tapestry of voices, though, would not be enough, and Dorfman decided that the play needed a dramatic antagonist who would provide tension for the work, a counter to these voices of courage and hope and defiance. He created what he calls an "Evangelist of evil," "who did not believe that the play itself, my word, the words of my heroes, would make a difference" (17). Like the anonymous male presence in *Konfidenz* or the anonymous superior to Tolgate in *Blake's Therapy*, Dorfman inserted a malignant character who could represent the two biggest threats to the defenders: the "repression of the State" and "those who do not care" (17). These two core ideas—blending the testimonial with the lyrical and inserting an antagonist—combined to form Dorfman's central aesthetic vision for the play, and they allowed him to explore a series of questions about the relationship between words, as representation and as denunciation, and the connection between the people who both utter and listen to those words. Dorfman's challenge was to find a way to circulate these questions throughout the play without having them overtake the voices themselves. The result is that the play presents the audience with a subtle counterpoint between the ambiguous questioning at the heart of Dorfman's work and the empowering intensity of the defenders' strength and success.

Dorfman creates this counterpoint in three ways, and these relate to the structure and lines of the cast, the intersections between the original text and the play, and the role of "the Man." Dorfman explains that there is some flexibility in casting, but the play is ideally written for nine performers, five male and four female. One of the male actors plays the Man, and all of the rest alternately speak the voices of the defenders according to their original gender. It is not unusual for playwrights to suggest that actors take on multiple speaking parts, but Dorfman's innovation is in having them all appear on stage together from the start of the play. The actors are to be grouped symmetrically, with the Man occupying the center of the stage. Dorfman specifically does not want the actors to change their appearance or mode of speech according to the identity of the defender they represent. He explains, "Each actor and actress is not pretending to be that person, but is the channel through which that person is reaching the audience. That is why it is not a good idea to attempt to create accents (Asian, African, Latino, etc.) for the voices" (80). This structure immediately calls attention to the act of representation since the actors are cautioned to avoid "acting out" the story (79). This absence of artifice—no costumes, no accents, no grand gestures—leaves the actor and the audience alone with the words of the defenders. By paring down the representation, Dorfman draws attention to it.

In addition to drawing attention to the words and to the actors' representation of them, the casting structure results in a complex technique of linguistic layering and difference, a strategy that adds a further level of questioning about words, representations, and human struggles. Each actor, apart from the Man, speaks the lines of various defenders. The simple tactic of having the same voice represent multiple voices underscores another representational dilemma that has interested Dorfman throughout his career. Since the actors are directed not to change their voices, the audience hears one voice representing many. Are these voices unique, irreducible, fundamentally different? Or do they have common links? What happens when the words of one person are spoken by someone else? Do they have the same effect? If not, why not? Again, Dorfman takes a relatively simple structure and embeds within it a series of intense questions about language and power. Then in a reverse gesture, he has actors repeat the words of defenders in a chorus that rhythmically flows throughout the play, creating a counterpoint between the poetic and the testimonial. For instance, the first lines of the play are spoken by the first male voice and later repeated by a number of actors: "Courage begins with one voice. It's that simple. I did what I had to do. Anything else would have tasted like ashes. That is what we know" (27). These lines are then repeated, sometimes only in parts, throughout the play by different actors. The repetitions reverse the action of having one voice speak for many because here many voices speak for one, reiterating one line, sharing it through collective speech. In some instances the lines are altered. "I did what I had to do," for example, becomes "We did what we had to do" (43). In this way Dorfman is able to draw attention to the relationship between the individual and the collective and between the original and its representation. The result is that Dorfman very gently pushes on the representational tensions regarding testimonial and authenticity without falling into skeptical nihilism.

The opening lines also hint at Dorfman's second strategy, where he creates a dialogue between the original text and the play. Without question the charge to turn fifty-one compelling stories of human rights defense into a brief play required that Dorfman make difficult choices about which sections of which voices to include. He strikes a balance between the voices of the famous and the marginal, and most of the play is dedicated to presenting brief vignettes of the defenders' testimonials. There are many lines like the opening lines, though, that are not attributed to any one defender. These are some of the most interesting parts of the play because in these lines Dorfman investigates the ties between the language of literature and of denunciation. When he combed through the original texts, he searched for phrases and passages that were inherently poetic and lyrically moving. He then placed these phrases, often uttered by different defenders, into a literary collage, merging the language of truth with the language of the imagination. For example, "Courage begins with one voice" belongs to Oscar Arias, and Desmond Tutu says, "Anything else would have tasted like ashes" in reference to Jeremiah (Kennedy Cuomo, 47, 60). Another line repeated and modified throughout the play comes from Samuel Kofi Woods: "You walk into the corridor of death and you know this moment might be your last" (Kennedy Cuomo, 124). This technique of making a collage of voices leads Dorfman to create a series of lines that circle around what the defenders "know":

Second Voice (Female):	You walk into the corridor of death . . .
First Voice (Male):	. . . and you know, you know this moment might be your last.
Second Voice (Female):	That's what you know.
Fourth voice (Female):	That is what I know. I know what it is to wait in the dark for torture and what it is to wait in the dark for truth. (28)

The last line of this passage, spoken by the fourth voice, merges the voice of Woods with that of the U.S.-Guatemalan nun Dianna Ortiz, who is the author of the last sentence. The play contains numerous such examples, and they all point to two of the essential messages of the play. First, there is no fundamental separation between the words of truth and the words of beauty. Art that is political does not need to be pedantic because the words of human struggle can and often do combine the power of the poetic with the power of the politically passionate. Second, by not attributing the lyrical lines to any one defender, Dorfman offers them up for collective ownership. He makes it possible for the audience to imagine that these words could be theirs as well.

These inspirational moments are balanced by the presence of the Man, who represents a threat to the defenders, first in the form of state repression and then in the form of public apathy.[75] The contrast between the Man and the voices of the defenders at first glance seems to follow a fairly predictable trajectory. The Man is ominous, threatening, and intimidating, allowing Dorfman to create dramatic tension through a quintessential source of evil. The

Man attempts to deflate the defenders' confidence and force them into self-doubt: "This is what they fear, what they really fear: that nobody cares, that nobody listens, that people forget, that people watch T.V. and say these are not their problems and then have dinner and go to sleep" (50). The Man, though, also plays a role in performing the representational struggles that plague human rights activism. As the defenders introduce themselves, they speak their names, but it is the Man who makes a gesture causing the names to appear on a screen. Here Dorfman stages the asymmetrical power of representational systems. The defenders speak their names, employing the oral, while the Man controls both the written word and the visual representation. Even when the defenders are trying to tell their stories to the public, their words are filtered through a signifying system that the Man controls. It is only when one of the defenders remains anonymous and unnamed that the Man ceases to hold that power. As the unnamed defender continues to speak, the lights fade on the Man. Then when the next defender speaks, another defender makes a gesture causing the defender's name to appear. It is no coincidence that the first defender to be "named" by another defender is Rigoberta Menchú, who says, "We have to reinvent hope all over again. These are things that are not going to be forgotten. They will not be forgotten. We are the ones that have the last words" (62). With the strategic positioning of Menchú's words, Dorfman makes a comment about the relationship between the voices of human rights defenders and the public sphere. For some time after this shift the Man remains silent. Then, near the end of the play, he speaks one last time to remind the audience members that while they might forget the defenders' names, men like him will remember them: "All those names. Names we won't forget, not me. Others will forget these names. They're already fading from memory, those names" (71). Through these lines Dorfman equates the struggle for signification with the struggle for memory. Whose memory will prevail? Those who want to destroy the defenders or those who want to support them?

The play first opened on September 19, 2000, at the Kennedy Center in Washington, D.C. President Bill Clinton opened the evening, and nine high-profile actors took the stage: Kevin Kline, Sigourney Weaver, John Malkovich, Rita Moreno, Alec Baldwin (who played the Man), Giancarlo Esposito, Hector Elizondo, Julia Louis-Dreyfus, and Alfre Woodard. According to Dorfman the evening was made unforgettable when, after the last words of the play, as the lights started to dim, a curtain opened to reveal, behind the Hollywood stars, the real defenders themselves. While Dorfman mentions that some were missing, like the Dalai Lama, most of those interviewed made the trip (19). Dorfman explains that "seeing some of the most visible beings on this planet hand in hand with some of the least visible," he had a "biting intuition of how precarious this moment really was" (20). How long would it take for the media attention to move to something more entertaining?

This staging of the play was broadcast by PBS on October 8, 2000. Since then, the play has been performed across the globe in a variety of settings, including Geneva, London, Helsinki, Athens, Madrid, Rome, Barcelona, Milan, Florence, New York, Sydney, and Doha, and often with the performances of high-profile actors at benefits for human rights. A second high-profile staging took place on January 14, 2005, at the Ebenezer Baptist Church in Atlanta, to celebrate Martin Luther King's birthday and the fortieth anniversary of his acceptance of the Nobel Peace Prize. This performance included Martin Sheen, Sean Penn, and Woody Harrelson, and it was the first performance with two actors playing the part of the Man. Similarly to *Death and the Maiden*, the play has linked Dorfman in highly visible ways to the global human rights struggle.

Desert Memories. *Manifesto for Another World* asks how the words of human rights defenders will be remembered when society seems disinclined to pay attention to the truths they represent. Similar meditations on memory and truth appear in Dorfman's next book, *Desert Memories*. Both texts unite a myriad of voices and both present the challenge of recuperating memory in an age of collective amnesia and apathy, but where *Manifesto for Another World* provides a global view of the voices of human rights activists, *Desert Memories* focuses on a particular geographical region. A book in the National Geographic literary travel series, *Desert Memories*, in a parallel to *Manifesto*, provided Dorfman with an opportunity to explore a new literary genre, that of travel writing. In keeping with his interest in experimenting with new types of texts, Dorfman used the opportunity to push on the limits of that literary form and to dialogue with the history of Latin American travel writing. Rather than travel to a foreign land, Dorfman writes his travel memoir about his own nation, but he chooses a region of Chile that he had previously ignored—a move that allows him to narrate the memoir from the perspective of an insider and an outsider at the same time.

Not only does Dorfman decide to narrate from a liminal, insider/outsider position, but his choice of location further allows him to develop another series of contrasts and complexities. The desert is an apt place to ponder the problem of memory since it both preserves and destroys everything, alternately conserving human history and eradicating it. The Atacama Desert—the driest desert in the world—allows Dorfman to use a specific geographic location as a grounding device for a wide range of questions about his identity, the identity of his nation, and the ways that memories are preserved and destroyed. He begins by making it clear that the trip is as much about the desert as it is about himself. The choice of the Atacama as the location forces Dorfman to confront a lifelong prejudice against deserts. When he had traveled through Latin America in 1962, embarking on the typical hitchhiking trip of those years, he had hurriedly rushed through the Atacama on his way to visit the region's *great* origins—the civilizations of the Inca and Tiawanaku (5). Even years later, when he recognizes that the Atacama may hold more clues to his past than the Andean highlands, he confesses to a lingering prejudice against deserts as travel destinations: "There was nothing there" (5). He also confesses his fear of them: "Perhaps I was afraid of precisely what so many others through history have found attractive in the emptiness: the solitude and extreme introspection that a landscape devoid of human habitation will force you to face with a vengeance, a truth about yourself that you can find nowhere else. . . . The desert, a place of death and testing, I thought, a place to avoid" (7).

In his quest to discover his origins and those of his country, though, Dorfman must return to the desert. He explains that the Atacama was the home of many indigenous groups, making it an important place to learn about the Americas' first peoples, but it was the discovery of nitrate that would convert the Atacama into a central factor in Chile's development as a nation (10). This discovery coincided not only with U.S. and European demand for nitrate for use in agriculture and later for gunpowder, but also with modern scientific methods that could expertly extract it. It thus provided an economic windfall for the Chilean elite and embedded a vicious class hierarchy in the region. Those same extreme class divisions would, in turn, give birth to the first Chilean democratic and socialist movements. The nitrate miners became the "the first social groups and trade unions in Latin America," and generations of Chilean leaders, including both Salvador Allende and Augusto Pinochet, began their careers in the desert (11). "The desert, therefore, had engendered contemporary Chile, everything that was good about it, everything that was dreadful. The Chile of inequality and misery I had witnessed as an adolescent, the Chile that gave me hope when I matured into a young man. . . . The desert was at the source of the world that I had inhabited" (12). By visiting the desert, Dorfman is able to explore his and his nation's origins by means of a physical space that is inherently contradictory.

The desert draws Dorfman for more personal reasons as well. Apart from its grand role in the shaping of Chilean history, the desert was also the location of a number of concentration camps during the Pinochet years. In a camp in Pisagua, Freddy Taberna, one of Dorfman's friends from the Allende years, was executed by a firing squad. His body was never found. Dorfman confesses that "his murder in the derelict concentration camp at Pisagua after the coup . . . came to symbolize for me, perhaps more than the loss of any other friend, the destruction of the country, the pillaging of the past" (16). Then in a parallel search for lost loved ones, Dorfman, accompanied by his wife Angélica, embarked on a second personal quest that, while less loaded by trauma, was equally obscure. Angélica's family had grown estranged from the relatives on her father's side, and since they had originally resided in the northern town of Iquique, the Dorfmans hoped to trace some links to relatives from her past. In seeking Angélica's past, Dorfman was searching for the roots of his children and grandchildren, who also had a tangled web of connections to the great Chilean north. Dorfman's memoir recounts, then, a layered trip to uncover multiple origins.

The memoir searches for these multiple origins in a structure that moves from History to history via a trajectory that becomes increasingly more personal and intimate the farther north Dorfman travels. Directly disobeying his own predetermined geographical boundaries, Dorfman begins the narrative symbolically, in the south of Chile at Monte Verde, the home of the oldest human footprint ever found in the Americas, dating back 12,500 years. The trip allows Dorfman to take in the lush landscape of the Chilean south and to procrastinate over his arrival in the dry, barren north. To justify the detour Dorfman rationalizes that if "this Chilean journey was to the origins . . . what could be more pertinent than to kick it off from the oldest human habitation in the Americas, the place where it all began?" (26). Dorfman playfully recounts that his enthusiasm for the footprint fails to convince Angélica, and she remains in Santiago during the excursion. Behind this jesting about his procrastination, though, lies a deeper reason for beginning in Monte Verde since the content and form of this opening section set the stage for Dorfman's narrative and establish the questions, concerns, and critical interventions that shape the text as a whole.

First and most obviously, the decision to begin a travel memoir about the northern desert in the south enables Dorfman to test the limits of the geographical space he has declared as his boundary. He reasons that the desert can be understood only via attention to this footprint to the south. Throughout the text Dorfman carefully structures a vision of geographical space that refuses to be contained by traditional categories. Not only is the south linked to the north by the movement of first peoples that traveled these lands on foot, but Dorfman also considers the connections between these places in order to offer another view of globalization. Monte Verde's links to Chile's past contrast with the homogenizing forces of globalization that increasingly draw the attention of Chileans away from their own history: "For a country whose identity in a world of accelerated globalization is under siege . . . here is an anchor in the past: ancestors who were centered in their own environment, who survived by depending on things they had created themselves" (42). Later, as he moves north, Dorfman will excavate memories of Chile's past that are at risk of being forgotten; many of these are linked to ghost towns, those of both miners and the disappeared. The desire to rescue memories from the onslaught of global superficiality, though, is not the only way that Dorfman's travel memoir tests the ties between the local and the global. He also considers the global exchange of products as a way for the Chilean desert to come into contact with other parts of the globe. While visiting a nitrate mine, he ponders how the minerals that are extracted become iodine for photos, lithium for batteries, borax for eyeglasses, toothpaste, and detergent. Those products then circulate the globe: "The Chilean desert scattered almost invisibly to every corner of the globe, stirring inside a snapshot taken in Sri Lanka and a tomato eaten in Chicago and a toy truck running on batteries in Tokyo" (98). This view of globalization suggests that the circulation of products in contemporary society is merely an intensification of the transport of Chilean materials that began in the nineteenth century.

Thus the first chapter, which takes place in Monte Verde and Valdivia, hints at the ways that Dorfman's text reconsiders the boundaries that demarcate geographical space and reassesses how spaces determine individual and national identities. It also establishes another central nexus of concerns that run throughout the text concerning the relationship among truth, science, and spirituality. The footprint is important for Dorfman to see not only because it represents the oldest sign of human life in the Americas, but also because it notoriously changed the scientific community's theory about the first people to walk the Americas. Prior to the discovery of the footprint the reigning theory about the first peoples of the Americas was the Clovis paradigm, a thesis that claimed that the first humans had arrived via the Bering Strait, going on to colonize the rest of what would later be known as the New World. The footprint, which dated at least one thousand years prior to the Clovis artifacts, disproved this thesis, "allowing a plethora of new and old speculations about multiple entries and landings and routes for the original settlement of the Americas to flourish" (30). Thanks to science, there is a new version of the truth about the origins of the peoples of the Americas, and unlike the scientific paradigms of the nineteenth century, which tended to reinforce the logic of empire and to contain and control the flow of knowledge, the science of the footprint has undermined that hegemonic structure and allowed for a reversal of its empirical orthodoxy.

The memoir goes on to trace the work of a number of scientists, thereby reviving in a revised form the historical link between science and travel writing in Latin America. As Roberto González Echevarría describes in *Myth and Archive*, nineteenth-century travel narratives were typically written by Europeans about Latin America: "The result is thousands of books describing, analyzing, and classifying the flora, fauna, landscape, social organization, ethnic composition, fossil formations, atmosphere, in short, everything that could be known to nineteenth-century science. The equation between power and knowledge, between collection and possession could not be clearer, particularly when one takes into account that many of the travelers . . . were representatives of corporations involved in some sort of economic exploitation, especially mining" (102). González Echevarría explains that this type of writing had a tremendous impact on the knowledge produced about Latin America: "Backed as they were by the might of their empires and armed with the systemic cogency of European science, these travelers and their writings became the purveyors of a discourse about Latin American reality that rang true and was enormously influential. Their entire discursive activity, from traveling itself to taxonomical practices, embodied truth and exuded authority through its own performance" (102).

Understanding this context is essential to appreciating the way that Dorfman structures the relationship between science and truth in his travel memoir. On the one hand, *Desert Memories* makes a point of signaling a new era of scientists whose work is no longer dictated by the empires of the north, but on the other hand, he suggests that the truths of science are incomplete without attention to intangible, spiritual, and emotional truths. Again the story of the footprint provides the memoir's readers with an interpretive map for the rest of the text since it teaches two lessons about alternative ways of producing knowledge. First, readers learn about the virulent opposition the scientific community had to the discovery of the footprint. "The defenders of the Clovis hypothesis . . . had offered fierce resistance, claiming the site had not been adequately protected from contamination" (30). Eventually, though, with the funding of an eccentric Texas millionaire, the truth of the discovery emerged, and the hegemony of "northern" science was displaced. The story reveals that science is no longer solely the domain of empire, and throughout the text Dorfman visits with Chilean scientists engaged in cutting-edge work, such as Miguel Roth, who runs an astrophysics observatory at Cerro Las Campanas, and Lautaro Núñez, an archeologist who lives in San Pedro de Atacama.

Against these scientists, who offer an alternative view of the role this discipline has had on the production of meaning about Latin America, Dorfman balances the work of the mining corporations he visits, which continue to follow the nineteenth-century model of using science as a means to exploit the land. Dorfman's point is that science in Chile is an ambivalent practice, depending on who is producing scientific knowledge and to what end.

Second, in addition to suggesting that the relationship between science and knowledge in Latin America has undergone a shift in power, the footprint provides Dorfman with an opportunity to establish the empirical limits of scientific knowledge. In recounting Mario Pino's tale of the discovery of the footprint, Dorfman emphasizes the spirituality and emotional impact of the moment. Pino tells him: "One thing is to see artifacts presumably made by somebody and another is to see the *pisada* someone made, what their foot left in the earth. That's what gives you a sense of humanity, right?" (34). Later Pino tells him that while showing a slide of the footprint to a group of young Chilean schoolgirls, he had said to the audience that the person who had made the footprint had been small, "like one of you, a girl like one of you" (39). Pino had then had the sensation that there was someone standing next to him and had inexplicably begun to cry, leading the entire room into uncontrollable sobs. He tells Dorfman he is a nonbeliever but that after that incident he couldn't shake a haunting feeling and has never used that slide again. This story is only one in a long line of stories Dorfman recounts throughout the text of moments of spiritual enlightenment, where knowledge is acquired through emotional intensity and human connection. The second lesson of the footprint, then, is that science provides only part of the story.

Written against the tradition of the nineteenth-century travel narratives of figures like Alexander Von Humboldt, Dorfman's travel memoir is not that of an outsider gathering scientific information about an exotic land. In a playful demonstration of the limits of his scientific knowledge, Dorfman advances a theory of "Desert Syndrome," a condition that makes it difficult for those who live in the desert to develop deep human connections, only to later have his theory refuted (57). It would be a mistake, however, to read this travel memoir as a purely oppositional text that writes against the tradition of producing scientific and authoritative knowledge about Latin America. In keeping with the nineteenth-century form, for instance, Dorfman supplies his readers with extensive descriptions of flora, fauna, and geographical landscapes—an attention to descriptive detail unusual for Dorfman, who typically shuns providing such information. Readers will note that this text is one of the first occasions where Dorfman narrates physical descriptions of any sort. We learn, for instance, that Miguel Roth has put on weight, and we receive a specific description of Freddy Taberna's face. Committed to an aesthetic that requires the reader's active imagination, Dorfman has historically avoided narrating any type of realistic detail, and it is rare for him to give any information about the physical features of characters in his stories or novels. Yet in order to situate his text both within and against the tradition of Latin American travel writing, Dorfman offers readers his own account, or *crónica*, of the natural history, landscape, and people he meets during his trip. These details progressively become more intimate and personal: flowing from the description of geographical and physical space, Dorfman recounts intimate details about his friend, Freddy, and about the family history of his wife, Angélica.

This style, which becomes apparent from the first chapter on the footprint, involves another important twist on the traditional travel narrative. Rather than replicate either the authoritative voice of the nineteenth-century traveler or the personal tone of the testimonial, Dorfman constructs a discursive counterpoint among a number of sources. Throughout much of the memoir he simply transmits the stories of others. These stories vary from those of scientists and corporate representatives of mining facilities to the accounts of old miners remembering their lives in abandoned mining towns. Dorfman's travel is both to the Atacama and to the people of the Atacama. He records, for instance, the stories of Hernán Rivera, who recounts his time living in the ghost town of Pampa Unión. Rivera has dedicated his life to keeping the history of his town alive in spite of the destruction of this segment of Chilean history, and Dorfman unites the voices of many people like Rivera. Alongside his own narrative power and authority he places the voices of others; most poignantly many of the other voices are those of the dead: they are the voices of Freddy, who hopes that when he is shot, it will not hurt; of the people who lived in mining towns like Humberstone and who danced in the desert; of the disappeared in Chacabuco; and of the mummies of Chinchorro, who were buried together in a ritual that reinforced the idea that in order to survive— both in life and in death—one needs community. But even though Dorfman records the voices of others, he does not attempt to entirely diminish his role as a writer. Just as he provides a counterpoint between the truths of science and the truths of the heart, the memoir alternates between his observations and those of others. As Dorfman concludes the last chapter, he reinforces the idea that this memoir has been both collective and personal: "So here is my prayer, my thanks for having completed this journey. My own writing, my own signposts, my own way of marking the road we took, recognizing the lives that were given to us to remember and care for and transmit. I want this book to be a small offering, a *gracias* for having been steered so softly through the ghost reaches of my country, the place where Chile and the family I married into and the world I inhabit, where it all had its origin" (276).

With these lines Dorfman emphasizes that even though he has tried to collect the many voices he encountered, this account is his, and it is not meant as a totalizing replacement for the grand narratives of history. It is meant as a challenge, a disruption, an *other* view. Dorfman's journey to the Atacama, then, is not only a critical engagement with nineteenth-century travel memoirs; it can also be read intertextually against the Latin American modernist novels that narrated a return to origins, especially, for example, Alejo Carpentier's *Los pasos perdidos* (*The Lost Steps*). Both *Desert Memories* and *The Lost Steps* undermine the scientific authority of Europe by providing a more autochthonous view of Latin America, but unlike the trajectory followed by Carpentier's protagonist, Dorfman's voyage is to multiple origins that cannot be located in his final destination. It is important to note that throughout the text Dorfman has highlighted a number of origins he seeks, but none of these are in fact found. Symbolically he never describes seeing the footprint; he only speaks about holding it in a closed-box (23). So, in a wink to Carpentier, while Dorfman finds the "paso" (footprint), he may not actually see it. Even though he searches to find more about the circumstances of Freddy's death, he does not find his body. Angélica searches through Iquique and is unable to locate any of her relatives. In fact, her success comes in Buenos Aires, not in the Chilean desert that supposedly was the original home of her family. Then, when Dorfman visits the sites of mines that hold keys to Chile's past, he is forced to acknowledge that these mines can be understood only in a geopolitical landscape that extends well beyond the borders of the desert. Each origin is displaced, projected elsewhere, or unknown. Against these origins Dorfman places a host of ghosts. For while the origins are elusive, the ghosts seem more tangible. On his search for origins he had wandered "through the avenues and armies of the dead and mostly what I had witnessed was violence, abandonment, betrayal, towns turned into ghosts and ghosts turned into emptiness as their destiny was decided from afar" (268). Dorfman learns, though, as he studies these tales of death, that the desert exposes the best and the worst of humanity. Most important, those that survive can survive only through solidarity: the desert tells "them to trust one another or die" (269). Bridging the redemptive journey of Carpentier's unnamed protagonist from *The Lost Steps* with a postmodern skepticism of origins, *Desert Memories* investigates the truth claims that define nations, communities, and individuals and attempts to inspire readers to recognize the traces of the Atacama desert in their own lives.

■ ■ ■

Dorfman's subsequent works, all at the time of this writing unpublished, continue to pursue the theme of redemption. A novel based on the life of Joaquín Murieta, the Chilean-Mexican bandit from the U.S.-Mexican border, is situated in the nineteenth century and builds on some of the critical interventions and stylistic explorations of *Desert Memories*. Three plays—*Purgatorio*, "Picasso's Closet," and "The Other Side"—all of which had U.S. premieres in 2005 and 2006, form what Dorfman has called the Redemption Trilogy.[76] The play "In the Dark," which was written for the Royal Shakespeare Company, further pursues themes of love and forgiveness in a society that has been tremendously wounded. These works continue many of the themes that Dorfman began to pursue after the official end of his exile in 1990.

As this chapter has shown, Dorfman has a constant set of critical concerns that morph and transform according to historical developments. Much of his work after the arrest of Pinochet and the 9/11 terrorist attacks on the United States has considered the problems of forgiveness, redemption, justice, and truth. For instance, in response to the U.S. decision to go to war in Iraq, Dorfman wrote a series of poems from "the other side of death" that proposed a dialogue between the past and the present. Pablo Picasso speaks to Colin Powell, Hammurabi speaks to Donald Rumsfeld, Christopher Columbus speaks to Captain John Whyte (who renamed Saddam Airport), and William Blake speaks to Laura Bush. The running theme throughout these poems is that one of the follies of the U.S. war on terror is its inattention to history and the lessons of art. The combined knowledge of Picasso, Hammurabi, Columbus, and Blake proves that art and history preserve the memory of the past even in the face of masterful efforts to silence dissent, critique, and social engagement.

These poems are evidence of Dorfman's increasingly global optic. As this chapter has shown, though, this global view has been counterbalanced throughout this period with a commitment to reflecting on Latin America. Of interest for scholars of Latin American literature and culture is the way that Dorfman's work in the period 1990–2005 has engaged in many of the core critical issues that shaped research on Latin American writing. Abril Trigo has written that "Four main theoretical trends emerged and dominated Latin American cultural studies in the early 1990s: subaltern studies, deconstructionist discourse analysis, postcolonialism, and transnational cultural studies with an emphasis on multiculturalism and the effects of globalization" (348). While all of these themes and concerns appear in his work, Dorfman has persistently attempted to provide readers with his own view of the intersections between art and politics, truth and representation, and structures of power and forces of resistance.

An example of this practice can be found in Dorfman's next identity transformation, which was to come after the end of his Chilean exile. In 2005 Dorfman became a U.S. citizen and voted in his first U.S. elections. In a multimedia project for PBS's POV entitled *American ID: Choice*, Dorfman explains his decision to become a U.S. citizen as stemming, to a certain extent, from a desire to highlight how U.S. identity is inherently multilingual and multicultural: "My life's experience has been a succession of geographic, cultural and linguistic border crossings. . . . I took on a multitude of identities, each one of them seemingly obliterating the other, each one a piece of that complex and contradictory modern puzzle we call the american [*sic*] identity" (n.p.). In yet another example of his interest in pushing language to perform critical work, Dorfman uses the lower case for "america," a move that reflects his desire to open up the meaning of American identity while simultaneously reducing its imperial force. Always searching for the other side, the point of tension, the irresolvable dilemma, Dorfman found in his new citizenship an opportunity to destabilize the concept of "America." In keeping with his motto that he is "a liar who always tells the truth," though, these destabilizations are not mere play; they are challenges to accepted ways of thinking. They are challenges to the rigidity of truth regimes and the naïve fluidity of nihilistic skepticism. They are challenges to use art and words and stories and messages to cure the poverty of the imagination.

If it had not been for Susana la Semilla, a cartoon character I invented, I would not have survived the coup.

—ARIEL DORFMAN, *Heading South, Looking North*

6. CREATIVE CRITICISM / CRITICAL CREATIVITY *Media Criticism and Cultural Journalism*

According to Ariel Dorfman, Susana la Semilla (Susana the Seed), a cartoon character he created, saved his life on the day of the coup (*Heading*, 30). At least that is one possible reason he gives for his survival. According to his memoirs, he had a meeting scheduled for ten thirty on September 11, 1973, with Augusto Olivares, the director of National Television, and that appointment kept him from being at the presidential palace, La Moneda, when it was bombed at the start of the coup. At this meeting Dorfman had planned to pitch Susana and her counterpart, Federico el Fertilizante (Fred the Fertilizer), who he hoped would appear in twenty-five one-minute weekly spots. During the infamous truckers' strike that weakened Allende's presidency, Dorfman was asked by Jaime Tohá, the minister of agriculture, to develop an advertising campaign to help convince the Chilean pubic that the strike was anti-patriotic and that it was the truckers who would be responsible for damaging the harvest if the fertilizer rotting in Chilean ports could not be transported in time for planting. Dorfman devised what he describes as an epic saga, a love story:

"I conjured up sexy, luscious, loquacious Susana, Susan the seed, a sort of Chilean version of Chiquita Banana, pining away in the lonely countryside, eager to bear fruit and be a mother. Her aspirations to multiply were, however, being frustrated by the fact that her faraway lover, Federico el Fertilizante, Fred the Fertilizer, is being held captive in a faraway port" (34). The characters were a socialist utopian depiction of the possibilities for growth and rebirth in Chile. They allowed Dorfman to imagine that he could use cartoon characters to conquer fear with love. Through the silly yet tragic tale of their relationship, he hoped to inspire the Chilean public to imagine a collective future.

Susana la Semilla is a significant figure in Dorfman's creative past not only because she ostensibly saved his life, but also because she provides an important clue to understanding Dorfman's relationship to media culture and cultural critique. Since his famous collaboration with Armand Mattelart on *Para leer al Pato Donald* (1971; *How to Read Donald Duck*), Dorfman has been a vociferous critic of media culture.[1] Dorfman's position vis-à-vis media culture, however, is not merely one of negative criticism; it is both critical and constructive. Moreover, he does not divide cultural discourse into neatly discrete categories. While he is well aware of the varied audiences that attend to distinct cultural forms and divide cultural registers according to social circumstances, Dorfman considers art, media culture, and critique as inseparable features of any progressive social project. As explained in my analysis of his aesthetics of hope, Dorfman is influenced by Frankfurt School theories about the hegemony of media culture, but in keeping with the Latin American tradition, he also sees culture as an integral source of resistance and community building. For instance, Dorfman considered media culture projects like that of Susana la Semilla to be an essential feature of revolutionary struggle. While Dorfman considers literature and other forms of "high" art to play a crucial function in the development of critical consciousness, he sees "lower" art forms, such as cartoons, children's stories, and advertisements as performing a major role as well. In this sense his theories about culture more closely resemble certain features of Ernst Bloch's aesthetic theory, elaborated in the three volumes of Bloch's *Principle of Hope*, than those of Adorno. Similarly to Bloch, Dorfman believes in the utopian potential of popularly accessible art forms, like myths, which have the ability to inspire their audience to hope for the future. Contrary to critical trends that view culture as a vehicle for reinforcing capitalist ideology, Bloch suggests that cultural forms are not only conduits for ruling-class ideas, but are also capable of inspiring social reform.

Dorfman's belief that culture plays a fundamental role in shaping identity, quelling dissent, and supporting state power and that it also inspires resistance and revolution is a consequence of his participation in a generation of leftist intellectuals who instigated a radical shift in critical appreciation of the social role of culture. What came to be known as the "cultural turn" represented a new-found interest in culture as a motor for mass consciousness and identity formation that moved beyond anthropology's understanding of culture as customs and bourgeois characterizations of culture as the elite arts of the privileged classes. The cultural turn marked not only a change in the definition of culture, but also a shift in intellectual appreciation of it. The intellectual work of the cultural turn is represented by a number of seminal studies like Walter Benjamin's "The Work of Art in the Age of Mechanical Reproduction" (1935), Adorno and Horkheimer's "The Culture Industry: Enlightenment as Mass Deception" (1944), Roland Barthes's *Mythologies* (1957), Raymond Williams's *Culture and Society* (1958), Marshall McLuhan's *Understanding Media* (1964), and Louis Althusser's "Ideology and Ideological State Apparatuses" (1969). Michael Denning explains that "with the discovery that culture was everywhere, the study and critique of culture became an increasingly central part of political and intellectual life" (2). He identifies fifty New Left intellectuals who played a significant role in shaping the cultural turn, and among them he lists both Dorfman and Mattelart (82). According to Denning, this generation of leftists was influenced by "the crisis of Stalinism, the triumphalism of the American century, and the electrifying new politics of the national liberation movements" (83). In response to the sense that social struggle was resisting the historical trajectory outlined by Karl Marx, the theorists of the cultural turn reversed the marxist hierarchy of economic base over ideological superstructure. No longer considered to be merely a superfluous feature of society, culture was now studied as the key to understanding how structures of power and domination maintained social control.

Many of the ground-breaking observations of this generation have become commonly accepted, but it is worth reviewing their initial innovations. First was the idea that culture mattered and that it played a fundamental role in shaping social relations. Prior to the cultural turn, culture was often perceived as customs and habits (via works such as E. B. Tylor's *Primitive Culture*, 1871) or as artistic interests and ideals (via works such as Matthew Arnold's *Culture and Anarchy*, 1869). Second, attention was drawn to the role of technology, mass media, and mass communication in post–Second World War society. Work by McLuhan, whose famous phrase "the medium is the message" influenced scores of studies on media and communications, called for attention to the new technologies that were rapidly changing the flow of communication.

Analyses of technology, media, and hegemony drew on the work of Antonio Gramsci and Raymond Williams. Third, the cultural turn began a "rethinking of economy and politics in cultural terms" (Denning, 84). Culture came to be known as the means by which states and markets acquired and maintained power. It was perceived as a form of both mass distraction and social control, leading to work by Michel Foucault on culture as surveillance and Guy Debord on culture and spectacle.

In the case of Latin America the cultural turn further signaled a deeper analysis of culture and imperialism via work by scholars such as Roberto Fernández Retamar, Ángel Rama, and Antonio Candido, whose analyses built on an earlier generation of Latin American critics of culture and society that included leftist theorists like José Carlos Mariátegui. This Latin American tradition also dialogued with other postcolonial critics like Frantz Fanon, Aimé Césaire, and C. L. R. James, whose work interrogated the ways that empires depended on establishing ideological structures that privileged imperial cultures over local ones. The Latin American intellectuals of the cultural turn considered the relationship among culture, mass media, and capitalist economics; cultural dependence and imperialism; and liberation and cultural autonomy. Dorfman's critique of media culture and his hopes that organic, politically progressive culture could aid struggles for social emancipation indicate the ways that he worked across many of these central questions.

George Yúdice points out that the two foundational texts of the Latin American cultural turn are Dorfman and Mattelart's *How to Read Donald Duck* and Roberto Fernández Retamar's *Caliban*, both of which appeared in 1971, launching a Latin American critical tradition dedicated to studying the relationship between culture and dependency (*Expediency of Culture*, 86).[2] Despite subsequent revisions to the rigid equation between U.S. media and U.S. imperialism suggested in later work by Dorfman and others, Dorfman and Mattelart's groundbreaking analysis of the ways that Donald Duck comics circulated in Chile influenced a wide range of intellectuals globally and in Latin America.[3] Latin American media analysts who study the connections among culture, identity, and social domination, such as Jesús Martín-Barbero and Carlos Monsiváis, have built on the early work of Mattelart and Dorfman. Analyses by Nestor García Canclini on hybridity and culture; by Beatriz Sarlo on urban spaces, media, and ideology; and by Daniel Mato on culture, power, and intellectual practices represent a new generation of critics engaged in analyzing the links between Latin American identity and media culture. Given that Latin America continues to be heavily dominated by cultural imports from the

United States, such research remains essential to understanding the tensions between local identities and global economic and political flows.

Many of these questions have also been taken up by media scholars working outside of Latin America. Dorfman and Mattelart's work on Donald Duck heralded a wave of research on Walt Disney and other mass cultural forms aimed at children. These studies consider the connections among the Disney Corporation, global economics, children's imaginations, consumer culture, and mass marketing. Works like Henry Giroux's *The Mouse That Roared*; Eric Smoodin's *Disney Discourse*; and Wasko, Phillips, and Meehan's *Dazzled By Disney?* illustrate a wave of research that grew out of Dorfman and Mattelart's revolutionary study of the ideological world of Disney comics and its impact on "third world" identity.

Dorfman stands apart from most of the critics originally associated with the cultural turn and those that have continued in their wake because of his commitment to combining critique with creative work, his persistent faith in the emancipatory possibilities of engaged art, and his relentless efforts to re-define the discursive boundaries that shape social communication. As Dorfman himself has pointed out, one of the defining features of the literary writers of his generation has been their use of the media "as a framework, as a challenge, as a source of inspiration, as a purveyor of characters, as a dilemma" (*Other Septembers*, 171). In order to draw attention to the pivotal role that Dorfman played in the cultural turn, this chapter focuses on his extra-literary work—that is, projects that are not strictly speaking works of literature. It begins by providing an overview of Dorfman's collections of essays, which broadly fall into the categories of media criticism, literary criticism, and cultural journalism. Following is an analysis that outlines the main components of his major works in media theory and reads these in relation to his work creating media culture. (Given that much of this book, especially chapters 2 and 3, has compared Dorfman's literary production to the ideas expressed in his essays of literary criticism, I have not included analysis of those works here.) I then analyze his work with cultural journalism. Few media critics also produce media, and even fewer write novels, plays, poetry, short stories, and literary criticism. In this sense Dorfman's work is quite unusual, and its interdisciplinary range has challenged scholarly consideration of the full range of his work.

One challenge relates to understanding the relationship between Dorfman's critical and creative work. Dorfman's dual dialectical intentions—to at one and the same time criticize the alienating effects of media culture while also creating viable cultural alternatives—are at the core of his aesthetic project. A second challenge is that Dorfman works across a broad range of cultural registers from "high" to "low" art forms. So not only does he produce criticism and creative works, but he also engages in these activities via a vast array of cultural forms from children's stories to novels, from comic books to film. By way of an illustration of these challenges, it is useful to remember that Dorfman's two most influential works to date are *How to Read Donald Duck* and *Death and the Maiden*. At first glance it may seem difficult to reconcile that these two texts originate from the work of the same person since they appear to have little in common. What links a critical assessment of the cultural imperialism of Disney comics and a play about the trauma of recovering from dictatorship? The key connection, I argue, is Dorfman's aesthetic project, which links critical art and artistic criticism.

For the most part studies of Dorfman ignore or gloss his essays and focus solely on his literature.[4] Studies that do engage with his essays tend to ignore his other work in media and film, often overlooking his journalism as well. I briefly examine the other types of extra-literary cultural production in which Dorfman has engaged, such as work with fine arts, photography, and music, in order to illustrate the range of his cultural production and the ways that this assortment of activities relates to his overall aesthetic project. Because Dorfman tests the boundaries of cultural forms, mixing journalism with memoir or cultural criticism with storytelling, it is particularly difficult to place generic designations on his works. Consequently, on the one hand, I will argue that all of these projects form part of an integrated aesthetic vision; on the other hand, in the interest of clarity, this chapter will perpetuate some of the divisions that Dorfman himself has tried to dismantle. Accordingly, this chapter will trace two broad trends in Dorfman's work—his media criticism and cultural journalism—and show how each of these indicates his interest in creative critique and critical creativity. Certainly Dorfman is not the first writer to work across these discursive forms. These projects are noteworthy in Dorfman's oeuvre because of the way that he links the critical, analytic, and objective with the creative, imaginative, and personal. In this way Dorfman troubles the binaries between theory and practice, artist and critic, and observer and participant.

To date, Dorfman has published sixteen books of "nonfiction," thirteen of which can be divided roughly according to the three trends of media criticism, literary criticism, and cultural journalism and three of which are more overtly hybrid texts that aggressively combine these critical modes. The following schema indicates the books that fall into the three main categories.

Media Criticism

1. *Para leer al Pato Donald* (co-authored with Armand Mattelart; 1971; *How to Read Donald Duck*). Contains six chapters analyzing Disney comics created for a Chilean audience. The English edition also includes a prologue by the authors and a bibliography.
2. *Superman y sus amigos del alma* (co-authored with Manuel Jofré; 1974; Superman and His Bosom Buddies). Prologue and part one by Dorfman; the latter analyzes the Lone Ranger.
3. *Culture as Democratic Resistance in Chile Today* (1977). Includes an analysis of the potential of cultural resistance.
4. *Reader's nuestros que estás en la tierra: Ensayos sobre el imperialismo cultural* (1980; Our Reader's Digest Who Art on Earth: Essays on Cultural Imperialism). Includes essays on *Reader's Digest*, children's literature, the Lone Ranger, and comic books during the Allende presidency.
5. *The Empire's Old Clothes: What the Lone Ranger, Babar, and Other Innocent Heroes Do to Our Minds* (1983). Contains essays on Babar, Donald Duck, the Lone Ranger, *Reader's Digest*, and pop culture during the Allende presidency.
6. *Patos, elefantes y héroes: La infancia como subdesarrollo* (1985; Ducks, Elephants, and Heroes: Infancy as Underdevelopment). Spanish version of *The Empire's Old Clothes*, absent the chapter titled "The Innocents March into History . . . and Overthrow a Government."[5]

Literary Criticism

1. *El absurdo entre cuatro paredes: El teatro de Harold Pinter* (1968; The Absurd within Four Walls: The Theater of Harold Pinter). A study of the work of Harold Pinter.
2. *Imaginación y violencia en América* (1970; Imagination and Violence in America). Contains seven essays on Latin American literature, with analysis of works by Borges, Asturias, Carpentier, García Márquez, Juan Rulfo, José María Arguedas, and Mario Vargas Llosa.
3. *Hacia la liberación del lector latinoamericano* (1984; Toward the Liberation of the Latin American Reader). Contains five essays on Latin American literature (on Carpentier, Skármeta, Neruda, and Cardenal), one of which (on Pablo Neruda) previously appeared in *La última aventura del Llanero Solitario*.
4. *Some Write to the Future: Essays on Contemporary Latin American Fiction* (1991; trans. George Shivers). Contains seven essays, including two

from *Imaginación y violencia en América* (on Borges and Asturias) and two from *Hacia la liberación del lector latinoamericano* (on Carpentier and Arguedas).

Cultural Journalism

1. *Los sueños nucleares de Reagan* (1986; Reagan's Nuclear Dreams). Includes articles published previously in the Mexican periodical *Proceso*. Many were published in other magazines and newspapers as well. Some texts appeared previously in *De elefantes, literatura y miedo* and *Sin ir más lejos*, which are described below.

2. *Exorcising Terror: The Incredible Unending Trial of Augusto Pinochet* (2002). An account of the Pinochet trial that combines historical events, testimonials, and Dorfman's personal memories of Pinochet.[6]

3. *Other Septembers, Many Americas: Selected Provocations, 1980–2004* (2004). Contains an introduction and forty-two short works. Many of the pieces were previously published in periodicals.

In addition to testing the boundaries of scholarly research by working across fields, Dorfman in many of these books includes reprints and translations. In some cases the essays are rewritten, in others not. In each edition Dorfman selected the texts according to the context of publication, which explains why certain texts repeat and why certain ones are rewritten.[7] Moreover, a number of Dorfman's books of essays, while favoring one of these three critical trends, break with the genre. For example, *La última aventura del Llanero Solitario* contains ten essays, nine of which are dedicated to media criticism. The last essay in the volume, though, is a reprint of his analysis of Neruda's *Canto General*. For another example, *Other Septembers, Many Americas* consists of poems alongside cultural journalism. One of the most moving examples of Dorfman's efforts to push on the boundaries of textual discourse, *Exorcising Terror* (which will be analyzed in more detail below), combines the reporting of historical events with personal testimony.

In addition to the thirteen books that can be categorized as media criticism, literary criticism, or cultural journalism, Dorfman has published three volumes that more openly combine these discursive forms. The first, *Ensayos quemados en Chile: Inocencia y neocolonialismo* (1974; Essays Burned in Chile: Innocence and Neocolonialism), combines all three forms and presents a number of the texts Dorfman was unable to publish because of Pinochet's coup. It includes prefaces to books by Fidel Castro and Ernesto Cardenal that were to be released by Quimantú, as well as an essay on mass media and education that was to be published in the Chilean *Revista de Educación*. In addition to texts that were destroyed by the junta, Dorfman includes some that had already been censored. These consist of cultural journalism for newspapers and journals such as *Chile Hoy, Cuadernos de la Realidad Nacional, La Quinta Rueda, De Frente,* and *Más Fuerte.* He then adds two texts on Chilean literature that were written before Allende's election. By uniting a range of essays in this volume, he attempts to counteract the propaganda, censorship, and cultural hegemony of the Pinochet regime.

The second hybrid volume, *De elefantes, literatura y miedo: ensayos sobre la comunicación americana* (1986; Of Elephants, Literature, and Fear: Essays on American Communication), includes an introduction and eleven essays, and these are separated into literary essays, essays on communication, and cultural journalism. This volume is one of the few in which Dorfman makes a point of dividing his work across the three critical tendencies. The third hybrid volume is *Sin ir más lejos: Ensayos y crónicas irreverentes* (1986; Without Going Farther: Essays and Irreverent Chronicles), with a prologue and twelve previously published essays that represent all three discursive modes with no generic division. This volume was written as Dorfman was finally regaining access to a reading public in Chile after years of exile.

Given the vast body of nonfiction work published by Dorfman, the following analysis of his media criticism and cultural journalism highlights only the most salient examples in an effort to show how these projects illustrate Dorfman's aesthetics of hope. Each section also reads these works of nonfiction in conjunction with cultural projects that demonstrate Dorfman's commitment to combining criticism with creativity both within texts and across them.

MEDIA CRITICISM

Most of the main aspects of Dorfman's media criticism can be found in *How to Read Donald Duck* and *The Empire's Old Clothes.* In both of these texts Dorfman emphasizes the ideological role of mass-produced culture in influencing social consciousness. The first text dismantles the seemingly innocuous characters of Donald Duck and his pals and demonstrates how they serve to colonize Latin America through a repeated litany of tales favoring capitalism, U.S. imperialism, and the infantilization of the reader. One of the strengths of the text is a critical analysis of the world in which Disney characters live. Formulaic in their ethics, Disney characters are always able to resolve their problems in simplistic ways. Dorfman and Mattelart critique not only this facile view of the world, but also the role that the third world and the working classes play in Disney comics.

Dorfman and Mattelart's text carried the subtitle "A Manual of Decolonization," and its mission was to "raise consciousness." By analyzing the internal ethical logic of Disney, the writers hoped to unmask its false innocence and provoke its readers—both young and old—to reject Disney's ideology. Like the exiled Frankfurt School writers, who were responding to a moment of historical crisis, Dorfman and Mattelart created their critique of Disney as Chilean society was undergoing rapid and intense change. And they brought to their analysis their insider/outsider status: neither one of them had been born in Chile, but both of them were committed to the success of Allende's government.[8] They explain in the preface to the English edition that after the Chilean government nationalized the copper industry, the United States imposed an "invisible blockade" and an embargo against Chilean copper was organized—moves that devastated the Chilean economy. However, two products were not a part of the blockade: military support and media culture. John Berger notes that in Chile before the coup, "Disney comics claimed a million readers a week," an astonishing number given that the Chilean population at the time was 10 million (478). Writing from exile after the coup, Dorfman and Mattelart explain: "In the words of General Pinochet, the point was to 'conquer the minds,' while in the words of Donald Duck . . . the point was to 'restore the king'" (9). According to Dorfman and Mattelart, imperialism, military intervention, and hierarchical social structures depend on media culture to create the ideological support systems they require.

The comics of Disney are particularly insidious because they masquerade as pure innocence and fun. Dorfman and Mattelart set out to unpack the supposed innocence and fun of these comics in order to reveal the ways that they supported capitalism and imperialism. First of all, they asked, why are there no parents in Disney comics, only uncles and cousins? Disney's destruction of the family denies the potential dialectic between father and son, mother and daughter. Because children never grow up to be parents, social authority is endless and unchallenged. The lack of parents and any hint of sexual reproduction relates to the lack of material production. In the land of Disney the only work is in the service sector. There is no labor, and those with money simply find pots of "loot." The only exchange of commodities is between ignorant "savages" and crafty imperialists. For instance, when Donald and his cousins travel to other lands, like "Inca-Blinca" or "Aztecland," they easily dupe the locals into trading their precious resources for items of no value. The reason why certain nations are wealthy and others are poor is due to the barbaric ignorance of those who live in places like "Unsteadystan." The last major insight Dorfman and Mattelart have into Donald's world is that there is no pleasure. There is no labor and no leisure. Instead Donald is constantly bored and wishing he were off having an adventure. Those adventures invariably include having fun while deceiving someone else. By describing Donald's antics as innocent fun, Disney manages to gloss the real conflicts behind social struggle. The power of Dorfman and Mattelart's analysis is that once revealed, it is blatantly obvious.

It is not an exaggeration to say that this text has been one of the most influential works of cultural criticism both in Latin America and abroad. It has appeared in thirty-nine Spanish-language editions via the Mexican publishing house Siglo XXI since its release, and it has been translated into English, French, German, Portuguese, Dutch, Italian, Greek, Turkish, Swedish, Finnish, Danish, Japanese, and Korean. It was burned in Chile in 1973 and blocked from circulation in the United States in 1975.[9] As explained above, *How to Read Donald Duck* remains one of the essential classics of the cultural turn, and it continues to influence research on culture and social relations. Even though the text inspired many later works, few scholars have been able to replicate its style and methods. Drawing on the combined strengths of Mattelart's background in social sciences and communication studies and Dorfman's skills as a scholar of literature and creative writer, the text's methods include detailed close reading, analysis of empirical data, and leftist cultural critique. The work stands as one of the few examples of the cultural turn to combine historical, theoretical, and political analysis with detailed empirical data. It also serves as an example of the early interdisciplinary efforts of cultural studies, which were dedicated to breaking down the barriers between the social sciences and the humanities.

A further important innovation is the text's style. It is highlighted in the first paragraph, when the authors claim that their mission is not only to strip naked an icon of childhood innocence but also to disrupt the cold, solemn tone of intellectual writing: "El tipo de lenguaje que aquí se utiliza intenta quebrar la falsa solemnidad con que la ciencia por lo general se encierra su propio quehacer" (9); ("The kind of language we use here is intended to break with the false solemnity that generally cloaks scientific investigation"; 25). The authors criticize intellectual writing that shrouds itself in jargon and inaccessibility while attempting to analyze society, thereby replicating social divisions and hierarchies that distance leftist academic works from the people they hope to influence. They suggest that such writing betrays the goals of revolutionary critique: "Este miedo a la locura de las palabras, al futuro como imaginación, al contacto permanente con el lector, este temor a hacer el ridículo y perder su 'prestigio' al aparecer desnudo frente a su particular reducto público, traduce su aversión a la vida y, en definitiva, a la realidad total. El científico quiere estudiar la lluvia y sale con un paraguas" (9); ("This fear of breaking the confines of language, of the future as a conscious force of the imagination, of a close and lasting contact with the reader, this dread of appearing insignificant and naked before one's limited public, betrays an aversion for life and for reality as a whole. We do not want to be like the scientist who takes his umbrella with him to go study the rain"; 25). The playfulness of these lines combined with the text's accessible and clear language is one of its significant achievements. The style is fun, irreverent, witty, and concise. The authors refuse to mimic the dry, distant, abstruse language of academic discourse. Written when Dorfman was not yet thirty years of age, the text displays youthful exuberance and a sense of play that continues to be characteristic of much of Dorfman's work.[10]

Years later Dorfman recast his thoughts from *How to Read Donald Duck* in *The Empire's Old Clothes*. This work includes criticism of the characters of Babar and the Lone Ranger and analyzes the ways that the overly reductive resolutions to conflict offered by these cultural products serve to reinforce capitalist ideology.[11] Dorfman's work in this text also indicates how the experience of exile from Chile affected his understanding of media culture. In the prologue to the text he explains that he observed how Chile had been used by imperialist culture as a test case to experiment economically and culturally (10). He also differentiates his work in *The Empire's Old Clothes* from *Donald Duck* by articulating a broader audience for his critique; history has taught him that successful political activism requires that one's message go beyond the sphere of the already convinced (11). The text also reveals the influence of both Brecht and Althusser on Dorfman's cultural criticism: he argues that the recipient should be actively involved in the production of meaning, and he analyzes ways that the cultural content of most mass media is aimed at fortifying the strength and ideological hold of the social system. An elaboration of these thoughts can be found in the chapter "The Infantilization of the Adult Reader." Analyzing *Reader's Digest*, Dorfman details the ideological world fostered by such "light" reading: "Whatever is faraway and famous is reduced incessantly to its most comprehensible, immediate, not to say vulgar, form. . . . Whatever the reader might not be able to handle is never presented" (144–45). The consequences of creating a reading public that has no skills in critical thinking are that the public loses its ability to interpret other forms of information received via the media. In an interview from 1991 Dorfman explains that media culture closes the universe and presents a distorted image of the world, one that keeps the reader in the position of naïve and pre-critical child (Incledon, 100).

The transition from Dorfman's critique of Disney comics to his analysis of media culture in *The Empire's Old Clothes* also reflects a historical shift in the cultural turn. Denning notes that after 1968 the left critique of culture consisted mainly of "denunciations of the dominant culture, as ideological state apparatus, cultural imperialism, consciousness industry, or society of the spectacle" alongside "theorizations of cultural revolution" (8). Dorfman and Mattelart's work is a key example of post-1968 cultural critique. By the time of *The Empire's Old Clothes*, though, the cultural turn was entering a new phase, which developed in response to the repressive backlash against 1960s and '70s revolutionary politics. This new phase "gave way to reflections on the failures of popular nationalisms and the contradictions of popular cultures" (Denning, 8). Denning notes the increased interest in Gramsci in this phase, which resulted in new approaches to cultural studies, such as that found in postcolonial theory and subaltern studies. Following the work of subaltern studies in South Asia, Latin Americanists like John Beverley applied subaltern studies theory to Latin America in conjunction with postmodern/postcolonial critiques of master narratives and of the privileging of literature over oral traditions (especially the testimonial). Indicative of this turn is Beverley's highly influential work *Against Literature*, which expressed profound skepticism toward all forms of literature and turned to the testimonial as a more politically powerful form of writing. Beverley explains that "there is always a danger that even the most iconoclastic or 'progressive' literature is simply forging the new forms of hegemony" (xiv). As a professor at Duke University and a colleague of scholars like Fredric Jameson, Stanley Fish, Barbara Hernstein Smith, and Alberto Moreiras, Dorfman was well aware of the theories that often underpinned this new wave of research. He, however, would never be thoroughly convinced of the theoretical moves of the Latin American subaltern studies group, nor would he succumb to the extreme skepticism that characterized much critical theory in the United States in the 1980s and '90s. While his position called for "permanent criticism and revision" and while he recognized that once in exile and after the violent crush of many of the revolutionary movements of the '60s and '70s it was no longer possible to feel that he had all of the answers, he was reluctant to relegate literature to the realm of social oppression (*Empire's Old Clothes*, 11).

Beyond attempting to reach a broader audience and in addition to stressing questions over answers, *The Empire's Old Clothes* signals a change in Dorfman's theories about culture and society that indicates both his affinity for and his departure from a number of the postmodern theories circulating at the time. From this moment forward Dorfman comes to perceive that social relations refuse manicheistic categories of good and evil. He begins to emphasize, instead, the degree to which all members of all social sectors are capable of violence, betrayal, and evil. He explains in the preface to *The Empire's Old Clothes*: "I have also been discovering and exploring, through my poetry and fiction, that jungle which each of us can become. These violent undergrowths of imaginary characters are successful because in our own provinces and sewers, they match and accompany deep-seated tendencies and fears" (12). The conclusion echoes this point: "The enemy is inside, and we find it hard to distinguish him from our innermost thoughts and nurturings" (207). This observation signals the end for him of romantic, nostalgic notions about masses versus elites, victims versus oppressors. It no longer makes sense to divide the world into "good guys and bad guys," which further means that there are no "good texts" versus "bad texts." After exile, after the postmodern turn, Dorfman comes to consider that more attention needs to be paid to human shortcomings and failures of the imagination. If, as Foucault claimed, power flows in all directions in micro and macro degrees, then it no longer makes sense to pit an evil power elite against the good oppressed masses. Furthermore, the idea that certain cultural forms oppress and others liberate places too much stress on the cultural product and misses the necessary interaction between cultural form and audience.

This move away from such value claims implies that the stories of Superman or the Lone Ranger or Donald Duck cannot be the sole sources of blame for social tendencies to stereotype, to envy, and to dominate, even though they play an important role in cultivating these tendencies and in reinforcing social inequities. So, in contrast to postmodern critics who turned to testimonials or other popular cultural forms as antidotes to the failures of the revolutionary movements of the '60s and '70s, Dorfman followed a different track that refused to place the power in the cultural product but instead moved toward the study of representation, discourse, and cultural dialogue. This meant that Dorfman, along with other postmodern theorists who emphasized the need to problematize representation, increasingly stressed that progressive cultural forms could not be understood in the abstract but acquired meaning only when studied in concrete, material cases. Certain cultural forms that engage in complex aesthetics and require the active participation of the audience hold promise and hope, but these potentialities depend entirely on the interaction among culture, audience, and specific context.

One of the best signs of this transition in Dorfman's cultural theory is in *The Empire's Old Clothes* and appears in most of his nonfiction works after exile. Like the stylistic innovations of *Donald Duck*, *The Empire's Old Clothes* reveals an important poetics that integrally links Dorfman's theory to his style. Perhaps as a consequence of Dorfman's belief that his life was spared during the coup so that he could be its storyteller or perhaps as a sign of Dorfman's postmodern transitions, his nonfiction work after exile always incorporates multiple voices. Dorfman includes in these works the testimonials, anecdotes, phrases, and memories of others, which he places in dialogue with himself. At times these voices serve to illustrate his position, and at others they speak in opposition. They serve as interruptions of Dorfman's voice, and they connect his theories to the world outside the text. For instance, *The Empire's Old Clothes* begins by recounting Dorfman's experiences with a Chilean "slum dweller" who chastised him for his critique of mass-media culture because he was stealing her dreams, only to later thank him, after Allende's election, because now she didn't read that trash; now she was "dreaming reality" (5). But this is not the end of her story. In fact Dorfman does not know what happened to her after the coup. He asks his readers to remember her courage and, most of all, to remember that unlike the characters in the comics who die on one page and appear alive on the next, the violence she was sure to have suffered is no laughing matter. Of course, idealistic as it may be, this practice runs the same risks as that of testimonial because even though Dorfman is opening the text to other voices, ultimately he is the "compiler" of the text, and eventually it is his voice that is most dominant. Ultimately the reader must decide whether this practice unravels the hegemony of the critical voice or simply rearranges it. It is perhaps worth emphasizing, though, that Dorfman's style lays this practice bare, facilitating the critical engagement of the reader and encouraging, through its own self-reflexivity, questioning of the ideas put forth.

This interest in returning theory to practical contexts is a central feature of Dorfman's personal take on the postmodern turn. Another important element is his persistent commitment to using theory to support vision and imagination. His utopian vision changes after exile and becomes more nuanced to reflect his sense that drawing value-laden boundaries on cultures and social sectors is impossible. Nevertheless, while the postmodern turn has often been associated with skepticism, nihilism, and negative, deconstructive critique, Dorfman remains committed to using theory at the service of imagining a better world and struggling for social change. These goals, which are fundamental to his aesthetics of hope, explain his interest in children's culture and link his version of postmodern cultural theory to scholars like Henry Giroux, who argue that social change depends on creating an environment that enables children to become active and engaged in their world. Consequently, Dorfman's version of postmodernism associates his theories with those of other critics of the cultural turn, like Giroux, Ira Shor, and Paulo Freire, who have insisted that any serious commitment to understanding the relationship between culture and society necessarily has to be concerned with childhood and the cultural world of children. Giroux's theories resonate especially with Dorfman's: both authors stress the need to rescue hope from political cynicism, and they both consider utopia to be an essential feature of social engagement. Their visions of utopia, though, are grounded in practical realities and are dependent on breaking down the division between the individual and the community. Giroux writes in *Public Spaces, Private Lives* that "Utopian thinking matters, but not as a version of privatized hope or as a hope without realism" (120).[12]

Like Giroux, Shor, and Freire, Dorfman wrote early in his career about education and social change. While less work was expressly dedicated to the role of pedagogy for social change after his exile, Dorfman's interest in children's culture has remained constant throughout his career. From his work with Quimantú during the Allende years to his analysis of children's culture in *Donald Duck* and *The Empire's Old Clothes* a further feature of Dorfman's project has been to balance critique with creativity and to draw links between cultural projects that encourage children to develop their curiosity and playful spirit and ones that encourage adults to act like children—that is, to ask questions, take risks, and resist ideological assumptions. Dorfman differentiates media that infantilize adults (like *Reader's Digest*) and consequently stifle critical thinking from culture that encourages a childlike, curious engagement with the world.

One key example of this interest is Dorfman's children's book *La rebelión de los conejos mágicos* (*The Rebellion of the Magical Rabbits*). The story centers on a pack of wolves that takes over a community and prohibits the mention of rabbits. Will the rabbits disappear forever, or will they find a way to overthrow the wolves? Told with the express intention of imagining a world where the solidarity and questioning of children function as a positive metaphor for the ties between society and state, the story refuses to patronize its young readers. The rebellious rabbits, aided by an inquisitive girl, return despite the fact that the adults have simply resigned themselves to the wolves' rule. Dorfman wants to remind his readers—both young and old—that children's capacity to insistently ask questions makes them in many ways superior to adults. In the afterword to a reprinted edition of the book, Dorfman explains that "su falta de miedo para hacer preguntas que nosotros nos hemos cansado de hacer es esencial" (66); (their lack of fear at asking questions that we no longer have the energy for is essential). Similar to the book series written by Toni Morrison with her son that rewrites Aesop's fables, Dorfman's book takes on traditional tropes of children's stories and reverses the moral. In Dorfman's world the child who asks questions and disagrees with a parent makes the world a better place.

Rebellious children populate the realm of Dorfman's adult literature as well—for instance, those that lead the fetal rebellions of *Manuel Sendero*. In addition, children appear caught between their innocence and fear in stories like "A la escondida" ("My House Is on Fire"). These creative efforts to represent the hopeful potential of children and the challenges they face have been accompanied throughout Dorfman's career by efforts to create alternative forms of media that could appeal to children and adults and that most of all could be creative examples of his critical theories. In addition to Susana la Semilla, Dorfman worked on a number of creative projects during the Allende years that were meant to provide ideological support for his presidency. An important element of these efforts was his work with Quimantú, which, as noted, released inexpensive books in an effort to make literary and critical texts available to a wide Chilean readership.

As a further sign of his commitment to bridging theory and practice, Dorfman has worked extensively with visual media and film.[13] He has tried to use film as a form of cultural activism and a way to translate his writing into the visual. He has worked on scripts for three films that are versions of written texts: *Death and the Maiden*, *Dead Line* (based on the poetry of *Last Waltz in Santiago*), and *My House Is on Fire* (based on the short story of the same title). In 2005 he collaborated with his son Rodrigo, Patrick Adams, and Luis Navarro on a multimedia documentary, *In the Footsteps of September 11, 1973*. Part biography, part historical documentary, and part critique of contemporary events in Chile and abroad, it traces his steps on the day of the coup. Dorfman's work in creative arts extends to music, the fine arts, and photography. His poetry served, for instance, as the basis for James Macmillan's opera *Cantos sagrados*. He has collaborated with Eric Woolfson (creator of and writer for the Alan Parsons Project) on a musical, *Dancing with Shadows*, which is inspired by the Korean play *Forest Fire*, by Bum Suk Cha. He is also involved in a project to turn *Death and the Maiden* into an opera. In addition to musical projects, Dorfman has written accompanying texts for art shows and books of photography. Shortly after the Chilean plebiscite he lent his words to the photography of Susan Meisalas and others in the volume *Chile from Within*, where he expressed his solidarity with the "photographers who were not willing to let the image of hope and horror disappear" ("Memories of Hope," 121). In 1999 Peter Griffin, an artist who specializes in paintings that interrogate the human condition, collaborated with Dorfman on the exhibition *Identities*. In 2002 Dorfman was guest curator for a show at the Duke University Museum of Art that featured the work of Spanish-born Pedro Sanchez, who now resides in Chile. In the text that accompanied the show, Dorfman writes about his own interest in painting and recounts his early attraction and repulsion to the art of Goya, an affinity that he shares with Pedro Sanchez, whose art has been influenced by the Spanish master. Dorfman explains that Sanchez's art takes up some of the aesthetic visions of madness and monstrosity that occupied Goya but places those in a contemporary context ("Conjuros," 16). In the painting entitled *Tientos y diferencias* (Themes and Variations), Dorfman is drawn to the visual power of Sanchez's art, his stunning colors, and his use of light and shadows. Most important, Dorfman draws attention to the way that Sanchez's art displaces Goya's symbols of madness with those of modernity in order to comment on "globalization and the role of mass media" (16). As a sign of Dorfman's continued concern for the alienating effects of media culture, he is particularly interested in Sanchez's depiction of the devil as a television screen, where the "cold cathode rays of technology . . . create monsters" (16).

In addition to these efforts to merge his work with that of visual artists, Dorfman has placed significant energy into producing visual culture. He has made a number of films and has a number of film projects in progress. An interesting example of this commitment is a television ad on which he collaborated with his son Rodrigo. One day while out walking with Rodrigo during the campaign for the 2004 U.S. presidential election, he had an idea for an ad that would "reveal Bush's rhetoric, cowardice and hypocrisy."[14] Rodrigo later developed the idea and submitted it to MoveOn.org's "Bush in 30 Seconds" contest. The ad was entitled "Funerals for Us, Fundraisers for Him."[15] It begins with a black screen that reads, "Do you know how many military funerals George W. Bush has attended since the start of the Iraq War?" The answer is none. It then asks how many fund-raisers he has attended. The answer: forty-three. It is clear, we are told, that Bush cares more about the "soldiers of fortune" than about the "soldiers of freedom." Thirty-one years after Dorfman's work with Susana la Semilla, he was still looking for ways to use media culture to encourage critical reflection and public engagement.

CULTURAL JOURNALISM

Early in Dorfman's career he joined the long line of writers who had turned to journalism and periodical writing in order to earn a living while working on their own creative projects. From 1965 to 1967, for instance, Dorfman frequently wrote for the Chilean weekly news magazine *Ercilla*, covering stories on literature that ranged from the Beats to Chinese poetry, and the money earned was a welcome supplement to his meager pay from the university.[16] Once in exile, Dorfman followed in the footsteps of a number of Latin American exiles, like José Martí from the late nineteenth century and the boom writers Alejo Carpentier and Gabriel García Márquez, who used periodical writing to communicate their views to a public sphere that did not always include readers from their own nations. Studies by Julio Ramos and Aníbal González Pérez have considered the extent to which literature and journalism in Latin America have overlapped and influenced one another. In *Divergent Modernities* Ramos focuses on the Buenos Aires periodical *La Nación* in order to trace how Martí and Rubén Darío used their writing to develop a new literary form: the modernist chronicle. González Pérez's *Journalism and the Development of the Spanish-American Narrative* argues that journalism has been intimately tied to Latin American literature since the nineteenth century, and he traces the historical trajectory of these two discursive forms.

The following analysis of Dorfman's cultural journalism builds on the scholarly insights of those two studies. Ramos claims that Martí pushed on the boundaries of periodical writing and used it for formal and literary experimentation (103); in similar fashion Dorfman's cultural journalism is directly tied to his overall aesthetic project. Dorfman's efforts to blend testimonial with objective reporting and imaginative prose with stark observations speak to his commitment to use journalism as a critical mode that reinforces his vision for the social role of literature, where hopeful imagination and an aggressive pursuit of the truth productively complement one another. Furthermore, Dorfman's journalism during exile corresponds to González Pérez's observations that beginning with the boom writers, there was an increased interest on the part of narrative writers to use journalistic modes in their prose to explore an "ethics of writing" (120). While Dorfman does not incorporate such modes to the degree that Elena Poniatowska does, his fiction certainly investigates the role that literature plays in documenting historical events and archiving historical memory. More important, in the tradition of Martí, Dorfman's journalistic writing forcefully brings the metaphorical and passionate language of literature to journalism. In this sense, his "ethics of writing" is dedicated to recognizing that cold, sterile, "objective" words cannot capture the realities they pretend to transmit.

In addition to the ways that Dorfman's work relates to these traditions, his periodical writing includes two further features that are central to an appreciation of his cultural journalism. First is the fact that he writes in both English and Spanish, informing English readers about Latin America and Spanish readers about the United States. In the preface to *Other Septembers, Many Americas* he explains: "I could speak to the United States where I lived with the voice of a Latin American and to the Latin America that I inhabited only in my mind from the remoteness of living in North America" (xiv). To a certain extent, his double journalistic realms counter the divide noticed by Kirsten Silva Gruesz in *Ambassadors of Culture*, which documents the competing discourses that vied to narrate the nation in the nineteenth-century U.S. southwest. The second distinct feature of Dorfman's cultural journalism is its correlation to his media criticism. From his first works in exile to today Dorfman has written meta-critical pieces of journalism that draw attention to the fragile process of reporting news in a world that is always hostile to truths that threaten the status quo. He wonders how journalists can fight their own forms of self-censorship, which keep them from reporting because they worry that a piece might affect their next promotion or might cause even worse damage to their lives. Correspondingly, Dorfman raises questions about what happens when the public has lost interest in the news because it has come to represent nothing more than propaganda, entertainment, and manipulation.

As mentioned, Dorfman's early recourse to periodical writing follows a fairly typical path common to countless other writers. From his days in Chile to his writing in magazines like the Chilean *Hoy* while in exile, Dorfman often used cultural journalism to earn money and to work on forms of writing and themes of interest to his literature. Early pieces of cultural journalism in exile, however—such as his 1979 piece on *The Diary of Anne Frank* for *Hoy* and his 1982 article "Snow" for the *New York Times*—signaled that Dorfman had already begun to recognize that he could employ this powerful mode of communication to comment on issues of direct concern to him after the coup. Nevertheless, it would be the 1983 *New York Times* article "An Exile Finds Chile 'Struck by a Plague'" (which Dorfman dictated into the phone while visiting Chile) that would forever mark his cultural journalism as a distinct form of social intervention. Returning to Chile after ten years of exile, Dorfman boldly described what he observed, what had changed, and what had remained the same. There are the same birds, the food tastes the same, and life continues. But much has changed: "It is as if Chile had been struck by a plague. I am scandalized by the physical ruin of my country. The economic crisis, the worst in our history, touches everybody" (23). Such a claim was extraordinarily risky for Dorfman to make since the article would appear while he still was in Chile. From that moment forward Dorfman became highly visible as the voice that described Chile under Pinochet to the world at large. His journalism would also be marked by his willingness to take risks—in terms of both speaking the truth when it was unwelcome and taking stylistic risks that refused to relegate journalism to the realm of cold, objective, lifeless words.

Dorfman's need to characterize journalism as a form of communication that simultaneously reflects the state of the world and moves readers to imagine their role in shaping the future is visible in the 1983 *New York Times* article. After detailing the economic devastations caused by the Pinochet regime—devastations that surpass the typical class divide that has historically haunted Latin America—Dorfman ends his piece with a tone of hope and a rally to revolution. Calling attention to the fact that stories like the one he is writing cannot circulate in Chile, Dorfman begins his last paragraph by emphasizing an optimistic future: "And yet, in this land without a free press, this land where hundreds of thousands have been jailed and humiliated, where exile and violence and lying have become as natural as breathing air, the predominant mood is not despair" (23). Dorfman's use of the word "land" rather than "nation" or "country" to refer to Chile is indicative of his mixing of the literary with the journalistic. His last lines join an increasingly literary poetics with the subversive observation that the Chilean people are seeking ways to overthrow Pinochet: "People are no longer afraid. At night, they bang pots and pans to protest as if they were in front of the walls of Jericho, and in the daytime they march and congregate and openly discuss ways of ridding themselves of the tyrant" (23). Using the symbolism of Jericho, Dorfman describes the Chilean resistance to Pinochet in epic terms. These lines indicate the extent to which he used the piece to push on the traditional limits of journalism. Even though the article appeared in the editorial opinions section of the newspaper—an area that typically allows for more stylistic flexibility—Dorfman's style was an unusual combination of literary imagination and journalistic fact.

Dorfman described the process of writing this story in a piece entitled "Fear and the Word," which was written for a special issue of *Autodafe* that explored threats to creative expression after the terrorist attacks on the United States on September 11, 2001. Dorfman's essay provides background to the 1983 article and permits a glimpse into the fear that overwhelmed him when he decided to risk telling the story of how he saw Chile and how he hoped it would be. He explains that he carefully chose his words as a form of naked condemnation: "My words were harsh, blunt, calling things by their names, lamenting the blood and the pain and accusing the military of murder. This was the way I had written, outside Chile, for the last 10 years—it was, after all, to be free in expressing myself with unequivocal clarity that I had left my country. I told myself that now, when the dictator had allowed me to rejoin my homeland, I should not let any changes creep into my style or my vocabulary. I had to prove, more to myself than to others, that I could not be silenced" (219).

Dorfman explains that as he dictated the words of the article, he caught a glimpse of his son Rodrigo, who stared at him with a mix of admiration and alarm. It was then that the fear began. Waving his hand at Rodrigo in a gesture of calm that belied the pounding heart in his chest, Dorfman suddenly became acutely aware of how daring this act was. And then the voice from New York asked him to repeat the story because something had gone wrong with the recording. This time as he reread the words that had been hastily scribbled early that morning, Dorfman began to sweat and tremble: "I felt somehow naked, exposed—as if this sudden experience of fear had really returned me home, as if I could now really connect like lightning with what so many Chileans had been living, day in and day out, during my 10-year absence. . . . It was, in a way, a true homecoming for me, a way of understanding how repression can shape the shadow of our every word—a lesson in fear and what it does to us" (221).

What Dorfman appreciated in that moment was the ubiquitous combination of fear and political writing. The degree of fear varies according to context. One might be afraid of losing a promotion or a job or one's life. Instead of using the story of this moment in his life to contrast a free press with the challenges of presenting alternative views during dictatorships, Dorfman describes his experience as indicative of all journalism, and he urges his readers to ask questions about their own guilty avoidance of fear: "How many journalists in what we call the free world write everything they want to, speak the same words in public as they mutter to themselves softly in their own minds? How many bite their tongues, accommodate their views to those with more power? How many buck the trend toward infotainment, dare to disturb and transgress?" (224). In connecting the invisible censorship of media that are dominated by commercial interests to that of the plight of journalists living under dictatorship, Dorfman emphasizes the "ethics of writing" that is at the heart of his journalism.

In 1985 Dorfman wrote another key editorial for the *New York Times*, "A Rural Chilean Legend Come True," which displays many of the themes most noteworthy of his journalism. This article described the brutal crackdown of the Pinochet regime that followed the brief hopeful moments that Dorfman witnessed in 1983. He begins by describing the Chilean legend of the Imbunche, a creature that has been kidnapped by witches and has had all of his bones broken. The witches sew his body back together and turn his head around so that he must always look and walk backward. His eyes, ears, and mouth are stitched up. Pinochet has created, according to Dorfman, a nation of Imbunches (17). The military has declared a state of siege; it has engaged in raids, arrests, and manhunts. It has created a pervasive culture of fear. Most important, it has attacked the press, closing opposition magazines and severely limiting even the media that ostensibly support the regime. "By eliminating the news the government hopes to eliminate reality" (17). This censoring and silencing has led the Chilean people to stop reading the news since they have lost all faith that it will report anything of interest. "I have found many people who, like the disjointed bones of the Imbunche, float apart in fragments, reduced to private worries, merely trying to survive the worst economic crisis in our history" (17). But again, Dorfman finds hope. He finds it in the association of journalists that publishes a newsletter every day of all of the material censored by the regime—what he calls Chile's own "samizdat," linking the Chilean press under Pinochet to that of censored writers from the Soviet bloc (17).

Dorfman's insistence that journalism requires bravery and commitment regardless of context runs throughout his periodical writing regarding the Pinochet regime. Dorfman wrote about Chile, about Pinochet, and about his hopes for Chile up to, during, and after Pinochet's rule. These concerns did not ebb after the elections that called an end to Pinochet's dictatorship because even though Pinochet was no longer head of state, he was directly involved in the transition government as head of the military and later as a senator for life. During these years Dorfman continued to describe the challenges that faced the Chilean road to democracy amid the endlessly haunting specter of Pinochet. In a piece for *Harper's* published in 1989, Dorfman explained the persistent centrality and complexity of the image of Pinochet sixteen years after his initial takeover: "In all cases, the general weighs at the center of one's life, a dark anchor narrowing the range of every choice. . . . He is burned into our memory, in our customs, into the way we speak, into our dreams. How are we to exorcise him?" ("Adiós General," 76). Dorfman's obsession with Pinochet and Pinochet's influence on the Chilean imagination would reach a climactic turn on October 16, 1998, when Pinochet was arrested on charges of torture and genocide in London on extradition orders from Spain. The event provided Dorfman with an irresistible opportunity to explore not only the bizarre twists in the Pinochet case, but also the symbolic role of Pinochet in Chilean consciousness. The result was *Exorcising Terror*.

The book is a highly hybrid text that weaves together a number of stories. First is the journalistic recounting of the details of the Pinochet case. This portion of the text is told like a suspense novel; Dorfman highlights the twists and turns of the case as Pinochet battled the legality of his arrest in the British courts, claimed he was a political prisoner, argued that he was unfit to stand trial, was freed in London, returned to Chile, was arrested in Chile, and then was deemed unfit to stand trial. Dorfman's account brings the reader to July 2001, when it seemed that all avenues for prosecuting Pinochet had been pursued.[17] Dorfman religiously listens to the radio news, watches broadcasts of the trial, and even sits in the House of Lords as he follows the case that will determine whether Pinochet will be held accountable for his crimes. The book would have made a valuable contribution to public understanding of the case if it had covered only the factual events, but Dorfman goes beyond the mere reporting of events in an effort to investigate the deeper question of what Pinochet represents to the Chilean people and to the global community.

In a move that parallels his memoir, Dorfman refuses to allow Pinochet to occupy the center of his own story.[18] Instead he interweaves the details of the Pinochet case with his own recollections, the testimonials of Pinochet victims, his memories of those victims, and his investigation into "the mind" of Pinochet. These additional discursive registers follow two paths, which complement the reporting of the details of Pinochet's arrest and depart from the traditional confines of documentary narrative: Dorfman strays from the simple reporting of facts, and he measures the story of Pinochet against the voices of his victims. By structuring the text to begin with his own relationship to Pinochet, to next move on to that of his friends, only to later open it up to other voices of Pinochet's victims, Dorfman purposefully violates the law of objectivity that typically characterizes nonfictional accounts, suggesting that the only way to understand the Pinochet case is through attention to that which is subjective, intimate, and unverifiable.

The dedication of the book makes this point clear. Dorfman begins by describing the Wall of Memory, which was erected in Santiago in 1994. It includes the names of victims of the military regime, more than a thousand of whom lack dates of death. The wall also carries a large blank space for names that the sculptors knew would emerge over the years. Dorfman explains that he wants to dedicate the book to five friends whose names appear on that wall, but that is not all because the wall—even with its open space for names to be identified—is still missing the names of those who lost their jobs, their homes, their loved ones, and their dignity in the years of the coup. Most important, "the wall does not include hundreds of thousands who were tortured and who survived, it does not include their memories" (10). The wall, then, like the facts of Pinochet's arrest, represents only one small segment of the story. If Dorfman were to report the facts only, then he would perpetuate the crime of silence and he would contribute to a communicative mode that fails to register the complexity of state violence.

In this sense Dorfman's text, as it engages in documentary narrative as a form of political denunciation and as a means to bring the voices of the silent to public consciousness, dialogues with the genre of the *testimonio*, if only to reverse two of its central trends. Dorfman suggests that the story of Pinochet, since it is the story of a brutal dictator, cannot be told using the techniques of the *testimonio*; it requires a different textual strategy. It cannot be told through attention to a "life," nor can it be told through attention to truth, veracity, or authenticity—features of the testimonial that have been highlighted by both Beverley and Yúdice.[19] In traditional testimonial the speakers' identities as social agents are a source of struggle, and the facts of their experience are a direct challenge to official history. Dorfman, himself an advocate of the testimonial form, finds in Pinochet's story an opportunity to invert these narrative gestures by showing that understanding Pinochet requires understanding his social context and that the boundaries of his individual life are inextricably tied to that of the Chilean community.[20] Consequently, in a move that parallels—yet reverses—the testimonial effort to reinforce the subjectivity of the subaltern, Dorfman unravels the privileged identity of the tyrant by narrating Pinochet through a variety of voices. Moreover, in a gesture that repeats his use of poetry as a way to express the horror of torture, Dorfman emphasizes that reporting the story of Pinochet requires that one report more than the facts.[21] It requires attention to all that is not represented on the Wall of Memory.

Consequently *Exorcising Terror* does not center on Pinochet, but rather on what Pinochet represents, on how a man who had been considered to be "honeyed and even groveling" orchestrated a reign of violence and terror (165). Interspersed with Dorfman's coverage of the arrest are a series of stories about Pinochet, like that of Moy Tohá, who had socialized with Pinochet during Allende's presidency and who confronted him twice after the coup (51, 164). Dorfman also writes about those who followed Pinochet, those who professed and continue to profess his innocence. Dorfman relates, for instance, a conversation with an acquaintance before the plebiscite to determine whether Pinochet would continue as head of state in 1989. Gracia tells Dorfman that she plans to vote for Pinochet (95). Dorfman is shocked and asks her how she can do that in the face of all the torture and violence. She responds, "Oh . . . he doesn't know about any of that. Just look at him, our *Tata*, he has such beautiful blue eyes" (96). This story is told in order to investigate why Pinochet was able to maintain popular support, for without that he would not have been able to hold power. But Dorfman is not simply interested in condemning Pinochet's supporters. That would be too easy. Rather than highlight the chasm between Pinochet and himself, Dorfman wonders how much of Pinochet lives in everyone. "Maybe what is frightening about Pinochet is not how far from us he has been all of this time, but how very close. . . . Maybe my need to exorcise him, to put him on trial, is really the need to banish that closeness, set him apart from the rest of humanity, punish in him what we fear we might also do, we might be horribly tempted to do, may the Lord help us, under the wrong circumstances" (141). Pinochet as representative of the human weakness for using violence to ensure power, to maintain authority, and to silence opposition runs throughout the text and ties Dorfman's analysis of the Pinochet case to his postmodern belief that the province of evil cannot be contained and that any hope for social change requires that we all face our own demons.

Not only does Dorfman expand the realm of traditional information included in such a text, but he also makes a concerted decision to intercalate the facts of the Pinochet arrest with the very facts that the arrest hoped to uncover. In all of his writing on the violence and horror of the coup Dorfman has never recounted the brutal details of those tortured under Pinochet to the extent that he does in this book. Beginning with the dedication, readers familiar with Dorfman's writing know that he has decided to break that silence and tell those stories in a way he never has before. In explaining what is missing from the Wall of Memory, he tells us the story of a man who was brutally tortured: "And then they attached something—a wire, a clasp, what was it?—they attached it to my genitals and then that voice said, Let's make him dance, let's make him sing, let's fuck him over. And then they made me dance. And they made me sing" (10). This story and its absence from official memory begin the text and indicate to the reader that this book is dedicated to reminding its audience that the facts of the arrest should not supersede the reasons behind it. Throughout the text these stories continue. Some of them come from the 249-page indictment prepared by the Spanish judge Baltasar Garzón (94). These contain lists and details of horror and violence. Added to that are stories from Dorfman's own admittedly imperfect memory. In his recounting of a meeting with the family of Eugenio Ruiz Tagle, who was brutally murdered, he confesses that his memory might be unreliable: "Angélica says I am mistaken . . . and yet that memory burns within me still" (178). By pointing out that he may not be remembering the story exactly, Dorfman is pushing on the limits of what constitute the important "facts" in the Pinochet case. He is also engaging in a debate over testimonial and truth that parallels his play *Death and the Maiden*. What happens when certain stories cannot be proven according to the standards of the Western legal system? What happens to the stories that are not a part of the legal documents? Dorfman stresses that any effort to account for the horror of Pinochet will always be incomplete, will always ignore a story that should be preserved. He makes it clear that this book itself is only the beginning. He also underscores the fact that while his memory and that of other victims of Pinochet may be imperfect, that does not mean that what they misremember did not happen. Memory in cases of mass trauma becomes fluid, fragile, and imprecise, but, as Dorfman shows, this does not make memory any less essential to the process of recovery. To a certain extent *Exorcising Terror* is a deep meditation on how societies attempt to come to terms with the various ways that the horrors of dictatorship are remembered, recorded, and prosecuted.

As much as *Exorcising Terror* is a book about Pinochet's arrest, it is equally a confession of Dorfman's personal obsession with him. Perhaps the biggest journalistic taboo broken in this text is that Dorfman makes the story of Pinochet personal. Dorfman's reporting of facts that were still officially in question, his delving into the mind of Pinochet, and his concern about the ties between Pinochet and Chile, while stretching the boundaries of nonfiction, still fall within the range of acceptable documentary writing. But Dorfman is interested in crossing the line even further and breaking down the boundaries between objective journalism and personal reflection. This gesture is made clear from the first chapter, where Dorfman gives a personal account of when he first learned about the arrest of Pinochet. He briefly hears of the arrest and then has to catch a flight. In limbo spatially and intellectually, Dorfman muses during the flight about his own knowledge of Pinochet. He replays events in his mind: a brief phone call while Allende was still president, reading Pinochet's memoir, a chance encounter during a visit to Chile after exile. He is filled with memories of the ways that Pinochet continued to haunt him and his nation. "Was I finally going to get a chance, was my country to be allowed, to wave good-bye to General Augusto Pinochet?" (26). As if to reinforce the ways that he hopes to use narrative to interrogate the limits of justice and the lines between fact and fiction, Dorfman then makes a stylistic shift. The next section is narrated in the first person and directed at Pinochet, who, in occupying the second person, forces an identification between the reader and the dictator.

> I've wanted so much for this to come to pass: that at least once before your death those eyes of yours would have to look at the clear and black eyes of the women whose sons and husbands and fathers and brothers you kidnapped and disappeared, one woman and then another woman and then one more. . . . Do you know something, Don Augusto? As far as I am con-

cerned that would be enough. It would be punishment enough. And think of what a great contribution it would be to the country you say you love, you say you did all of this for: You could help our shared motherland take one more step in the arduous, tentative task of reconciliation, which is only possible if the terrible truth of what has been done is revealed and acknowledged, if you participate in this bruising search for the truth without lying to us or yourself. (29–30)

This book, then, is meant as a supplement to the Wall of Memory. For by the time that Dorfman wrote these lines, he knew that full disclosure by Pinochet was not and would not be forthcoming now or ever. *Exorcising Terror* places the intimately personal into direct contact with facts both known and ignored.

The arrest of Pinochet was a landmark event that shattered the supposed code of impunity that had allowed despots to roam free. Dorfman explains the ramifications: "I have slowly come to the conviction that what happens to Pinochet's contingent and uncertain body is ultimately not as important as what this never-ending trial has already changed in the vast mind of humanity" (191). Bringing all of his years as a human rights activist to bear on the arrest, Dorfman explores the implications of the Pinochet case for the myriad tyrants that enjoy impunity. He wonders, for instance, if Pinochet's arrest frightened Slobodan Milošević: "Did Milosevic . . . tremble at the idea that a foreign court could put former heads of state on trial in the name of the very humanity that those rulers had violated? Did he foresee in the Chilean General's fate what might befall him? Could he suspect that less than four years later he would be facing the International Criminal Court in The Hague?" (195). Dorfman clearly holds much hope for international courts and global struggles for human rights. His account of the Pinochet case examines the future implications for holding tyrants accountable for their crimes. The arrest of Pinochet represented an extraordinary reversal of public accountability. That Pinochet spent even one night under arrest was more than many could have ever hoped to witness. His arrest, then, portends tremendous potential for the future of international human rights law, and it teaches the public that these tyrants are not above the law: "This is Pinochet's irrefutable gift to humanity" (192).

Dorfman ultimately considers the Pinochet case in terms of its implications for the world at large. And, in fact, its broader implications were already becoming evident before Dorfman had finished the manuscript. Slobodan Milošević was arraigned on July 3, 2001, clearly following the precedent set by

Pinochet's arrest. Then on September 11, 2001, terrorist attacks on the United States set into motion a series of events that tested global support for international human rights. Would the attacks on the United States and the U.S. response to them reverse the gains of the Pinochet arrest? Dorfman suggests wariness and vigilance: "We will be seeing, I believe, a recrudescence of violations against the rights of people" (199). These musings are part of the book's second epilogue, mere supplements to the text itself, and they are not elaborated on extensively. Brief mentions are made throughout of how the events of September 11, 2001, had a historical twin moment of terror in Chile: "Yes, there are more Septembers of terror in history than most people remember; yes, there exists another Tuesday, the eleventh of September that descended from the sky" (30). Exploring the uncanny historical coincidence of terror and September 11, however, is not the goal of *Exorcising Terror*. Dorfman leaves that task to his next book of nonfiction, *Other Septembers, Many Americas: Selected Provocations 1980–2004*.

In many ways *Other Septembers* is an apt text with which to end this section on Dorfman's journalism because it represents a broad range of Dorfman's periodical writing, delves into many of the themes that are at the heart of his cultural criticism, and provides a survey of almost a quarter century of his writing. The book unites a range of short texts—"provocations" as Dorfman describes them—that includes (among others) editorials from newspapers, book reviews, commencement addresses, speeches to the United Nations, and poems inspired by the events of the Iraq war. Purposefully eschewing a chronological layout, Dorfman groups the pieces around core themes that allow him to speak directly to the convergences and divergences between the two September 11's. The goal of the text is to use Dorfman's own experience as a hemispheric American, an American of the South and of the North, of Spanish and of English, as a way to "break down the barriers that separate Americans and foreigners," as a way to "envision a different dialogue, another sort of relationship" (xvi). He hopes that these writings, originating as they do in a double homelessness and a double vision, can play a role in encouraging a form of "collective imagining" that can challenge the divisions prompted by the September attacks (xvi).

The first section, "I Have Been through This Before," includes a series of pieces and one poem, all of which were published after the terrorist attacks on the United States. Dorfman thinks through the post-9/11/2001 crisis in light of his own experience of a similar yet different tragedy. From the moment of the attacks on the United States he is driven to "extract the meaning of the juxtaposition and coincidence of these two September 11ths, which in my case becomes even more enigmatic and personal because it is a violation that conjoins the two foundational cities of my existence—the New York which gave me refuge and joy during ten years of my infancy and the Santiago which protected my adolescence under its mountains and made me into a man" (39). In the outpouring of international support for the United States that immediately followed the attacks and in the extraordinary strength shown by the citizens of New York, Dorfman locates enormous possibility within the horror of the attacks. "Strange as this may sound, I see a dreadful form of hope in the dark blizzard of photos that began to cover the streets of New York precisely after those criminal acts of terror that devastated that city after September 2001" (8). What if the inhabitants of the United States were to respond to the attacks by finally recognizing that we were all vulnerable, that we all shared the same planet, that we shared a common humanity? These hopes, of course, did not come to fruition, and instead of using the attacks as a call to actively struggle for global peace, the United States declared war on Iraq.

The next section of the book, "Yesterday Is Still Here," presents pieces that consider the devastating consequences of historical amnesia. Beginning with a piece originally published in the *Los Angeles Times* during the Gulf War that imagines a corporal reading *Moby Dick*, Dorfman stresses that the only reason that the war could be fought was because the Iraqis were nameless, faceless, and lifeless. "It is the stark fact of his very absence from our awareness that prepares his death" (47). Reminding readers that Saddam Hussein and George Bush, Sr. would likely emerge from the battle unscathed and "that it will be their people who will have to pay for this absurd conflagration," Dorfman's piece, positioned as it is at the start of the section, gives harsh testimony to the ways that the post-9/11 war on terror mirrored earlier conflicts (47). Readers are then prepared for the next piece, a poem that imagines Hammurabi speaking to Donald Rumsfeld. Dorfman reminds readers of another Iraq, where Hammurabi once ruled by the first written legal code that defined a just society. The poem asks: What might Rumsfeld gain from listening to Hammurabi? What have we lost by forgetting him?

The third section, "Troubled Bridges," returns to questions essential to Dorfman's aesthetics of hope, including a piece by that name. In an essay on "Memory and Fate in Latin America" Dorfman explores difficult questions about how the historical legacy of cultural conflict hinders the potential for societies to consider themselves part of a larger human community. After the violence of colonialism, war, and dictatorship and the violence of a consumer society that reduces the struggles of Che Guevara to nothing more than an icon for a T-shirt, how is it possible to create bridges among diverse groups of people, many of whom have defined themselves in opposition to others? As explained in detail in chapter 3, these questions are essential to Dorfman's aesthetics of hope. For bridges across communities, nations, and individuals to be meaningful and lasting, culture must play a central role, and that role must emphasize again and again that "individualistic answer[s] to communal frustration" will only bring more of the same, unproductive, stagnant communication (170). Also hopeful but resolutely determined to expose the challenges that face a global commitment to peace, this section delves into the difficult work that is at the heart of Dorfman's search for an *other* America, one that can be a utopian space of possibility.

The last section of the book, "Imagining a Way Out," includes a number of texts that attempt the task of building bridges. The section presents pieces by Dorfman about other artists, writers, and culture workers whose art models aesthetic interventions that uncompromisingly ask audiences to imagine "a possible peace" and to recognize that the "world does not have to be the way it is" (254). In analyses of film, photos, journalism, literature, painting, and bilingualism (among other categories) Dorfman reiterates his commitment to engaged art. Alongside these pieces are works by Dorfman, such as "Voices from Beyond the Dark" (the preface to the *Speak Truth to Power Play*) and the epilogue to *Death and the Maiden*. These are accompanied by two texts that focus on how the decisions of today affect the children of tomorrow. The first, a commencement address, refuses to treat the audience of recent graduates as innocent children. Instead it speaks of responsibility, work to be done, and difficult decisions in a world overwhelmed by pain. Dorfman undermines the typical format for such speeches, which assumes a wise orator in the face of a youthful and ingenuous audience, by speaking to the audience as his peers: "I take for granted that you, the young who are graduating, are part of a collective that must confront the grief of the world, that you are accountable, along with your elders, for our common fate" (236). Dorfman does not give his audience an alibi to evade responsibilities: "Because from this solemn and joyous moment onwards, you will be faced every day with the decision of whether to rise up against that pain or whether to stand by the wayside and let it continue" (237). Dorfman asks the graduates to think of the children who will be watching them, who will learn from them, and who will inherit the world from them. "Will the world you hand them be better than the world you inherited?" (238). Continuing on the same themes, the second piece, a playful "Letter to the Six Billionth World Citizen," invokes the fetal rebellion of *Manuel Sendero* and promises the newly born children that even though they are born into a world that is far from perfect, that promises to stifle—at least a little bit—the heroic, rebellious spirit of the babies who still reside in their mothers' wombs, humanity awaits them. Do not be afraid, he writes, because you will not be alone. Far from it.

Throughout these texts Dorfman weaves an aesthetic commitment to bridge facts with literary language and to combine a powerful discursive intervention with a vision of hope, beauty, and utopian possibility. It is interesting that unlike Dorfman's literary texts, which range in style from the epic to the absurd and from the picaresque to the thriller, his essays and journalism share a more cohesive stylistic unity. When he writes in this mode, Dorfman tends to join a linguistic gentleness typical of his poetry with incisive commentary. He balances the poetic with an intense language of intervention and provocation. One remarkably consistent stylistic practice Dorfman employs throughout these pieces is an extreme use of conjunctions to begin sentences. In *Other Septembers*, which represents a broad spectrum of Dorfman's writing, sentences begin with "and" in a way that creates rhythm and defies the laws of grammar.[22] These sentences stand in contrast to those that begin with "or" or "but" or that repeat these conjunctions of opposition, contradiction, and distinction.[23] The practice of beginning sentences with linking words allows Dorfman to use language as a model for social relations and as a way to emphasize his interest in using writing to call attention to the ties between history and storytelling. Since a new sentence is meant to be a beginning, by starting a sentence with a linking word Dorfman emphasizes that each beginning is also a continuation, that each story has a history and each history has a story.

For instance, in "Globalizing Compassion," which asks if the events of September 11, 2001, will enable the United States to see itself in a global context where all humanity is vulnerable and where the events of September 11, 2001, have historical precursors, Dorfman begins sentences with "and," "but," and "or" on various occasions. After he explains that the photos carried by the loved ones of the victims of the 2001 attacks may provide a model for making this world a "less threatening home for us all," he follows with a strategically placed one-sentence paragraph: "And yet," he writes, "a note of caution" (7). The caution emphasizes that not all people are photographed. In the case of Chile, for instance, many of the disappeared had never been photographed. The use of "and yet" to signal Dorfman's caution about the limits of the photograph as a source of memory allows him to emphasize the moment as a bridge via the word "and," which must be qualified via the word "yet." It is as if Dorfman were making these conjunctions stand in for the larger social questions that trouble him. Will society favor "and," or will it be overtaken by "or" and "but"? This question is perhaps too simplistic because in fact Dorfman is trying to see if these conjunctions can weave together and collaborate. So his use of conjunctions to start and repeat within sentences might be better questioned this way: Is it possible to nuance and be critical while simultaneously building connections and nurturing a collective vision? Dorfman very carefully chooses his words to provoke his readers.

This practice appears as well in the last paragraph of "Globalizing Compassion," which has three sentences that begin with "but," "and," and "yes," respectively. Each word that begins these last sentences allows Dorfman to deliberately chart a path for global compassion. I have reproduced this last paragraph in its entirety in order to show the aesthetic interaction between Dorfman's ideas and his word choices.

> But that is the challenge of the moment: to find ways to make this new global tragedy draw us closer to each other, not because we can now kill one another more easily and with more devastating effects, but closer because we share the same need to mourn, the same flesh that can be torn, the same impulse toward compassion. And closer to the day when the most powerful members of humankind can pin to our clothes that blank photo of the disappeared, that image of an emptiness and absence that threatens to devour us all. Yes, perhaps our species is oh so slowly getting ready for the day when enough of us will want to wander the boundaries of this Earth until we have brought back the lost souls of modernity, like the other missing of the world, back from death and oblivion. (10)

The word sequence that ends this piece is quite strategic. After pointing out that the terrorist attacks on the United States did not naturally lead to empathy but rather that horror and pain lead to rage and vengeance, Dorfman begins the last paragraph with "but." The word choice helps Dorfman explain that changing the historical cycle of violence requires a break, a beginning of contrast and opposition to what has come before. This break with the past will then set up the possibility of connecting humanity, a vision that Dorfman highlights with his symbolic use of "and" to start the second sentence. Once those bridges have been built, the affirmation of "yes" functions as a rally toward collective agency.

Beyond the specific poetics of Dorfman's nonfiction writing that complement his aesthetics of hope, he also makes pointed use of literary language in venues that are prone to the type of dry, scientific, and objective writing that he and Mattelart railed against in *Donald Duck*. By consistently writing for newspapers and journals whose language tends to be formulaic and monotonous in a style that is literary, metaphorical, and moving, Dorfman reaffirms his commitment to writing as a form of subversive engagement. For example, poetic word choices, like the use of "land" over "nation" to refer to Chile in the *New York Times*, or repetitive phrasing, like "somewhere in the world today," which appears numerous times in "The Hidden Censors" from *Other Septembers*, indicate Dorfman's commitment to calling attention to the power and vulnerability of linguistic expression. On the one hand, poetic language reminds readers of the intense power of evocative words. On the other hand, it draws attention to the artifice of writing, to the distance between the text and what it represents, to the imperfect tools available to the writer.

"The Hidden Censors," which was originally delivered as a speech to the United Nations Assembly on World Press Freedom Day in 1997 and is printed in *Other Septembers*, unites many of Dorfman's concerns. Aware that his audience was accustomed to a specific discursive register, Dorfman unabashedly chose a different one. His first lines read: "Somewhere in the world today. A journalist is being beaten. Policemen are beating him, beating her, somewhere in the world today, on the shoulders, on the head, on the hands. Somewhere in the world today, another journalist, yet another, is being thrown in jail, joining so many others who have spent days, months, years in prison" (228). Here Dorfman brings the poetic into direct contact with the horrifying. At one and the same time he employs an evocative language rarely heard in the General Assembly alongside a language of truth that many politicians and diplomats seem to find difficult to utter. He then goes further. He speaks directly to the audience, saying that these unnamed journalists could easily be named, their places and dates of harassment detailed. In words that must have been quite uncomfortable for the delegates to hear he accuses many of them of representing nations that violate the universal right to free speech and a free press: "It would take more time than we have right now to examine, even briefly, each violation . . . so I will leave with you, Mr. Secretary General, a list of those nations, 142 of them, to be exact" (229). He makes his position clear: I may be a poet, but I have my facts. As if that were not enough, Dorfman pushes his audience even more. If there is so much repression of the press and of the word, there must be a good reason. "Censorship is only ferociously necessary because, in spite of all of the barriers, stories are incessantly being told" (229). Censorship, he explains, also takes many forms, and it persists in countries that claim to have a free press, via corporate control and other forms of fear and social pressure. If the world has become so hostile to words, images, and stories that threaten the status quo, then what hope is there that the courageous journalist who is beaten after writing a story does not suffer in vain? Not only do these heroic acts have to take place, but they also require an audience and interlocutors. "Symbols matter. Words *do* matter. We are congregated today to symbolically alleviate the loneliness of all those who, around the world, struggle against enormous odds to give birth to the weight of those words that are as necessary to our survival as the air we breathe" (231). In order to ensure that his audience is prepared to listen, Dorfman ends his intervention with a reading of his poem "Simultaneous Translation," which asks how we can "listen to the stones that bleed, hidden, at the bottom of the rivers of silence of humanity" (232). Both in style and in content, this address most certainly shocked its audience. Connecting poetry to journalism and censorship to corporatism, Dorfman reminds his audience that the struggle to protect free expression knows no bounds.

Uncomfortable placing all of his hope in his own writing, Dorfman has also supported a number of alternative media projects. Alongside public intellectuals like Howard Zinn and Noam Chomsky, he has published various texts with Seven Stories Press, an independent book publisher that provides an alternative to corporate publishing. He has lent his support to Tom Englehardt's work with TomDispatch.com, an independent news source that is dedicated to providing readers with information ignored or censored by the mainstream media. In addition, he has his own blog on *The Guardian*'s "Comment Is Free" Web site, a collective group blog that is dedicated to expanding the comment section of the British newspaper.[24] And these are only a few examples. From *Donald Duck* to his blog, Dorfman has been a tireless critic of mainstream media and an ardent activist for using any and all forms of communication.

I have suggested that these myriad activities be read as an organic whole because they combine to support Dorfman's aesthetic project, but it is important to point out that this exceedingly broad range of projects, while not necessarily unusual for a writer, might border on the extreme. In describing his childhood, Dorfman tells his readers that he "was always performing, partly because of my exuberant personality (today I would be diagnosed as having a mild form of ADD, Attention Deficit Disorder), but also, I believe, as a way of incessantly staking my claim to the public space in an English that I knew I had not been born to, endlessly acting out for the benefit of my fellow Americans" (*Heading*, 82). But as we know from his memoir, his confidence as a speaker of Spanish and his identity as a Chilean were hard won as well. When Dorfman was attending an English-language school in Chile, his Spanish teacher forced him to repeat the phrase "'*Hablo este idioma en forma execrable.*' I speak this language execrably" (111). These childhood experiences of unease and displacement combined with his energetic personality and led him as a young boy to "play with words and horse around endlessly," so much so that he was slow to read because he was "unable to sit quietly, unable to concentrate" (82). It is possible, then, that Dorfman's extensive span of projects as an adult follows a pattern of activity visible in his childhood.

In a sense Dorfman's broad range of critical and creative projects can be understood as a consequence of his frantic desire to reinforce his connection to his community and to constantly use his creative talents as a way of enacting a "ritual of belonging" and combating loneliness (*Heading*, 82). Dorfman's incessant level of creative activity and his fearless forays into a variety of critical and creative projects are probably best understood as personally and politically motivated. What began as the constant performances of a restless boy has become artistic engagement and impassioned critical intervention. And there is no question that such behavior calls attention to itself since any writer who represents ethical crises and calls on readers to reflect on their own ethics is sure to receive intense scrutiny and much potential backlash. As James Dawes explains in *That the World May Know*, writers who represent human rights issues are always stuck in a paradox: they feel that they must write about what they have seen, and they are certain to receive criticism for presuming to do it (166). Such writers, claims Dawes, know that their work can never be enough, but their work stems from their hope that their writing can make a difference and their sense of responsibility not to be silent. It is a calling they can't refuse and a process that requires idealism, skepticism, and perseverance. From *Donald Duck* to *Death and the Maiden* to *Exorcising Terror*, from Susana la Semilla to his Internet blog, Dorfman's works reveal his aesthetic commitment to providing readers with an unflinchingly intense view of a world where hope for the future depends on a combination of critical reflection and creative imagination.

CONCLUSION. ONE AMONG MANY

I began this book by claiming that Ariel Dorfman's work is dedicated to breaking rules. Over the course of this text I have shown how Dorfman's writing and other creative projects attempt to break conventional forms of cultural communication. Unwilling to conceive of art and politics as separate spheres of activity, Dorfman has always created an engaged art. But contrary to the assumption that political art must be propaganda, Dorfman's art is highly experimental and aesthetically complex.

To a certain extent this approach is a consequence of Dorfman's historical and social experiences. Throughout this book I have tried to link Dorfman's creative efforts to his sociopolitical context. Responding to the Latin American revolutionary movements of the 1960s, accompanied as these were with the extraordinary artistic innovations of the boom writers, the New Latin American cinema, and the "boom" of the testimonial genre, writers from Dorfman's generation often created literature that oscillated among the highly intellectual aesthetics of the boom writers, the critique of media culture of Latin American cinema, and the direct form of political denunciation found in *testimonio*.

These writers, known as the "post-boom" generation, constructed texts that were aesthetically hybrid and politically motivated.

Of course these interests were not unique to Latin America, and it is possible to find points of comparison between Dorfman and a global community of writers. Dorfman's experience of multiple exiles, political activism, and his witnessing of a number of major historical events, coupled with his exposure to theories of postmodernism, globalization, trauma, and memory, link his work to other writers who experienced a similar confluence of events and theories. Dorfman can be productively compared to diaspora writers who use formal experimentation to communicate political commitment and concern. Writers like Juan Goytisolo (Spain), Tahar Ben Jelloun (Morocco), Derek Walcott (St. Lucia), Salman Rushdie (India), George Lamming (Barbados), J. M. Coetzee (South Africa), Assia Djebar (Algeria), Ngugi Wa Thiong'o (Kenya), Naruddin Farah (Somalia), and Gao Xingjian (China) also engage in aesthetic innovation in conjunction with political writing intended to challenge the status quo. The connections between these writers and Dorfman suggest that diaspora writers from the latter part of the twentieth century have often turned away from literary realism and have considered complex aesthetics to be an essential literary tool for critiquing society. In this way the work of Dorfman is exemplary of a global cultural trend.

Nevertheless, while Dorfman shares the rejection of realism and the interest in constructing complex and political art with a number of other writers, his aesthetics of hope is unique. One of the purposes of this book has been to mine Dorfman's writing, both fiction and nonfiction, for clues to his aesthetic project. In the process I have found that his texts combine to form a theory of art and its relationship to society that includes six main features. First, art with an aesthetics of hope draws attention to the relationship between art and history. At once utopian and dystopian, such an art indicates the social appreciation of historical time as a problem. Second, an aesthetics of hope produces art that links reason and emotion and that refuses to privilege one over the other. Third, an aesthetics of hope draws attention to the relationship between the individual and a collective. Each of these three features of Dorfman's aesthetic project is dedicated to dismantling binary constructions—between history and myth, reason and emotion, and the self and society—a critical practice that leads to the fourth characteristic, which is that art with an aesthetics of hope is dialectical. Such art is internally dialectical, presenting ideas in tension, and it is externally dialectical as it creates a confrontational relationship between the work and its audience. Thus the fifth feature of this theory of art is that it should be provocative, contestatory, and that it requires the active engagement of the reader. For this reason, Dorfman always leaves his texts open and inconclusive. Finally, art with an aesthetics of hope strives to be revolutionary, artistically and socially, and uses a guerrilla strategy of shifting representational practices.

In chapters 3–5 I traced Dorfman's use of these aesthetic strategies over the course of his writing from the 1970s to the early twenty-first century. The survey and analysis of these texts yielded yet another distinctive feature of Dorfman's work, one that has confounded scholarly efforts to synthesize his literary project into a coherent whole. Dorfman's incessant experimentation with genre, form, and poetics has frustrated any effort to pinpoint a specific Dorfman textual practice. If anything, his "signature style" is characterized best by its absence. This constantly shifting technique, which derives from a broad range of literary and cultural influences (as described in chapter 2), flows across a variety of narrative genres. For instance, Dorfman's novels, as noted, creatively intertext with (among other styles) classical tragedy, the baroque, the picaresque, and the political thriller.

In addition to creatively adapting a broad range of literary techniques and approaches, Dorfman also works across a wide array of textual forms. So not only does he combine (for instance) the baroque and the theater of the absurd, but he also writes novels, poetry, essays, journalism, and advertisements. One of the most important features of this spectrum of projects is that Dorfman has always tried to combine creativity with critique and critique with creativity. One of the best examples of this tendency, as described in detail in chapter 6, is Dorfman's interest in infusing his nonfiction writing with literary language. Alternatively, Dorfman uses much of his literature as a way of exploring critical ideas. *Hard Rain*, for example, is a meditation on the relationship between art and revolution, and *Blake's Therapy* explores the ethical dilemmas of "socially responsible" capitalism.

By way of illustrating these points, I would like to end this book by describing a speech Dorfman delivered to the 2005 Modern Language Association (MLA) convention, held in Washington, D.C. (He published an essay describing the event entitled "Homeland Security Ate My Speech.") Dorfman presented at a roundtable on the role of the public intellectual, accompanied by Ngugi Wa Thiong'o and the words of Julia Kristeva (she could not attend, so her essay was read in her absence). The other presenters seriously mulled over the question of how to be a public intellectual in a time of crisis, offering interesting and provocative ideas for the audience to consider. Dorfman took a different tack. He tried humor. He explained that he couldn't read the text he had prepared because on his way to the convention, he was stopped in the airport by home-land security and interrogated. The agents who stopped him confiscated his speech. So instead of reading his missing text, he would describe his experience of defending his speech and his work to his two interrogators. Over the course of describing the conversation, he managed to hit many of his intellectual concerns and make a number of critical interventions, but these were all embedded in a larger tale about the practical limits of intellectual work in a public sphere disinclined to opt for critical thinking as an antidote to the global crisis caused by the events of September 11, 2001.

The most astonishing consequence of Dorfman's presentation was the audi-ence's reaction. Despite his having adopted a witty, wry tone and despite his constant references to literary masters of deception (like Borges), many in the audience failed to appreciate that he was telling a story and that, moreover, he was trying to be funny. As he explains: "Everybody seemed absolutely ready to credit my absurd story as perfectly real, as not, in fact, at all absurd. When I lamented the naiveté of such a sophisticated audience to friends at the MLA, when I declared my amazement at the reaction I had gotten, the answer was unanimous: I was the naïve one" ("Homeland," n.p.). As Dorfman goes on to analyze the consequence of his talk, he comes to conclude that the joke was lost on so many in the audience only because, in fact, it was too close to the truth:

Amazed? Why should I be amazed? Of course, people had found my version of events—to use an Aristotelian category—a paragon of verisimilitude. Isn't art, according to my master Picasso, a lie that always tells the truth? To those friends, my fraudulent story was terrifyingly plausible, all-too-unfortunately representative of a country where citizens and non-citizens can indeed be kept forever and a day in custody without charges, where illegal wiretapping is rampant, where that obscene word "rendition" (or the even more perverse "extraordinary rendition") has crawled into our every-day vocabulary, where the Vice President insists that certain suspects may have to be tortured in order to defeat terrorism, where the President lies and invades another country under sham pretences and is not impeached, where polls indicate that a majority of Americans are willing to give up their civil liberties in order to be "secure." . . . And wasn't I as responsible as my gullible audience? Wasn't I also laboring under the anxiety that this could truly befall me? Wasn't my story, my telling of it, filled with an underlying panic? Wasn't that what had made it so credible? ("Homeland," n.p.)

Not only did Dorfman use the presentation as a way to combine storytelling with critical intervention, to mix humor with panic, to be provocative as well as elusive, but he also used the experience as a way to remind himself of the ongoing struggle to find a way to use art to inspire the imagination. Dorfman tells the homeland security agents that he hopes his speech will motivate his audience to "think through the crisis," and yet he purposefully avoids explaining what he means because such a project cannot be dictated. All of his work, in fact, attempts to inspire his audience to "think through the crisis." Dorfman's aesthetics of hope is dedicated to constructing art that encourages memory and imagination to triumph over amnesia and apathy.

APPENDIX 1. AN ARIEL DORFMAN CHRONOLOGY

1903 Ariel Dorfman's maternal great grandfather is murdered in a pogrom in Kishinev (today the capital of the Republic of Moldova). This death eventually leads to his grandmother's family's decision to emigrate. They choose Argentina as a consequence of Baron Maurice de Hirsch's Jewish Colonization Association, which helped many East European Jews emigrate to Argentina and Brazil.

1907 Adolfo Dorfman is born in Odessa (now in Ukraine).

1909 Fanny Zelicovich Vaisman (Ariel's mother) is born in Kishinev.

1909 Three-month-old Fanny departs with her parents for Argentina, fleeing the pogroms.

1911 Adolfo and his mother leave Odessa for Argentina.

1914 Dorfman's paternal grandmother, Raissa, and his father, Adolfo, return to Russia and are caught in the eruption of the First World War and the Russian Revolution.

1920 Raissa and Adolfo Dorfman return to Argentina.

Early 1930s Dorfman's father joins the Communist Party in Argentina. He is expelled for a difference of opinion in the late 1930s.

May 6, 1942 Vladimiro Ariel Dorfman is born in Buenos Aires.

June 1943 General Pedro Ramírez overthrows the conservative government of Ramón Castillo in Argentina. This pro-Axis coup will soon cause problems for Dorfman's family when the military takes over the Universidad de la Plata, where Adolfo Dorfman teaches industrial engineering.

February 1944 Adolfo Dorfman receives a Guggenheim Fellowship and flees Argentina after he is expelled from the university as a consequence of his political beliefs and heightened anti-Semitism.

February 1945 Dorfman, his mother (Fanny), and his sister (Eleonora) join Adolfo in New York. Adolfo Dorfman is conscripted into the U.S. Army but avoids service because he is reclassified. Nelson Rockefeller determines that the work of Adolfo Dorfman in the office of Inter-American Affairs (housed in the State Department) is "essential."

February 1945 Dorfman catches pneumonia and spends three weeks in a New York hospital. Upon release he does not speak Spanish for ten years.

April 1945 Dorfman's mother is institutionalized for depression shortly after Franklin Delano Roosevelt dies. Dorfman and his sister go to a foster home.

November 1, 1945 Dorfman's parents pick up their children from the foster home, and they all move to an apartment on Morningside Drive.

August 1946 Adolfo Dorfman accepts a job as deputy head with the Council for Economic Development at the newly formed United Nations.

November 1, 1947 The family moves to Parkway Village, a housing development in Queens that had been created for UN staff. Dorfman attends the International School for children of UN staff.

September 1949 Dorfman attends New York City public school PS117 after having been a student at the UN school. Here he is confronted with a conservative climate and the atmosphere of the "red scare."

June 1951 Dorfman's family takes a trip to Europe and Argentina. On the cruise to Europe aboard the *De Grasse*, Dorfman decides to change his first name from "Vladimiro" to "Edward." He meets Thomas Mann aboard the ship and begins his first diary. After this trip, at the age of nine, Dorfman begins to imagine life as a writer.

June 19, 1953 Dorfman and his family keep a vigil outside of Sing Sing the night that Ethel and Julius Rosenberg are executed.

November 1953 After Maurice Halperin and his wife, Edith, spend the night in the Dorfman's apartment as they flee the House Un-American Activities Committee, Adolfo Dorfman is forced to take a post with the UN in Santiago.

Summer 1954 Dorfman endures his second exile as he and his family join his father in Santiago.

1954 Guatemala is invaded by a U.S.-trained force in order to oust democratically elected Jacobo Arbenz. Dorfman meets Arbenz later, when he comes to dinner with his family.

March 1955 Dorfman begins high school at The Grange, a school modeled on British public schools, where classes are taught in English and Spanish.

1956 Dorfman first hears of Salvador Allende, who was a senator at this time.

1958 Salvador Allende barely loses the presidential election to right-wing candidate Jorge Alessandri.

December 1959 Dorfman graduates from The Grange and wins an award for excellence in the Spanish language.

1960 Even though he is admitted to Columbia University with a scholarship, Dorfman decides to stay in Chile, and he begins to study literature at the University of Chile. In another effort to redefine himself, he changes his name from "Eddie" to "Ariel."

June 1960 Dorfman is at a soccer match in the National Stadium when Chile is rocked by an earthquake. He and his fellow students organize a massive rescue operation, collecting food, blankets, building materials, and money for the south of Chile, where the earthquake has hit the hardest. This is Dorfman's first experience of involvement in a communal project, and it sparks his decision to become more actively political.

1965 Dorfman graduates summa cum laude in literature from the University of Chile with a thesis on Shakespeare. His degree is a *licenciatura*, roughly the equivalent of a U.S. master's degree. He begins teaching as an assistant professor in Spanish and journalism at the University of Chile.

1965–67 Dorfman writes regularly for the literary and cultural magazine *Ercilla*.

May 6, 1965 Dorfman celebrates his twenty-third birthday protesting the U.S. invasion of the Dominican Republic in front of the U.S. Embassy in Santiago. This is the period of the Johnson Doctrine, which brought increased U.S. military action and intervention in Latin America, leading Dorfman to distance himself even further from the United States.

January 7, 1966 Dorfman marries Angélica Malinarch.

1967 Dorfman becomes a Chilean citizen.

February 11, 1967 Dorfman's first son, Rodrigo Fidel, is born.

October 9, 1967 Che Guevara is murdered by the Bolivian Army. The event has a tremendous impact on young revolutionaries, like Dorfman, throughout the Americas.

1968 Dorfman and his family go to Berkeley for a year on a research fellowship. Dorfman works on a book on Latin American literature.

1968 Dorfman's first book, a critical study of the theater of Harold Pinter, is published.

1968 Dorfman is promoted to associate professor at the University of Chile.

1969 Dorfman returns to Chile. He creates the first seminar at the University of Chile on "Subliteratura y formas de combatirla" (Subliterature and Ways to Combat It).

Mid-August 1970 Dorfman is shot in the back and legs with buckshot at a protest and has to seek a friendly doctor to treat him outside of a hospital in order to avoid arrest and interrogation.

September 4, 1970 Salvador Allende is elected president of Chile. Dorfman celebrates in the streets.

1970 Dorfman is promoted to full professor at the University of Chile. His first book of essays on Latin American literature is published, *Imaginación y violencia en América* (Imagination and Violence in America).

1971 Dorfman and Armand Mattelart's critical study of the ideology of Disney comics, *Para leer al Pato Donald* (*How to Read Donald Duck*), is published.

1971–73 Dorfman is consultant to Quimantú, the state publishing house, which produces magazines for young people and an inexpensive literary collection. He is also active in a number of other cultural projects, including several television programs.

September 1972 Dorfman begins work on his first novel, *Moros en la costa* (*Hard Rain*).

1973 Dorfman's first novel, *Moros en la costa*, is published in Argentina and wins an award from *La Opinión* (Buenos Aires). The novel also receives strong support from Julio Cortázar.

September 11, 1973 As a consequence of a number of coincidences, Dorfman is not at La Moneda, the governmental palace, the morning of the coup launched by Augusto Pinochet against Salvador Allende. Allende dies later that day.

September 25, 1973 Pablo Neruda dies. Dorfman is unable to attend his funeral because he is in hiding.

September 1973 After the coup Dorfman is on the run, hiding out with friends and at the residence of the Israeli ambassador.

October 1973 Dorfman takes refuge in the Argentine Embassy in Santiago. While at the embassy, he witnesses the murder by snipers of Sergio Leiva.

October 1973 Dorfman goes into exile, first to Argentina, then to France.

1974 Dorfman publishes *Ensayos quemados en Chile: Inocencia y neocolonialismo* (Essays Burned in Chile: Innocence and Neocolonialism) and, with Manuel Jofré, *Superman y sus amigos del alma* (Superman and His Bosom Buddies).

1974 In the United States the Longshoreman's Union and other protesters succeed in turning the Chilean tall-ship-turned-torture-chamber, *La Esmeralda*, away from the port of San Francisco. Dorfman uses the event as the basis for his story "Putamadre."

1975–76 Dorfman teaches Latin American literature at the Sorbonne in Paris.

1976 Dorfman goes from Paris to exile in the Netherlands.

1976–80 Dorfman teaches at the University of Amsterdam.

February 16, 1979 Joaquín Emiliano, Dorfman's second son, is born in Amsterdam.

1979 Dorfman publishes *La última aventura del Llanero Solitario* (The Last Adventure of the Lone Ranger), *Pruebas al canto* (Soft Evidence), and *Cría ojos* (Raising Eyes). The last two, a volume of poetry and a collection of short stories, are his first creative publications since exile.

1980 Dorfman is awarded a Woodrow Wilson Fellowship at the Smithsonian and moves to Washington, D.C. He publishes *Reader's nuestro que estás en la tierra: Ensayos sobre el imperialismo cultural* (Our Reader's Digest Who Art on This Earth: Essays on Cultural Imperialism).

1981 Dorfman publishes his second novel, his first in exile, *Viudas* (*Widows*). He also publishes a collection of poetry, *Missing*.

1981–84 Dorfman is a visiting fellow at the Institute for Policy Studies in Washington, D.C.

1983 As a result of international protests, Dorfman's exile is lifted, and he is able to return to Chile. He publishes his third novel, *La última canción de Manuel Sendero* (*The Last Song of Manuel Sendero*) and *The Empire's Old Clothes: What the Lone Ranger, Babar, and Other Innocent Heroes Do to Our Minds*. Dorfman and his son Rodrigo personally deliver 535 copies of the English version of *Widows* to all U.S. senators and congressmen.

1984 Dorfman becomes a post-doctoral fellow at Duke University. He publishes *Hacia la liberación del lector latinoamericano* (Toward the Liberation of the Latin American Reader).

1985–89 Dorfman becomes a visiting professor at Duke University.

1986 Dorfman is reported dead by the Chilean media. After this he returns only briefly to his country. He publishes three books of essays: *Los sueños nucleares de Reagan* (Reagan's Nuclear Dreams), *Sin ir más lejos: Ensayos y crónicas irreverentes* (Without Going Farther: Essays and Irreverent Chronicles), and *De elefantes, literatura y miedo: Ensayos sobre la comunicación americana* (Of Elephants, Literature, and Fear: Essays on American Communication). Dorfman also publishes a children's book, *La rebelión de los conejos mágicos* (*The Rebellion of the Magical Rabbits*).

1988 Dorfman publishes his fourth novel, *Máscaras* (*Mascara*). He flies to Chile to vote in the plebiscite and joins 55 percent of the Chilean public who vote against Pinochet continuing in power.

1989–96 Dorfman is promoted to research professor at Duke University.

1989 Patricio Aylwin is elected president of Chile in the first presidential elections since 1970.

1990 Patricio Aylwin establishes the Rettig Commission, which will investigate cases of disappearance and death during the Pinochet dictatorship. Dorfman's play *La muerte y la doncella* (*Death and the Maiden*) has a reading in London and opens in London and Santiago in 1991 and on Broadway in 1992.

1991 Dorfman publishes a collection of literary criticism in English entitled *Some Write to the Future*. Many of the essays were originally written in Spanish.

November 1991 The Chilean Navy sends one of its ships, the *Lautaro*, to Antarctica to hack an iceberg and then bring it to Seville, Spain, where it is reassembled and displayed for six months to visitors of the Chilean Pavilion in the World's Fair of 1992. This event plays a central role in Dorfman's novel *La nana y el iceberg* (*The Nanny and the Iceberg*).

1994 Dorfman is on the set during the filming of *Death and the Maiden* in France. While traveling between Paris and Durham, North Carolina, he writes and publishes his first post-exile novel, *Konfidenz*.

1995 Dorfman works with his son Rodrigo on the screenplay for *Prisoners in Time*.

1996 Dorfman becomes the Walter Hines Page Distinguished Professor of Literature and Latin American Studies at Duke University.

1998 Dorfman publishes his memoir, *Heading South, Looking North*, in both English and Spanish.

March 10, 1998 General Pinochet "steps down" as head of the Chilean military and becomes senator-for-life.

October 16, 1998 General Pinochet is arrested in London and awaits extradition to Spain on charges of torture and genocide.

1999 Dorfman publishes two novels, *Terapia* (*Blake's Therapy*) and *La nana y el iceberg* (*The Nanny and the Iceberg*).

September 19, 2000 Premiere of *Voices from Beyond the Dark: The Speak Truth to Power Play* (later titled *Manifesto for Another World: Voices from beyond the Dark*), Dorfman's play based on *Speak Truth to Power*, by Kerry Kennedy Cuomo.

March 3, 2000 Pinochet returns to Chile after avoiding prosecution by Spanish authorities. Shortly thereafter legal proceedings attempting to try him for crimes in Chile begin in Chilean courts.

May 2000 Chilean courts strip Pinochet of his immunity from prosecution for crimes committed during his dictatorship.

July 2001 Pinochet is ruled unfit by Chilean courts to stand trial.

September 11, 2001 Terrorists attack the United States and cause Dorfman to reflect on the connections and divergences between this event and September 11, 1973, in Chile.

2002 Dorfman's account of the Pinochet trial, *Exorcising Terror*, is published.

2003 Dorfman co-authors a novel with his son Joaquín, *The Burning City*.

February 5, 2003 Standing in front of a shrouded replica of Picasso's *Guernica* Colin Powell announces at UN headquarters that the United States will go to war in Iraq. This event inspires Dorfman to write the poem "Pablo Picasso Has Words for Colin Powell from the Other Side of Death."

March 19, 2003 The United States and Britain attack Iraq. Dorfman writes numerous editorials, poems, and essays protesting the war.

2004 Dorfman publishes a travel memoir about the North of Chile, *Desert Memories*; re-releases his play *Voices from the Dark* in a volume with an introduction and epilogue entitled *Manifesto for Another World*; and publishes a book of essays, *Other Septembers, Many Americas*.

January 14, 2005 *Manifesto for Another World: Voices from beyond the Dark* is performed at the Ebenezer Baptist Church in Atlanta to celebrate Martin Luther King's birthday and the fortieth anniversary of his acceptance of the Nobel Peace Prize, with performances by Martin Sheen, Sean Penn, and Woody Harrelson.

October 29, 2005 Dorfman's play "Purgatorio" has its U.S. premiere at the Seattle Repertory Theater.

November 2005 Dorfman casts his first vote as a U.S. citizen. The event is filmed as part of the PBS program *POV: Borders*.

December 6, 2005 Dorfman's play "The Other Side" has its U.S. premiere at the Manhattan Theater Club.

June 21, 2006 Dorfman's play "Picasso's Closet" has its U.S. premiere at Washington, D.C.'s Theater J.

2006 Dorfman's short story "Gringos" is selected for the O. Henry Prize Stories 2007. The prize is given to the twenty best short stories published in English in North America each year. Dorfman's story about a South American couple's unpleasant encounter with a man on a back street of Barcelona first appeared in 2006 in the inaugural issue of the journal *Subtropics*, published by the University of Florida English Department and edited by David Leavitt, who submitted the story.

Late 2006 Dorfman is in Chile with Peter Raymont, filming a documentary based on his life and his memoir: *A Promise to the Dead: The Exile Journey of Ariel Dorfman*.

December 10, 2006 Augusto Pinochet dies of heart failure. Dorfman is present in front of the hospital where Pinochet dies. He uses the occasion to try to reach out to a Pinochet supporter.

December 11, 2006 Pinochet receives a military funeral but not a state funeral.

2007 *A Promise to the Dead* is named one of the best Canadian films of the year. It is placed on the short list of fifteen films under consideration for an Academy Award nomination but does not make it into the final five.

May 15, 2008 The North American Congress on Latin America (NACLA) awards Dorfman the Latin America Peace and Justice Award.

APPENDIX 2. AN ARIEL DORFMAN BIBLIOGRAPHY

This bibliography is broken down into the following categories: novels; memoir, travel memoir, and testimonial essay; drama; unpublished plays; poetry; short stories; children's stories; excerpts; libretti; miscellaneous; books of essays; audio recordings; film and video; essays; contributions by Ariel Dorfman to other volumes; periodical publications in English and in Spanish; and secondary sources on Ariel Dorfman's work (published sources, dissertations and theses, and interviews). All entries are listed by date, with most recent first, except in the last section of secondary sources, where the entries are alphabetized. In cases where complete bibliographic references were unavailable, the text is still listed.

NOVELS

Americanos. Bueno Aires: Seix Barral, 2009. (Unpublished manuscript, "Americanos," cited in text.)

(and Joaquín Dorfman). *The Burning City*. New York: Random House, 2003; London: Doubleday, 2003.

Blake's Therapy. New York: Seven Stories Press, 2001, 2002; Waterville, Maine: Thorndike Press, 2001, 2002.

Terapia. Barcelona: Seix Barral, 2001.

Terapia. Trans. Anna Olga de Barros Barreto. Rio de Janeiro: Objetiva, 1999.

La nana y el iceberg. Mexico City: Seix Barral Biblioteca Breve, 1999; Barcelona: Editorial Seix Barral, 2000; Buenos Aires: Seix Barral, 2000.

The Nanny and the Iceberg. London: Sceptre, 1999; New York: Farrar, Straus, and Giroux, 1999; New York: Seven Stories Press, 2003.

Konfidenz (English). New York: Farrar, Straus, and Giroux, 1995; New York: Vintage International, 1995, 1996; Normal, Ill.: Dalkey Archive, 2003.

Konfidenz. Buenos Aires: Planeta, 1994; Mexico City: Editorial Planeta Mexicana, 1994; Santiago: Editorial Planeta, 1994; London: Sceptre, 1995; Madrid: Alfaguara, 1995, 1997.

Hard Rain. Trans. George Shivers. Los Angeles: Reader's International, 1990. English version of *Moros en la costa*, 1973.

Máscaras. Buenos Aires: Sudamericana, 1988; Mexico City: Seix Barral, 1997.

Mascara. New York: Penguin Books, 1988, 1989; New York: Seven Stories Press, 2004.

The Last Song of Manuel Sendero. Trans. George Shivers and Ariel Dorfman. New York: Viking Penguin, 1987, 1988.

La última canción de Manuel Sendero. México City: Siglo XXI, 1982; Santiago: Planeta, 1990.

Widows. Trans. Stephen Kessler. New York: Pantheon Books, 1981; London: Abacus, 1983; London: Pluto, 1983; New York: Vintage Books, 1983, 1984; New York: Penguin Books, 1989; New York: Viking, 1988; New York: Seven Stories Press, 2002.

Viudas. Mexico City: Siglo XXI, 1981, 1985, 1987; Santiago: Melquíades, 1988; Madrid: Alfaguara/Santillana, 1998; Buenos Aires: Seix Barral, 2000.

Moros en la costa. Buenos Aires: Editorial Sudamericana, 1973.

MEMOIR, TRAVEL MEMOIR, TESTIMONIAL ESSAY

Memorias del desierto. Barcelona: Ediciones RBA, 2004.

Desert Memories: Journeys through the Chilean North. Washington, D.C.: National Geographic, 2004.

Exorcising Terror: The Incredible Unending Trial of General Augusto Pinochet. New York: Seven Stories Press, 2002; London: Pluto, 2003.

Más allá del miedo: El largo adiós a Pinochet. Madrid: Siglo XXI, 2002; Santiago: Editorial Planeta, 2003.

Heading South, Looking North: A Bilingual Journey. London: Sceptre, 1998; London: Hodder and Stoughton, 1998; New York: Farrar Straus, and Giroux, 1998; New York: Penguin Books, 1999.

Rumbo al sur deseando el norte: Un romance en dos lenguas. Buenos Aires: Planeta, 1998; New York: Siete Cuentos Editorial, 2001. *Rumbo al sur deseando el norte: Un romance bilingüe.* Barcelona: Planeta 1998; Madrid: Planeta, 2003.

DRAMA

"The Prey." *Storie* 52–53 (2004): 12–47. Act 1 of "Picasso's Closet."

Manifesto for Another World: Voices from beyond the Dark. New York: Seven Stories Press, 2003, 2004. Reprint of *Speak Truth to Power: Voices from beyond the Dark* with a long introduction.

Purgatorio. London: Nick Hern, 2006.

Speak Truth to Power: Voices from beyond the Dark. Based on *Speak Truth to Power,* by Kerry Kennedy Cuomo. London: Index on Censorship, 2000, 2001. Reprinted with introduction by author, New York: Umbrage, 2000.

The Resistance Trilogy: Widows; Death and the Maiden; Reader. London: Nick Hern, 1998.

(and Tony Kushner) *Widows.* London: Nick Hern, 1997.

(with Tony Kushner). *Teatro 2: Lector, Viudas.* Buenos Aires: Ediciones de la Flor, 1996.

Reader. London: Nick Hern, 1995, 1998.

Teatro 1: La muerte y la doncella. Buenos Aires: Ediciones de la Flor, 1992, 2000, 2002; Mexico City: Seix Barral, 1995; Madrid: Ollero y Ramos, 1995; Santiago: LOM Ediciones, 1997; New York: Siete Cuentos Editorial, 2001.

Death and the Maiden. New York: Penguin Books, 1991, 1992, 1994; London: Nick Hern, 1991, 1992, 1994, 1995, 1996.

"Lector." *Conjunto* 83 (April–June 1990): 55–90.

UNPUBLISHED PLAYS

"In the Dark." Commissioned by the Royal Shakespeare Company.

"Dancing with Shadows." Text by Ariel Dorman; music and lyrics by Eric Woolfson. (Inspired by the Korean play *Forest Fire,* by Bum Suk Cha.)

(with Rodrigo Dorfman). "Who's Who."

(with Rodrigo Dorfman). "Mascara."

——. *The Other Side*. London: Nick Hern Books, 2006. (Unclear if ever released.) "Picasso's Closet."

POETRY

"William Blake tiene palabras desde más allá de la muerte para Laura Bush, amante de la literatura." *Página 12*, July 18, 2004; *El País*, July 31, 2004. http://www.pagina12web.com.ar/diario/contratapa/13-38316.html. Accessed August 2, 2004.

"William Blake Has Words from the Other Side of Death for Laura Bush, Lover of Literature." *San Francisco Chronicle*, July 25, 2004, E3. http://www.sfgate.com/cgi-in/article.cgi?file=/c/a/2004/07/25/ING947QF1P1.DTL. Accessed August 2, 2004.

"Hammurabi, the Exalted Prince Who Made Great the Name of Babylon, Has Words for Donald Rumsfeld from the Other Side of Death." *Tom Dispatch*, May 7, 2003. http://www.tomdispatch.com/index.mhtml?pid=650. Accessed August 2, 2004.

"Cristóbal Colón tiene palabras desde el otro lado de la muerte para el capitán John Whyte, que cambió el nombre del aeropuerto internacional Saddam cuando sus tropas se apoderaron de él." *Página 12*, April 13, 2003. http://www.pagina12web.com.ar/diario/elmundo/4-18775-2003-04-13.html. Accessed June 11, 2004.

"Christopher Columbus Has Words from the Other Side of Death for Captain John Whyte." *openDemocracy*, April 11, 2003. http://www.opendemocracy.net/debates/article-2-95-1148.jsp. Accessed July 20, 2004.

"Pablo Picasso tiene palabras para Colin Powell desde el otro lado de la muerte." *Página 12*, March 16, 2003. http://www.pagina12web.com.ar/diario/elmundo/4-17661-2003-03-16.html. Accessed June 28, 2004.

"Pablo Picasso Has Words for Colin Powell from the Other Side of Death." *openDemocracy*, February 25, 2003. http://www.opendemocracy.net/themes/article.jsp?id=1&articleId=1002. Accessed July 20, 2004.

"Esperanza," "Hope." In *Los poetas y el general: Voces de oposición en Chile bajo Augusto Pinochet 1973–1989*, 173–77. Ed. Eva Goldschmidt Wyman. Santiago: LOM Ediciones, 2002.

"Identidad," "Identity." In *Los poetas y el general: Voces de oposición en Chile bajo Augusto Pinochet 1973–1989*, 293–96. Ed. Eva Goldschmidt Wyman. Santiago: LOM Ediciones, 2002.

In Case of Fire in a Foreign Land. Trans. Ariel Dorfman and Edith Grossman. Durham: Duke University Press, 2002.

"Ten Minutes." In *Pomeriggio/Afternoon*, 102–4. Ed. Gianluca Bassi. Rome: Leconte, 2001.

Último vals en Santiago. Barcelona: Germania Serveis, 2000.

"Hope." In *Captured Voices: An Anthology of Prose and Poems*, 53. Ed. Janna Letts and Fiona Whytehead. London: Victor Gollancz, 1999.

"Simultaneous Translation." *Civilization* 6, no. 3 (1999): 79.

"La guardia interior tampoco se rinde." In *El gran libro de América Judía*, 392–93. San Juan: Editorial de la Universidad de Puerto Rico, 1998.

"Nothing Nada." In *El gran libro de América Judía*, 1000–1003. San Juan: Editorial de la Universidad de Puerto Rico, 1998.

"Nupcias." In *El gran libro de América Judía*, 543–44. San Juan: Editorial de la Universidad de Puerto Rico, 1998.

"Pies." In *El gran libro de América Judía*, 303–4. San Juan: Editorial de la Universidad de Puerto Rico, 1998.

"Sol de piedra." In *El gran libro de América Judía*, 479. San Juan: Editorial de la Universidad de Puerto Rico, 1998.

"Vocabulario." In *El gran libro de América Judía*, 628–31. San Juan: Editorial de la Universidad de Puerto Rico, 1998.

"Last Will and Testament." *Jewish Quarterly* 39, no. 145 (1992): 13.

"Something Must Be Happening to My Antennas." In *Hauling Up Morning: Poetry and Images of Latin America*. Ed. Martin Steingesser. New York: War Resisters League/New Society, 1990. (Calendar).

Last Waltz in Santiago and Other Poems of Exile and Disappearance. Trans. Edith Grossman. New York: Viking, 1988; New York: Penguin, 1988.

"First We Set Up the Chairs." *Harper's Magazine*, February 1988, 33.

Pastel de choclo. Santiago: Editorial Sinfronteras, 1986.

"Identidad." In *Campo abierto: Lecturas sociopolíticas de Hispanoamérica*, 96–100. Ed. Mary Jane Treacy and Nancy Abraham Hall. Boston: Houghton Mifflin, 1984.

Missing. London: Amnesty International British Section, 1981.

Pruebas al canto. Mexico City: Nueva Imagen, 1979, 1980.

"Que busca en el monte amparo." *Revista Casa de las Américas* 20, no. 116 (1979): 117.

"Abecedario." *Revista Casa de las Américas* 19, no. 111 (1978): 108–11.

(and Jorge Teillier). "Dos poetas chilenos: Ariel Dorfman ("Sol de piedra," "Testamento") y Jorge Teillier ("Algeria," "La ultima isla"). *Plural* 6, no. 78 (1978): 16–17.

Poems ("Vocabulario," "Sí sí sí," "El día está azulísimo en Amsterdam"). *Hispamérica* 7, no. 19 (1978): 61–65.

"Sol de piedra," "Esperanza", "Dos mas dos," "No hay lugar." *Revista Casa de las Américas* 18, no. 106 (1978): 128–31.

"Sol de piedra," "Testamento." *Plural: Revista Cultural de Excelsior* 6 (1978): 16.

SHORT STORIES

"Gringos." *Subtropics* 1 (winter/spring 2006): 119–27.

"Travesía." In *Cuentos en Dictadura*, 51–64. Ed. E. Ramón Díaz and V. Diego Muñoz. Santiago: LOM Ediciones, 2003.

Acércate más y más: Cuentos casi completos. Madrid: Siglo XXI, 2002.

"A Candle for Kerala." *Moment* 26, no. 6 (2001): 44.

"A la escondida." In *Escribiendo el Sur Profundo*, 153–64. Santiago: Empresas El Mercurio, 1989.

"Dorando la píldora." In *Cuento chileno contemporáneo: Breve antología*, 67–77. Ed. Poli Délano. Mexico City: UNAM, 1996.

Rojos Copihuex. Santiago: Pluma y Pincel, 1993.

"Warning." In *Columbus Egg: New Latin American Stories on the Conquest*, 107–19. Ed. Nick Caistor. London and New York: Serpent's Tail, 1992.

"Warning Signals." *Queen's Quarterly: A Canadian Review* 99, no. 1 (1992): 134–45.

"Warning Signals." *Mother Jones* 17, no. 1 (1992): 62–66.

Cuentos casi completos. Buenos Aires: Ediciones Letra Buena, 1991.

"A Matter of Time." Trans. George Shivers. *Rethinking Marxism* 3, no. 1 (spring 1990): 8–13.

My House Is on Fire. Trans. George Shivers and Ariel Dorfman. London: Methuen, 1990, 1992; New York: Viking Penguin, 1990, 1991; London: Abacus, 1990, 1993.

"Trademark Territory." *Index on Censorship* 17, no. 5 (1988): 122–24; *Mississipi Review 52* 18, no. 1 (1989): 92–100.

"Travesía." In *Cuentos Chilenos*, 201–18. Berlin: Editorial Kinkulén/Comité Chile Antifascista Berlin RDA, 1988.

"Trademark Territory." Trans. George Shivers with Ariel Dorfman. In *An Embarrassment of Tyrannies: 25 Years of Index on Censorship, 1972–1997*, 139–46. Eds. W. L. Webb and Rose Bell. London: Victor Gollancz, 1987.

Travesía: Cuentos. Montevideo: Ediciones de la Banda Oriental, 1986.

Cuentos para militares: La batalla de los colores y otros cuentos. Santiago: Emisión, 1986.

Dorando la píldora. Santiago: Ediciones del Ornitorrinco, 1985.

"Reader." *Ethos* 1, no. 3 (1984): 51–61.

"To Miss, Be Missing, Be Missed." *This Magazine* 16, no. 3 (1982): 20–21.

"With the Family." *Review 27: Latin American Literature and Arts* 27 (1980): 16–24.

Cría ojos. Mexico City: Editorial Nueva Imagen, 1979.

"Missing." *Index on Censorship* 8, no. 3 (1979): 12–16.

"En familia." *Suplemento* 4 (1978): 27–36.

"Y qué oficio le pondremos." *Revista Universidad de Mexico* 33, no. 1 (1978): 16–18.

"Chilex and Company: Nueva guía." *Cambio* 5 (October–December 1976): 10–14.

"Nothing Nada." *Crisis*, July 1976, 52–53.

CHILDREN'S STORIES

"The Rebellion of the Magical Rabbits." In *Animal Farm and Related Readings*, 115–27. George Orwell et al. Evanston, Ill.: McDougal Littell, 1997; London: Transworld/Doubleday/Random House, 2001.

"The Rebellion of the Magical Rabbits." In *Globe Fearon's World Literature*, 346–54. Ed. Nancy Davidson. Upper Saddle River, N.J.: Globe Fearon/Simon and Schuster, 1998. "The Rebellion of the Magical Rabbits." In *Global Issues: The Issues Collection*, 131–40. Ed. Bryan Shelly. Toronto: McGraw-Hill Ryerson, 1993.

"The Rebellion of the Magical Rabbits." In *Where Angels Glide at Dawn: New Stories from Latin America*, 7–25. Eds. Lori M. Carlson and Cynthia L. Ventura. New York: Harper Trophy/J. B. Lippincott, 1990.

La rebelión de los conejos mágicos. Buenos Aires: Ediciones de la Flor, 1986; Barcelona: Ediciones B, 1988; Madrid: Anaya, 2001.

EXCERPTS

"Reader." *Blood and Aphorisms* 24 (1996): 31–36.

"Konfidenz." *Fiction etc.* 5 (1995): 260–72.

"Death and the Maiden." *Index on Censorship* 20, no. 6 (1991): 5–20.

"Lector." *Nueva Sociedad* 100 (1989): 44–59.

"Reader." *Salmagundi* 82–83 (1989): 162–84.

"The X-Factor." *Blatant Artifice: An Anthology of Short Fiction by Visiting Writers, 1985–1987* 2–3 (1988): 147–51.

"Viudas: Capítulo de la novela." *Cuadernos Americanos* 238, no. 5 (September–October 1981): 223–34.

LIBRETTI

(and James McMillan, Ana Maria Mendoza et al.). *Cantos Sagrados: For SATB Chorus and Organ*. New York: Boosey and Hawkes, 1995.

(and others). *Sinfonía Testimonial: For Choir, Orchestra and Tape, 1987*. Comp. Tera de Marez Oyens. Amsterdam: Donemus, 1987.

MISCELLANEOUS

"Conjuros: The Bull in the Labyrinth of Spain and Chile" *Duke University Museum of Art* Durham, spring 2002.

Widows, Last Waltz in Santiago. Trans. Edith Grossman, Ariel Dorfman, and Stephen Kessler. London: Sceptre, 1997.

Donald, P. [pseudonym for Ariel Dorfman]. "Furioso cantabile." Fictitious book review of *The Last Song of Manuel Sendero*. *Hispamérica* 10 (1981): 19–23.

BOOKS OF ESSAYS

Other Septembers, Many Americas: Selected Provocations, 1980–2004. New York: Seven Stories Press, 2004.

Some Write to the Future: Essays on Contemporary Latin American Fiction. Trans. George Shivers. Durham: Duke University Press, 1991.

Los sueños nucleares de Reagan. Buenos Aires: Editorial Legasa, 1986.

Sin ir más lejos: Ensayos y crónicas irreverentes. Santiago: Pehuen-CENECA, 1986.

De elefantes, literatura y miedo: Ensayos sobre la comunicación americana. Havana: Casa de las Américas, 1986, 1988.

Patos, elefantes y héroes: La infancia como subdesarrollo. Buenos Aires: Ediciones de la Flor, 1985; Mexico City: Ariel, 1997; Madrid: Siglo XXI, 2002 (with additional essay).

Hacia la liberación del lector latinoamericano. Hanover, N.H.: Ediciones del Norte, 1984.

The Empire's Old Clothes: What the Lone Ranger, Babar, and Other Innocent Heroes Do to Our Minds. Trans. Clark Hansen. New York: Pantheon Books, 1983; London: Pluto, 1983; Reinbeck bei Hamburg: Rowohlt, 1988; New York: Penguin Books, 1996.

Reader's nuestro que estás en la tierra: Ensayos sobre el imperialismo cultural. Mexico City: Editorial Nueva Imagen, 1980, 1982.

La última aventura del Llanero Solitario. Buenos Aires: Editorial Galerna, 1974; San José, Costa Rica: EDUCA, 1979; Ciudad Universitaria Rodrigo Facio, Costa Rica: Editorial Universitaria Centroamericana, 1982.

Culture as Democratic Resistance in Chile Today. Geneva: IDAC, 1977.

Sobre las artes del espectáculo y fiestas en América Latina. Havana: UNESCO, Oficina Regional de Cultura para América Latina y el Caribe, Centro de Documentación, 1976.

(and Armand Mattelart). *How to Read Donald Duck: Imperialist Ideology in the Disney Comic*. Trans. David Kunzle. New York: International General, 1975, 1984, 1991.

(and Manuel Jofré) *Superman y sus amigos del alma*. Buenos Aires: Editorial Galerna, 1974.

Ensayos quemados en Chile: Inocencia y neocolonialismo. Buenos Aires: Ediciones de la Flor, 1974.

(and Armand Mattelart). *Para leer al Pato Donald: Comunicación de masa y colonialismo*. Valparaíso: Ediciones Universitarias de Valparaíso, 1971; Buenos Aires: Siglo XXI Argentina Editores, 1973; Havana: Editorial de Ciencias Sociales, 1974; Mexico City: Siglo XXI, 1979, 1987, 1998, 1990.

Imaginación y violencia en América. Santiago: Editorial Universitaria, 1970; *Imaginación y violencia en América: Ensayos sobre Borges*. Barcelona: Anagrama, 1972, 1974.

El absurdo entre cuatro paredes: El teatro de Harold Pinter. Santiago: Editorial Universitaria, 1968.

AUDIO RECORDINGS

(and others). *Chile: Promise of Freedom*. AK Press; Freedom Archives, 2003.

"Testamento." *Donde estás*. Patricio Rivera. 2002.

"Identity" and "Sun Stone." *Coro Allegro: Sacred Songs*. Dir. David Hodgkins. 2002.

"A Candle for Kerala." *NPR's Chanukah Lights*. Susan Stamberg and Murray Horwitz. NPR, 2001.

"Bringing General Pinochet to Justice." *¡Justicia!* By Bay Area Veterans of the Abraham Lincoln Brigade. Alba, 1999.

"Hope." In *Voices: An Evening of Words and Music*. London: John Waite Publishers, 1997.

"Last Waltz in Santiago." In *Pieces by Stephen Davismoon*. 1997.

Death and the Maiden. Dir. Robert Robinson. L.A. Theatre Works, 1999.

Cantos sagrados. Comp. James McMillan. Catalyst/BMG, 1995.

"The Politics of South American Fiction." In *Houses on Fire: Chaos and Culture*. National Humanities Center, 1990.

Challenges from the Land of the Missing. Ithaca, N.Y.: Cornell University, 1989.

(and others). *Sinfonía testimonial; Charon's gift; Litany of the victims of war*. Comp. Tera de Marez Oyens. Composers' Voice, 1988.

The Unborn Make History, Literature, and Social Change. Ames, Iowa: Institute on World Affairs, Iowa State University, 1987.

Chilean Writer Ariel Dorfman Reading from His Poetry and Prose. Washington, D.C.: Archive of Hispanic Literature on Tape, 1978.

FILM AND VIDEO

Screenplays and Directing

An Evening with Ariel Dorfman. Dir. Ariel Dorfman. Corcoran Gallery of Art and Theater J, 2002.

Speak Truth to Power. Dir. Marc Levin. PBS Home Video, 2000.

(and Rodrigo Dorfman). *Deadline*. London: ITV, 1998.

My House Is on Fire. Dir. Ariel Dorfman and Rodrigo Dorfman. First Run/Icarus/Calama Films, 1997.

Prisoners in Time. Dir. Stephen Walker. London: BBC, 1995.

(and Rafael Yglesias). *Death and the Maiden*. Dir. Roman Polanski. Warner Bros., 1992.

(and Pablo Fernández). *Behind the Two Poets There Is a White House*. Washington, D.C.: Video del Sur, 1983.

Film Appearances

A Promise to the Dead: The Exile Journey of Ariel Dorfman. Dir. Peter Raymont. White Pine Pictures, 2007.

American ID: Choice. Multimedia Web site with videos written, produced, and directed by Rodrigo Dorfman. Web site text by Ariel Dorfman. For PBS, 2006. http://www.pbs.org/pov/borders/2006/choice.html.

In the Footsteps of September 11, 1973. Multimedia Web site created by Rodrigo Dorfman with photography by Luis Navarro. September 2005. (Follows Dorfman's return to Santiago, Chile, to trace his footsteps thirty-two years after the coup.)

An Evening with Ariel Dorfman. Corcoran Gallery of Art. Taped October 7, 2002.

Human Wrongs. Dir. Michael Chanan, 2001. (Dorfman visits Washington, D.C. in September 2000 for a series of events on human rights, including the presentation of his play *Speak Truth to Power*.)

Can the Margins Take Over the Center? A Journey from Santiago to Broadway to Hollywood. Sherman, Tex.: Austin College, 1990. (Lecture by Dorfman delivered on October 5, 2000. An introduction by Dr. Johanna Bartow is included.)

Interview. *Harto the Borges*. Eduardo Montes-Bradley and Soledad Liendo. Princeton, N.J.: Films for the Humanities and Sciences, 2000. (Dorfman and other writers are interviewed on Borges.)

(and Imamu Amiri Baraka). *Amiri Baraka*. Princeton, N.J.: Films for the Humanities and Sciences, 1995. (Ariel Dorfman interviews twentieth-century American writer Amiri Baraka about his writing and politics. Part of a series for Literati/CBC.)

Interventions in the Field of Dreams. Dir. Jon Beller. New York: Paper Tiger Television, 1990. (Dorfman critiques the baseball motion picture *Field of Dreams*.)

"Los demás compañeros de la celda están dormidos." In *VHS-20 años, 20 poemas, 20 artistas: Video homenaje a las Madres de la Plaza de Mayo*. Buenos Aires: *Página 12*/Asociación Madres de la Plaza de Mayo, 1987. (Video homage to the Mothers of the May Plaza.)

ESSAYS

Many of these essays have later been included in books, have been translated into other languages, and/or have become parts of anthologies.

(and David Ball, Sophia A. McClennen, Gordon O. Taylor). "Forum: Poetry and Torture." *World Literature Today* 81, nos. 1–2 (May–August 2005): 6–7.

"Fear and the Word." *Autodafe: The Journal of the International Parliament of Writers* 3–4 (2003): 219–23.

"El miedo y la palabra." *Autodafe: The Journal of the International Parliament of Writers* 3–4 (2003): 303–8.

"What We Think of America." *Granta* 77 (spring 2002): 29–32.

"The Nomads of Language." *American Scholar* 71, no. 1 (2002): 89–94.

(and others). "On Translation." *PEN-America: A-Journal-for-Writers-and-Readers* (*PENA*) 1, no. 2 (2001): 208–16.

"Touched by Terror: America through Humanity's Mirror." *New Internationalist*, no. 340 (2001): 28.

"The Defenders: Voices from Beyond the Dark." *El Andar* 11, no. 4 (2001): 10–11.

"Voci divise: La doppia vita della paura." *Problemi dell'informazione* 26, nos. 2–3 (2001): 273–79.

"Salvador Allende." In *Revolution: Faces of Change*, 110–15. Ed. John Miller and Aaron Kenedi. New York: Thunder Mouth Press, 2000.

"Afterword from *Death and the Maiden*." *Southwest Review* 85, no. 3 (2000): 350–54.

"Cómo se gesta un 'manual de descolonización': Disney desde una perspectiva tercermundista." *Educación y Biblioteca* 11, no. 10 (1999): 66–70.

"Dulces círculos." Trans. Esther Pérez. *Revolución y Cultura* 41, no. 6 (1999): 48–49.

"La feroz lealtad de Antonio." *Revista de Crítica Literaria Latinoamericana* (1999): 271–73.

"A la espera." *Sekai* 8 (1999): 160–65.

"No Longer Hostage." *Creation and Criticism* 103 (1999): 254–61.

"Pinochet's Mirror." *Mediations: (Dis)locations of Culture and Chile after Pinochet* 22 (spring 1999): 112–25.

"Postfacio a *La muerte y la doncella*." *Periplo: Revista Hispanoamericana de Literatura* 7 (1999): 3–7.

"Süsse Kreise: Von Franco Zu Pinochet." *Lettre Internationale* 45 (1999): 94–95.

"Sweet Circles." *The Volunteer: Journal of the Veterans of the Abraham Lincoln Brigade* 21, no. 3 (1999): 12–15.

"Writing the Deep South." *Unisa Latin American Report* 15, no. 1 (1999): 4–7.

"Celebrando una vida y llorando una muerte." *Patrimonio Cultural* 3, no. 12 (1998): 3–4.

"Los duendes." *Realidad Económica* 155 (April–May 1998): 88–91.

(and others). "Melange: An Unevolved Paradise; Playing the Part of Farce; Looking beyond Looks; Language as an Instrument of Intolerance; The Best of Students and the Worst." *Chronicle of Higher Education* 43, no. 43 (1997): B7.

"September, 1973." *Granta* 60 (winter 1997): 65–95. Online *Granta* 60: 36 pars. 2004. http://www.granta.com/extracts/717. Accessed June 12, 2004.

"Language of Survival." *Index on Censorship* 26, no. 3 (1997): 20–24.

"La ballena en el desierto." *Textos: Revista semestral de creación y crítica* 2, no. 2 (1991): 49–50.

"Comments (on the panel 'Liberty and Justice for All: Human Rights and Democratization in Latin America')." SALALM *Papers* 36 (1991): 209–12.

"Some Write to the Future: Meditations on Hope and Violence in García Márquez." *Transition: An-International-Review* 52 (1991): 18–34.

"Advertencia." *Revista Casa de las Américas* 29, no. 174 (May–June 1989): 69–77.

"Messages from Afar." *Monthly Review*, fortieth anniversary issue (1989): 13.

"Shouts above the Silence." *American Theatre* 5, no. 9 (December 1988): 22–29.

"Máscara." *Hispamérica* 17, no. 49 (April 1988): 85–99.

"Into Another Jungle: The Final Journey of the Matacos?" *Grassroots Development* 12, no. 2 (1988): 2–15.

"Las caras pintadas de la muerte." *Crisis* 44 (1986): 8–9.

"Estamos aquí para quedarnos." *Culturas: Identidad cultural en América Latina.* UNESCO special issue (1986): 109–11.

"Otro golpe de orejas." *Revista Casa de las Américas* 26, nos. 155–56 (March–June 1986): 104–5.

"El fuego purificador de Augusto Pinochet." *Araucaria de Chile* 35 (1986): 15–20.

"Into Another Sort of Jungle: The Last Voyage of the Matacos." *Massachusetts Review* 27, nos. 3–4 (1986): 673–92.

"Little Reagan Is Watching Us: A View on *Nineteen Eighty-Four* from the Third World." *1984, Vision and Reality, Papers in Comparative Studies* 4 (1985): 167–76.

"Bread and Burnt Rice: Culture and Economic Survival in Latin America." *Grassroots Development* 8, no. 2 (1984): 2–25.

"Notes from Chile." *Granta* 11 (1984): 232–43.

"Isla negra." *Oasis: Semiotext(e)* 4, no. 3 (1984): 57–58.

"Duas crônicas norte-americanas." *Novos Estudos* CEBRAP 1, no. 3 (1982): 68–70.

"How to Read the Comics." *Granta* 6 (1983): 241–60.

"Entre Proust y la momia americana: Siete notas y un epílogo sobre *El Recurso del Método.*" *Revista de Literatura Iberoamericana* 47, nos. 114–15 (1981): 95–128.

"El cartero del exilio." *Revista Universidad de México* 35, nos. 2–3 (October–November 1980): 85.

"Edipo entre los árboles." *Revista Universidad de México* 34, no. 11 (July 1980): 16–21.

"With the Family." Trans. Marcelo Montecino and Paz Cohen. *Review* 27 (1980): 16–24.

"El estado chileno actual y los intelectuales: Acercamiento preliminar a algunos problemas impostergables." *Araucaria de Chile* 10 (1980): 35–50.

"Puentes y padres en el infierno: Los ríos profundos de José Maria Arguedas." *Revista de Crítica Literaria Latinoamericana* 6, no. 12 (1980): 91–137.

"Versos de amor para Santiago." *Cuadernos de Marcha* 2, no. 7 (1980): 90–94.

"Frage der Zeit." Trans. Ursula Roth. *Neue Deutsche Literatur* 27, no. 12 (1979): 119–25.

"Tiempo de amor, tiempo de lucha: Los epigramas de Ernesto Cardenal." *Texto Crítico* 5, no. 13 (1979): 3–44.

"Problemas para la liberación del lector en América Latina." *Revista de la* UNAM 33, no. 11 (1979): 10–13.

"Pequeñas alamedas: La lucha de la cultura chilena actual." *Revista Casa de las Américas* 20, no. 115 (1979): 60–75.

"Condizionamenti politici sui 'mass-media': Il caso del fumetto 'Mapato.' " Trad. Gabriella Lapasini. *Política Internazionale*, 1979, 63–78.

"In the Concentration Camps of Chile." *Canadian Theatre Review* 22 (1979): 48–66.

"Chile: Kultura przeciw imperializmowi." *Literatura na Swiecie* 9 (1978): 306–19.

"Innocence and Neo-Colonialism: A Case of Ideological Domination in Children's Literature." *Black Phoenix: Third World Perspective on Contemporary Art and Culture* 2 (1978): 4–11.

"The Invisible Chile: Three Years of Cultural Resistance." *Praxis 4: A Journal of Radical Perspectives on the Arts* 2, no. 4 (1978): 191–97.

"Jaguares y helicópteros: La literatura como disfraz." *Diálogos* 14, no. 84 (1978): 19–22.

"Jorge Edwards: Máscara non grata." *Plural* 6, no. 76 (1978): 76–80; *Crítica, Arte, Literatura* 76 (1978): 76–80.

"Niveles de la dominación cultural en América Latina: Algunos problemas, criterios y perspectivas." *Ideologies and Literature* 2, no. 6 (1978): 54–89.

"Om jaguarer och helikoptrar: Litteraturen förklädd i Latinamerika." Trans. Sven Ahman. *Litteraturens Förklädnader: Internationella* PEN 43 (1978): 61–69.

"¿Podemos establecer relaciones entre los escritores eurocéntricos y los latino-americanos?" *Nueva Sociedad* 35 (1978): 16–28.

"Teatro en los campos de concentración chilenos: Conversación con Oscar Castro del *Aleph*." *Conjunto* 37 (1978): 3–34.

"Niveles de la dominación cultural en América latina: Algunos problemas, criterios y perspectivas." *Iberoamericana* 7, no. 1 (1977): 29–79.

"Literatura chilena y clandestinidad." *Escritura: Teoría y Crítica Literarias* 2, no. 4 (1977): 307–14.

"Profeta en su tierra: Un poema/clandestino desde Chile." *Revista de Crítica Literaria Latinoamericana* 6 (1977): 111–36.

"Changing PEN, *Changing the World? The Case of a Generation of Young Latin American Writers*." *BZZZletin* (1976): 28–34.

"Chile: Tres años de resistencia cultural." *Plural: Crítica, Arte, Literatura* 63 (1976): 7–11.

"Chile: La resistencia cultural al imperialismo." *Revista Casa de las Américas* 17, no. 98 (1976): 3–11.

"Salvation and Wisdom of the Common Man: The Theology of *The Reader's Digest*." *Praxis 3: A Journal of Radical Perspectives on the Arts* 1, no. 3 (1976): 41–56.

"Men of Corn: Myth as Time and Word." Trans. Paula Speck. *Review* 75, no. 15 (1975): 12–22.

"Correspondencia americana: Poeta, pueblo y naturaleza en un poema del *Canto General*." *Nuestra Sociedad* [Costa Rica] 18 (1975): 47–64.

"Todo el poder a dios-proletariado: Ernesto Cardenal." *Crisis*, 1974, 49–52.

"Salvación y sabiduría del hombre común: La teología de *Selecciones del Reader's Digest*." *Cuadernos de la Realidad Nacional*, 1972, 186–201. *Revista Casa de las Américas* 13, no. 77 (1973): 81–92; *Textual* 8 (1973): 44–55.

"Del buen salvaje al subdesarrollado: *Para leer al Pato Donald*." *Textual* 4 (1972): 2–11.

"Inocencia y neocolonialismo: Un caso de dominación ideológica en la literatura infantil." *Cuadernos de la Realidad Nacional* (1971): 223–53.

"El fugitivo." *Textual* 2 (1971): 53–56.

"Notas para una aproximación marxista a la novela chilena de los últimos treinta años." *Revista Casa de las Américas* 12, no. 69 (1971): 65–83.

"Mario Vargas Llosa y José Maria Arguedas: Dos visiones de una sola América." *Revista Casa de las Américas* 11, no. 64 (1971): 6–19.

"La actual narrativa chilena: Entre ángeles y animales." *Los libros* 15–16 (1971): 15–17, 20–21.

"¿Volar? Un estudio comparativo de Jorge Edwards y Antonio Skármeta." *Revista Chilena de Literatura* (1970): 59–78.

"El Patas de Perro no es tranquilidad para mañana." *Revista Chilena de Literatura* 2, no. 3 (1970): 167–97.

"*Hombres de maíz*: El mito como tiempo y palabra." *Atenea: Revista de Ciencia, Arte y Literatura de la Universidad de Concepción* 45, no. 167 (1968): 129–53.

"Borges y la violencia americana." *Amaru* 7 (1968): 44–51.

"Perspectivas y limitaciones de la novela chilena actual." *Anales de la Universidad de Chile* 140 (1966): 110–67.

"En torno a Pedro Páramo." *Mapocho* 15 (1966): 289–95.

"La última obra de Truman Capote, ¿un nuevo género literario?" *Anales de la Universidad de Chile* 124 (1966): 94–117.

"El 'Lycidas' de Milton, ¿poema barroco o manierista?" *Anales de la Universidad de Chile* 123 (1965): 194–210.

CONTRIBUTIONS BY ARIEL DORFMAN TO OTHER VOLUMES

"Where the Buried Flame Burns." Afterword to *Poems from Guantánamo: The Detainees Speak*, 69–72. Ed. Marc Falcoff. Iowa City: University of Iowa Press, 2007.

"The Black Hole." In *The Impossible Will Take a Little While: A Citizen's Guide to Hope in A Time of Fear*, 241–50. Ed. Paul Rogat Loeb. New York: Basic Books, 2004.

"The Tyranny of Terror: Is Torture Inevitable in Our Century and Beyond?" Foreword to *Torture: A Collection*, 3–18. Ed. Sanford Levinson. Oxford: Oxford University Press, 2004.

Foreword. In *My Neighbor, My Enemy: Justice and Community in the Aftermath of Ethnic Cleansing*, xiii–xv. Ed. Eric Stover and Harvey M. Weinstein. New York: Cambridge University Press, 2004.

"Footnotes to a Double Life." In *The Genius of Language: Fifteen Writers Reflect on Their Mother Tongues*, 206–17. Ed. Wendy Lesser. New York: Pantheon, 2004.

"A Bilingual Journey." In *Unrooted Childhoods: Memoirs of Growing Up Global*, 277–84. Ed. Faith Eidse and Nina Sichel. London and Yarmouth, Maine: Nicholas Brealey Publishing/Intercultural Press, 2004.

"Fear and the Word." In *Autodafe3/4*, 219–24. New York: Seven Stories Press, 2003.

"Hope." In *Responding to Literature: Stories, Poems, Plays and Essays*, 981–82. Ed. Judith A. Stanford. New York: McGraw Hill, 2003.

"The Nanny and the Iceberg." In *Chile: A Traveler's Literary Companion*, 36–48. Ed. Katherine Silver. Berkeley: Whereabouts Press, 2003.

"Purgatorio." In *Cúirt Annual: Snapshot of the Cúirt International Festival of Literature*, 57–60. Galway, Ireland: Galway Arts Centre, 2003.

"The Wandering Bigamists of Language." In *Lives in Translation: Bilingual*

Writers on Identity and Creativity, 29–37. Ed. Isabelle de Courtivron. New York: Palgrave MacMillan, 2003.

"The Last September 11." In *Chile: The Other September 11*, 1–5. Ed. Pilar Aguilera and Ricardo Fredes. Melbourne: Ocean Press, 2003.

"El último once de septiembre." In *Chile: El otro 11 de septiembre*, 1–4. Ed. Pilar Aguilera and Ricardo Fredes. Melbourne: Ocean Press, 2003.

"Christopher Columbus Has Words from the Other Side of Death for Captain John Whyte, Who Rebaptized Saddam International Airport as His Troops Rolled into It." In *Africa and Its Significant Others: Forty Years of Intercultural Entanglement*, 77–81. Amsterdam: Rodopi, 2002.

"The Empire's New Games." In *Appeal to Reason: 25 Years of In These Times*, 329–30. Ed. Craig Aaron. New York: Seven Stories Press, 2002.

"L'esprit de paix au quotidien." In *Imaginer la paix/Académie Universelle des Cultures*, 157–61. Ed. Françoise Barret-Ducrocq. Paris: Editions Grasset et Fasquelle, 2002.

"Resisting Hybridity." In *Voice-overs: Translation and Latin American Literature*, 55–57. Ed. Daniel Balderston and Marcy E. Schwartz. New York: SUNY Press, 2002.

"Esperanza/Hope"; "Identidad/Identity." In *Los poetas y el general: Voces de oposición en Chile bajo Augusto Pinochet 1973–1989*, 173–77, 293–97. Ed. Eva Goldschmidt Wyman. Santiago: LOM Ediciones, 2002.

"I Have Been through This Before." In *Strike Terror No More: Theology, Ethics and the New War*, 18–20. Ed. Jon L. Berquist. St. Louis: Chalice Press, 2002.

"Fictionalizing the Truth in Latin America." In *Cinema Nation: The Best Writing on Film from The Nation, 1913–2000*, 242–49. Ed. Carl Bromley. New York: Thunder's Mouth/Nation, 2002.

"Les disparus et la photographie: Utilité et détournement de la mondialisation." In *Quelle mondialisation? Académie Universelle des Cultures*, 226–33. Paris: Editions Grasset et Fasquelle, 2001.

"Once Upon a Time." In *Light Among Shadows: A Celebration of Orlando Letelier, Ronni Karpen Moffitt, and Heroes of the Human Rights Movement*, 52–54. Ed. Scott Williams. Washington, D.C.: Institute for Policy Studies, 2001.

"El último once de septiembre." In *¿Apocalipsis Ahora?: Chile y el mundo tras el derrumbe de las Torres Gemelas*, 77–82. Ed. Carlos Orellana. Santiago: Editorial Planeta Chilena, 2001.

"El último once de septiembre." In *El mensaje del 11 de septiembre*, 38–43. Havana: Editorial de Ciencias Sociales, 2001.

"Celebration from America." In *Celebración de nuestra América: Rewriting America: Colonialismo y neocolonialismo*, 25–36. Chicago: DePaul University Press, 1999.

"L'intolérance et les dilemmes de l'identité: Une perspective bilingue." In *L'intol-*

érance/Académie Universelle des Cultures, 119–24. Paris: Editions Grasset et Fasquelle, 1998.

(and Arthur Miller). "Mi primer encuentro, mi perpetuo encuentro con Jacobo." In *Preso sin nombre, celda sin número*, 9–12. Ed. Jacobo Timerman. Buenos Aires: Ediciones de la Flor, 2000. Trans. Toby Talbot, New York: Knopf, 1981.

"Ariel Dorfman on Roman Polanski." In *Writers on Directors: An Artists' Choice Book*, 16–21. Ed. Susan Gray. New York: Watson-Guptill/BPI, 1999.

"The Birth Dodger." In *Letters to the Six Billionth World Citizen*, 7–26. Ed. Toef Jaeger and Joke van Kampen. Amsterdam: Podium, 1999.

"Dealing with the Discovery of Death inside an Embassy in October of 1973, in Santiago de Chile." In *In Brief: Short Takes on the Personal*, 69–73. Ed. Judith Kitchen and Mary Paumier Jones. New York: W. W. Norton, 1999.

"The Discovery of Life and Language at an Early Age." In *King David's Harp: Autobiographical Essays by Jewish Latin American Writers*, 121–39. Ed. Stephen A. Sadow. Albuquerque: University of New Mexico Press, 1999.

"A punto de nacer." In *Carta al ciudadano 6.000 millones*, 15–39. Ed. Toef Jaeger and Joke van Kampen. Barcelona: Ediciones B, S.A., 1999.

"Meric." In *El gran libro de América Judía*, 200–202. San Juan: Editorial de la Universidad de Puerto Rico, 1998.

"Novela-objeto." In *El gran libro de América Judía*, 604–7. San Juan: Editorial de la Universidad de Puerto Rico, 1998.

"What I Always Knew." In *Celebrating Elie Wiesel: Stories, Essays, Reflections*, 15–18. Ed. Elie Weisel and Alan Rosen. Notre Dame, Ind.: University of Notre Dame Press, 1998.

"Adiós, General." In *The Oxford Book of Latin American Essays*, 468–73. Ed. Ilan Stavans. New York: Oxford University Press, 1997.

"En algún lugar del mundo." *Realidad Económica* 148 (1997): 7–12.

"Homenaje." In *Libros, personas, vida: Daniel Divinsky/Kuki Miler y Ediciones de la Flor (Buenos Aires 1967–1997)*, 77–80. Ed. Jesus R. Anaya Rosique. Guadalajara: University of Guadalajara, 1997.

"Hombres de maíz: El mito como tiempo y palabra (con una postdata)." In *Miguel Ángel Asturias: Hombres de maíz*, 657–74. Ed. Gerald Martin. Madrid: Colección Archivos/CEP de la Biblioteca Nacional, 1996.

"Soft Evidence." In *The Sky Never Changes: Testimonies from the Guatemalan Labor Movement*, vii-viii. Ed. Thomas F. Reed and Karen Brandow. New York: ILR/Cornell University Press, 1996.

"Death and the Maiden." In *Actresses' Audition Speeches for All Ages and Accents*, 50–51. Ed. Jean Marlow. London: A and C Blackman/Heinemann/Reed, 1995.

"Konfidenz." In *Sceptre: The Best of Contemporary Fiction*, 24–31. London: Hodder and Stoughton/Sceptre, 1995.

(and Jonathan L. Beller) "Interventions in the *Field of Dreams* with Ariel Dorf-man." In *Learning History in America: Schools, Cultures, and Politics*, 161–85. Ed. Lloyd Kramer, Donald Reid, and William L. Barney. Minneapolis: University of Minnesota Press, 1994.

Commentary on "Interventions in the *Field of Dreams* with Ariel Dorfman." In *Learning History in America: Schools, Cultures, and Politics*, 180–85. Ed. Lloyd Kramer, Donald Reid, and William L. Barney. Minneapolis: University of Minnesota Press, 1994.

Introduction to "Interventions in the *Field of Dreams* with Ariel Dorfman." In *Learning History in America: Schools, Cultures, and Politics*, 161–63. Ed. Lloyd Kramer, Donald Reid, and William L. Barney. Minneapolis: University of Minnesota Press, 1994.

"Haïti." In *Intervenir? Droits de la personne et raisons d'état/Académie Universelle des Cultures*, 43–48. Paris: Editions Grasset et Fasquelle, 1993.

"I Just Missed the Bus and I'll Be Late for Work." In *Against Forgetting: Twentieth Century Poetry of Witness*, 613. Ed. Carolyn Forché. London and New York: W. W. Norton, 1993.

"Last Waltz in Santiago." In *Against Forgetting: Twentieth Century Poetry of Witness*, 614. Ed. Carolyn Forché. London and New York: W. W. Norton, 1993.

"Vocabulary." In *Against Forgetting: Twentieth Century Poetry of Witness*, 615. Ed. Carolyn Forché. London and New York: W. W. Norton, 1993.

"farland" and "intervaland." In *In a Word: A Dictionary of Words That Don't Exist but Ought To*, 65, 91–92. Ed. Jack Hitt. New York: Harper's Magazine/Laurel Trade/Dell Publishing, 1992.

"Of Elephants and Savages." In *Stories and Readers: New Perspectives on Literature in the Elementary Classroom*, 33–55. Ed. Charles Temple and Patrick Collins. Norwood, Mass.: Christopher-Gordon, 1992.

"Posmodernos en el patio trasero." In *Rebeldes y domesticados: Los intelectuales frente al poder*, 123–29. Ed. Raquel Ángel. Buenos Aires: Ediciones el Cielo por Asalto, 1992.

"Cien primaveras." In *El mundo de Ana Frank, 1929–1945*, 65–71. Ed. Dieter Strauss. Santiago: Goethe Institut/Pehuén, 1991.

"Hymn for the Unsung." In *The Gulf War Reader*, 326–28. Ed. Micah L. Sifry and Christopher Cerf. New York: Time/Random House, 1991.

"Afterword." In Pablo Neruda, *The House in the Sand: Prose Poems*. Buffalo: White Pine Press, 1990, 2004.

"Memories of Hope." In *Chile from Within 1973–1988*, 93–121. Ed. Susan Meiselas. New York: W. W. Norton, 1990.

"Myth as Time and Word." In *Modern Latin American Fiction*, 59–73. Ed. Harold Bloom. New York: Chelsea House Publishers, 1990.

"Der Tod als Phantasie- und Denkgeschehen in "Hundert Jahre Einsamkeit." In *Ansichten zu Gabriel García Márquez und Einmischungen des Autors*, 50–90. Ed. Jochen Martin. Berlin and Weimar: Aufbau-Verlag 1989.

"Afterword." In Pablo Neruda, *The House at Isla Negra*. Fredonia, N.Y.: White Pine Press, 1988.

"Foreword." In Augusto Roa Bastos, *Son of Man*, 7–10. New York: Monthly Review Press, 1988.

(and Armand Mattelart) "How to Read Donald Duck and Other Innocent Literature for Children." In *How Much Truth Do We Tell the Children? The Politics of Children's Literature*, 22–31. Ed. Betty Bacon. Minneapolis: MEP/University of Minnesota Press, 1988.

"Intervenciones." In *Los Veteranos del 70: Antologia*, 51–59. Ed. Carlos Olivarez. Santiago: Ediciones Melquíades, 1988.

"Wandering on the Boundaries of Development." In *Direct to the Poor: Grassroots Development in Latin America*, 166–85. Ed. Sheldon Annis and Peter Hakim. Boulder: Lynne Rienner, 1988.

"Beyond Satan and a Siesta: A Preface." In *Reviewing Histories: Selections from New Latin American Cinema*, 2–3. Ed. Coco Fusco. Buffalo: Hallwalls, 1987.

"Carta a Miguel Otero Silva de Neruda." In *Nuevas aproximaciones a Pablo Neruda*, 171–95. Ed. Angel Flores. México City: Fondo de Cultura Económica, 1987.

(and Armand Mattelart). "The Great Parachutist." In *American Media and Mass Culture: Left Perspectives*, 530–39. Ed. Donald Lazere. Berkeley: University of California Press, 1987.

"The Infantilizing of Culture." In *American Media and Mass Culture: Left Perspectives*, 145–53. Ed. Donald Lazere. Berkeley: University of California Press, 1987.

"José Maria Arguedas y Mario Vargas Llosa: Dos visiones de una sola América." In *Monografías del Maiten* 5, 187–208. Santiago: Instituto Profesional del Pacífico, 1986.

"We're Here to Stay." In *Cultures: Dialogue between the Peoples of the World*, 109–11. Paris: UNESCO, 1986.

"Código político y código literario: El género testimonio en Chile hoy." In *Ideologies and Literature*, 170–234. Ed. René Jara and Hernán Vidal. Minneapolis: Society for the Study of Contemporary Hispanic and Lusophone Revolutionary Literatures, 1986.

"Soft Evidence." In *Conspire: To Breathe Together*, 94. Ed. Merle Bachman and John Benson. San Francisco: Fire in the Lake/Amnesty International, 1985.

"Two Times Two." In *Conspire: To Breathe Together*, 94. Ed. Merle Bachman and John Benson. San Francisco: Fire in the Lake/Amnesty International, 1985.

"Last Will and Testament." In *They Shoot Writers, Don't They?*, 186–87. Ed. George Theiner. London: Faber and Faber/Index on Censorship/Writers and Scholars International, 1984.

"Oedipus among the Missing." In *First Harvest: The Institute for Policy Studies, 1963–83*, 297–305. Ed. John S. Freidman. New York: Grove Press, 1983.

"Cultural Survival." In *The Case of the Mapuche in Chile: Indian Populations under Authoritarian Regimes*, 7–11. Washington, D.C.: Institute for Policy Studies, 1980.

"Putamadre." Trans. Stephen Kessler. In *Chilean Writers in Exile: Eight Short Novels*, 139–60. Ed. Fernando Alegría. Trumansburg, N.Y.: Crossing Press, 1982.

"Presentación." In Marcelo Montecino, *Con sangre en el ojo*, 5–7. Mexico City: Editorial Nueva Imagen, 1981.

"Chilenische Literatur im Untergrund." Trans. Dagmar Ploetz. In *Unsere Freunde die Diktatoren: Lateinamerikanische Schriftsteller heute*, 90–98. Ed. Curt Meyer-Clason. Munich: Verlag Autoren Edition, 1980.

"El estado como intelectual, el intelectual como una especie de estado: Reflexiones sobre la cultura chilena de la década del setenta." In Ariel Dorfman and Orlando Albornoz, *El intelectual y el estado*, 37–69. College Park: University of Maryland Press, 1980.

"Cultural Resistance in Chile Today." In *Chile: A Report to the Freedom to Write Committee*, 10–25. New York: PEN American Center, 1980.

(and Armand Mattelart). "The Noble Savage: Cultural Imperialism in the Disney Comics." In *Dialectics of Third World Development*, 122–34. Ed. Igolf Vogeler and Anthony De Souza. Newark, N.J.: Allanheld, Osmun, 1980.

"Widerstand in Chile: Kultur gegen imperialistische Politik." In *Wir Haben Keine Zeit Zu Verlieren: Ateinamerikanische Autoren im Exil*, 55–71. Ed. Jacinta Vera and Mario Trejo. Wuppertal: Peter Hammer Verlag, 1978.

"El hombre en el camino." In *Recopilación de textos sobre Alejo Carpentier*, 373–83. Ed. Dominica Diez. Havana: Casa de las Américas, 1977.

"Die Welt verändern, PEN verändern? Zur Situation der jungen lateinamerikanischen Literatur." In *Kunst und Kultur des demokratischen Chile*, 123–33. Ed. Martin Jürgens and Thomas Metscher. Munich: Verlag Atelier im Bauernhaus, 1977.

"Aspectos de Chilex." In *Joven narrativa chilena después del golpe*, 23–33. Ed. Antonio Skármeta. Clear Creek, Ind.: American Hispanist, 1976.

"La derrota de la distancia: La obra de Antonio Skármeta." In *Del cuerpo a las palabras: La narrativa de Antonio Skármeta*, 81–99. Ed. Raúl Silva Cáceres. Madrid: Literatura Reunida, 1976.

"La historia nos sigue absolviendo, Fidel." Prologue to Fidel Castro, *La historia me absolverá*, 7–51. Oviedo: Ediciones JUCAR, 1976, 1978.

"Inocencia y neocolonialismo: Un caso de dominio ideológico en la literatura infantil." In *Cultura y comunicaciones de masa: Materiales de la discusión chilena 1970–1973*, 155–90. Ed. Manuel A. Garretón. Barcelona: Editorial Laia, 1976.

"La muerte como acto imaginativo en *Cien años de soledad*." In *Novelistas Hispano-americanos de hoy*, 291–324. Ed. Juan Loveluck. Madrid: Taurus, 1976.

(with Franz Hinkelammert). "Cultural Repression in Chile." In *Repression in Latin America: A Report on the First Session of the Second Russell Tribunal, Rome, April 1974*, 82–91. Ed. William Jerman. Nottingham: Spokesman Books/Betrand Russell, 1975.

"Das letzte Projekt." Trans. Dagmar Ploetz. In *Kürbiskern: Literatur, Kritik, Klassenkampf*, 48–51. Munich: Damnitz Verlag, 1974.

PERIODICAL PUBLICATIONS

Many of Dorfman's periodical contributions appear in more than one venue. In most cases these publications have been listed only once in order to avoid repetition. Dorfman has written numerous book reviews for periodicals. Not all of these have been included.

English-Language Periodical Publications

"Mission Akkomplished." *New Statesman*, May 8 and 15, 2006. http://www .newstatesman.com/nssubsfilter.php3?newTemplate=NSArticle_NS&new DisplayURN=200605080023.

"Waving the Star-Spanglish Banner." *Washington Post*, May 7, 2006, B02.

"Would I Lie to You?" *The Guardian,* January 18, 2006, 2.

"Homeland Security Ate My Speech." *TomDispatch*, January 15, 2006. http:// tomdispatch.com/index.mhtml?pid=49432.

"It's No Joke Anymore." *Los Angeles Times*, January 15, 2006, 3.

"A Morse Code Signal for 2006." *San Francisco Chronicle*, January 8, 2006, D-2.

"An Einstein Strings Theory." *Los Angeles Times*, August 16, 2005, 13.

"Love Song for London." *Washington Post*, July 9, 2005, A15.

"Adieu to a Philosopher." *Los Angeles Times*, April 11, 2005, B11.

"The Five Minutes of Pope John Paul II." *openDemocracy*, April 8 and May 23, 2005. http://www.opendemocracy.net/faith-catholicchurch/article_2412.jsp.

"Echoes of King's Dream Ring True in Chile." *San Francisco Chronicle*, January 16, 2005, C-2.

"Why Chile Is Hopeful." *New York Times*, September 11, 2004, A31.

"Protest: Liberty's Language." *Los Angeles Times*, August 29, 2004, M6.

"Fear and the Word." *Utne*, May–June 2004, 70–72.

"Price We Pay for Paradise Is Torture." *The Australian*, May 10, 2004, 9.

"Untying an Ethical Question on Torture: Happiness for All Is One Justification." *San Francisco Chronicle*, May 9, 2004, E1.

"Words the Pulse among Madrid's Dead: Neruda's Verses Howl against Terror Today and Yesterday—Testimony to the Courage of Spain's People." *Los Angeles Times*, March 21, 2004, home ed., M5.

"Lessons of a Catastrophe." *The Nation*, September 29, 2003, 18.

"Pablo Neruda, Shaping the World with His Words." *Washington Post*, September 26, 2003, final ed., C01.

"The True 'Desaparecidos.'" *Chronicle Review*, September 5, 2003, B7. http://chronicle.com/free/v50/io2/02b00701.htm. Accessed June 12, 2004.

"A Reply to an Iraqi Dissident Urging Invasion." *The Independent*, February 26, 2003, 18.

"The Urge to Help. The Obligation Not To." *Washington Post*, February 23, 2003, final ed., B02.

"A Different Drum: With the World on the Brink of War, the Need for Stories of Peace Is Paramount." *The Guardian*, January 11, 2003, 36.

"Letter to America." *The Nation*, September 30, 2002, 22.

"You Gave Me, an Americano from the Latino South, This Language of Love That I Return to You." *The Observer*, September 8, 2002, 31.

"Dark Blizzard of Photos Connects Those Left Behind." *Los Angeles Times*, December 24, 2001, home ed., B11.

"America Looks at Itself through Humanity's Mirror." *Los Angeles Times*, September 21, 2001, home ed., B15.

"Americans Must Now Feel What the Rest of Us Have Known: One Way for Americans to Overcome Their Trauma Is to Admit That Their Suffering Is Not Unique." *The Independent*, October 3, 2001, 5.

"A Voice for the Voiceless: Ariel Dorfman's New Play Has Its European Debut in London Tomorrow. He Explains How the Work Grew out of an Urgent Need to Celebrate the Defenders of Human Rights." *The Guardian*, June 2, 2001, 2.

"The General's Handiwork: This Week, His Fingers Will Get the Treatment They Deserve." *Washington Post*, May 13, 2001, final ed., B04.

"Blame the Killing on Armies of the SiiY." *Los Angeles Times*, May 4, 2001, B9.

"Dictators Will Not Sleep Easy: Did Milosevic Shudder When Pinochet Was Arrested? If He Didn't He Should Have, as Must All Tyrants Now." *The Observer*, April 8, 2001, 27.

(and Adolfo Gilly, JoAnn Kawell, Fred Rosen et al.). "The Americas React to Terror." NACLA Report on the Americas 35, no. 3 (November–December 2001): 6.

"The General Is Hoist on His Own Petard: Victory against Impunity for the

Chilean Dictator Belongs to the Disappeared and Their Families." *The Observer*, December 3, 2000, 31.

"Chilean Courts Finally Ready to Face Pinochet." *Times Union*, August 10, 2000, A15.

"Justice for Pinochet Seems like the Impossible Dream." *The Record*, August 10, 2000, final ed., A11.

"Moral Good Triumphs in Chile." *Milwaukee Journal Sentinel*, August 9, 2000, final ed., 15.

"In Chile, the Cries for Justice Are Heard: Pinochet Loses Immunity." *Plain Dealer*, August 9, 2000, final ed., 11.

"Who Thought We'd Get This Close to Justice?" *Washington Post*, August 6, 2000, final ed., B01.

"He Has Been a Symbol for Too Long: Now Let Elian Be a Boy Once More; It Is for Bill Clinton to Dare to Build on the Tiny Bridge That Elian Has Now Created." *The Independent*, June 30, 2000, 4.

"Pinochet Hoisted by His Own Petard." *Contra Costa Times*, June 4, 2000, final ed., P11.

"The Missing Return to Haunt Pinochet." *Sun-Sentinel*, May 31, 2000, Broward metro ed., 23A.

"Perspective on Chile: 'Los Desaparecidos' Are Returning to Haunt Gen. Pinochet; to Get off the Hook, Former Dictator Must Prove That He Ordered the Assassination of Prisoners." *Los Angeles Times*, May 30, 2000, home ed., 7.

"Pinochet's Mind." NACLA Report on the Americas 33, no. 5 (March–April 2000): 4.

"It Is up to Chile to Try the General Now." *The Independent*, March 6, 2000, 5.

"No Rest for the Wicked: Pinochet's Gift to Us All; Chile: His Detention Elevates the Principle of Universal Prosecution for Human Rights Crimes." *Los Angeles Times*, January 16, 2000, home ed., 5.

"The General's Gift to Humanity." *The Independent*, January 14, 2000, 4.

"Let Pinochet Back Only on His Deathbed; Chile: He's a Monster Who Should Face a Reckoning before the Families of Those Who Were His Victims." *Los Angeles Times*, November 28, 1999, home ed., 5.

"Whatever Pinochet's Fate, His Name Means Disgrace." *Houston Chronicle*, October 5, 1999, three star ed., 23.

"Pinochet Has Lived to See His Name Despised." *The Journal Gazette*, 1 October 1, 1999, final ed., 10A.

"Never Again Will a Torturer Shrug and Walk Away." *The Observer*, September 26, 1999, 31.

"Truth and Reconciliation." *New York Times*, September 12, 1999, 14.

"Pinochet, the Lincoln Brigade, and Me." *The Progressive* 63, no. 5 (1999): 20.

"A Despot's Last Shot at Redemption." *Harper's Magazine* 298, no. 1784 (1999): 17.

"The Guerrilla: Che Guevara." *Time Magazine*, June 14, 1999, 210–12.

"The Spirit of the Future." *Time Magazine*, May 24, 1999, 50–51.

"Pinochet's Bad Name Will Be His Legacy; World Politics: Former Chilean Dictator's Fate Is in Question, but He's Already Lost the Battle Over How He Will Be Remembered." *Los Angeles Times*, September 26, 1999, home ed., 5.

"People: Che Moi?; I Saw Myself as the Guevara of Chile, Fist Raised in Protest against the Forces of Tyranny. And Then the Shot Rang Out." *The Observer*, March 28, 1999, 2.

"I Was Blessed to Be Here on this Happy Day; the Pinochet Ruling: Chile's Leading Author and One of Britain's Top Barristers Comment on Yesterday's Judgement: A Third of the Country Has Ruled Chile for Decades but Has Found It Doesn't Rule Abroad." *The Independent*, March 25, 1999, 5.

"Tell Us Where the Bodies Are." *Miami Herald*, December 18, 1998, 17.

"Chile Can Still Get Its General Home; If Pinochet Dies Abroad, It Will Be Because His Followers Did Not Try to Deal with the Past." *The Independent*, December 14, 1998, 4.

"My Plea to Mr. Straw: Listen to Chile's Damaged People; Yesterday He Told My Wife about the Worst Event of His Life—Being Tortured by Pinochet's Police." *The Independent*, November 27, 1998, 4.

"No Safe Havens: A Noted Chilean Author Applauds the Judgment on the General." *The Guardian*, November 26, 1998, 24.

"Repent Now, While You Can; Chilean Writer Ariel Dorfman Makes a Personal Plea to Pinochet." *The Observer*, November 1, 1998, 28.

"Perspectives on Dictators; Have Chileans Become Strong Enough to Grow Up? Pinochet Was Like an Abusive Parent; The Children Still Are Addicted to the Toxic Relationship." *Los Angeles Times*, October 28, 1998, home ed., 7.

"Chile's Democracy Needs to Nail the Torturers." *Evening Standard*, October 27, 1998, 11.

"U.S. Will Falter in Global Arena If It Becomes a Monolingual Society." *Desert News*, June 27, 1998, metro ed., A11.

"If Only We All Spoke Two Languages." *New York Times*, June 24, 1998, late ed., 25.

"Perspectives on the Summit of the Americas; Will the Duendes Prowl in Santiago? The Assembled Heads of State Must Not Forget Who They Represent in the Relentless March of Modernization." *Los Angeles Times*, April 17, 1998, home ed., 9.

"Last Chance for Redemption in Chile." *The Guardian*, September 17, 1997, 17.

"Perspective on Chile; The Calendar Brings Pinochet His Last Chance to Be Heroic; Like Achilles, Only the Bloodstained General Can Return the Bones of His Enemy to the Bereaved." *Los Angeles Times*, September 11, 1997, home ed., 9.

"Death and the Playwright: My Big Night with General Pinochet." *The Observer*, May 18, 1997, 1.

"To Have and Have Not during the Dictatorship of General Pinochet." *The Guardian*, February 22, 1997, 6.

"For Sarajevo, after a Thousand and One Days and Nights of Siege." *Los Angeles Times*, February 13, 1995, record ed., B5.

"But Even Yet, Chile's Pain Remains; Only Pinochet Can Mitigate the Sorrow by Ordering His Soldiers to Reveal the Whereabouts of the 'Disappeared.' " *Los Angeles Times*, October 3, 1993, home ed., 5.

"Ban the Bard." *New York Times*, July 28, 1991, sec. 7, 24.

"Silence Emerges as a Tragedy of Our Times." *Ottawa Citizen*, May 6, 1992, final ed., A11.

"Pinochet Never Far from Limelight." *San Francisco Chronicle*, 3 April 3, 1991, final ed., 5.

"For Chile, Dangerous Question Must Be Asked." *Houston Chronicle*, March 28, 1991, two star ed., 11.

"A Belated Obituary with No End." *Los Angles Times*, March 26, 1991, record ed., B7.

"Perspective on Chile: A Belated Obituary with No End; the Fate of 2,000 Victims of Pinochet Is Finally Told, and the Country, Newly Freed to Speak, Wonders What to Say." *Los Angeles Times*, March 26, 1991, home ed., 7.

"Hymn for the Unsung." *Los Angeles Times*, February 1, 1991, record ed., B7.

"Perspective on the Gulf War Hymn for the Unsung: What Obsessions, What Mythic Readings of Good and Evil, Bring Young Strangers Together in the Embrace of Death?" *Los Angeles Times*, February 1, 1991, home ed., 7.

"Dead and Alive." *New Statesman*, 3, no. 119 (1990): 22.

"The Autumn of a Dictator: A Chilean Diary by Ariel Dorfman." *Los Angeles Times*, May 13, 1990, home ed., 17.

"Can a Dictator Tell Us Something about Ourselves?" *New York Times*, February 25, 1990, late ed., 5.

"Burying Allende: Death and Rebirth in Chile." *The Nation*, 251, no. 11 (1990): 365.

"Dancing in the Streets—But Dancing Alone Chile: The Euphoria of Shedding 16 Years of Dictatorship Is Tempered by the Sound of Thousands of Voices Forever 'Disappeared.' " *Los Angeles Times*, December 17, 1989, home ed., 7.

"Pinochet's Departure Won't End Pall He Cast over Chile." *Dallas Morning News*, December 10, 1989, home final ed., 9J.

"Adios, General." *Harper's Magazine*, December 1989, 72–76.

"Beyond the Blackout: How Chile Beat Pinochet with a Pencil." *Village Voice*, October 18, 1988, 20–22.

"Reports from the Heart of the No." *Village Voice*, 33, no. 40 (1988): 25.

"Pinochet Didn't Get the Message: Chileans Demand Freedom." *The Record*,
   October 16, 1988, 04.

"We Reconquered Our Dignity." *Washington Post*, October 9, 1988, final ed., D7.

"Would You Trust Someone Like Gen. Pinochet?" *Houston Chronicle*, September
   15, 1988, two star ed., 15.

"A Holiday for Exiles in Chile." *Los Angeles Times*, September 11, 1988, home ed., 5.

"The Eyes of the World Must Focus on Chile's Struggle for Free Election: Offers
   Only Opportunity to Overcome General's Tyranny." *Seattle Post-Intelligencer*,
   June 5, 1988, final ed., F3.

"Keep an Eye on Chile." *New York Times*, June 2, 1988, late ed., 27.

"Pinochet's Reign of Terror Claiming New Victims in Chile." *Seattle Post-
   Intelligencer*, November 22, 1987, final ed., F3.

"New Intimidation in Chile." *New York Times*, November 20, 1987, final ed., 39.

"Pry Letelier's Killers Out of Chile." *New York Times*, March 9, 1987, final ed., 15.

"Crossing the Street in Chile." *Tikkun* 4, no. 6 (1987): 13–17, 83–84.

"Time Quickly Running Out for Chile's Gen. Pinochet." *Dallas Morning News*,
   September 11, 1986, home final ed., 27A.

"Behind Chile's Wall of Darkness." *Houston Chronicle*, September 10, 1986, no
   star ed., 27.

"Pinochet Has Reaped What He Has Sown." *New York Times*, September 9, 1986,
   late city final ed., 27.

"Exile's Death Ignites a New Fire in Chile." *San Francisco Chronicle*, August 6,
   1986, final ed., C5.

"The Burning of Rodrigo Rojas/Background Report on a Victim of Military Brutality in Chile." *The Guardian*, July 26, 1986, 17.

"Chileans Challenge Pinochet's Rule/Give the Dictatorship the Blade." *San Francisco Chronicle*, July 2, 1986, 1.

"Strike! Showdown in Chile." *Toronto Star*, June 29, 1986, H4.

"The Challenge in Chile." *New York Times*, June 29, 1986, late city final ed., 23.

"Chile Poised for Showdown with Pinochet." *Seattle Post-Intelligencer*, June 29,
   1986, final ed., F3.

"Reports of My Death." *The Nation*, 243, no. 12 (1986): 370–74.

"In Chile, a Show of Hands." *New York Times*, November 23, 1985, late final ed., 27.

"Learn from the Trees about Dictators." *Houston Chronicle*, September 17, 1985,
   no star ed., 19.

"A Rural Chilean Legend Come True." *New York Times*, February 18, 1985, late
   final ed., A17.

"Roman Emperor Pinochet Must Go." *New York Times*, September 11, 1984, late
   final ed., A31.

"An Exile Finds Chile 'Struck By A Plague.' " *New York Times*, September 11, 1983, late final ed., 23.

"Strangers in a Strange Land." *Washington Post*, July 24, 1983, final ed., 3.

"Mother's Day." *New York Times*, May 7, 1983, late final ed., 23.

"I Am Not an L." *New York Times*, November 5, 1982, late final ed., A27.

"Snow." *New York Times*, January 15, 1982, late final ed., A23.

Spanish-Language Periodical Publications

Many of the pieces in *El País* (Spain) also appear in *El Proceso* (Mexico). Some of Dorfman's earliest periodical writing was for the Santiago cultural weekly magazine *Ercilla*. Numerous pieces appeared from 1965 to 1967. Because of limited access to the archives of *Ercilla*, these pieces have not been included.

"Una llamada de auxilio para el año nuevo." *El País*, January 5, 2006, 14.

"El violinista en el tejado del cosmos." *El País*, September 5, 2005, 16.

"Los cinco minutos de Juan Pablo II." *El País*, April 7, 2005, 18.

"El perdón y los pingueinos." *El País*, November 29, 2004, 16.

"Juegos de la memoria." *El País*, October 31, 2004, 21.

"Más allá de la pantalla." *El País*, October 15, 2004, 17.

"Yuxtaposiciones." *El País*, September 8, 2004, 13.

"Emergencias." *El Proceso*, August 15, 2004, 56.

"La tentación de Iván Karamazov." *Página 12*, May 7, 2004. http://www. pagina 12web.com.ar/diario/contratapa/13-34991-2004-05-07.html. Accessed June 11, 2004.

"Neruda frente al terror en Madrid." *El País*, March 20, 2004, 14.

"Un almuerzo con Kerry." *El País*, March 5, 2004, 13.

"Miller: La muerte de un fabulador." *El Proceso*, February 20, 2005, 82.

"Carta abierta al presidente Batlle." *Página 12*, January 21, 2004. http://www .pagina12web.com.ar/diario/contratapa/13-30578-2004-01-21.html. Accessed June 11, 2004.

"Despidiendo a Pablo." *El País*, September 24, 2003, Andalucia ed., 42.

"30 años del golpe de estado en Chile, lecciones de un naufragio." *El País*, September 7, 2003, 12.

"Martin Luther King, cuarenta años más tarde: El camino a la justicia." *Página 12*, August 24, 2003. http://www.pagina12web.com.ar/diario/elmundo/ 4-24542-2003-08-24.html. Accessed June 11, 2004.

"La ballena en el desierto." *Página 12*, March 31, 2003. http://www.pagina12web .com.ar/diario/contratapa/13-18234-2003-03-31.html; accessed June 11, 2004. *Página 12*, February 1991.

"De Pablo Picasso a Colin Powell." *El Proceso*, March 23, 2003, 8.

"Irak y Moby Dick." *El Proceso*, March 23, 2003, 70.

"Carta a un disidente iraqui anónimo." *El País*, February 25, 2003, 6.

"Imaginando una paz posible." *Página 12*, December 22, 2002. http://www
.pagina12web.com.ar/diario/elmundo/4-14479-2002-12-22.html. Accessed
June 11, 2004.

"El mundo tras el 11 de septiembre: Las heladas aguas del terror." *El País*, September 4, 2002, 11–12.

"Globalicemos la compasión." *El País*, December 10, 2001, 17.

"El último once de septiembre." *El Diario La Prensa*, September 25, 2001, 15.

"La terapia de los que sólo ven." *Clarín*, September 2, 2001. http://
old.clarin.com/suplementos/cultura/2001/09/02/u-00611.htm. Accessed
August 23, 2004.

"Aquella noche tan lejana." *El País*, May 3, 2001, 13.

"El largo adiós a los tiranos." *El País*, April 9, 2001, 9.

"Esas manos." *El Nuevo Heráld*, February 4, 2001, final ed., 24A.

"Los múltiples retornos de Julio Cortázar." *El País*, December 11, 2000, 16.

"Las otras olimpiadas." *El Proceso*, October 1, 2000, 56.

"Mi primer encuentro, mi perpetuo encuentro." *El País* (Madrid), October 1,
2000, 18–19.

"Increíble pero cierto." *El País*, August 3, 2000, 11.

"Pinochet y los muertos de la historia." *El Proceso*, May 28, 2000, 64.

"No a términos inciertos: El milagro de Elían." *El Sol de Texas*, May 11, 2000, 2.

"El milagro de Elían." *El País*, May 2, 2000, 13.

"El día en que no logré ser 'Che' Guevara." *El País*, March 26, 2000, 16–17.

"Esto recién comienza." *El País*, March 4, 2000, 18.

"Las cuentas claras." *El País*, February 16, 2000, 5–6.

"¿Y la mente de Pinochet?" *El País*, January 13, 2000, 14.

"Un brindis por Pinochet." *El Proceso*, November 20, 1999, 50.

"Más allá de Pinochet." *El País*, March 25, 1999, 17–18.

"A la espera." *El País*, March 11, 1999, 15–16.

"Buscando el sur-Sur-Sur." *Brecha* (Montevideo), December 23, 1998, 8+.

"La alegría y el abismo." *El Proceso*, November 29, 1998, 46–48.

"Más allá del miedo." *El País*, November 26, 1998, 16.

"Dejemos de ser rehenes." *El País*, November 1, 1998, 4.

"Carta de veras abierta al General Pinochet." *El País*, October 26, 1998, 16; *El Proceso*, November 15, 1998, 47.

"Terminemos con la prisión del idioma único." *Clarín*, August 7, 1998. http://
old.clarin.cim/diario/1998/08/07/i-01403d.htm. Accessed August 23, 2004.

"Cumbre de las Américas: Entre la exaltación de la codicia y la avidez com-
petitiva." *El Proceso*, April 19, 1998, 50–51.

"Cuidado con los duendes." *El País*, April 17, 1998, 15–16.

"Recomendación para Pinochet: Leer la 'Iliada,' imitar a Aquiles, y devolver cadáveres y desaparecidos a sus familias." *El Proceso*, September 14, 1997, 51.

"Una conversación con Alan Ginsberg poco antes de morir, en torno de la 'generación beat' y de su celebre poema 'Aullido.' " *El Proceso*, May 4, 1997, 60–61.

"Como y por que Michael Ondaatje escribió 'El paciente inglés,' esa novela sobre los nómadas de la historia." *El Proceso*, April 13, 1997, 13–14.

"Resurrección a pesar de Pinochet." *El País*, November 9, 1986, 16–17.

"Miedo a una guerra civil." *El País* (Madrid), July 4, 1986, 4.

"Pinochet y sus dos rivales." *El País* (Madrid), July 3, 1986, 4.

"Chile, entre el miedo y la impotencia." *El País* (Madrid), July 2, 1986, 4.

"El cometa Halley apunta a Pinochet." *El País* (Madrid), July 1, 1986, 6.

"Madre hay más que una sola." *La Razón* (Buenos Aires), May 29, 1986.

"Un rito de reencuentro y desconsuelo." *Clarín* (Buenos Aires), April 10, 1986, 16.

"Es una dramatización." *Clarín* (Buenos Aires), June 23, 1983, 2–3.

"De un mito." *Clarín* (Buenos Aires), March 24, 1983, 5.

"Un diario para Ana." *Revista Hoy*, June 20–26, 1979, 35–41.

SECONDARY SOURCES ON ARIEL DORFMAN'S WORK

Published Sources

Avelar, Idelber. "Five Theses on Torture." *Journal of Latin American Cultural Studies* 10, no. 3 (2001): 253–71. Trans. of "La práctica de la tortura y la historia de la verdad." In *Retrazos de la transición*. Ed. Nelly Richard and Alberto Moreiras. Santiago: Cuarto Propio, 2001.

———. *The Letter of Violence: Essays on Narrative, Ethics, and Politics*. New York: Palgrave Macmillan, 2004.

———. "*La muerte y la doncella*, o la hollywoodización de la tortura." *Revista de Crítica Cultural* 22 (2001): 20–23.

———. "La práctica de la tortura y la historia de la verdad." In *Pensar en/la postdictadura*, 175–91. Ed. Nelly Richard and Alberto Moreiras. Santiago: Cuarto Propio, 2001.

Ball, David, Sophia A. McClennen, Ariel Dorfman, and Gordon O. Taylor. "Forum: Poetry and Torture." *World Literature Today* 81, nos. 1–2 (May–August 2005): 6–7.

Barr, Lois Baer. "Deconstructing Authoritarian Codes: Ariel Dorfman." In *Isaac Unbound: Patriarchal Traditions in the Latin American Jewish Novel*, 131–58. Tempe: ASU Center for Latin American Studies, 1995.

Barsky, Robert F. "Outsider Law in Literature: Construction and Representation in *Death and the Maiden.*" *SubStance: A Review of Theory and Literary Criticism* 84 (1997): 66–89.

Beller, Jonathan L. "Interventions in the *Field of Dreams* with Ariel Dorfman." In *Learning History in America: Schools, Cultures, and Politics,* 161–85. Ed. Lloyd Kramer, Donald Reid, and William L. Barney. Minneapolis: University of Minnesota Press, 1994.

Berger, Peter. "A Disney World." *New Society* 20 (August 1975): 478–80.

——. "The Hour of Poetry." In *The Sense of Sight: Writings by John Berger,* 243–52. Ed. Lloyd Spencer. New York: Vintage Books, 1985.

Blum, Bihla. "Desde Chile a Israel: *La muerte y la doncella* por el teatro 'Habima.'" *Revista de Artes, Letras y Filosofía* 15 (1999): 147–56.

Cajiao Salas, Teresa. "Algunas consideraciones sobre la narrativa chilena en el exilio." *Cuadernos Hispanoamericanos* 375 (1981): 600–615.

Campos, Javier. "Literatura, testimonio, cine y derechos humanos en los tiempos del neoliberalismo global." *MACLAS: Latin American Essays* 14 (2001): 27–37.

Castillo, Debra. "Arrival: Dorfman, Salazar, Sainz, Rivera-Valdés." In *Redreaming America: Toward a Bilingual American Culture,* 99–143. Ed. Debra Castillo. Albany: SUNY Press, 2004.

Castro, Pércio B. de., Jr. "*La muerte y la doncella* de Ariel Dorfman: Cuarteto en D[olor] Mayor." *Acta Literaria* 22 (1997): 131–39; *Alba de America Revista Literaria* 16, nos. 30–31 (1998): 73–83.

——. "*La muerte y la doncella*: ¿De quién son las bolas? Opresor oprimido y viceversa." *Revista Chilena de Literatura* 52 (1998): 61–67.

Cheadle, Norman. "Los intelectuales y el caso Pinochet: ¿Canto de cisne de una figura centenaria?" *A contracorriente* 1, no. 2 (2004): 63–81. http://www.ncsu .edu/project/acontracorriente/spring_04/Cheadle.pdf.

Claro-Mayo, Juan. "Dorfman, cuentista comprometido." *Revista Iberoamericana* 47, nos. 114–15 (1981): 339–45.

Coddou, Marcelo. "Konfidenz, de Ariel Dorfman." *Acta Literaria* 19 (1994): 107–13.

——. "Una nota sobre 'Konfidenz' de Ariel Dorfman." *Textos: Revista Semestrial de Creación y Crítica* 4, no. 1 (1995): 29–34.

Codrescu, Andrei. "Introduction: Note on a Filament." In Ariel Dorfman, *Konfidenz,* v-vii. Normal, Ill.: Dalkey Archive, 2003.

Coetzee, J. M. "Afterword." In Ariel Dorfman, *Mascara,* 131–36. New York: Seven Stories Press, 2004.

Crnkovic, Gordana. Review of *Death and the Maiden,* by Roman Polanski. *Film Quarterly* 50, no. 3 (1997): 39–45.

Cusato, Domenico Antonio. "La denuncia de los desaparecidos en *Viudas* de Ariel Dorfman." In *La dittatura di Pinochet e la transizione alla democrazia in*

Cile, atti del convegno (11–12 novembre 2003), 57–69. Ed. Domenico Antonio Cusato. Messina: Lippolis, 2004.

——. "*La muerte y la doncella* de Ariel Dorfman: Una música de fondo para no olvidar." In *Las páginas se unieron como plumas: Homenaje a Hernán Loyola*, 85–97. Ed. Domenico Antonio Cusato and A. Melis. Messina: Lippolis, 2002.

Doloughan, Fiona J. "Translating the Self: Ariel Dorfman's Bilingual Journey." *Language and Intercultural Communication* 2, no. 2 (2002): 147–52.

Ferrera, Myriam. "La giustizia sospesa in *La muerte y la doncella* di Ariel Dorfman." In *La dittatura di Pinochet e la transizione alla democrazia in Cile, atti del convegno (11–12 novembre 2003)*, 22–32. Ed. Domenico Antonio Cusato. Messina: Lippolis, 2004.

Flora, Cornelia Butler. "Roasting Donald Duck: Alternative Comics and Photonovels in Latin America." *Journal of Popular Culture* 18, no. 1 (1984): 163–83.

Galán, Eduardo. "*La muerte y la doncella*. ¿Perdonar los crímenes del fascismo?" *Primer Acto* 249 (1993): 116–17.

Glickman, Nora. "Los gritos silenciados en el teatro de Aida Bortnik, Alberto Adellach, Eduardo Pavlovsky y Ariel Dorfman." *Revista Hispánica Moderna* 50, no. 1 (1997): 180–89.

Gregory, Stephen. "Ariel Dorfman and Harold Pinter: Politics of the Periphery and Theater of the Metropolis." *Comparative Drama* 30, no. 3 (1996): 325–45.

Hassett, John J. "Dictatorship, Memory and the Prospects for Democracy: The Fiction of Ariel Dorfman." *Third World Quarterly* 13, no. 2 (1992): 393–98.

Jofré, Manuel Alcides. "*La muerte y la doncella* de Ariel Dorfman: Transición democrática y crisis de la memoria." *Atenea: Revista de Ciencia, Arte y Literatura de la Universidad de Concepción* 469 (1994): 87–99.

Kim, Euisuk. "La representación de la muerte viva y la reconciliación nacional en *La muerte y la doncella* de Ariel Dorfman." *Céfiro* 2 (2002): 9–18.

——. *Una reconstrucción alternativa del pretérito: Una aproximación psicoanalítica a la obra de Ariel Dorfman*. New Orleans: University Press of the South, 2003.

Kohut, Karl. "Política, violencia y literatura." *Anuario de Estudios Americanos* 59, no. 1 (2002): 193–222.

Maree, Cathy. "Truth and Reconciliation: Confronting the Past in *Death and the Maiden* (Ariel Dorfman) and *Playland* (Athol Fugard)." *Literator: Tydskrif vir Besondere en Vergelykende Taal-en Literatuurstudie/Journal of Literary Criticism* 16, no. 2 (1995): 25–37.

McClennen, Sophia A. "Ariel Dorfman." *Review of Contemporary Fiction* 20, no. 3 (2000): 81–132.

——. "Chilex: The Economy of Transnational Media Culture." *Cultural Logic: An Electronic Journal of Marxist Theory and Practice* 3, nos. 1–2 (1999). http://

eserver.org/clogic/3–1%262/mcclennen.html; May 17, 2004. *Mediations* 22 (1999): 90–111.

——. *The Dialectics of Exile: Nation, Time, Language, and Space in Hispanic Literatures.* West Lafayette, Ind.: Purdue University Press, 2004.

——. "The Diasporic Subject in Ariel Dorfman's *Heading South, Looking North.*" *MELUS* 30, no. 1 (spring 2005): 169–88.

——. "Poetry and Torture." *World Literature Today* 78, nos. 3–4 (2004): 68–70.

Morace, Robert A. "The Life and Times of *Death and the Maiden.*" *Texas Studies in Literature and Language* 42, no. 2 (2000): 135–53.

Moreno, Fernando. "Notas sobre la novela chilena actual." *Cuadernos Hispanoamericanos* 386 (1982): 381–95.

Munro, Andrew. "Recalling Voice: *La muerte y la doncella.*" *Ciberletras* 6 (2002). http://www.lehman.cuny.edu/faculty/guinazu/ciberletras/v06/munro.html. Accessed June 12, 2004.

Nelson, Alice A. *Political Bodies: Gender, History, and the Struggle for Narrative Power in Recent Chilean Literature.* Lewisburg, Pa.: Bucknell University Press, 2002.

Newman, Robert D. *Transgressions of Reading: Narrative Engagement as Exile and Return.* Durham: Duke University Press, 1993.

Oropesa, Salvador A. *La obra de Ariel Dorfman: Ficción y crítica.* Madrid: Pliegos, 1992.

Payne, Judith A. "Anima Rejection and Systematic Violence in *La ciudad y los perros.*" *Chasqui: Revista de Literatura Latinoamericana* 20, no. 1 (1991): 43–49.

Pinet, Carolyn. "Retrieving the Disappeared Text: Women, Chaos and Change in Argentina and Chile after the Dirty Wars." *Hispanic Journal* 18, no. 1 (1997): 89–108.

Reynolds, Bonnie Hildebrand. "Voz y memoria en el teatro hispanoamericano reciente." *Latin American Theatre Review* 30, no. 2 (1997): 3, 31–43.

Schulz, Bernard. "Lo difuso de la política en la versión cinematográfica de *La muerte y la doncella.*" *Revista Chilena de Literatura* 56 (2000): 127–34.

Shivers, George. "Textual Unity in Ariel Dorfman's *The Last Song of Manuel Sendero.*" *Washington College Review* (spring 1989): 19–20.

Silva Cáseres, Raúl. "Sentido del antiautoritarismo en el cuento latinoamericano (Cortázar, Skármeta, Dorfman)." *Cuadernos Americanos* 243 (1982): 202–13.

Sotomayor, Ana Maria. "(To Be) Just in the Threshold of Memory: The Founding Violence of the Victim in Diamela Eltit's *Lumpérica* and Ariel Dorfman's *Death and the Maiden.*" *Nomada: Creacion, Teoria, Critica* 3 (1997): 23–29.

Vidal, Hernán. "Sacrificios primordiales: Ariel Dorfman, *La muerte y la don-*

cella." In *Política cultural de la memoria histórica,* 286–304. Santiago: Mosquito Comunicaciones, 1997.

Walder, Dennis. "The Necessity of Error: Memory and Representation in the New Literatures." In *Reading the "New" Literatures in a Postcolonial Era,* 149–70. Ed. Susheila Nasta. Cambridge: Brewer, 2000.

Waldman, Gilda M. "Ariel Dorfman: De la identidad nómada a la identidad múltiple." *Híspamerica: Revista de Literatura* 30, no. 90 (2001): 107–12.

Wallace, Jennifer. "We Can't Make More Dirt . . . : Tragedy and the Excavated Body." *Cambridge Quarterly* 32, no. 2 (2003): 103–11.

West, Paul. "Ariel Dorfman: *The Last Song of Manuel Sendero.*" In *Sheer Fiction,* 131–34. New York: McPherson, 1987.

Dissertations and Theses

Babson, Jane Hall. "Voices: A Study of Diversity and Transition in Narrative Discourse." PhD diss., University of Wisconsin, Madison, 1990.

Bass, Leith Sinclair. "Three Chilean Writers' Views of Women under Oppression: Women and the Pinochet Regime." PhD diss., Wake Forest University, 1995.

Elbirt, Susana Inés. "Ariel Dorfman: Literatura en el exilio o el exilio de la literatura." Master's thesis, George Mason University, 1991.

Hynick, Harold. "*Death and the Maiden*: A Director's Approach." Master's thesis, University of South Dakota, 1995.

Jensen, Andrew Blaine. "Paradise Split: Binaries of Division in the Works of Ariel Dorfman." PhD diss., University of Utah, 2001.

Jolley, Jason. "Genealogy as Personal Criticism: Tracing Theories in the Self-Writings of José Donoso, Antonio Skármeta, Isabel Allende, and Ariel Dorfman." PhD diss., Pennsylvania State University, 2003.

Kim Euisuk. "Una reconstrucción alternativa del pretérito: Una aproximación psicoanalítica a la obra de Ariel Dorfman." PhD diss., University of Minnesota, 2001.

Little, Scott E. "An Environmental Light and Sound Design for Ariel Dorfman's *Death and the Maiden.*" PhD diss., University of South Dakota, 1995.

McClennen Expósito, Sophia. "Out of Bounds: Exile and the Crisis of Cultural Identity in Contemporary Hispanic Literature." PhD diss., Duke University, 1996.

McCracken, David Scott. " 'To Dream Reality': The Reification of History in the Novels of Ariel Dorfman." PhD diss., Texas A&M University, 1995.

Morello, Henry James. "Masking the Past: Trauma in Latin American and Peninsular Theatre." PhD diss., University of Illinois, Urbana-Champaign, 2006.

Nelson, Alice. "The Body Politic: Gender and the Struggle for Narrative Power in Chilean Literature of the Pinochet Years." PhD diss., Duke University, 1994.

Novak, Amy Louise. "Conceptualizing History in Postmodern Narrative: Don Delillo and Ariel Dorfman." Master's thesis, San Francisco State University, 1993.

Oropesa, Salvador Antonio. "An Appraisal of Ariel Dorfman's Fiction and Cultural Criticism," PhD diss., Arizona State University, 1990.

Porter, Amanda Jo. "A Comprehensive Record of the Directoral Process for a Production of Ariel Dorfman's *Death and the Maiden*." PhD diss., North Dakota State University, 1994.

Rabideau, Susan. "Directing 'Death and the Maiden.'" PhD diss., Mankato State University, 1997.

Romo, Leticia-Isabel. "Autor y lector: Representación de la realidad en tres novelas del post-boom (Esquivel, Dorfman y Martinez)." PhD diss., University of North Carolina, Chapel Hill, 2001.

Sandoval, Roberto Castillo. "La imaginación como praxis liberadora: Lecturas de la obra de Ariel Dorfman." PhD diss., Vanderbilt University, 1985.

Interviews

Abdala, Verónica. "Mi desafío es convertir al lector en un personaje más, que se busque a sí mismo." *Página 12* (Buenos Aires), September 9, 2001, 35–36.

Ángel, Raquel. "Ariel Dorfman: Posmodernos en el patio trasero." In *Rebeldes y domesticados: Los intelectuales frente al poder*, 123–29. Buenos Aires: El Cielo por Asaltado, 1992.

Arenes, Carolina. "Dialogo con Ariel Dorfman." *Suplemento Cultura La Nación*, March 26, 2000, 8.

"Ariel Dorfman." *Literatura y Lingüística* 4 (1990): 191–202.

"Ariel Dorfman on Culture, Democracy, and Development." *Development International* 1, no. 1 (1986): 37.

Berger, Beatriz. "Ariel Dorfman: Escribo libros perturbadores." *Revista de Libros El Mercurio*, August 7, 1994, 1, 4–5.

Berlanga, Ángel. "Entrevista a Ariel Dorfman, un autor chileno con resonancias mundiales: 'Una vez terminadas, las novelas salen a andar por el mundo.'" *Página 12*, February 15, 2004. http://www.pagina12web.com.ar/diario/elpais/1-31533-2004-02-15.html. Accessed June 11, 2004.

Berman, Jennifer. "Ariel Dorfman." *Bomb* 50 (1994–1995): 30–33. Reprinted in *Speak Fiction and Poetry!: The Best of Bomb Magazine's Interviews with Writers*, 251–61. Ed. Betty Sussler with Susan Sherman and Ronalde Shavers. New York: G&B Arts International, 1998.

Boyers, Peggy, and Juan Carlos Lectora. "Ideology, Exile, Language: An Interview with Ariel Dorfman." *Salmagundi* 82–83 (1989): 142–63.

Casimir, Jean, and Carlos Fazio. *El militarismo en América Latina: Entrevistas con*

Jean Casimir, Julio Cortázar, Ariel Dorfman, Theotonio Dos Santos, Gabriel García Márquez, Pablo González Casanova, Carlos Quijano y René Zavaleta. México City: Proceso, 1980.

Cooper, Marc. "Blake's Therapy." Radio Nation, July 31, 2001. http://www .webactive.com/radionation/rn20010704.html. Accessed May 27, 2004.

———. "The Art of Exile." Interview, 1988, 126–27.

Dillon, John. "The Anatomy of Fear." American Theatre 5, no. 9 (December 1988): 26, 51.

Epple, Juan Armando. "La literatura chilena del exilio." Texto Crítico 22–23 (July–December 1981): 209–37.

Esquivada, Gabriela. "Rechazo el silencio como solución." Puentes 2, no. 6 (2002): 52–55.

Farhi, Moris. "One True Word Is Worth Five Thousand Lies." Jewish Quarterly 39, no. 145 (1992): 8–15.

Graham-Yooll, Andrew. "Dorfman: A Case of Conscience." Index on Censorship 20, no. 6 (1991): 3–4.

Graña, Rolando. "Del Pato Donald a Polanski." Página 12 (Buenos Aires), September 26, 1993, 29–30.

Incledon, John. "Liberating the Reader: A Conversation with Ariel Dorfman." Chasqui: Revista de Literatura Latinoamericana 20, no. 1 (1991): 95–107.

———. "Morality and Politics: A Conversation with Ariel Dorfman." Albright 2, no. 2 (1989): 17–23.

"Interview with Korean Journal." Creation and Criticism 100 (1998): 430–61.

Isola, Laura. "Oigo voces." Página 12 (Buenos Aires), October 1, 2000. http://old .pagina12web.com.ar/2000/suple/radar/00-10/00-10-01/nota3.html.

Kafka, Paul. "On Exile and Return: An Interview with Ariel Dorfman." Bloomsbury Review, 1989, 12–15.

Makdisi, Sara. "Conversations with Ariel Dorfman." Sapina Newsletter 3, nos. 2–3 (1991): 50–63.

Martínez-Tabares, Vivian. "Ariel Dorfman: Si supiera quien soy no lo diría." Conjunto 120 (2001): 82–87.

McClennen, Sophia A. "An Interview with Ariel Dorfman." Context 15 (2004): 7–8.

———. "An Interview with Ariel Dorfman." World Literature Today 78, nos. 3–4 (2004): 64–67.

Minnemann, Joachim. "So wird die Dichtung nicht vergeblich gesungen haben" (Pablo Neruda) Eine Umfrage unter chilenischen Autoren im Exil." In Sammlung 3: Jahrbuch für antifaschistische Literatur und Kunst, 45–59. Ed. Uwe Naumann. Frankfurt am Main: Röderberg Verlag, 1980.

Muñoz, Silverio. "Entrevista a Ariel Dorfman." *Prismal/Cabral: Revista de Literatura Hispanica/Cabral Afro-Brasileiro Asiatico Lusitano* 3, no. 4 (1979): 60–76.

Pacheco, Cristina. "Conversation with Ariel Dorfman." *Al Pie de la Letra* 1, no. 1 (2001): 441–47.

Pezzopane, Barbara, and Laura Petruccioli. "Interview with Ariel Dorfman." *Storie* 52–53 (2004): 49–61.

Ploetz, Dagmar. "Gesucht wegen 'Bewußtmachung.'" *Kürbiskern: Literatur, Kritik, Klassenkampf* 3 (1974): 52–58.

Polak, Maralyn Lois. "Ariel Dorfman. The Intellectual-in-Exile." *Philadelphia Inquirer Sunday Magazine*, August 14, 1988.

Postel, Danny. "Ariel Dorfman." Trans. Gregori Dolz Kerrigan and Danny Postel. *The Progressive*, 1998. http://www.progressive.org/poste19812.htm. Accessed May 27, 2004.

Prieto Castillo, Daniel. "Ariel Dorfman: Evaluación del desarrollo de la lectura crítica en Latinoamérica." *Chasqui: Revista Latinoamericana de Comunicación* 15 (July–September 1985): 9–13.

Reyes, Carlos, and Maggie Paterson. "Ariel Dorfman on Memory and Truth." July 15, 2002. http://www.amnesty.org.uk/journal_july97/carlos.html. Accessed May 10, 2004.

Ruffinelli, Jorge. "Las batallas de Ariel Dorfman contra los demonios de adentro y los demonios de afuera." *Nuevo Cine Latinoamericano* 2 (2001): 11–18.

Sadowska-Guillón, Irene. "Ariel Dorfman: Una entrevista." *ADE Teatro* 75 (1998): 182–83.

Santana Dias, Maurício. "Ariel Dorfman." *Folha de S. Paulo*, August 30, 1998, 5.

Smith, R. J. "Chile Is Sort of Insane Now." *Alternative Media* 15, no. 1 (1985): 13, 19.

Smith, Wendy. "Ariel Dorfman." *Publishers Weekly*, October 21, 1988, 39.

Stavans, Ilan. "The Gringo's Tongue: A Conversation with Ariel Dorfman." *Michigan Quarterly Review* 34, no. 3 (1995): 303–12.

——. "Thorn at the Core: A Conversation with Ariel Dorfman." *Metamorphoses: Journal of the Five College Seminar on Literary Translation* 4, no. 1 (1995): 8–15.

Tagliaferro, Eduardo. "Diversidad en una humanidad única." *Página 12* (Buenos Aires), January 30, 2001, 7–8.

Thwaites Rey, Mabel. "Con el tiempo descubrí que las historias personales sí importan." *Clarín*, February 8, 2004. http://old.clarin.com/suplementos/zona/ 2004/02/08/z-03715.htm. Accessed August 23, 2004.

Villareal, Ana. "Dorfman: de vuelta." *La Razón* (Buenos Aires), January 6, 1985, 10–11.

Wallace, Jennifer. "Howls from a Thicket of Blood." *Times Higher Education Supplement* April 10, 1998, 13.

Waters, Mike, and Alex Wilde. "Art, Authenticity and Latin American Culture: A Dialogue with Mario Vargas Llosa and Ariel Dorfman." Washington, D.C.: Latin American Program, Wilson Center, 1980.

Wisenberg, S. L. "Ariel Dorfman: A Conversation." *Another Chicago Mag* 18 (1988): 196–221.

NOTES

1. THE POLITICAL IS PERSONAL

1 Dorfman mentions relatively little about his sister in his memoir. In fact, despite revealing many intimate details about his own life, he tends to avoid describing much about his family and loved ones.

2 Dorfman attributes the reclassification to David Rockefeller in his memoir (*Heading*, 27). He later realized that such was his father's recollection and that it had to have been Nelson (e-mail communication from Dorfman).

3 This chapter uses the memoir as a source of information especially about Dorfman's early life. Even though I point to moments when readers should be skeptical about the details offered by Dorfman in his memoir, detailed analysis of the text itself as a form of life writing is provided in chapter 5.

4 Douglas Kellner explains the difficult terminology relating to the topic of "media culture." In his opinion, and mine, "media culture" more adequately describes the form of culture that is mass-produced and mass-consumed. Rather than refer to this culture as "mass," which suggests a value judgment between high and low culture, or as "popular," which could mean that it is of the people, the term "media culture" refers more specifically to the conditions of production and dissemination of these cultural forms and makes a clear distinction between this type of "low" art and that

of folklore or mythology. Moreover, Kellner's definition of his favored terminology suggests a strong parallel with Dorfman's approach to the study of culture. According to Kellner, "The term 'media culture' also has the advantage of signifying that our culture *is* a media culture, that the media have colonized culture, that they are the primary vehicle for the distribution and dissemination of culture" (35).

5 Parkway Village, where Dorfman lived at the time, was a few blocks away from PS 117 and close to Lake Success, where the United Nations was lodged initially. The UN Manhattan headquarters was first occupied in 1950.

6 These interests will be discussed in greater detail in the following chapter on Dorfman's literary influences.

7 Rodó's position was subsequently critiqued by Roberto Fernández Retamar, who suggested that Caliban, due to his rebellious spirit, provided a better intellectual role model for Latin America.

8 Dorfman did write other plays prior to *Death and the Maiden* when he was young. His first plays were composed while a student at Dalton in New York City and were inspired by Pirandello.

9 Salma Hayek's production company, Ventanazul, which is dedicated to Latin-based themes and Latino talent on both sides of the camera, announced in early 2008 plans to release a film version of *Blake's Therapy*.

10 The English version of the story appeared in the collection *My House Is on Fire*.

11 Dorfman holds citizenship from three countries: Argentina, Chile, and the United States.

12 It ultimately did not make the final five.

2. LITERARY AND CULTURAL INFLUENCES

1 In *Reclaiming the Author* Lucille Kerr makes a similar point when she argues that the concept of the author in Latin American boom and post-boom texts varies from European versions.

2 In fairness to Benjamin, it is worth considering that he exaggerated the opposition between the novelist and the storyteller in order to emphasize the social role he believed literature could and should play.

3 Even though Barthes would later qualify his rejection of the author when he signaled his "return" in the preface to the 1971 text *Sade, Fourier, Loyola*, Sean Burke argues in *The Death and Return of the Author* that "The Death of the Author" was often taken unreflectively at face value as a sign that any effort to narrate was inevitably tyrannical (21). Indeed there has been significant rethinking of the "death" of the author. See, for example, *The Author*, by Andrew Bennett, as well as Jane Gallop's unpublished manuscript, "My Unfinished Book Should Not Feel like Death: Mortal Authors Writing in Time."

4 Dorfman makes a point that he is not the voice of the voiceless in an interview with Maya Jaggi: "I've never thought of myself as a 'voice for the voiceless.' People aren't voiceless; we're deaf—we don't hear them" (n.p.).

5 To complicate matters still further, this constant questioning of the role of the writer can be read as overwrought and has the potential to further alienate his audience (see Barr).

6 In this chapter I rely on a number of sources: (1) Dorfman's literature and essays; (2) interviews with him; (3) my experience as his student and teaching assistant; and (4) my extensive correspondence with him.

7 In a nod to Cervantes, Dorfman's chapter titles in his memoir mirror the style of *Don Quijote*, whose chapter titles themselves mirror the titles of famous medieval tales of chivalry. For more on this intertextuality, see my essay on Dorfman's memoir, "The Diasporic Subject" (172–73).

8 As I know from firsthand experience, Dorfman feels that all students of literature should know *Tristram Shandy*.

9 Stephen Gregory's impressive article on the two writers emphasizes the lack of scholarly attention to how these authors have mutually influenced one another.

10 Dorfman cites Esslin and was well aware of his reading of Pinter. He makes a point of differentiating his reading of Pinter from that of critics like Esslin.

11 Stephen Gregory makes this point as well.

12 See Castillo for more on Dorfman's depiction of the woman as trope.

13 According to Dorfman, Pinter's work was always political.

14 This reference is to Dorfman's adult writing. In an interview with Silverio Muñoz, Dorfman explains that when he was about ten years old, he began to write plays (71).

15 This genre—*testimonio*—receives fuller treatment in chapter 5.

16 The genre is a frequent subject of the courses that he has taught at Duke University.

17 The word "style" can refer to both a form of literary practice and a specific literary language, like diction or sentence length. Given that Dorfman himself uses "style" in the former sense, I will also occasionally use the term that way.

3. AN AESTHETICS OF HOPE

1 In his article on the Latin American aesthetics of hope, which is a translation from Spanish, the phrase "aesthetics of hope" is left for the most part in the original Spanish.

2 Dorfman experiences a similar situation in *Interventions in the Field of Dreams*.

3 The second phrase—"that was giving me a beginning"—is not in the English translation.

4 From Kant and Schiller to Hegel and Marx a central strain of aesthetic theory has focused on the dialectics of artistic mediation. Where Kant focused on the way that art mediates between a concrete particular and an abstract universal, Schiller's *Aesthetic Education* emphasized the way that art facilitates a "play" between the individual and society. Hegel's aesthetics is grounded on a productive dialectic between thought and feeling, and he believed that art plays a key role in the development of "self-consciousness" (Singer and Dunn, 259). Marx's aesthetics focuses on the dialectic between form and content. Eagleton explains that "an interfusion of form and content, in fact, may be taken as Marx's aesthetic ideal" (210).

5 An appendix to the English edition of *How to Read Donald Duck* provides a selected bibliography on cultural imperialism and the mass media with a number of Latin American authors.

6 For a more elaborate discussion of this historical development, see my introduction to *The Dialectics of Exile*.

7 For more analysis of these distinct versions of postmodernism, see Best and Kellner, 247, and McClennen, *The Dialectics of Exile*, 17–20.

8 See Lawrence for the details of a Disney lawsuit in U.S. courts that accused the English translation of copyright infringement. Eventually the book was admitted into the United States from England.

9 In *The Dialectics of Exile* I explore the dialectical tensions of nation, time, language, and space in Dorfman's exile writing.

10 This essay was originally presented to Chilean professors during a seminar on art, media, and politics that took place prior to Allende's election.

11 For more on the ways that Latin American literature adapted and responded to the avant-garde, see Greg Dawes's *Aesthetics and Revolution*.

12 See Bell-Villada for more on the political ambivalence of the avant-garde, especially chapter 5.

13 I am using Dorfman and Edith Grossman's translation for the poem that also provides the title for the volume. While that volume itself has not been translated, the poem has appeared in translation in a variety of venues, including *In Case of Fire in a Foreign Land*. The Chilean dish *pastel de choclo* is actually more like a casserole than a cake. The gloss translation loses the literal reference to the dish and instead offers a similarity through the idea of comfort food.

14 This story was recounted to me by a close friend of Dorfman's who accompanied him on the trip.

15 These particular techniques are analyzed in detail in the sections dedicated to each text in the following chapters.

16 From correspondence with Dorfman.

4. FROM POPULAR UNITY TO EXILE

1 Since I will be treating the original Spanish and the English translation of works in this chapter as two related yet distinct texts, when referring specifically to the original, I will use the Spanish title for clarity.

2 As mentioned in chapter 1, the text also uncannily seemed to predict future events. It highlighted antagonisms among members of the left at a time when Dorfman himself was highly committed to the success of Allende's government. While Dorfman would be criticized for his dark vision and overly complex style, he responded that the grim world of *Moros en la costa* was a fictional exploration of disharmony, the challenges of peaceful revolution, and the social impotence of a politically committed bourgeoisie.

3 The novel received the support of Julio Cortázar when it won a literary prize offered by *La Opinión*, which at the time was under the direction of Jacobo Timmerman. According to Dorfman, Rodolfo Walsh voted against awarding the novel the prize because he did not think that "we needed a socialist Borges" (personal communication with Dorfman). Walsh's reading of the novel reveals important features of its aesthetics.

4 One of Oropesa's most useful contributions to the study of the novel is his schematization of the various fragments (22–25).

5 It is worth remembering that Dorfman's favorite novel is Cortázar's *Rayuela* (*Hopscotch*) because both *Moros en la costa* and *Rayuela* are über-novels structured by meta-narratives that focus on the problem of representation. *Moros en la costa* attempts to apply *Rayuela*'s problems of representation to the revolution.

6 Dorfman also attributes imaginary novels to writers, taking real authors and pairing them with made-up texts.

7 Dorfman's story was wrong about who would be in exile from Chile in the future, but his vision of the future accurately foreshadowed the consequences the left would suffer at the hands of the extreme right.

8 It is important to note that George Shivers worked with Dorfman on the translation. After Dorfman rearranged and edited the Spanish text, Shivers did much of the original translation into English, and then Dorfman made changes to the English. The translation was a collaborative effort, with Dorfman approving all changes to the original syntax and style. I do not mean to diminish Shivers's considerable labor as translator when I attribute the differences between the original and the translation to Dorfman, but considering Dorfman's bilingualism, I believe that it is safe to assume that he either approved or instigated all departures from the original version.

9 Appearing in the same year, and ostensibly the first publication of Dorfman's poetry, was the bilingual German-Spanish edition *Desaparecer*, which includes the poems that appear in the first section of *Pruebas al canto* together with illustrations by Guillermo Nuñez.

Dorfman has published five poetry collections—two in Spanish, two in English, and one bilingual. Many of these collections have included new and previously published works. A more detailed study of the promiscuity among these poetry collections would be useful but is beyond the scope of this volume. The following outlines the poetry collections and the appearance and reappearance of particular poems in them.

> *Missing*. A collection of English-language versions of the poems collected in the first section of *Pruebas al canto*.
>
> *Pastel de choclo*. A collection of poems previously published in *Pruebas al canto*. Poems from *Pruebas al canto* not included here are "Traducción simultánea," "Comunicando," "Hay que armar una campaña," "Vocabulario," "Cono sur," "Sexo siglo XX," "Pájaro de cuentas," "Hambre de muchas cosas," "La misma

semana en que 26 personas," "La vida afuera, hermano," "Herencia," "Veo algunas nubes, es verdad," "Solidaridad, Jericó," "Carta de identidad," "Pies," and "Epílogo: Misión posible."

Last Waltz in Santiago and Other Poems of Exile and Disappearance. An English-language translation of *Pastel de choclo*; part 1 was previously published in English as *Missing*. Poems from *Pastel de choclo* that do not appear here are "Mañana," "Política cultural," "Que venga yo mismo a cargar mi batería," "La guardia interior tampoco se rinde," "Comunicando," "Hay que armar una campaña," "Vocabulario," "El día está azulísimo en Ámsterdam," "Cono sur," "Sexo siglo XX," "Pájaro de cuentas," "Hambre de muchas cosas," "La misma semana en que 26 personas," "Presente," "La vida afuera, hermano," "Que busca en el monte amparo," "Herencia," "Veo algunas nubes, es verdad," "Solidaridad, Jericó," "Carta de identidad," "Pies," and "Epílogo: Misión posible."

In Case of Fire in a Foreign Land. English- and Spanish-language versions of the poems first collected in *Pruebas al canto* with the addition of a preface, dedication, and the following poems: "Drowning/Ahogos," "Gracias/Gracias," "In Case of Fire in a Foreign Land/En caso de incendio en una tierra extraña," "Voices from beyond the Dark/Voces contra el poder," and "Ten Minutes/Diez minutos." The poems from *Pruebas al canto* that do not appear here are "Mañana," "Política cultural," "Cono sur," "Sexo siglo XX," "Pájaro de cuentas," "Hambre de muchas cosas," "La misma semana en que 26 personas," "La vida afuera, hermano," "Que busca en el monte amparo," "Herencia," "Veo algunas nubes, es verdad," "Solidaridad, Jericó," "Carta de identidad," "Pies," and "Epílogo: Misión posible."

10 Poetry also appeals to Dorfman in exile because the poem is short, can circulate easily, and can be memorized. It is an agile yet intimate form of literary expression. (Personal correspondence with Dorfman.)

11 Henry James Morello suggests a number of functions that literature can serve in the mediation of trauma.

12 Given that all of the poems I will highlight appear in the bilingual edition, *In Case of Fire in a Foreign Land,* page references to individual poems will be from this more recent edition. This collection of new and collected poems was also translated by Edith Grossman. The translations of poems from *Pruebas al canto* that appeared in *Missing* were not changed.

13 Dorfman described the volume in these terms in e-mail correspondence with me.

14 Dorfman engages in a similar project when he writes *Manifesto for Another World.*

15 It is also worth noting that Dorfman's first three published literary works invoke colloquial expressions for their titles, the third being his first collection of short stories, *Cría ojos.* (This title is discussed in the text below.) Used albeit with different intent, these expressions underscore Dorfman's desire to use his writing to bridge highbrow literature with orality.

16 Dorfman often includes poems in his essays and fiction. This particular poem

appears in the Spanish version of the play version of *Widows*, *Viudas*. It also was included in a speech Dorfman delivered to the United Nations on censorship. That text is included in *Other Septembers*.

17 The newer poems that end the collection *In Case of Fire in a Foreign Land* return to the problem of the difficulty of narrating in combination with the need to narrate moments of extreme historical crisis. These, in addition to the poems that Dorfman wrote after the U.S. invasion of Iraq in 2003 under the series "The Other Side of Death," demonstrate his ongoing interest in these issues.

18 Carlos Saura's film *Cría cuervos* (Raise Crows) also uses the phrase in order to explore the relationship between family structure and authoritarianism.

19 The word "Putamadre" is not translated. It could have maybe been rendered as "asshole," but after some dialogue on the matter, Shivers and Dorfman decided to leave it in the original Spanish.

20 Similar to the case of Dorfman's poems, his short story collections often include a combination of new and reprinted pieces. To date, Dorfman has published seven collections of stories, one of which is an English translation. The following outlines the new and reprinted works.

> *Dorando la píldora*. Contains seven stories previously published in *Cría ojos*, along with the new stories "Nothing Nada," "Feliz aniversario," "Dorando la píldora," and "Despidiendo a John Wayne."
> *Cuentos para militares: La batalla de los colores y otros cuentos*. Contains the remaining seven stories from *Cría ojos* not collected in *Dorando la píldora*, as well as "Raigambre" and "Botánica clandestina."
> *Travesía: Cuentos*. Five stories from *Cría ojos* with the addition of a prologue by Elbio Rodríguez Barilari.
> *Cuentos casi completos*. Contains twelve stories originally from *Cría ojos*, four from *Dorando la píldora*, and one new piece, "Advertencia."
> *My House Is on Fire*. Trans. George Shivers. London: Methuen, 1990, 1992; New York: Viking. Contains English versions of eleven stories from *Cría ojos*.
> *Rojos Copihuex*. Contains four stories from *Cría ojos*, three from *Dorando la píldora*, and one from *Cuentos casi completos*, as well as "Rojos Copihuex" and "Primera vez."
> *Acércate más y más: Cuentos casi completos*. Contains the stories from *Cuentos casi completos* with the addition of a short glossary.

21 Oropesa is the only other scholar to study these stories, but he focuses on isolated stories rather than looking at the shape of an entire collection.

22 Lucho is the common nickname for Luis.

23 Here it is worth remembering Walsh's description of Dorfman's *Moros en la costa* as a text that reads like a socialist Borges.

24 Scholarship on this novel has been conducted by Lois Baer Barr (on patriarchy and authoritarianism), Cusato (on denouncing the military's strategy of disappearance), Kim (on the construction of community), McClennen (on the relationship to exile),

Nelson (on gender ideology), Oropesa (on heroism and Manichaeism), Pinet (on women's resistance), and Wallace (on representing the disappeared).

25 Two towns by the name of Longa exist: one is in Greece and the other in Angola.

26 For more on the technique of doubling and mirroring as an essential feature of Dorfman's aesthetics of hope, see chapter 3.

27 Again the difference between the original and the translation indicates that the original Spanish was far more vague and ambiguous than the English translation. In this example, Alejandra simply says that the grandmother is "wrong," but in the translation Sofía's mistake is specifically translated as an accusation that she is responsible for "killing" the men.

28 Oropesa's analysis of the novel suggests that the women's rebellion exemplifies a Manicheistic struggle of good over evil.

29 Social agency is Henry Giroux's term, which appears throughout his works, to describe a form of collective empowerment that does not deny the individual.

30 Scholarship on the novel has focused on Jewish themes and patriarchy (Barr), the representation of the future perfect (Kim), postmodernism (Oropesa), exile (McClennen), and textual unity (Shivers).

31 This structure has led some critics such as Barr to criticize the novel's complexity (140). The various narrative lines, though, converge in shared themes. The novel's English translator, George Shivers, makes this point clear in a brief essay on the novel's "textual unity." Dorfman himself concedes that one of the novel's major flaws may be its complex structure, but he also has said in a number of interviews that it is his favorite novel. (See, for instance, his interview with Incledon and his essay written under the pseudonym P. Donald.)

32 As Barr points out, the multiple meanings of the original Spanish complicate translation into English (142). The English words hint more subtly at the birth metaphor than the original Spanish, which uses terms commonly used to describe pregnancy and birth.

33 Dorfman has compared the act of writing to birth on a number of occasions, most especially with regard to his memoir; he confesses that it took him nine months to write the first few lines ("Footnotes," 206).

34 The essay was published in 1981, and the novel first appeared in 1982.

35 See Barr and Kim for more on the connections between Manuel Sendero and Víctor Jara.

36 According to Dorfman, he had originally titled the novel *Ojos que no ven* (Eyes That Don't See), and when he called his publisher to tell him he wanted to change the title, the publisher misunderstood him. He had decided on a title that would be the same in English and Spanish: *Máscara* and *Mascara*. But his Argentine publisher mistook his pronunciation of "*Máscara*" for "*Máscaras*" since Chileans often aspirate the last "s." Thus Dorfman was surprised by the title when he saw his first copy of the published novel. The Mexican edition (1997), consequently, has the Spanish title Dorfman originally intended. (Personal communication from Dorfman.)

Research on the novel has been conducted by Oropesa (on deconstruction), Barr (on Jewish themes), and McClennen (on themes of exile).

37 For more of Dorfman's comments on the novel, see his interview with Incledon.

38 Both the English and the Spanish versions of the novel play with the name of the doctor. To add to the confusion the dominant name used in the Spanish text is "Mavirelli," and the dominant one in the English is "Mirarelli." Here Dorfman plays with the idea that the signifier might change but the signified remains the same. Oropesa has done a meticulous accounting of the various spellings used by the faceless man when he speaks to the doctor in the Spanish version (109). In an interview with Ilan Stavans, Dorfman explains that he wrote the novel first in Spanish, revised it as he translated it into English, and then retranslated it back into Spanish (305). The novel appeared simultaneously in English and Spanish.

5. FROM EXILE TO DIASPORA

1 Fukuyama's *The End of History and the Last Man* was published in 1992. His article "The End of History?" appeared in the *National Interest* in the summer of 1989. Homi Bhabha's *Nation and Narration* appeared in 1990.

2 The epigraph from Cocteau cited above is on Ariel Dorfman's Web site, http:www.adorfman.duke.edu/.

3 Alongside theories about the changing role of the nation were theories that focused on the postcolonial condition and that also worked to remap the way that global relations were studied. After Edward Said's groundbreaking work, *Orientalism* (1978), a growing number of scholars began to work in postcolonial studies. *The Empire Writes Back: Theory and Practice in Post-Colonial Literatures* (1989), by Bill Ashcroft, Gareth Griffiths, and Helen Tiffin, is a key example of the intersections of globalization theory with postcolonial theory. Dorfman had begun to work on many of these themes in the 1970s in works like *How to Read Donald Duck* and in the essays that appeared later in English in *The Empire's Old Clothes*. Dorfman recounts that when *The Empire's Old Clothes* first appeared in English translation in 1983, a reviewer mistakenly suggested that the book was an example of the influence of Edward Said's critique of colonial structures of knowledge in *Orientalism*, a book that appeared in print a few years after Dorfman's original text. (Personal communication.)

4 For more on the role of nationalism in defining the identity of the exile, see McClennen, *The Dialectics of Exile*, 35–57.

5 It is important to note that Dorfman believes that these two often competing ways of recording the past have a long history in Latin America and that for him literature has played a pivotal role in bringing these versions of the past into contact and conflict. For more on this, see especially *Imaginación y violencia*.

6 See Quinn on the establishment of truth commissions in the 1990s. The Wall of Memory in Chile was erected in 1994. Legislation to construct Memory Park in Buenos Aires was passed in 1998.

7   In an interview with me for *Context* Dorfman describes the start of the Second World War as "the turning point of the twentieth century—the most important date of the twentieth century" (7).

8   Two texts provide important background to the debate over the *testimonio* and especially in relation to the veracity of Rigoberta Menchú's text: *The Real Thing*, edited by Georg M. Gugelberger, and *The Rigoberta Menchú Controversy*, edited by Arturo Arias.

9   For more, see Elzbieta Sklodowska's analysis of this point in her essay in the Arias volume and Doris Sommer's essay in the Gugelberger volume.

10 It is worth remembering that Dorfman was a professor at Duke University during this period and a colleague of scholars like Fredric Jameson, Stanley Fish, and Alberto Moreiras. Not only was he acutely aware of these debates, but he also fostered them himself. For instance, he was the first professor at Duke to teach a graduate seminar on the *testimonio*.

11 John Beverley positions *testimonio* discretely apart from literature. In contrast, Sklodowska explains that she always approached *testimonio* "with an awareness of the text's artifactual nature, including the inevitable embroidering of the facts for dramatic, political, or aesthetic effect" (256). Dorfman's ideas about *testimonio* are more akin to Sklodowska's.

12 For more detailed analysis of Dorfman's work in media criticism, see chapter 6.

13 See, for example, my analysis of this tension in his earlier works in *The Dialectics of Exile*, 175–83.

14 The Rettig Commission was established in 1990 and released its final report in March 1991. *Death and the Maiden* was written before the final report.

15 A number of his subsequent texts would also follow in these two extremes, especially *The Nanny and the Iceberg*.

16 All quotations of the English version of the play come from *The Resistance Trilogy*.

17 From Dorfman's Web site: http://www.adorfman.duke.edu.

18 See the secondary bibliography on Dorfman for reference details for these works. Only texts that are quoted are included in the works cited.

19 Dorfman has been writing avidly since he was a young boy, so it is technically a mistake to refer to *Death and the Maiden* as his first play. It is, however, his first produced and published theatrical work, a fact I use to suggest that this is his first play because it is his first *public* play.

20 For more detailed analysis of this turn to poetry, see chapter 4.

21 Personal communication from Dorfman.

22 Dorfman states that the play had a mixed reception in Chile. It was successful in free showings, but received very negative reviews and did not appeal to the Chilean theatergoing elite (*La muerte y la doncella*, 97). Idelber Avelar, who critiques the film version, writes that the play "was a resounding failure among the public that it had attempted, secretly and in bad faith, to translate and express, the Chilean population" (45). In contrast, Robert A. Morace provides a more subtle critique, recognizing that the play meant to "provoke, not please" and that it failed with the elites, not with what

Avelar calls the "Chilean population." Chilean critic Manuel Jofré says that the play is "sin duda alguna, la obra de teatro chileno y latinoamericano que más ha llegado en la historia latinoamericana" (98); (without any doubt the Chilean and Latin American play that has gone the farthest in Latin American history). Maya Jaggi writes that for Carlos Fuentes, who deemed *Death and the Maiden* Sophoclean in its power and simplicity, no other play in Latin America has achieved its universal resonance (n.p.).

23 Dorfman refers to the two main groups who did not like the play in the Spanish version of the afterword (97). I do not mean to suggest that the exiles suffered in the same ways as those who were tortured, although many who survived torture later went into exile so that these two groups overlapped. I simply want to note that they were equally ignored by the official reconciliation process.

24 See Morello for an analysis of De la Parra's theater and Nelson for Benavente and Eltit.

25 For more on the public reception of Gambaro's play, see Morello and Taylor.

26 In Act I, Scene 2, Paulina eavesdrops on the conversation between Miranda and Gerardo. In Scene 4 of the same act, Miranda is gagged and must listen to Paulina and later to Paulina and Gerardo. In the second act, shortly after Gerardo ungags Miranda, Paulina and Gerardo leave Miranda alone to talk privately on the terrace. In the second scene, Paulina watches the men talk from the terrace. And in the first scene of the third act, Miranda watches Paulina tell her story to Gerardo and the scene shifts to Miranda's confession. Later in the scene Gerardo leaves while Paulina talks to Miranda. In the second scene Paulina is silent while Gerardo speaks about the successes of the commission. When Miranda appears, they are all silent.

27 It is important to note that none of these cited expressions of affection are in the English translation. While the word play with "gata," which can mean both pussycat and car jack, would obviously have to change, the other terms could have been translated but were not.

28 Much is made of whether Miranda is actually guilty. I agree with Vidal that he is guilty, but I also think that the play is written so as to allow for a degree of ambiguity for those who wish to remain skeptical.

29 The absence of this phrase in the English is very interesting. A number of significant changes between the two versions merit a more thorough study.

30 To Chilean ears the phrase might also remind one of the word "huevón," a commonly used vulgar term roughly equivalent to "asshole."

31 Nietzsche is famous for two sets of quotes that refer negatively to women. In *Thus Spoke Zarathustra* he suggests that women's sole function is to reproduce. Numerous references in that text call for women to submit to men. And *Beyond Good and Evil* opens with the line, "Supposing that truth is a woman—what then?" (ix).

32 The original quote is: "The great question that has never been answered, and which I have not yet been able to answer, despite my thirty years of research into the feminine soul, is 'What does a woman want?'" (cited in Jones, 474).

33 http://www.scribd.com/doc/46681/On-Truth-and-Lies-in-a-Nonmoral-Sense-by-Friedrich-Nietzsche

34 E-mail correspondence with David Schroeder.

35 Scholarship on *Konfidenz* has been conducted by Kim (on psychoanalytic transference) and Coddou (on authorship). The 2003 Dalkey edition includes an interesting preface by Andrei Codrescu.

36 This technique is a key feature of his aesthetic practice, and it is especially visible in this work. See chapter 3 for more on how this is a common Dorfman practice.

37 According to personal correspondence from Dorfman, the source of the author/narrator is the narrator figure from the theatrical version of *Widows*. The narrator remains in the Spanish version of the play and was omitted in the definitive English version.

38 All English references are from the Dalkey 2003 reprint.

39 Detailed study of the differences between the English and Spanish versions would be highly valuable for future research on Dorfman's work.

40 The English here departs significantly from the Spanish. In the Spanish there is no mention of the need to have a story with a "good, decent man"; instead in the Spanish the narrator describes him as the man that "alguna vez me tuvo confianza" (166; at one time trusted me).

41 To add a further twist to these multiple versions, the Spanish version of the play, published by Ediciones de la Flor, retains the narrator. This difference may be a consequence of the distinct theatrical traditions in English and Spanish, but it certainly merits further study. Because the narrator speaks about his existence in exile, he offers readers further insight into this theme in Dorfman's work. Readers will also want to note that the seventeenth scene in the Spanish version, which is the narrator's third appearance, rewrites Dorfman's poem "Traducción simultánea" (Simultaneous Translation). The narrator also adds significant commentary on the theme of storytelling and resistance.

42 For detailed analysis of the novel, see chapter 4.

43 Technically the opening scene of the novel follows Dorfman's explanation of the frame followed by the frame.

44 This as yet unpublished play was written for the Royal Shakespeare Company.

45 In yet another level of layering, the original story is about Don Alfonso, who reads about another censor named José Cordova. Dorfman seems to be playfully suggesting to readers to read these texts as simulacra of one another.

46 These comments may also be an oblique reference to the fact that Dorfman was criticized by some in the Latino community when non-Latinos were cast in the Broadway production of *Death and the Maiden*.

47 Research on the memoir has been done by Castillo (on gender and *latinidad*), Doloughan (on language and identity), and Waldman (on the description of identity as multiple). Those interested in studying *Heading South, Looking North* will want to read Dorfman's "Footnotes to a Double Life," which describes his struggle to find the right language for the memoir. My comments in this section are a revised version of McClennen, "The Diasporic Subject."

48 John Beverley and Marc Zimmerman also support an oppositional view of northern versus southern forms of life writing in their study of *testimonio*, but the fallacy of

this binary has been pointed out by Silvia Molloy and Steven Hunsaker. It is important to note that Dorfman envisions these discourses of identity as largely oppositional, only to then expose the ways that they intertwine.

49 See chapter 2 for a discussion of the role of Renaissance literature in Dorfman's literary formation.

50 Most reviews refer to the text as a memoir. In all of my correspondence with Dorfman he has never used "autobiography" to describe the text.

51 While my references to the Spanish version will be occasional, it is important to point out that this text was originally written in English and then was translated and adapted by Dorfman into Spanish. I have noted more than one hundred discrepancies between the two versions. A future study might look at the relationship between the ways identity is constructed in the two versions and how they complement one another.

52 The Spanish version keeps these same phrases.

53 See table 1 in chapter 3 for a chart of the book's structure.

54 While in exile, Dorfman would use both English and Spanish for "noncreative" writing, such as the journalistic. The memoir is his first published creative work originally written in English. For more on this tension, see his essay "Footnotes to a Double Life."

55 The subtitle in Spanish ("Un romance en dos lenguas") is considerably different and suggests further interpretive possibilities.

56 This novel was originally published in English in 1999. It was then translated by Dorfman into Spanish and published in 2000. When he translated it, he made changes, the most notable of which was the shortening of the epilogue. Then he reissued it in English in 2003 with the shortened epilogue. I will be quoting primarily from the 2003 English edition. The original British English version also has the shortened epilogue.

57 In-depth comparison of these two novels yields a number of interesting links. For example, in *The Last Song*, Manuel's son was nameless and had no identity, just as Gabriel McKenzie has a face that does not age. The breakdown of distinct masculine identities as representative of social sectors takes place in both novels, just as both novels depend on the loving, maternal support of female characters for salvation and redemption. Both texts also include numerous connections to other literary works.

58 Novels in nineteenth-century Europe also took up these themes, but their role in the New World was somewhat distinct, as explained by Doris Sommer in her study *Foundational Fictions*, because of the New World urge to link reproduction with population growth and racial purity.

59 Chilean novelist Diamela Eltit's novel *El cuarto mundo* (*The Fourth World*) provides another interesting link on this point.

60 For more detail on the way the novel adapts the picaresque to the postmodern, see the section on the picaresque in chapter 2.

61 Gabriel's social alienation might also be interestingly read as a commentary on the young generation of Latin American writers who were gaining acclaim during this

time and who in general were less radically political than the writers of the post-boom. The writers that would later come to be known as the "McOndo generation" wrote their first novels in this period. For instance, Alberto Fuguet's novel *Mala onda* (*Bad Vibes*) was published in 1996. In one of the later scenes of Fuguet's novel father and son have sex with different women while in the same room, a sexual link that might be productively compared to Gabriel's contradictory desire to both be sexually similar yet independent of his father.

62 *The Nanny and the Iceberg* was preceded by *Heading North, Looking South*, and it is important to understand the two as complementary. The memoir attends to history, and the novel seems to abandon it. In the novel, a young man who has been revealed as immoral and immature performs the abandonment of history. His character is not meant to function as a role model but as a foil that renders the apathy of youth culture as destructive and, in the case of Gabriel, suicidal. Such moral weakness contrasts with *Heading North, Looking South*, which elaborates on the need to tell one's story and to be responsible for one's actions and their impact on history.

63 Gabriel twice mentions that he has two fathers, each time referring to different fathers. First he refers to Cris and to Che and then to Cris and Barón. In a sense my schema merges these two versions.

64 It might be interesting to read Octavio Paz's discussion of the Mexican colloquial use of "chingar" in *El laberinto de la soledad* against the use of Chilean equivalents in *The Nanny and the Iceberg*, especially in terms of the ties between these expletives and colonial violence.

65 A famous case of a novelist using the word was D. H. Lawrence in *Lady Chatterley's Lover* (1928).

66 When Gabriel and Amanda Camila go to visit the mission linked to the Ona tribe, they learn that the mission often tried to keep the Ona from reproducing. They pay particular attention to a sculpture of a woman who has no genitals (227).

67 An earlier, much shorter version was published in Portuguese in a series on the seven deadly sins.

68 In an uncanny foreshadowing the novel's release predated by only a few months the Enron scandal, which drew public attention to the way that massive corporate greed had destroyed the lives of many workers.

69 The novel also provides Dorfman's readers to links to his earlier works, especially to *Mascara*. Both Blake and the nameless protagonist of *Mascara* do not like to be photographed, and both are obsessed by the power of capturing the images of others. Another interesting link is to *The Last Song of Manuel Sendero*: Blake says that he wants to develop a diet pill, called the Gobbler, which allows people to lose weight the more that they eat (92). Readers will recall that an identical pill was advertised on the television program *Search, Search* in *The Last Song*. Dorfman uses the symbolic pill as an analogy for consumer culture.

70 Other intertextual references are to Alfred Hitchcock's *Vertigo* and to the poetry of William Blake. The paranoia and psychological tension of the novel connect with *Vertigo*, while the protagonist's name and his fascination with Rose are an homage

to William Blake. Furthering this connection, Dorfman wrote a poem dedicated to Laura Bush from William Blake in response to the events of the Iraq War.

71 *Exorcising Terror* is analyzed in detail in the following chapter.

72 Readers will note that Dorfman has spoken almost these exact same words in reference to his exile. See, for instance, *Heading South, Looking North*, 275–76.

73 An earlier published edition of the play was released in 2000 via Amnesty International. In that first appearance the play was entitled *The Speak Truth to Power Play: Voices from beyond the Dark*. It was then re-released in 2004 in a new edition and with a title change to *Manifesto for Another World: Voices from beyond the Dark*.

74 For more on this point, see chapter 3.

75 In the most recent (as yet unpublished) and, according to Dorfman, definitive version of the play this character is now divided into two men. They share the features of this one character, and they are able to exchange dialogue, thereby adding a further element of drama to the work.

76 Personal communication from Dorfman.

6. MEDIA CRITICISM AND CULTURAL JOURNALISM

1 See note 4 of chapter 1.

2 Despite Yúdice's designation of Dorfman and Mattelart's text as seminal for Latin American cultural studies and Denning's inclusion of Dorfman as one of the fifty most influential members of the New Left, it is worth noting that his work is not included in the massive anthology of Latin American cultural studies edited by Abril Trigo, Alicia Ríos, and Ana del Sarto. It is possible that his absence from the text reveals his continued outsider status among U.S. Latin Americanists. This point becomes especially clear when one notes that his work is included in the anthology *Media and Cultural Studies*, edited by Meenakshi Gigi Durham and Douglas Kellner, a volume that also includes the work of Jesús Martín-Barbero and Néstor García Canclini within an international lineup of influential cultural studies scholars.

3 In the introduction to *The Empire's Old Clothes* Dorfman critiques some of the central assumptions in his earlier work (10–11). He also reassesses *Donald Duck* in his memoir (250–52). Denning explains that the utopian leanings of this wave of cultural theory were later reconsidered in light of the massive wave of repression and dictatorship in Latin America, Africa, and Asia and the free-market fundamentalism of Margaret Thatcher and Ronald Reagan (8).

4 Scholarship on his critical work has been conducted by Oropesa (on Dorfman's critique of popular culture), Berger (on *How to Read Donald Duck*), Flora (on *How to Read Donald Duck*), and López-Calvo (on Dorfman's essays).

5 To give a brief sense of how these various editions morph, the Mexican edition of *Patos, elefantes y héroes* (1998) does include the chapter "The Innocents March into History," and Siglo XXI's reprint (2003) also includes a brief new introduction to the chapter, which draws parallels to the 9/11 terrorist attacks on the United States.

6 The text did not appear previously in periodicals, but it flows from the type of cul-

7 Even though the reprints can be explained by the complexities of Dorfman's publishing history (problems with censorship and international circulation), it should be noted that the multiple reprints can make it appear as though Dorfman were simply recycling texts.

8 Armand Mattelart is Belgian. He lived in Chile from 1962 to 1973, during which time he taught sociology in the Universidad Católica in Santiago. In 1973 he went to Paris.

9 See John Shelton Lawrence's account of the text's blocked circulation in the appendix to the 1991 English edition.

10 For instance, in the multimedia documentary *In the Footsteps of September 11, 1973* (2005), which traces Dorfman's movements that day, he tries to reenter the university where he used to teach, only to find that the university's gates are locked, just as they were locked thirty-two years prior. This time, though, they are locked for different reasons. Accompanied by his good friend Manuel Jofré, who was Dorfman's colleague in 1973, Dorfman playfully convinces the university's guard to let the two men step inside the gates. Wearing a wide grin, he symbolically places his feet on the university campus in an act meant to remember and reconsider the past.

11 Dorfman first published on these topics while living in Chile. His work on Babar appeared before *Donald Duck*, and his work on the Lone Ranger was conducted simultaneously to his work with Mattelart.

12 Giroux's notion of "educated hope" is indebted to Freire's theories in *Pedagogy of Hope* and *Pedagogy of Freedom*.

13 The majority of these projects are collaborative, especially with his son Rodrigo.

14 E-mail communication from Dorfman describing this project.

15 See http://www.bushin30seconds.org/150/view.html?ad_id=360.

16 Personal communication from Dorfman. According to Dorfman, when *Ercilla* censored a piece of his on Nicolás Guillén, he resigned.

17 The case was reopened in May 2004. When Pinochet died on December 10, 2006, he had not been convicted of any crimes.

18 For more on the way that Dorfman displaces Pinochet as the center of his own life story, see my analysis of the memoir in chapter 5.

19 As I have noted, the definition of *testimonio* has been quite contentious, but the two elements mentioned here are common features of many definitions. Beverley emphasizes that *testimonio* represents a "life" (70). Yúdice emphasizes truth and authenticity ("Testimonio and Postmodernism," 44).

20 In particular see his chapter on Chilean testimonial in *Some Write to the Future*.

21 For more on this point see my analysis of his poetry in chapter 4.

22 See for example on pages 7, 14, 27, 39, 59, 65, 79, 89, 94, 99, 105, 116, 149, 160, 166, 176, 191, 220, 229, 237, 242, 245, 246, 247, 251, 252.

23 See for example on pages 10, 12, 13, 18, 25, 26, 46, 48, 54, 60, 69, 71, 77, 124, 163, 169, 224, 236, 244, 245, 247, 248.

24 See the blog at http://commentisfree.guardian.co.uk/about.html.

WORKS CITED

Adorno, Theodor W. *Aesthetic Theory*. Trans. Gretel Adorno and Rolf Tiedeman. Minneapolis: University of Minnesota Press, 1997.

——. *Prisms*. Trans. Samuel and Shierry Weber. Cambridge, Mass.: MIT Press, 1981.

Adorno, Theodor W., and Max Horkheimer. "The Culture Industry: Enlightenment as Mass Deception" (1944). http://www.marxists.org/reference/archive/adorno/1944/culture-industry.htm. Accessed August 1, 2004.

Aguilera, Pilar, and Ricardo Fredes. *Chile: The Other September 11*. New York: Ocean Press, 2003.

Ahmad, Aijaz. *In Theory: Literatures, Classes, Nations*. London: Verso, 1992.

Alazraki, Jaime, and Ivar Ivask, eds. *The Final Island: The Fiction of Julio Cortázar*. Norman: University of Oklahoma Press, 1978. In the Gale Literary Database: http://galenet.galegroup.com. Accessed August 8, 2005.

Althusser, Louis. "Ideology and Ideological State Apparatuses (Notes towards an Investigation)." In *Lenin and Philosophy and Other Essays*, 127–86. New York: Monthly Review Press, 1972.

Anzaldúa, Gloria, and Cherríe Moraga, eds. *This Bridge Called My Back: Writings of Radical Women of Color*. New York: Kitchen Table Press, 1983.

Arenas, Reinaldo. *Antes que anochezca*. Barcelona: Tusquets, 2001.

Arias, Arturo, ed. *The Rigoberta Menchú Controversy*. Minneapolis: University of Minnesota Press, 2001.

Arnold, Matthew. *Culture and Anarchy*. 1869. Landmarks in the History of Education. Cambridge: Cambridge University Press, 1960.

Ashcroft, Bill, Gareth Griffiths, and Helen Tiffin. *The Empire Writes Back: Theory and Practice in Post-Colonial Literatures*. London: Routledge, 1989.

Avelar, Idelber. *The Letter of Violence: Essays on Narrative, Ethics, and Politics*. New York: Palgrave Macmillan, 2004.

Bakhtin, Mikhail. "Discourse in the Novel" (1934–35). In *The Dialogic Imagination: Four Essays*, 259–422. Ed. Michael Holquist. Trans. Caryl Emerson and Michael Holquist. Austin: University of Texas Press, 1981.

Ball, David, Sophia A. McClennen, Ariel Dorfman, and Gordon O. Taylor. "Forum: Poetry and Torture." *World Literature Today* 81, nos. 1–2 (May–August 2005): 6–7.

Barr, Lois Baer. "Deconstructing Authoritarian Codes: Ariel Dorfman." In *Isaac Unbound: Patriarchal Traditions in the Latin American Jewish Novel*, 131–58. Tempe: ASU Center for Latin American Studies, 1995.

Barthes, Roland. "The Death of the Author." In *Image, Music, Text*, 142–48. Ed. and trans. Stephen Heath. New York: Hill, 1977.

——. *Mythologies* (1957). New York: Hill and Wang, 1972.

——. *Sade, Fournier, Loyola*. Trans. Richard Miller. New York: Farrar, Straus, Giroux, 1976.

Baudrillard, Jean. *The Gulf War Did Not Take Place*. Bloomington: Indiana University Press, 1995.

Baumgarten, Alexander. *Aesthetica* (1750). New York: G. Olms, 1970.

——. *Reflections on Poetry* (1735). Trans., intro., and notes by Karl Aschenbrenner and William B. Holther. Berkeley: University of California Press, 1954.

Beebee, Thomas O. "Ballad of the Apocalypse: Another Look at Bob Dylan's 'Hard Rain.' " *Text and Performance Quarterly* 2, no. 1 (January 1991): 18–34.

Bell-Villada, Gene H. *Art for Art's Sake and Literary Life*. Lincoln: University of Nebraska Press, 1998.

Benjamin, Walter. "The Storyteller." In *Illuminations: Essays and Reflections*, 83–109. Trans. Harry Zohn. New York: Schocken-Random House, 1988.

——. "The Work of Art in the Age of Mechanical Reproduction." In *Illuminations: Essays and Reflections*, 217–51. Trans. Harry Zohn. New York: Schocken-Random House, 1988.

Bennett, Andrew. *The Author*. New York: Routledge, 2005.

Berger, John. "A Disney World." *New Society*, August 20, 1975, 478–80.

——. "The Hour of Poetry." In *The Sense of Sight: Writings by John Berger*, 243–52. Ed. Lloyd Spencer. New York: Vintage Books, 1985.

——. "The Storyteller." In *The Sense of Sight: Writings by John Berger*, 13–18. Ed. Lloyd Spencer. New York: Vintage Books, 1985.

Berman, Jennifer. "Ariel Dorfman." *Bomb* 50 (1994–95): 30–33.

Best, Steven, and Douglas Kellner. *Postmodern Theory: Critical Interrogations*. New York: Guilford Press, 1991.

Beverley, John. *Against Literature*. Minneapolis: University of Minnesota Press, 1993.

Beverley, John, and Marc Zimmerman. *Literature and Politics in the Central American Revolutions*. Austin: University of Texas Press, 1990.

Bhabha, Homi, ed. "Introduction: Narrating the Nation." In *Nation and Narration*, 1–7. London: Routledge, 1990.

Bloch, Ernst. *The Principle of Hope*. Studies in Contemporary German Social Thought. Cambridge, Mass.: MIT Press, 1986. 1st American ed.

Blum, Bihla. "Desde Chile a Israel: *La muerte y la doncella* por el teatro 'Habima.' " *Revista de Artes, Letras y Filosofía* 15 (1999): 147–56.

Boal, Augosto. *Teatro del oprimido y otras poéticas políticas*. New York: Urizen Books, 1979.

Boyers, Peggy, and Juan Carlos Lertora. "Ideology, Exile, Language: An Interview with Ariel Dorfman." *Salmagundi* 82–83 (1989): 142–63.

Brotherston, Gordon. *Book of the Fourth World*. New York: Cambridge University Press, 1992.

Bürger, Peter. *Theory of the Avant-Garde*. Trans. Michael Shaw. Minneapolis: University of Minnesota Press, 1984.

Burke, Peter. "History as Social Memory." In *Memory: History, Culture and the Mind*, 97–113. Ed. T. Butler. Oxford: Blackwell, 1989.

Burke, Sean. *The Death and Return of the Author: Criticism and Subjectivity in Barthes, Foucault, and Derrida*. Edinburgh: Edinburgh University Press, 1992.

Carpentier, Alejo. *Los pasos perdidos*. Madrid: Cátedra, 1985.

Castillo, Debra. "Arrival: Dorfman, Salazar, Sainz, Rivera-Valdés." In *Redreaming America: Toward a Bilingual American Culture*, 99–143. Albany: SUNY Press, 2004.

Cervantes, Miguel de. *Don Quijote de la Mancha*. Trans. Burton Rafael. Ed. Diana de Armas Wilson. New York: Norton, 1999.

——. *El ingenioso hidalgo don Quijote de la Mancha*. April 1, 2004. http://www.donquixote.com/texto.html. Accessed May 1, 2005.

Claro-Mayo, Juan. "Dorfman, cuentista comprometido." *Revista Iberoamericana* 47, nos. 114–15 (1981): 339–45.

Coddou, Marcelo. "Konfidenz, de Ariel Dorfman." *Acta Literaria* 19 (1994): 107–13.

Codrescu, Andrei. "Introduction: Note on a Filament." In Ariel Dorfman, *Konfidenz*, v–vii. Normal, Ill.: Dalkey Archive, 2003.

Coetzee, J. M. "Afterword." In Ariel Dorfman, *Mascara*, 131–36. New York: Seven Stories Press, 2004.

——. *Boyhood: Scenes from Provincial Life*. London: Secker and Warburg, 1997.

Cohn, Deborah. Review of *Blake's Therapy*, by Ariel Dorfman. *Review: Latin American Literature and Arts* 65 (fall 2002). http://www.counciloftheamericas.org/as/literature/br65dorfman.html. Accessed June 10, 2005.

Cuomo, Kerry Kennedy. *Speak Truth to Power: Human Rights Defenders Who Are Changing Our World*. New York: Crown, 2000.

Dawes, Greg. *Aesthetics and Revolution: Nicaraguan Poetry 1979–1990.* Minneapolis: University of Minnesota Press, 1993.

——. "Realism, Surrealism, Socialist Realism and Neruda's 'Guided Spontaneity.' " In *Verses against Darkness: Neruda's Poetry and Politics.* Lewistown: Bucknell University Press, 2006. http://eserver.org/clogic/2003/dawes.htm. Accessed May 1, 2005.

Dawes, James. *That the World May Know: Bearing Witness to Atrocity.* Cambridge, Mass.: Harvard University Press, 2007.

de la Campa, Román. "On New American Subjects and Intellectual Models." *Nepantla: Views from South* 4, no. 2 (2003): 235–43.

De la Parra, Marco Antonio. *Lo crudo, lo cocido, lo podrido.* In *Teatro chileno contemporáneo,* 809–65. Ed. Juan Andrés Piña. Madrid: Fondo de Cultura Económica, 1992.

del Sarto, Ana, Alicia Rios, and Abril Trigo, eds. *The Latin American Cultural Studies Reader.* Durham: Duke University Press, 2004.

de Man, Paul. "Autobiography as De-facement." In *The Rhetoric of Romanticism,* 67–81. New York: Columbia University Press, 1984.

Deleuze, Gilles, and Félix Guattari. *Nomadology: The War Machine.* Trans. Brian Massumi. New York: Semiotext(e), 1986.

Denning, Michael. *Culture in the Age of Three Worlds.* New York: Verso, 2004.

Donald, P. [pseudonym for Ariel Dorfman]. "Furioso cantabile." Review of *The Last Song of Manuel Sendero. Hispamérica* 10 (1981): 19–23. (Fictitious book review).

Dorfman, Ariel. *El absurdo entre cuatro paredes: El teatro de Harold Pinter.* Santiago: Editorial Universitaria, 1968.

——. "Adios, General." *Harper's Magazine,* December 1989, 72–76.

——. *American ID: Choice.* Multimedia Web site with videos written, produced, and directed by Rodrigo Dorfman. Web site text by Ariel Dorfman. For PBS. 2006. http://www.pbs.org/pov/borders/2006/choice.html.

——. "Americanos." Unpublished manuscript.

——. "Are There Times When We Have to Accept Torture?" *The Guardian,* May 8, 2004, n.p.

——. *Blake's Therapy.* New York: Seven Stories Press, 2001.

——. "Christopher Columbus Has Words from the Other Side of Death for Captain John Whyte." *open Democracy,* April 11, 2003. http://www.opendemocracy.net/debates/article-2–95–1148.jsp. Accessed July 20, 2004.

——. "Conjuros: The Bull in the Labyrinth of Spain and Chile." *Duke University Museum of Art,* spring 2002.

——. *Death and the Maiden.* New York: Penguin Books, 1991; London: Nick Hern, 1991.

——. *De elefantes, literatura y miedo: Ensayos sobre la comunicación americana.* Havana: Casa de las Américas, 1986.

——. *Desert Memories: Journeys through the Chilean North.* Washington, D.C.: National Geographic, 2004.

——. "Un diario para Ana." *Revista Hoy,* June 20–26, 1979, 35–41.

——. *The Empire's Old Clothes: What the Lone Ranger, Babar, and Other Innocent Heroes Do to Our Minds.* Trans. Clark Hansen. New York: Pantheon Books, 1983.

———. *Ensayos quemados en Chile: Inocencia y neocolonialismo*. Buenos Aires: Ediciones de la Flor, 1974.

———. "An Exile Finds Chile 'Struck by a Plague.' " *New York Times*, September 11, 1983, 23.

———. *Exorcising Terror: The Incredible Unending Trial of General Augusto Pinochet*. New York: Seven Stories Press, 2002.

———. "Fear and the Word." *Autodafe* 3/4: 219–24.

———. "Footnotes to a Double Life." In *The Genius of Language: Fifteen Writers Reflect on Their Mother Tongues*, 206–17. Ed. Wendy Lesser. New York: Pantheon, 2004.

———. *Hacia la liberación del lector latinoamericano*. Hanover, N.H.: Ediciones del Norte, 1984.

———. "Hammurabi, the Exalted Prince Who Made Great the Name of Babylon, Has Words for Donald Rumsfeld from the Other Side of Death." *TomDispatch*, May 7, 2003. http://www.tomdispatch.com/index.mhtml?pid=650. Accessed August 2, 2004.

———. *Hard Rain*. Trans. George Shivers. Los Angeles: Readers International, 1990.

———. *Heading South, Looking North: A Bilingual Journey*. New York: Farrar, Straus and Giroux, 1998.

———. "Homeland Security Ate My Speech." *TomDispatch*, January 15, 2006. http://tomdispatch.com/index.mhtml?pid=49432. Accessed August 2, 2006.

———. *Imaginación y violencia en América*. Santiago: Editorial Universitaria, 1970.

———. *In Case of Fire in a Foreign Land*. Trans. Ariel Dorfman and Edith Grossman. Durham: Duke University Press, 2002.

———. *Interventions in the Field of Dreams*. Dir. Jon Beller. New York: Paper Tiger Television, 1990.

———. "In the Dark." Unpublished play.

———. *Konfidenz*. Buenos Aires: Planeta, 1994.

———. *Konfidenz*. Normal, Ill.: Dalkey Archive, 2003.

———. *The Last Song of Manuel Sendero*. Trans. George Shivers and Ariel Dorfman. New York: Viking Penguin, 1987.

———. *Last Waltz in Santiago and Other Poems of Exile and Disappearance*. Trans. Edith Grossman. New York: Viking, 1988.

———. *Manifesto for Another World: Voices from beyond the Dark*. (2004) Reprint of *Speak Truth to Power* with extended introduction. New York: Seven Stories Press, 2003.

———. *Mascara*. New York: Penguin Books, 1988, 1989; New York: Seven Stories Press, 2004.

———. *Máscaras*. Buenos Aires: Sudamericana, 1988; Mexico City: Seix Barral, 1997.

———. "Memories of Hope." In *Chile from Within 1973–1988*, 93–121. Ed. Susan Meiselas. New York: Norton, 1990.

———. *Moros en la costa*. Buenos Aires: Editorial Sudamericana, 1973.

———. *La muerte y la doncella (Teatro 1)*. Buenos Aires: Ediciones de la Flor, 1992.

———. *My House Is on Fire*. Trans. George Shivers and Ariel Dorfman. New York: Viking Penguin, 1990.

———. *La nana y el iceberg*. Mexico City: Seix Barral, 1999.

———. *The Nanny and the Iceberg*. New York: Seven Stories Press, 2003.

——. *Other Septembers, Many Americas: Selected Provocations, 1980–2004*. New York: Seven Stories Press, 2004.

——. "The Other Side." Unpublished play.

——. "Pablo Picasso Has Words for Colin Powell from the Other Side of Death." *open Democracy*, February 25, 2003. http:// www.opendemocracy.net. themes/article.jsp? id=1&articleId=1002. Accessed July 20, 2004.

——. *Pastel de choclo*. Santiago: Editorial Sinfronteras, 1986.

——. *Patos, elefantes y héroes: La infancia como subdesarrollo*. Buenos Aires: Ediciones de la Flor, 1985.

——. "Picasso's Closet." Unpublished play.

——. *Purgatorio*. London: Nick Hern, 2006.

——. *Reader's nuestro que estás en la tierra: Ensayos sobre el imperialismo cultural*. Mexico City: Editorial Nueva Imagen, 1980.

——. *La rebelión de los conejos mágicos*. Buenos Aires: Ediciones de la Flor, 1986.

——. "The Rebellion of the Magical Rabbits." In *Where Angels Glide at Dawn: New Stories from Latin America*, 7–25. Ed. Lori M. Carlson and Cynthia L. Ventura. New York: Harper Trophy/J. B. Lippincott, 1990.

——. *The Resistance Trilogy: Widows; Death and the Maiden; Reader*. London: Nick Hern Books, 1998.

——. *Rumbo al sur deseando el norte: Un romance en dos lenguas*. Buenos Aires: Planeta, 1998.

——. "A Rural Chilean Legend Come True." *New York Times*, February 18, 1985, A17.

——. "Snow." *New York Times*, January 15, 1982, A23.

——. *Some Write to the Future: Essays on Contemporary Latin American Fiction*. Trans. George Shivers. Durham: Duke University Press, 1991.

——. Speak Truth to Power: Voices from Beyond the Dark. Based on *Speak Truth to Power*, by Kerry Kennedy Cuomo. London: Index on Censorship, 2000.

——. Los sueños nucleares de Reagan. Buenos Aires: Editorial Legasa, 1986.

——. *Terapia*. Trans. Anna Olga de Barros Barreto. Rio de Janeiro: Objetiva, 1999.

——. *La última aventura del llanero solitario*. Buenos Aires: Editorial Galerna, 1974.

——. *La última canción de Manuel Sendero*. México City: Siglo XXI, 1982.

——. *Viudas*. Mexico City: Siglo XXI, 1981.

——. "Viudas." In *Teatro 2*. Buenos Aires: Ediciones de la Flor, 1996.

——. *Widows*. Trans. Stephen Kessler. New York: Pantheon Books, 1983.

——. "William Blake Has Words from the Other Side of Death for Laura Bush, Lover of Literature." *San Francisco Chronicle*, July 25, 2004, E3.

Dorfman, Ariel, and Joaquín Dorfman. *The Burning City*. New York: Random House, 2003; London: Doubleday, 2003.

Dorfman, Ariel, Joaquín Dorfman, and Rodrigo Dorfman. *Los Angeles, Open City*. Undirected screenplay.

Dorfman, Ariel, and Rodrigo Dorfman. "About 'Who's Who.'" http://www.adorfman .duke.edu/pages/THEATREPAGE/pages/who_is_who.htm. Accessed August 5, 2006.

——. *Dead Line*. Video, December 1998.

——. *My House Is on Fire*. First Run/Icarus/Calama Films, 1997.

——. *Paradise II*. Undirected screenplay.

——. *Prisoners in Time*. Screenplay.

——. "Who's Who." Unpublished play.

Dorfman, Ariel, and Manuel Jofré. *Superman y sus amigos del alma*. Buenos Aires: Editorial Galerna, 1974.

Dorfman, Ariel, and Armand Mattelart. *How to Read Donald Duck: Imperialist Ideology in the Disney Comic*. Trans. and intro. David Kunzle. New York: International General, 1991.

——. *Para leer al pato Donald: Comunicación de masa y colonialismo*. Valparaíso: Ediciones Universitarias de Valparaíso, 1971.

DuBois, Page. *Torture and Truth*. New York: Routledge, 1991.

Durham, Meenakshi Gigi, and Douglas Kellner. *Media and Cultural Studies*. Keyworks. New York: Blackwell, 2005.

Eagleton, Terry. *The Ideology of the Aesthetic*. New York: Blackwell, 1990.

Eco, Umberto. *The Role of the Reader: Explorations in the Semiotics of Texts*. Bloomington: Indiana University Press, 1979.

Eltit, Diamela. *El cuarto mundo*. Santiago: Planeta, 1988.

Esslin, Martin. *The Theater of the Absurd*. Garden City, N.Y.: Doubleday, 1961.

Feitlowitz, Marguerite. *A Lexicon of Terror: Argentina and the Legacies of Torture*. Oxford: Oxford University Press, 1998.

Foster, Hal. *The Anti-Aesthetic: Essays on Postmodern Culture*. Port Townsend, Wash.: Bay Press, 1983.

Foucault, Michel. *History of Sexuality*, vol. 1. Trans. Robert Hurley. New York: Pantheon Books, 1978.

——. "What Is an Author?" Trans. Donald F. Bouchard and Sherry Simon. In *Language, Counter-Memory, Practice*, 124–27. Ithaca, N.Y.: Cornell University Press, 1977.

Fuguet, Alberto. *Mala onda*. Santiago: Planeta, 1992.

Fukuyama, Francis. *The End of History and the Last Man*. New York: Free Press, 1992.

García Márquez, Gabriel. *Cien años de soledad*. (1967). Madrid: Espasa-Calpe, 1990.

——. *One Hundred Years of Solitude*. Trans. Gregory Rabassa (1970). New York: Avon, 1971.

Gallop, Jane. "My Unfinished Book Should Not Feel like Death: Mortal Authors Writing in Time." Unpublished ms.

Gilmore, Leigh. *Limits of Autobiography: Trauma and Testimony*. Ithaca, N.Y.: Cornell University Press, 2001.

Giroux, Henry. *The Mouse That Roared: Disney and the End of Innocence*. Lanham, Md.: Rowman and Littlefield, 1999.

——. *Public Spaces, Private Lives: Beyond the Culture of Cynicism*. Lanham, Md.: Rowman and Littlefield, 2001.

——. *The Terror of Neoliberalism*. Boulder, Colo.: Paradigm, 2004.

González Echevarría, Roberto. *Myth and Archive: A Theory of Latin American Narrative*. Cambridge: Cambridge University Press, 1990.

González Pérez, Aníbal. *Journalism and the Development of the Spanish-American Narrative*. Cambridge: Cambridge University Press, 1993.

Gregory, Stephen. "Ariel Dorfman and Harold Pinter: Politics of the Periphery and Theater of the Metropolis." *Comparative Drama* 30, no. 3 (1996): 325–45.

Grinberg, Leon, and Rebeca Grinberg. *Psychoanalytic Perspectives on Migration and Exile*. Trans. Nancy Festinger. New Haven, Conn.: Yale University Press, 1989.

Gugelberger, Georg M., ed. *The Real Thing: Testimonial Discourse and Latin America*. Durham: Duke University Press, 1996.

Hart, Francis R. "Notes for an Anatomy of Modern Autobiography." *New Literary History* 1 (spring 1970): 486–511.

Hunsaker, Steven. *Autobiography and National Identity in the Americas*. Charlottesville: University of Virginia Press, 1999.

Huyssen, Andreas. *Present Pasts: Urban Palimpsests and the Politics of Memory*. Stanford, Calif.: Stanford University Press, 2003.

Incledon, John. "Liberating the Reader: A Conversation with Ariel Dorfman." *Chasqui: Revista de Literatura Latinoamericana* 20, no. 1 (1991): 95–107.

Jacobs, Louis. "Jeremiah: Prophet of Judgment and Hope." http://www.myjewishlearning.com/texts/bible/TO_Prophets_1460/TOLiteraryProphets/JeremiahJacobs.htm. Accessed June 5, 2006.

Jaggi, Maya. "Speaking for the Dead." *The Guardian*, June 14, 2004. http://books.guardian.co.uk/review/story/0,12084,975904,00.html. Accessed June 10, 2005.

Jameson, Fredric. *The Cultural Turn: Selected Writings on the Postmodern, 1983–1998*. London: Verso, 1998.

——. *The Political Unconscious: Narrative as a Socially Symbolic Act*. Ithaca, N.Y.: Cornell University Press, 1972.

——. *Postmodernism; or, The Cultural Logic of Late Capitalism*. Durham: Duke University Press, 1991.

Jofré, Manuel Alcides. "*La muerte y la doncella* de Ariel Dorfman: Transición democrática y crisis de la memoria." *Atenea: Revista de Ciencia, Arte y Literatura de la Universidad de Concepción* 469 (1994): 87–99.

Jones, Ernest. *The Life and Work of Sigmund Freud*. Ed. Lionel Trilling and Stephen Marus. Harmondsworth: Penguin Books, 1961.

Kant, Immanuel. *The Critique of Judgment* (1790). Trans. James Creed Meredith. Oxford: Clarendon Press, 1961.

Kellner, Douglas. *Media Culture*. New York: Routledge, 1995.

Kennedy Cuomo, Kerry. *Speak Truth to Power*. New York: Crown, 2000.

Kerr, Lucille. *Reclaiming the Author: Figures and Fictions from Spanish America*. Durham: Duke University Press, 1992.

Kim, Euisuk. *Una reconstrucción alternativa del pretérito: Una aproximación psicoanalítica a la obra de Ariel Dorfman*. New Orleans: University Press of the South, 2003.

Kunzle, David. "Introduction." In Dorfman and Mattelart, *How to Read Donald Duck*, 11–23.

Laub, Dori, and Shoshana Felman. *Testimony: Crisis of Witnessing in Literature, Psycho-analysis, and History*. New York: Routledge, 1992.

Lawrence, John Shelton. "Donald Duck vs. Chilean Socialism: A Fair Use Exchange." In Dorfman and Mattelart, *How to Read Donald Duck*, 113–19.

Lejeune, Philippe. *On Autobiography*. Trans. Katherine Leary. Minneapolis: University of Minnesota Press, 1989.

Lionnet, Françoise. *Autobiographical Voices: Race, Gender, Self-Portraiture*. Ithaca, N.Y.: Cornell University Press, 1989.

Lopez Calvo, Ignacio. "Ariel Dorfman: El hombre y su obra." Proyecto ensayo hispánico. http://www.ensayistas.org/filosofos/chile/dorfman/introd.htm. Accessed September 5, 2008.

Lyon, Ted. "Review of *Moros en la costa*." *Books Abroad* 49, no. 11 (1975): 84–85.

Marcuse, Herbert. *The Aesthetic Dimension: Toward a Critique of Marxist Aesthetics*. Boston: Beacon Press, 1978.

Matthews, Chris. *Hardball with Chris Matthews*. MSNBC, Seacaucus, N.J., May 18, 2004. http://msnbc.msn.com/id/5013391/. Accessed June 10, 2005.

McClennen, Sophia A. *The Dialectics of Exile: Nation, Time, Language, and Space in Hispanic Literatures*. West Lafayette, Ind.: Purdue University Press, 2004.

———. "The Diasporic Subject in Ariel Dorfman's *Heading South, Looking North*." *MELUS* 30, no. 1 (spring 2005): 169–88.

———. "An Interview with Ariel Dorfman." *Context* 15 (2004): 7–8.

———. "An Interview with Ariel Dorfman." *World Literature Today* 78, nos. 3–4 (2004): 64–67.

McIrvin, Michael. *Whither American Poetry*. San Diego: Cedar Hill, 2000.

McLuhan, Marshall. *Understanding Media: The Extensions of Man*. 1st ed. New York: McGraw-Hill, 1964.

Mendieta, Eduardo. "What Can Latinas/os Learn from Cornel West? The Latino Post-colonial Intellectual in the Age of the Exhaustion of Public Spheres." *Nepantla: Views from South* 4, no. 2 (2003): 213–33.

Miller, Nancy K. *Bequest and Betrayal*. Bloomington: Indiana University Press, 2000.

Miller, Nancy K., and Jason Daniel Tougaw. *Extremities: Trauma, Testimony, and Community*. Urbana: University of Illinois Press, 2002.

Molloy, Silvia. *Autobiographical Writings in Spanish America: At Face Value*. Cambridge: Cambridge University Press, 1991.

Morace, Robert A. "The Life and Times of *Death and the Maiden*." *Texas Studies in Literature and Language* 42, no. 2 (2000): 135–53.

Moraga, Cherríe. *Loving in the War Years: Lo que nunca pasó por sus labios*. Boston: South End, 1983.

Morello, Henry James. "Masking the Past: Trauma in Latin American and Peninsular Theatre." PhD diss., University of Illinois, Urbana-Champaign, 2006.

Morgan, Fiona. "Telling the Truth through Lies." *Independent Weekly*, February 19, 2003. http://indyweek.com/durham/2003–02–19/ae.html. Accessed June 10, 2005.

Morrison, Toni. *Beloved*. New York: Plume, 1987.

Muñoz, Silverio. "Entrevista a Ariel Dorfman." *Prismal/Cabral: Revista de Literatura Hispanica/Cabral Afro-Brasileiro Asiatico Lusitano* 3, no. 4 (1979): 60–76.

Nelson, Alice A. *Political Bodies: Gender, History, and the Struggle for Narrative Power in Recent Chilean Literature.* Lewisburg, Pa.: Bucknell University Press, 2002.

Neruda, Pablo. *Confieso que he vivido: Memorias.* Buenos Aires: Editorial Losada, 1974.

Nietzsche, Friedrich Wilhelm. *Beyond Good and Evil: Prelude to a Philosophy of the Future.* Trans and ed. Walter Arnold Kaufmann. New York: Vintage Books, 1966.

——. *Thus Spoke Zarathustra: A Book for All and None.* Trans. Walter Arnold Kaufmann. New York: Modern Library, 1995.

Nora, Pierre. "Between Memory and History." In *Realms of Memory: The Construction of the French Past*, 1–20. Ed. Pierre Nora. Trans. Arthur Goldhammer. New York: Columbia University Press, 1996.

Omang, Joanne. "Killer Cure" (review of *Blake's Therapy*). *Washington Post*, July 15, 2001.

——. Review of Dorfman, *The Nanny and the Iceberg. Washington Post*, August 15, 1999. http://www.washingtonpost.com/wp-srv/style/books/reviews/thenannyandtheiceberg0815.htm. Accessed June 10, 2005.

Onís, Federico de. *España en América: Estudios, ensayos y discursos sobre temas españoles e hispanoamericanos.* Río Piedras: University of Puerto Rico Press, 1968.

O'Regan, Nadine. "Escaping Pinochet's Shadow." *Sunday Business Post Online*, May 11, 2003. http://archives.tcm.ie/businesspost/2003/05/11/story46571874.asp. Accessed August 1, 2004.

Oropesa, Salvador. *La obra de Ariel Dorfman: Ficción y crítica.* Madrid: Pliegos, 1992.

Pezzopane, Barbara, and Laura Petruccioli. "Interview with Ariel Dorfman." *Storie* 52–53 (2004): 49–61.

Pinet, Carolyn. "Retrieving the Disappeared Text: Women, Chaos and Change in Argentina and Chile after the Dirty Wars." *Hispanic Journal* 18, no. 1 (1997): 89–108.

Pinter, Harold. *The New World Order* (1981). In *Plays 4*. London: Faber, 1993.

——. *One for the Road.* London: Grove, 1985.

Pozo, Mike Alexander. "An Educator's Reflections on the Crisis in Education and Democracy in the United States: An Interview with Henry A. Giroux." *Axis of Logic*, September 21, 2004. http://www.axisoflogic.com/artman/publish/article_11970.shtml. Accessed June 10, 2005.

A Promise to the Dead: The Exile Journey of Ariel Dorfman. Dir. Peter Raymont, White Pine Pictures, 2007.

Puig, Manuel. *Boquitas pintadas.* Buenos Aires: Sudamericana, 1969.

Quinn, Joanna R. "Lessons Learned: Practical Lessons Gleaned from inside the Truth Commissions of Guatemala and South Africa." *Human Rights Quarterly* 25, no. 4 (November 2003): 1117–49.

Rama, Ángel. *La ciudad letrada.* Hanover, N.H.: Ediciones del Norte, 1984.

——. *Transculturación narrativa en América Latina.* México City: Siglo XXI, 1982.

Ramos, Julio. *Divergent Modernities: Culture and Politics in Nineteenth-Century Latin America.* Durham: Duke University Press, 2001.

Redgrave, Vanessa. Video publicity. *My House Is on Fire*. First Run/Icarus 1997. http://www.frif.com/new97/my_house_.html. Accessed August 3, 2004.

Retamar, Roberto Fernández. *Calibán: Apuntes sobre nuestra cultura*. Mexico City: Editorial Diógenes, 1971.

Reyes, Carlos, and Maggie Paterson. "Ariel Dorfman on Memory and Truth." http://www.amnesty.org.uk/journal_july97/carlos.html, July 15, 2002. Accessed May 10, 2004.

Rich, Adrienne. *Blood, Bread, and Poetry: Selected Prose 1979–1985*. New York: Norton, 1986.

Ricouer, Paul. *Memory, History, Forgetting*. Chicago: University of Chicago Press, 2004.

Rodó, José Enrique. *Ariel*. Montevideo: Dornaleche y Reyes, 1900.

Rodriguez, Richard. *Days of Obligation*. New York: Penguin Books, 1992.

Said, Edward. *Orientalism*. New York: Vintage Books, 1988.

Sartre, Jean-Paul. *Les mots*. Paris: Gallimard, 1998.

Schiff, Stephen. "Pinter's Passions." *Vanity Fair*, September 1990, 218–22, 300–303.

Schroeder, David. "Ariel Dorfman, Franz Schubert, and *Death and the Maiden*." In *Representing Humanity in an Age of Terror*. Special Issue of *CLC WEB: Comparative Literature and Culture* 9, no. 1 (2008). Ed. Sophia A. McClennen and Henry James Morello. http://docs.lib.purdue.edu/clcweb/vol9/iss1/.

Shaw, Donald. *Post-Boom in Spanish American Fiction*. Saratoga Springs, N.Y.: SUNY Press, 1998.

Shivers, George. "Textual Unity in Ariel Dorfman's *The Last Song of Manuel Sendero*." *Washington College Review*, spring 1989, 19–20.

Silko, Leslie Marmon. *Ceremony* (1977). New York: Penguin Books, 1986.

Silva Gruesz, Kirsten. *Ambassadors of Culture: The Transamerican Origins of Latino Writing*. Princeton, N.J.: Princeton University Press, 2002.

Singer, Alan, and Allen Dunn. *Literary Aesthetics: A Reader*. Oxford: Blackwell, 2000.

Sklodowska, Elzbieta. "The Poetics of Remembering, the Politics of Forgetting: Rereading *I, Rigoberta Menchú*." In *The Rigoberta Menchú Controversy*, 251–69. Ed. Arturo Arias. Minneapolis: University of Minnesota Press, 2001.

Smith, Sidonie, and Julia Watson. *Reading Autobiography: A Guide for Interpreting Life Narratives*. Minneapolis: University of Minnesota Press, 2002.

Smoodin, Eric Loren. *Disney Discourse: Producing the Magic Kingdom*. New York: Routledge, 1994.

Sollers, Werner. *Beyond Ethnicity: Consent and Descent in American Culture*. New York: Oxford University Press, 1986.

Sommer, Doris. *Foundational Fictions: The National Romances of Latin America*. Berkeley: University of California Press, 1991.

——. "No Secrets." In *The Real Thing: Testimonial Discourse and Latin America*, 130–57. Ed. Georg M. Gugelberger. Durham: Duke University Press, 1996.

Stavans, Ilan. "The Gringo's Tongue: A Conversation with Ariel Dorfman." *Michigan Quarterly Review* 34, no. 3: 303–12.

Steiner, George. *Language and Silence: Essays on Language, Literature, and the Inhuman* (1958). New Haven, Conn.: Yale University Press, 1998.

Taylor, Diana. *Disappearing Acts*. Durham: Duke University Press, 1997.

Tharoor, Shashi. "Blame It on Chile" (review of *The Nanny and the Iceberg*). *New York Times*, June 13, 1999. http://www.nytimes.com/books/99/06/13/reviews/990613.13tharoot.html. Accessed August 1, 2006.

Trigo, Abril. "The 1990s: Practices and Polemics within Latin American Cultural Studies." In *The Latin American Cultural Studies Reader*. Ed. Ana del Sarto, Alicia Rios, and Abril Trigo, 347–73. Durham: Duke University Press, 2004.

Twain, Mark. *The Prince and the Pauper* (1882). New York: Modern Library–Random, 2003.

Vidal, Hernán. "Sacrificios primordiales: Ariel Dorfman, *La muerte y la doncella*." In *Política cultural de la memoria histórica: Derechos humanos y discursos culturales en Chile*, 286–304. Santiago: Mosquito Comunicaciones, 1997.

Wallace, Jennifer. "We Can't Make More Dirt . . . : Tragedy and the Excavated Body." *Cambridge Quarterly* 32, no. 2 (2003): 103–11.

Wasko, Janet, Mark Phillips, and Eileen R. Meehan. *Dazzled by Disney? The Global Disney Audiences Project*. London: Leicester University Press, 2001.

Williams, Raymond Leslie. *The Postmodern Novel in Latin America: Politics, Culture, and the Crisis of Truth*. New York: St. Martin's Press, 1995.

World Economic Forum. "Our Organization." Created July 24, 2006. http://www.weforum.org/en/about/Our%20organisation/index.htm. Accessed August 5, 2006.

Yúdice, George "Contrapunteo estadounidense/latinoamericano de los estudios culturales." In *Estudios y otras prácticas intelectuales latinoamericanas en cultura y poder*, 339–52. Ed. Daniel Mato. Caracas: Consejo Latinoamericano de Ciencias Sociales y CEAP, FACES, Universidad Central de Venezuela, 2002.

——. *The Expediency of Culture: Uses of Culture in the Global Era*. Durham: Duke University Press, 2003.

——. "*Testimonio* and Postmodernism." In *The Real Thing: Testimonial Discourse and Latin America*, 42–57. Ed. Georg M. Gugelberger. Durham: Duke University Press, 1996.

INDEX

aesthetics of hope (*cont.*)
48, 52–53; questions essential to, 273–74; revolutionary aspect of, 79–81; self-collective relationship in, 63–64; stylistic traits in, 65–69; three elements of hope fundamental to, 62–65, 75; utopian longing in, 63, 80, 92; writing to the future with, 61, 69, 92

Against Literature (Beverley), 158, 256

Alberti, Rafael, 47

Alemán, Mateo, 41

Allen, Woody, 146

Allende, Salvador, administration: bourgeoisie–working class tensions, 104; Castro's support for, 97; changes accompanying, 97; election (1970), 13–14; Dorfman's involvement with, 13–14, 16, 32, 244–45, 260; election described in *The Last Song of Manuel Sendero* (*La última canción de Manuel Sendero*), 14; *Moros en la costa* on the art–revolution relationship, 99–103, 133; petit-bourgeoisie during, 106; processes for creating social change, 103–4; solidarity of supporters as public force, 97; U.S. relations, 78, 99, 252–56. *See also* Pinochet military coup (1973)

Ambrosio, Rodrigo, 106, 108

Amnesty International, 18, 26, 27, 56

Antes que anochezca (*Before Night Falls*) (Arenas), 193

Argentine Embassy, 29, 40

Arguedas, José María, 55

Ariel (Rodó), 10

Arnold, Matthew, 246

art: with an aesthetics of hope, 75–79, 89–92, 174, 176; community building through, 81, 95–96, 176, 245; determining authenticity of, 83; dialectical and political implications of, 71–72, 76–77; Dorfman's theory of, 61–62; emancipatory, 71–72, 248; engaged, 248, 274; as a form of resistance, 138–39; fostering di-

alogue through, 99; inspiring the imagination, 60, 63, 284; language-subjectivity intertwined in, 182–83; mass-produced media compared with, 76, 83; propaganda compared with, 76; purpose of, 78, 81, 96; reconstruction and reconciliation using, 173–74, 176; revolutionary aspect of, 79–81; social function of, 32–33, 64–65, 70–76, 173–74, 176; sublimation of reality in, 76; subversive, 46; utopian potential of popularly accessible forms of, 245

art, in relation to: activism, 11–12, 100, 133, 245; audience, 63; literature, 75–76, 101; politics, 38, 45–46, 100, 120–21, 122, 243, 248; revolution, 133; social change, 72–74, 122–24; truth, 124, 173–74, 190; war, 45–46

Artificial Respiration (*Respiración artificial*) (Piglia), 59, 95

artist, the, 47, 92

Asturias, Miguel Ángel, 54, 55

Atacama Desert, 235–36

audience: art and, 63; Jeremiah's message to, 94; *Mascara*, 150; *Other Septembers, Many Americas* (Dorfman), 274; post-traumatic theater for intervention in public consciousness, 165; respecting through rejection of catharsis, 91; staging *Death and the Maiden* for the Chilean, 164, 165, 177

audio recordings, 303

Auschwitz, 80, 176

authorial agency, 59

authoritarianism–society relationship, 117

author(s), 34–35, 47, 123. *See also* writer(s)

autobiography studies, 191–92

autobiography vs. memoir, 193–94

Autodafe (periodical), 264

avant-garde aesthetic, 79–81

avant-garde movement, 45–47

Aves sin nido (*Torn from the Nest*) (Matto de Turner), 207 awards: Academy Awards (2008) documentary short list, 29; Edinburgh film festival, 25; Human Rights Watch film festival, 29; Laurence Olivier Award, 23; Telluride film festival, 35; Toronto film festival, 25

Aylwin, Patricio, 22, 152, 163

babies, as symbols, 134–35, 188, 221, 274–75

Bakhtin, Mikhail, 35, 140, 200

Baldwin, Alec, 233

Barnet, Miguel, 56, 72

Barr, Lois Baer, 84, 90, 123, 134, 146–47

Barthes, Roland, 34, 35, 159, 246

Baudrillard, Jean, 153, 159

Baumgarten, Alexander, 70

Beebee, Thomas O., 108

Before Night Falls (*Antes que anochezca*) (Arenas), 193

Bell-Villada, Gene, 79

Beloved (Morrison), 199

Benavente, David, 165

Benjamin, Walter, 33, 45–46, 71, 246

Berger, John, 34, 74, 109, 253

Berkeley, California, 11–12, 107, 199

Berlin Wall, fall of the, 24, 152, 154

Beso de la mujer araña, El (*The Kiss of the Spiderwoman*) (Puig), 95

betrayal: capacity of the individual for, 257; in *Death and the Maiden* (*La muerte y la doncella*), 160–76; in *Konfidenz*, 176–85; in *Reader* (theatrical adaptation), 188–91; in *Widows* (theatrical adaptation) (Dorfman and Kushner), 186–88

Beverley, John, 158, 256

Beyond Good and Evil (Nietzsche), 171

Bianchi, Soledad, 29

bilingualism/biculturalism and dual identity, 24; Dorfman's, 4–6, 8–12, 14, 194, 199–201, 262–63. See also *Heading South, Looking North*

Biografía de un cimarrón (Barnet), 56

Biography of a Runaway Slave (Barnet), 56

birth: as accident motif, 44

Blake, William, 242

Blake's Therapy (Dorfman): Calderón de la Barca and, 43, 77, 218, 219; confined spaces in, 53; epigraph of, 78; literary technique of, 217–18; reaching the audience, 91; structure of *The Divine Comedy* (Dante) in, 39, 43, 84, 218, 219; technological change and the global social structure in, 24–25, 213–22

Bloch, Ernst, 62, 71, 245

Boal, Augusto, 72, 91

book, consumer culture of the, 33

boom writers. *See* Latin American literary boom

Borges, Jorge Luis, 35, 55, 120–21

"Borges and I" ("Borges y yo") (Borges), 35

boundaries: creating for survival, 60–61; discursive, 248; geographic, 26, 39, 126, 153, 242; hope in bridging, 62; ideological, 26; "The Other Side," 26, 39, 242; spatial, 32, 53, 153, 236–37; temporal, 32, 44, 86–87, 121, 141–43, 197; words for creating, 7

bourgeois, 45, 79–80, 95

Brando, Marlon, 146

Braque, Georges, 106–7

Brecht, Bertolt, 46, 108, 255–59

Brink, André, 57

Bum Suk, Cha, 260

Bürger, Peter, 45–46

Burke, Peter, 155

Burning City, The (Dorfman and J. Dorfman), 25, 223–27

Burroughs, William, 147

Buscón, El (Quevedo), 41

Bush, George W., 273

Bush, Laura, 242

"Bush in 30 Seconds" (MoveOn.org), 261

Cabro Chico (comic book, Dorfman et al.), 78

Calderón de la Barca, Pedro, 43, 77, 218, 219

Death and the Maiden (*La muerte y la doncella*) (Dorfman): aesthetic of, 165–66;
aesthetics of hope in, 52, 163, 174–75;
audience role in, 172, 175; bridge to previous work, 155; Chilean response to, 21,
23, 81; collaboration with R. Dorfman
on, 25; contextual location on, 163–165;
continuing influence of, 22–23; core element of, 172–73; dialogue in, 167, 202;
foretelling history in, 22; forgetting in,
21–22, 79; global-local dialectic in, 161,
167; historical context of, 161; intertextuality of, 39, 174–76; language–truth
relationship in, 111, 173–74; literary
techniques of, 51–52, 86–88, 162, 167–73,
175; Pinter's influence on, 50–52; plot
line of, 161–62; role of art in, 161, 163,
173–76; scholarship on, 162–63; international success of, 21–22, 51; techniques
of realism in the service of the unspeakable, 21–23; themes, 26, 155, 167–72;
trust, betrayal, and storytelling in,
160–76
Death and the Maiden (*La muerte y la doncella*) (Dorfman), adaptations: film, 177,
260; opera, 260; theatrical, 167, 269;
transformation through, 260
Death and the Maiden (*La muerte y la doncella*) (Dorfman), compared: *Konfidenz*,
176–77, 179, 183; *Mascara*, 150; *The
Nanny and the Iceberg*, 202; *Reader* (theatrical adaptation), 190–91
Death of a Salesman (Miller), 188–89
"Death of the Author" (Barthes), 34
deception. *See* betrayal
De Frente (Dorfman), 252
De Grasse, 6
De la Cruz, Sor Juana Inés, 42
De la Parra, Marco Antonio, 165
Deleuze, Gilles, 153
De Man, Paul, 195
Denning, Michael, 246, 256
depression, 17–19, 33, 109

*Desert Memories: Journeys through the
Chilean North* (Dorfman), 27, 234–42
Desert Syndrome, 239
dialogue: lack of as literary technique, 98–
99, 103–4, 166–67; and the power–
communication relationship, 183–85,
202. *See also* communication
diaspora: experience forming Dorfman's
identity, 20, 31, 94; *Heading South, Looking North*, 191–201. *See also* exile
diaspora writers, 281
Díaz de Castillo, Bernal, 42, 56
"Discourse in the Novel" (Bakhtin), 35
dislocation, separation, and isolation in
Dorfman's sense of identity, 2–6, 9–10,
12, 23, 29, 31, 43, 192, 198–99, 253, 278
Disney corporation, 248, 253. See also *How
to Read Donald Duck*
Disney Discourse (Smoodin), 248
Divergent Modernities (Ramos), 262
Divine Comedy, (Dante), 39, 43, 84, 218,
219
Donald Duck ideology. See *How to Read
Donald Duck*
Don Juan Tenorio (Zorrilla), 42
Don Juan theme, 205–11
Donoso, José, 54
Don Quijote (Cervantes), 40, 77, 193
doppelganger, 2. *See also* doubling, as liter-
ary technique
Dorando la píldora (Dorfman). *See* Coating the Pill
Dorfman, Adolfo (father), 2–3, 6–8, 18
Dorfman, Angélica (wife), 11, 17, 27, 236,
241, 269
Dorfman, Ariel (Dorfman): chronology,
285–93; death reported in Chile, 19;
fears and obsession with death, 32; inability to face personal loss, 28; personality, 9, 278–79; Picasso compared to,
46–47; Pinter's writing compared, 49–
50; pneumonia, hospitalization for, 4,
32; public vs. personal face, 28, 35; sense

of rejection by the Chilean community, 178

Dorfman, Ariel, background: Chile (1954–73), 8–15, 198–99, 278; education, 6, 8–9, 11, 40, 259, 278; friendships, 8; New York (1945–54), 1–7, 32, 198; political, 7–8, 9–11; religious, 2

Dorfman, Ariel, identity: bicultural/bilingual identity, 4–6, 8–12, 14, 194, 199–201, 262–63; in community, 14–15, 164, 178, 279; defining moments, 2–4, 6, 8–10; of dislocation, separation, and isolation, 2–6, 9–10, 12, 23, 29, 31, 43, 192, 198–99, 253, 278; as expatriate, 177; guilt of the survivor and, 15–16, 32–33, 196; identification with Jeremiah, 94; Jewish, 2, 20, 31; Latin American, 11, 12; monolingualism in establishing, 4–5, 12–13; name changes in reframing, 1–3, 6–10; Native American culture and, 31; as an outsider, 9–10, 12, 23, 29, 234, 253; post-exile, 153, 243; self-determined, 4, 12–13, 16; shaped through the voices of others, 200–201; as a storyteller, 31–37, 97, 200; U.S. citizenship, 27, 243; as a writer, 10, 14–15, 31, 57, 196, 200. See also *Heading South, Looking North*

Dorfman, Eleonora (sister), 4

Dorfman, Fanny Zelicovich (née Vaisman) (mother), 2, 4–5, 32

Dorfman, Joaquín (son), 18, 20, 25–26

Dorfman, Rodrigo (son), 11, 25–28, 32, 156, 260–61, 264

doubling, as literary technique in: *Death and the Maiden* (*La muerte y la doncella*), 86; *Exorcising Terror: The Incredible Unending Trial of General Augusto Pinochet*, 86; *Konfidenz*, 86, 180; *The Last Song of Manuel Sendero* (*La última canción de Manuel Sendero*), 86, 142; *The Nanny and the Iceberg* (*La nana y el iceberg*), 86, 204; *Other Septembers, Many Americas*, 272; *Reader* (theatrical adaptation), 189–90; time and place questioned through, 86–89; *Widows* (*Viudas*) (novel), 125–27

dreams vs. hopes, 64–65

Dreyfus, Richard, 23

DuBois, Page, 172–73

Ducks, Elephants, and Heroes (*Patos, elefantes y héroes*) (Dorfman), 64

Duke University, 18, 21, 29, 256

Dunn, Allen, 76, 83

Duvauchelle, María Elena, 51, 166

Dylan, Bob, 107–8

Eagleton, Terry, 70, 79

earthquake relief efforts, 64

Echevarría, Roberto González, 238

echoing, as literary technique, 127, 167

Eco, Umberto, 90

economic change, 19

Editorial Sudamericana, 143

education, Dorfman's, 6, 8–9, 11, 40, 259, 278

Egan, Bob, 186

"Ejército de ocupación" (Dorfman). *See* "Occupation Forces" ("Ejército de ocupación") (Dorfman)

Elefantes, literatura y miedo, De. See Elephants, Literature, and Fear

Elephants, Literature, and Fear, Of (*De elefantes, literatura y miedo*) (Dorfman), 252

Elizondo, Hector, 233

Eloy Martínez, Tomás, 56

Eltit, Diamela, 158, 165

Empire's Old Clothes, The (Dorfman), 20, 61, 64, 74, 78, 83, 255–59

"En familia" (Dorfman). *See* "Family Circle"

Englehardt, Tom, 278

Ensayos quemados en Chile (Dorfman). *See* Essays Burned in Chile

epistolary genre, 202

Ercilla (magazine), 38, 261

Eros, 80

"Escondida, A la" (Dorfman). *See* "My House is on Fire"

Esmeralda (ship), 119

esperar, 64. *See also* hope

Esposito, Giancarlo, 233

Essays Burned in Chile (*Ensayos quemados en Chile*) (Dorfman), 20, 77, 251

Esslin, Martin, 48, 53

ethics of writing, 262

ethnic literature, scholarship on, 191

Euripides, 39, 118–19

European Union, 154

evil, individual's capability for, 79, 123–24, 257

exile: Dorfman, Adolfo (father), 2–3, 8, 18; Dorfman, Fanny, 4–5; fracturing of identity, meaning, and language caused by, 114–16; illness and, 4–6, 32; language describing, 116. See also *A Promise to the Dead*; diaspora

exile, Dorfman's: in Amsterdam (1976–79), 18; Argentine Embassy sanctuary, 40; celebrity and alienation during, 23; in France (1973–75), 17–18; guilt experienced during, 16; lifting of (1983), 19; official ending of, 150–51; reconciled to, 16–18; in Santiago slums, 61; survival as consequence of creativity, 16, 108–9; in the United States (1980–), 18–21, 150–51

exile, Dorfman's writing while in: aesthetics of loss and hope in, 19; depression affecting, 17–19, 32–33, 109; poetry, 18, 47, 108–17, 163; political disempowerment reflected in, 18–19; return to, 33, 47; shift in genre during, 47, 163–64; short stories, 116–21; using language to bear witness of, 18, 33, 47; using literature as a political weapon, 109; works of (1990–2005), 152–60. See also *specific genres*; *specific titles*

exiled, the: Dorfman's help to, 109; challenges faced, 5, 16, 19; diasporic subject in the life writing of, 192; disillusion-

ment and frustration of, 19; identity and, 153; suspicion of by Chileans, 164

"Exile Finds Chile 'Struck' by a Plague, An" (Dorfman), 263

exile journalism, 251, 261–79

exile novels: *The Last Song of Manuel Sendero* (*La última canción de Manuel Sendero*), 133–43; *Mascara* (*Máscaras*), 143–51; *Widows* (*Viudas*) (novel), 124–33

Exorcising Terror: The Incredible Unending Trial of General Augusto Pinochet (Dorfman), 27, 56, 123, 155, 222, 266–72

expatriate, 177

expatriate, Dorfman as, 21

extra-literary works, Dorfman's, 248–49

"Eyelids" ("Párpados") in *Cría ojos* (Dorfman), 117–18

"Eyes" ("Ojos") in *Cría ojos* (Dorfman), 117–18, 120

family: challenges of the exiled, 5; dialectic vision of, 134–35; as a metaphor for Chile, 204; as a metaphor for society, 117–19, 122–23, 130–33, 153–54

"Family Circle" ("En familia") (Dorfman), 117, 118, 131

Fanon, Frantz, 247

Faulkner, William, 45

"Fear and the Word" (Dorfman), 264–65

Feitlowitz, Marguerite, 167

Felman, Shoshana, 157

Fernández de Oviedo, Gonzalo, 42–43

Fernández Retamar, Roberto, 42–43

Ferré, Rosario, 57

fiction, 101–4

Flores, Fernando, 16, 33

Footsteps of September 11, 1973 (Dorfman et al.), 260

Forest Fire (Bum Suk), 260

Foster, Hal, 70

Foucault, Michel, 35, 72, 123, 257

"Fourth Version" ("Cuarta versión") (Valenzuela), 95

Frankfurt School, 45, 71–72, 78, 245, 253

free trade agreements, 154

Free Trade Area of the Americas (FTAA), 24, 154

Frei, Eduardo, 107

Freire, Paulo, 72, 259

Freud, Sigmund, 171

Frondizi, Arturo, 9

Fuentes, Carlos, 54

"Funerals for Us, Fundraisers for Him" (R. Dorfman), 261

Gabriel, Peter, 23

Galeano, Eduardo, 57

Gambaro, Griselda, 166

García Canclini, Néstor, 72

García Espinosa, Julio, 107, 108

García Lorca, Frederico, 47

García Márquez, Gabriel: hope in writing of, 58; on hybrid nature of Latin American identity, 54–55; intertextuality with *The Nanny and the Iceberg* (Dorfman), 207; literary practice to "write to the future," 62, 68, 80; shifting use of tenses by, 67–68; unity of style, 59; use of periodicals to communicate with the public by, 262

Garcilaso de la Vega, El Inca, 42

Garzón, Baltasar, 269

gender issues, 162, 191, 206–7

General Agreement on Tariffs and Trade (GATT), 218

Getino, Octavio, 72

Ghosh, Amitav, 57

Gilmore, Leigh, 195

Gimeno, Claudio, 16

Giroux, Henry, 63, 214, 248, 258–59

globalization: *Blake's Therapy* and, 24–25, 213–22; *The Burning City* (Dorfman and J. Dorfman) and, 223–27; the decline of community and, 42, 202, 208–9; era of, 152–57, 160; *The Nanny and the Iceberg* (*La nana y el iceberg*) (Dorfman), 202–13

globalization theory, 191

"Globalizing Compassion" in *Other Septembers, Many Americas* (Dorfman), 275–76

"Godfather" ("Y qué oficio le pondremos") (Dorfman), 117, 119

González Pérez, Aníbal, 262

Gordimer, Nadine, 57

Goya, Francisco, 261

Gramsci, Antonio, 72, 247, 256

Grange, The, 8, 9

Grass, Günter, 136

Gregory, Stephen, 49

Griffin, Peter, 260

Grinberg, Leon, 16

Grinberg, Rebecca, 16

Grossman, Edith, 109

Guardian, "Comment Is Free" Web site, 278

Guattari, Félix, 153

Guernica (Picasso), 26, 157

guerrilla art/aesthetics, 79–82

Guevara, Ernesto "Che," 202, 204, 205, 212, 273

Guggenheim, 18

guilt of the survivor, 15–16, 32–33, 196

Gulf War Did Not Take Place, The (Baudrillard), 153

Guzmán de Alfarache (Alemán), 41

Hacia la liberación del lector latinoamericano (Dorfman). *See* Toward the Liberation of the Latin American Reader

Hackman, Gene, 23

Halpern, Maurice and Edith, 8

Hammurabi, 242, 273

Hard Rain (Dorfman): award for, helps Dorfman get a passport, 17; complexity of the narrative project and, 44; historical context of, 156; intertextuality of, 44; intertwining humor with metacommentary on the nature of art in, 44; literature–self relationship in, 65–66;

ture" ("Medios masivos de comunicación y enseñanza de literatura") (Dorfman), 77

mass-media culture, 74–75, 78, 91–92, 136–37

mass-produced culture, 77–78, 91, 248, 252

Mato, Daniel, 247

Matrix, The (film), 219

Mattelart, Armand, 14, 74, 245, 246, 247, 248

"Matter of Time, A" ("Cuestión de tiempo") (Dorfman), 120–21

Matthews, Chris, 61

Matto de Turner, Clorinda, 207

McCarthyism, 7–8

McEwan, Ian, 57

McIrvin, Michael, 73

McLuhan, Marshall, 159, 246

media communications, 72

media criticism, 20–21, 250, 252–61, 347–48. See also *How to Read Donald Duck*; *The Empire's Old Clothes*

media culture: Dorfman's relationship to, 245, 247; distorted perceptions of humanity offered by, 215; to encourage critical reflection and public engagement, 261; infantalization of the public, 135, 259; Latin American identity and, 247–48; post-boom writers and, 57; reality television linked to dissolution of privacy, 216, 218. See also culture

"Medios masivos de comunicación y enseñanza de literatura" (Dorfman). See "Mass Media and the Teaching of Literature"

Meehan, Eileen R., 248

Meisalas, Susan, 260

Me llamo Rigoberta Menchú (I, Rigoberta Menchú) (Menchú and Burgos Debray), 56

Memento (film), 144

"Memories of Hope" (Dorfman), 260

memory: building a sense of fraternity, 197; dialectic of remembering and forgetting, 155; of the exile, 116; as fluid, fragile, imprecise, 155, 197, 269–70; forgotten, 21–22, 78, 79, 144–45, 148–149, 209, 273; geographic sources, 234–35; intertwining public history, 155–56, 267–68; negated, 144–45; photographs as a source of, 275; preserving, 20, 144–45, 149, 273–74; rebellion in the realm of, 124; recuperating, in an age of collective amnesia and apathy, 227–34; repressing through mass-produced fictions, 78; storytelling and, 20, 34; and trauma, complexity of, 28–29; truth and, 153, 183–84; unreliability of, 197; Wall of Memory, 156, 267, 268, 269, 271

memory, history, and truth: *The Burning City* (Dorfman and J. Dorfman), 223–27; *Desert Memories: Journeys through the Chilean North*, 234–42; *Manifesto for Another World: Voices from Beyond the Dark* (theatrical adaptation), 227–34

"Memory and Fate in Latin America" in *Other Septembers, Many Americas* (Dorfman), 273–74

Memory Park, 156

Menchú, Rigoberta, 152, 158, 233

Metzger, Deena, 208

Mexico, 18

Miller, Arthur, 188–89

Miller, Nancy K., 194

Milosevic, Slobodan, 271

mirroring, as literary technique: in *Blake's Therapy*, 217–18; in *Death and the Maiden* (*La muerte y la doncella*), 162, 173, 175; in *Konfidenz*, 179, 180–83; in *Mascara* (*Máscaras*), 144–45; in *The Nanny and the Iceberg* (*La nana y el iceberg*), 204, 210–12; in *Reader* (theatrical adaptation), 189–90; in *Widows* (*Viudas*) (novel), 125–26, 132

Missing (Dorfman), 18, 47, 56, 109

modernism, 44–57

Modern Language Association (MLA) convention, 282–84

monolingualism and identity, 4–5, 12–13

Monsiváis, Carlos, 247

Moraga, Cherríe, 191, 193

Morello, Henry James, 165

Moreno, Rita, 233

Morgan, J. P., 218

Moros en la costa (Dorfman), 65–66, 82–83, 96–108, 111–12, 133, 186; foretelling history in, 18; theme, 15. See also *Hard Rain*

Morrison, Toni, 199, 259

Mots, Les (*The Words*) (Sartre), 193

Mountain Language (Pinter), 50

Mouse That Roared, The (Giroux), 248

Movimiento de Acción Popular Unitaria (MAPU), 106

Mozart, 68–69, 175–76

Muerte y la doncella, La (Dorfman). See *Death and the Maiden*

Murieta, Joaquín, 30

"My House Is on Fire" ("A la escondida") (short story) (Dorfman), 25, 82, 117, 121, 260

My House Is on Fire (film) (Dorfman and R. Dorfman), 25, 26, 82, 260

"My House Is on Fire" (poem) (Dorfman), 82

myth, 74, 245

Myth and Archive (González Echevarría), 238

Mythologies (Barthes), 246

Nación, La (periodical), 262

name, relation to identity, 1–3, 6–10, 44

Nana y el iceberg, La (Dorfman). See *Nanny and the Iceberg*

Nanny and the Iceberg, The (*La nana y el iceberg*) (Dorfman), 24, 42, 44, 59; amnesia for handling the past in, 209; communication as possibility in, 205–6; compared to *Blake's Therapy*, 213, 218,

222; compared to *Death and the Maiden*, 202; criticism of, 90; duality in, 206–7; epigraph of, 208; gender issues in, 206–7; historical and literary reference and connections in, 205; historical context of, 202; incest as metaphor for destroying the future in, 207; intersections of sex, deceit, and society in, 206–9; intertextuality of, 203–5; linguistic techniques in, 41, 87, 90; literary technique of, 86, 89, 204, 209–13; media role in shaping public consciousness, 160; neoliberalism, technology and the global age in, 202–13; readers of, 205, 206, 208, 209–10; search for identity in, 202; self–community relationship, 205, 208–9; space fragmented and overflowing, 53; transformation through adaptation/translation, 89

narrative authority, 56

narrative voices, shifting, 65–67, 127–32, 147, 182, 209, 219–22, 270–71

National Commission for Truth and Reconciliation, 22

nation-state, legitimacy of the, 154

Native American culture, 31

Navarro, Luis, 260

Nave de los locos, La (*The Ship of Fools*) (Peri Rossi), 37

Nazi regime, 2, 80, 156, 167, 176, 185

Negri, Antonio, 159

Nelson, Alice A., 19, 165

neocolonialism, 20, 251

neoliberal economics: in *Blake's Therapy*, 213–22; in *The Nanny and the Iceberg*, 202–13

neoliberalism, 24, 208, 211, 214

Neruda, Pablo, 47, 60, 80, 251

New Latin American Cinema, 72

news media, 159, 263

New World Order, The (Pinter), 23, 50, 51

Nichols, Mike, 23

Nietzsche, Friedrich, 170, 171

"Simultaneous Translation" ("Traducción simultánea) (Dorfman), 112–14, 278

Singer, Alan, 75–76, 83

Sin ir más lejos (Without Going Farther) (Dorfman), 252

Skármeta, Antonio, 57, 97–98

slippage, linguistic, 167, 179

Smith, Sidonie, 191

Smoodin, Eric, 248

"Snow" (Dorfman), 263

social alienation, consumer society in creating, 208

social change: art and, 72–74, 122–24; birth process as metaphor for, 134–35; children and, 258–59; culture's role in, 11–12, 45, 245; difficulty of, 74; education and, 259; intersection with culture, 11–12; literature as a vehicle for, 57–59, 95, 100–102, 109, 121, 153; relationship of the body to, 148; storytelling for, 32

social consciousness, 252, 259

socialist irrealism, 78, 82

social oppression, 256

social relations, categorization of, 256–57

"Soft Evidence" (Dorfman), 109

solidarity, 13

Sollers, Werner, 191

Some Write to the Future (Dorfman), 45, 55–56

Soñé que la nieve ardía (*I Dreamt the Snow Was Burning*) (Skármeta), 98

Sophocles, 39

Soros, George, 24, 214, 218

Southern Common Market (MERCOSUR), 154

Soviet Union collapse, 154

Spanish Civil War (1936–39), 45, 47

Speak Truth to Power (Kennedy Cuomo), 27, 56, 93, 227–30

Speak Truth to Power Play: Voices from Beyond the Dark (Dorfman), 27. See also *Manifesto for Another World*

Spielberg, Steven, 227

spirituality–truth–science connections, 237–39

Stavans, Ilan, 23

Steiner, George, 167, 176

Sterne, Laurence, 44

Stevenson, Juliet, 23

Sting, 23

Stoll, David, 158

stories, commoditization of, 33

"Storyteller, The" (Benjamin), 33

"Storyteller, The" (Berger), 34

storytellers, storytelling: authorial conceit or privilege in, 36; author/novelist as distinct from, 33–34; combining with critical intervention, 282–84; creating community through, 32, 34; decline of, 33; Dorfman's self-identity tied to, 31–37, 97, 200; liberating possibilities of, 183–186; literary boom writers, 54; memory and, 20, 34; paradox in, 92; power of, 58, 61, 94; resistance and, 123; responsibilities of, 149–50; social role of, 133; survival of identity and, 185; *testimonio* as form of, 56; traditional, 31; as witness, 33; writers as, 31–37, 47, 58. *See also* writer, Dorfman as

strategy of aesthetic promiscuity, 188

structure, Dorfman's use of: complexity of, 62, 142; criticism of, 90–91; fragments and contradictions, 43, 59, 96, 99, 101; gestational, 84, 134–35, 188, 274–75; open, to engage the reader, 83–86; unity and consistency lacking in, 59

subaltern studies, 256

subject positions, shifting, 65–67, 127–32, 147, 182, 209, 219–22, 270–71

Sumario de la historia natural de las indias (Fernández de Oviedo), 42–43

superheroes, 63–64

Superman and His Soul Mates (Dorfman and Jofré), 20

Supermán y sus amigos de alma (Dorfman and Jofré), 20

surrealism, 160
survival: as consequence of creativity, 16, 108–9; through literature and storytelling, 60–61, 185
survivor's guilt, 15–16, 32–33, 97, 200
Susana the Seed (Susana la Semilla), 16, 244–45, 260

Taberna, Freddy, 27, 235–36, 239
Taylor, Diana, 165
technological change, global social structure: in *Blake's Therapy*, 213–22; in *The Nanny and the Iceberg*, 202–13
technology, 42, 159, 202, 217–18, 246
Tejas Verdes (Valdés), 158
Tempest (Shakespeare), 10, 43
testimonial texts, 111
testimonio genre, 55–56, 72, 158–60
Testimony (Laub and Felman), 157
That the World May Know (Dawes), 34, 279
Thayer, Willy, 29
theater: of the absurd, 47–50, 179; of the oppressed, 91; post-traumatic, 165–66
Themes and Variations (*Tientos y diferencias*) (Sánchez), 261
Thiong'o, Ngugi Wa, 282
tics, linguistic, 170–71
Tientos y diferencias (Themes and Variations) (Sánchez), 261
Tin Drum, The (Grass), 136
TIT theater collective, 165
Tohá, Jaime, 244
Tohá, Moy, 268
TomDispatch.com, 278
Torn from the Nest (*Aves sin nido*) (Matto de Turner), 207
Toronto film festival, 25
torture, 29–30, 51–52, 60, 109–10, 172
Toward the Liberation of the Latin American Reader (*Hacia la liberación del lector latinoamericano*) (Dorfman), 20, 60
"Traducción simultánea" (Dorfman). *See* "Simultaneous Translation"

transformation, through adaptation/translation: *Death and the Maiden* (*La muerte y la doncella*), 260; *Hard Rain* (*Moros en la costa*), 96–108, 186; *Heading South, Looking North: A Bilingual Journey* (*Rumbo al sur, deseando el norte*), 196; *Manifesto for Another World: Voices from Beyond the Dark* (theatrical adaptation), 228, 231–32; *The Nanny and the Iceberg* (*La nana y el iceberg*), 89; *Widows* (*Viudas*) (novel), 26, 286–88
trauma, results of, 195
travel memoir, 296–97
travel writing, 39, 240
Trigo, Abril, 158, 242
Trojan Women, The (Euripides), 39
"Troubled Bridges" in *Other Septembers, Many Americas* (Dorfman), 273
Truman Show, The (film), 219
trust and betrayal: in *Death and the Maiden* (*La muerte y la doncella*), 160–76; in *Konfidenz*, 176–85; in *Reader* (theatrical adaptation), 188–91; in *Widows* (theatrical adaptation) (Dorfman and Kushner), 186–88
truth: absolute, 56; crisis of, 157; and its representation, 124, 153, 160, 190, 243; memory and, 153, 183–84; as a process vs. democratic dialogue, 173
truth, memory, and history: in *The Burning City* (Dorfman and J. Dorfman), 223–27; in *Desert Memories: Journeys through the Chilean North*, 234–42; in *Manifesto for Another World: Voices from Beyond the Dark* (theatrical adaptation), 227–34
truth, to: art, 124, 163, 190; language, 167–72; memory, 153, 157
truth claims, 157–58
truth commissions, 22, 152, 156, 161–62, 172
truth–science–spirituality connections, 237–39

fluences on: avant-garde movement, 45–47, 79; baroque writers, 42–44, 99; classical theater, 39; colonial American literature, 42–43; Cortázar, Julio, 53–54; early modern, 39–44; early Renaissance writers, 40–42; late Italian Medieval, 39–40; Latin American literary boom writers, 54–57; modern, 44–57; 1960s revolutionary culture, 57; pattern in, 59; Pinter, Harold, 47–53; post-boom writers, 56–57; post-colonial writers, 57, 59; *testimonio* genre, 55–56; theater of the absurd, 47–50

writer(s): Dorfman's theory of, 31–32, 35–39, 41, 58, 59; connecting to regimes of signification, 35; creating literary autonomy, 47; defined, 34–35; diaspora, 281; as distinct from the narrator, 35; as the medium for heteroglossia, 200; modernistic version of, 34; power of, 43; reproduction linked to the craft of, 135;

social role and responsibilities of, 35, 58–59, 95, 114–16; as storyteller, 31–37, 47, 58

writing: fear and, 264–66; as a form of subversive engagement, 276–77; as inadequate effort at translating, 43; process of, 35; professionalization of, 33; purpose of, 32, 43; readerly, Barthes's advocacy of, 34; storytelling as distinct from, 33–34

writing to the future, 22, 61–62, 69, 92

"Yesterday Is Still Here" (Dorfman), 273
"Y qué oficio le pondremos" (Dorfman). *See* "Godfather"
Yúdice, George, 72, 247

Zelig (Allen), 146
Zinn, Howard, 278
Zorrilla, José, 42

Sophia A. McClennen is an associate professor
of comparative literature, Spanish, and women's studies
at Pennsylvania State University, University Park.

Library of Congress Cataloging-in-Publication Data
McClennen, Sophia A.
Ariel Dorfman : an aesthetics of hope / Sophia A. McClennen.
p. cm.
Includes bibliographical references and index.
ISBN 978-0-8223-4586-2 (cloth : alk. paper)
ISBN 978-0-8223-4604-3 (pbk. : alk. paper)
1. Dorfman, Ariel—Aesthetics. 2. Dorfman, Ariel—Criticism
and interpretation. I. Title.
PQ8098.14.07Z754 2010
863'.64—dc22
2009041158